"There are few 'eureka' moments in Psalms studies, but Steffen Jenkins has found one! The problem of retribution, especially the pesky imprecations ('curses'), has been a sore spot in biblical theology for centuries . . . Jenkins, powered by a canonical approach, argues that David, in book 5, . . . has become the master teacher of how to pray for Israel and the nations, both objects of Yahweh's undeserved 'steadfast love and plenteous redemption.'"

—C. HASSELL BULLOCK
Wheaton College (IL), emeritus

"With sustained and careful analysis of psalms 1–3 and the shape of book 5, Jenkins demonstrates persuasively that the imprecatory psalms should not be understood as self-righteous requests for revenge. Rather, they 'show concern for the welfare of the enemy, including . . . a desire for their repentance and blessing.' His work also clearly shows how attention to Psalter shape continues to yield illuminating and important results—very impressive!"

—J. CLINTON MCCANN JR.
Eden Theological Seminary

"Steffen Jenkins has produced a fresh and stimulating analysis of the imprecatory psalms that will greatly aid academics and students for years to come as they explore this difficult portion of the Psalter."

—JONATHAN GIBSON
Westminster Theological Seminary

"I am delighted to commend enthusiastically Steffen Jenkins's study on the imprecatory psalms. Steffen's commitment to the absolute trustworthiness of God's word shines through his insightful and always engaging exposition of this often much abused portion of Scripture. Jenkins writes not only with academic care but also with pastoral sensitivity. I look forward to more coming from his pen (or computer)."

—IAN HAMILTON
Westminster Presbyterian Theological Seminary

"This study makes an important contribution to the theology and ethics of the calls for divine retribution within the Psalter. It can also serve as an accessible introduction to reading the Psalter as a book and with an awareness of significant links to other parts of the Old Testament. Having studied and lectured on the Psalms for years, I have nevertheless learned much from this work which broadened my perspective on the Psalter, deepened my understanding of individual psalms, and changed my mind on a few issues."

—**THOMAS RENZ**
Oak Hill Theological College, retired

"Who hasn't wondered about why the imprecatory psalms are in the Bible? . . . Were the people who prayed them self-righteous or deluded? Were they unaware of the call to love one's enemies? Did they think they could simply say anything because they were suffering? Did they lack any idea of enemies turning to God? Jenkins shows that the answer to all these questions is no!"

—**JOHN GOLDINGAY**
Fuller Seminary, emeritus

"Imprecations in the Psalms have long posed a critical problem in their interpretation. Where the dominant approach in recent decades has been to look behind each individual poem, Steffen Jenkins suggests we look instead at the Psalter, which provides the context for interpretation. He shows that the final form of the Psalter provides the guardrails which guide how we are to read these prayers. This is a crucial work that will need to be considered by all who wrestle with this issue."

—**DAVID G FIRTH**
Trinity College, Bristol

"In line with the righteous man of psalm 1, Steffen Jenkins has clearly spent long hours meditating day and night on the Psalter, and among the fruits of this are a significant number of astute and important observations about the shape of the Psalter. He makes a case that needs to be heard that there are signs of careful arrangement of the Psalter and that this contributes to how we should understand imprecatory psalms. I would be very glad to see his research disseminated more widely."

—PETER J. WILLIAMS
Tyndale House, Cambridge

Imprecations in the Psalms

Imprecations in the Psalms

Love for Enemies in Hard Places

Steffen G. Jenkins

PICKWICK *Publications* · Eugene, Oregon

IMPRECATIONS IN THE PSALMS
Love for Enemies in Hard Places

Pickwick Publications
An Imprint of Wipf and Stock Publishers
199 W. 8th Ave., Suite 3
Eugene, OR 97401

www.wipfandstock.com

PAPERBACK ISBN: 978-1-7252-9239-0
HARDCOVER ISBN: 978-1-7252-9240-6
EBOOK ISBN: 978-1-7252-9241-3

Cataloguing-in-Publication data:

Names: Jenkins, Steffen G. [author]

Title: Imprecations in the Psalms : love for enemies in hard places / Steffen G. Jenkins.

Description: Eugene, OR: Pickwick Publications, 2022 | Includes bibliographical references and index.

Identifiers: ISBN 978-1-7252-9239-0 (paperback) | ISBN 978-1-7252-9240-6 (hardcover) | ISBN 978-1-7252-9241-3 (ebook)

Subjects: LCSH: Bible—Psalms—Criticism, interpretation, etc | Blessings and cursing in the Bible | Anger—Religious aspects | Bible—Psalms—Theology

Classification: BS1430.6 J46 2022 (print) | BS1430.6 (ebook)

01/25/22

Unless otherwise indicated, all translations are by the author.

In Memoriam

Brian David Foster
my dear father-in-law

irrevocably summoned into the presence of the ultimate
author, final subject and perfect performer of every Psalm

יָקָר בְּעֵינֵי יְהוָה
הַמָּוְתָה לַחֲסִידָיו

Contents

vii

List of Tables

Preface

THE BRICKS MAKING UP this humble book were quarried from doctoral research conducted at Trinity College, Bristol, under the supervision of Prof. Gordon Wenham. This publication gives me the excuse to offer hearty thanks more publicly to many!

How do I begin to thank Prof. Wenham for supervising me those four years, and for his and Mrs. Wenham's generous hospitality? He indefatigably read and commented on my work and guided me through every stage of the process with a sure, reassuring and experienced hand. Every visit to the Wenham home, sometimes by all the Jenkins, was a life-giving kindness and joy to us.

It was a great privilege to have Dr. Philip S. Johnston as my external supervisor. I cannot imagine how he found the time, while being the Senior Tutor of Hughes Hall, but he went well beyond the call of duty. From the minute detail to the overall claim of the work, he offered the most helpful criticisms with kind encouragement. I may not have convinced him of my case, but his warnings have made it less weak than it was. Proverbs 27:6a.

I would like to thank the thesis examiners, Dr. David Firth (then external to Trinity) and Dr. Knut Heim, for their enthusiastic and thorough evisceration and for their even more enthusiastic and prolonged encouragement to publish afterwards. Dr. Firth has been especially charitable in his ongoing spur to let some of the work see the light of day.

At Trinity and at Bristol University, I must thank the directors of Post-Graduate studies (Dr. Knut Heim and D.r Justin Stratis), the Dean of the Faculty of Arts and Humanities, and the Post-Graduate administrators (Mrs. Sam Hands and Mrs. Emma Crick de Boom).

I am immensely grateful for the privilege of enjoying study space and daily fellowship (sometimes from the shoulder, of course) at Tyndale House from 2011 to 2015. I would like to thank the Principal, Peter Williams, and the librarians, Elizabeth Magba and Simon Sykes, for allowing me to be part of the amazing community at the House. It was my undeserved pleasure to share a study carrel at various points with real scholars, men and women far above my station, and I will not debase their names by mentioning them in such a lowly book as this. They know who they are, and their friendship and encouragement, and that of their families to our whole family was a gift. Having them as "cell-mates" was a daily dose of delight.

I would like to thank Prof. Robert Gordon and Dr. Katherine Dell for suffering my attendance at the OT Senior Seminars at the Divinity Faculty in Cambridge, and Josh Harper, Kim Phillips, Brittany Melton, and Luke Wisely for organising the Tyndale House OT Graduate Seminar.

A love for Hebrew and for the Psalms were kindled and nurtured during my seminary education by Rev. Dr. James Robson, Dr. Charles Anderson, Rev. Dr. Thomas Renz, Dr. Bryan Howell and Dr. Seulgi Byun, and maintained on a weekly basis since then by the inclusive Psalmody of Cambridge Presbyterian Church, Chelmsford Presbyterian Church and now Bethel Presbyterian Church—the pattern in those names makes me wonder whether we should get the word out more widely about singing psalms once in a while! My whole family is grateful for the psalm settings of Jamie Soles, and not a few connections were spotted on car journeys as familiar words reappeared to different tunes.

In addition to faithful support in prayer a number of friends supported our family financially during the thesis (or, during its final year, supported my students when I took time out to run the "Cuba Hebrew Boot Camp" at Tyndale House) and we express our gratitude to God for them: Liz Capper, †Valerie Chambers, David & Sue Field, Martin Grinnell, Ian and Joan Hamilton, Phil and Ruth Heaps, †Gerv and Ruth Markham, Steve and Christine Martin, James and Liz Oakley, Mike and Ceri Payne, Mike and Lizzy Peach, Peter and Margaret Rae, Chad and Emily VanDixhoorn, and Neil and Sarah Yorke-Smith. I am most grateful to the Tyndale Fellowship for awarding me Erasmus Scholarships between 2011–15, and to the trustees of Emmanuel for a scholarship.

More recently, as I have tried to publish a book, rather than merely write a thesis, I confess that I have needed more encouragement and reassurance than a boy of my age perhaps ought. I am most grateful to Hassell Bullock, Peter Williams, Palmer Robertson, Jonny Gibson, James Hely-Hutchinson, Thomas Renz, Ian Hamilton, John Orchard and especially Cornelis Bennema, Stephen Moore, and Pieter Kwant. The now tragically late Donald Mitchell read extensively from an early draft, offered invaluable advice, and encouraged me to make the text accessible beyond those who read Hebrew.

Matt Wimer, the Editorial Production Manager, and EJ Davila and Robin Parry, the Pickwick editors, considered the proposal in the kindest and most hassle-free way imaginable, for which I thank them. Raj Sangha and Kevin Hale have kindly proof-read the volume and offered sage advice, as well as doing much thankless drudgery to bring the formatting of the manuscript up to scratch. Just a little while, and you too. . . . My faculty colleagues at Union School of Theology have selflessly encouraged me to keep a low profile and write for the last few months; I hope that this volume is a worthy product of their thoughtfulness!

Sally, Ben and Daniel: Proverbs 31:10 and Psalm 127:3. And the rest is silence.

Penultimately, all four of us express our gratitude to our parents for all their love and support in more ways than can be listed here.

Ultimately, in thankful worship and adoration, I express my indebtedness, devotion and love to the one who shows *hesed* to us on a daily basis.

Juravit Dominus, et non pœnitebit eum:
Tu es sacerdos in æternum
secundum ordinem Melchisedech.

Chiclana de la Frontera
August, AD 2021

Abbreviations

AB	Anchor Bible
AC	Goshen-Gottstein, Moshe, ed. *The Aleppo Codex: Part One: Plates*. Jerusalem: Magnes, 1976
ACCSOT	Ancient Christian Commentary on Scripture: Old Testament
AER	*American Ecclesiastical Review*
AJSL	*American Journal of Semitic Languages and Literature*
Alep	Aleppo Codex (cf. *AC*, *MGH*)
ALGHJ	Arbeiten zur Literatur und Geschichte des hellenistischen Judentums
AnBib	Analecta biblica
ANE	Ancient Near-East(ern)
ANF	*Ante-Nicene Fathers*
AOAT	Alter Orient und Altes Testament
ASV	American Standard Version
ATANT	Abhandlungen zur Theologie des Alten und Neuen Testaments

ATD	Das Alte Testament Deutsch
b. Berakot	*Berakot* in the Babylonian Talmud
BBB	Bonner biblische Beiträge
BBRSup	*Bulletin for Biblical Research* Supplements
BDAG	Bauer, Walter, F. W. Danker, W. F. Arndt, and F. W. Gingrich, eds. *A Greek-English Lexicon of the New Testament and Other Early Christian Literature*. 3rd ed. Chicago: University of Chicago Press, 2000
BDB	Brown, Francis, S. R. Driver, and Charles Briggs. *Hebrew and English Lexicon: With an Appendix Containing the Biblical Aramaic*. Oxford: Clarendon, 1906
BDF	Blass, F., A. Debrunner, and Robert W. Funk. *A Greek Grammar of the New Testament and Other Early Christian Literature*. Chicago: University of Chicago Press, 1961
BETL	Bibliotheca ephemeridum theologicarum lovaniensium
BEvT	Beiträge zur evangelischen Theologie
BHL	Dotan, Aron, ed. *[Torah Nevi'im u-Khetuvim]* = *Biblia Hebraica Leningradensia: Prepared According to the Vocalization, Accents, and Masora of Aaron Ben Moses Ben Asher in the Leningrad Codex*. Peabody, MA: Hendrickson, 2001
BHS	*Biblia Hebraica Stuttgartensia*. Edited by K. Elliger and W. Rudolph. 5th ed. Stuttgart: Deutsche Bibelgesellshaft, 1997
Bib	*Biblica*
BibInt	*Biblical Interpretation*
BibLeb	*Bibel und Leben*
BK	*Bibel und Kirche*

BKAT	Biblischer Kommentar, Altes Testament. Edited by M. Noth and H. W. Wolff
BL	*Bibel und Liturgie*
BN	*Biblische Notizen*
Brenton	Brenton, Lancelot Charles Lee. *The Septuagint Version of the Old Testament: English Translation*. London: Samuel Bagster and Sons, 1870.
BSac	*Bibliotheca sacra*
BTB	***Biblical Theology Bulletin***
BWANT	Beiträge zur Wissenschaft vom Alten und Neuen Testament
BZ	***Biblische Zeitschrift***
BZAW	Beihefte zur Zeitschrift für die alttestamentliche Wissenschaft
CahRB	Cahiers de la Revue biblique
CBQ	*Catholic Biblical Quarterly*
COS	*The Context of Scripture*. Edited by William W. Hallo and K. Lawson Younger. Leiden: Brill, 1997–
CurBS	*Currents in Research: Biblical Studies*
Darby	1890 Darby Bible
DCH	*Dictionary of Classical Hebrew*. Edited by David J. A. Clines. Sheffield: Sheffield Academic, 1993–
Delitzsch	Delitzsch, Franz. *Die Psalmen*. 5th ed. Leipzig: Dörflin u. Franke, 1894. Reprint, Giessen: Brunnen, 1984
Diodati, *Annotations*	Diodati, Giovanni. *Pious Annotations upon the Holy Bible: Expounding the Difficult Places Thereof Learnedly and Plainly*. London, 1664
DJD	Discoveries in the Judaean Desert

DOTWPW	*Dictionary of the Old Testament: Wisdom, Poetry & Writings*. Edited by Tremper Longman III and Peter Enns. Downers Grove, IL: InterVarsity, 2008
DSE	*Dictionary of Scripture and Ethics*. Edited by Joel B. Green. Grand Rapids: Baker Academic, 2011
DTIB	*Dictionary for Theological Interpretation of the Bible*. Edited by Kevin J. Vanhoozer. Grand Rapids: Baker, 2005
EHLL	*Encyclopedia of Hebrew Language and Linguistics*. Edited by Geoffrey Khan. 4 vols. Leiden: Brill, 2013
ESV	English Standard Version
ETL	*Ephemerides theologicae lovanienses*
ETS	Erfurter Theologische Schriften
EÜ	Einheitsübersetzung
EvQ	*Evangelical Quarterly*
EvT	*Evangelische Theologie*
ExAud	*Ex auditu*
ExpTim	*Expository Times*
FAT	Forschungen zum Alten Testament
FC	The Fathers of the Church, a new translation
FOTL	Forms of the Old Testament Literature
FRLANT	Forschungen zur Religion und Literatur des Alten und Neuen Testaments
GNB	Good News Bible
Goldingay 1/2/3	Goldingay, John. *Psalms*. Baker Commentary on the Old Testament Wisdom and Psalms. Grand Rapids: Baker Academic, 2006–8
GW	God's Word Translation
HALOT	Koehler, L., W. Baumgartner, and J. J. Stamm, *The Hebrew and Aramaic Lexicon of the Old*

	Testament. Translated and edited under the supervision of M. E. J. Richardson. 4 vols. Leiden: Brill, 1994–99
HAT	Handbuch zum Alten Testament
HBM	Hebrew Bible Monographs
HBS	Herders Biblische Studien
HBT	*Horizons in Biblical Theology*
HCSB	Holman Christian Standard Bible
Hossfeld-Zenger I/II/III	Hossfeld, Frank-Lothar, and Erich Zenger. *Die Psalmen I: Psalm 1–50.* NEchtB 29. Würzburg: Echter, 1993
	———. *Die Psalmen II: Psalm 51–100.* NEchtB 40. Würzburg: Echter, 2002
	———. *Die Psalmen III: Psalm 101–150.* NEchtB 41. Würzburg: Echter, 2012
Hossfeld-Zenger 2/3	———. *Psalmen 51–100.* HThKAT. Freiburg: Herder, 2000
	———. *Psalmen 101–150.* HThKAT. Freiburg: Herder, 2008
HThKAT	Herders theologischer Kommentar zum Alten Testament
HTR	*Harvard Theological Review*
HUCA	*Hebrew Union College Annual*
HUT	Hermeneutische Untersuchungen zur Theologie
Int	*Interpretation*
Jastrow	Jastrow, M. *A Dictionary of the Targumim, the Talmud Babli and Yerushalmi, and the Midrashic Literature.* Authorised ed. New York: Choreb, 1926
JBVO	*Jenaer Beiträge zum Vorderen Orient*
JBQ	*Jewish Bible Quarterly*
JET	*Jahrbuch für Evangelische Theologie*

JETh	*Jahrbuch für evangelikale Theologie*
JETS	*Journal of the Evangelical Theological Society*
JNES	*Journal of Near Eastern Studies*
JNSL	*Journal of Northwest Semitic Languages*
Joüon	Joüon, P. *A Grammar of Biblical Hebrew.* Translated and revised by T. Muraoka. 2 vols. Subsidia biblica 14/1–2. Rome: Pontifical Biblical Institute, 1991
JPSTC	JPS Torah Commentary
JSOT	*Journal for the Study of the Old Testament*
JSOTSup	Journal for the Study of the Old Testament: Supplement Series
JSS	*Journal of Semitic Studies*
JTS	*Journal of Theological Studies*
K&D	Keil, Carl Friedrich, and Franz Delitzsch. *Commentary on the Old Testament.* Translated by J. Martin et al. 25 vols. Edinburgh: T&T Clark, 1857–78. Reprint, 10 vols. Peabody, MA: Hendrickson, 1996
Kirkpatrick	Kirkpatrick, A. F., ed. *The Book of Psalms.* Cambridge: Cambridge University Press, 1892–1901
KJV	King James Version
Kraus	Kraus, Hans-Joachim. *Psalmen.* 5., grundlegend überarbeitete und veränderte Aufl. BKAT 15. Neukirchen-Vluyn: Neukirchener, 1978
L	Leningrad Codex (cf. *BHL, LC, BHS*)
L&N	Louw, Johannes P., and Eugene A. Nida, eds. *Greek-English Lexicon of the New Testament: Based on Semantic Domains.* 2nd ed. New York: United Bible Societies, 1989.
LC	Freedman, David Noel, ed. *The Leningrad Codex: A Facsimile Edition.* Grand Rapids: Eerdmans, 1998

LCC	Library of Christian Classics.
LEB	Lexham English Bible
LHB/OTS	Library of Hebrew Bible/Old Testament Studies
LSJ	Liddell, Henry George, and Robert Scott. *A Greek-English Lexicon*. Revised and augmented throughout by Sir Henry Stuart Jones, with the assistance of Roderick McKenzie. Oxford: Clarendon, 1940
LXX	Septuagint
McCann	McCann, J. Clinton, Jr. "Psalms." In Vol. 4 of *The New Interpreter's Bible*, edited by Leander E. Keck, 639–1280. Nashville: Abingdon, 1996
MdB	Le Monde de la Bible
MGH I/II	Cohen, Menachem, ed. *Psalms: Part I*. Mikra'ot Gedolot 'Haketer': A Revised and Augmented Scientific Edition of 'Mikra'ot Gedolot'. Based on the Aleppo Codex and Early Medieval MSS. Ramat Gan, Israel: Bar Ilan University Press, 2003
	———, ed. *Psalms: Part II*. Mikra'ot Gedolot 'Haketer': A Revised and Augmented Scientific Edition of 'Mikra'ot Gedolot'. Based on the Aleppo Codex and Early Medieval MSS. Ramat Gan, Israel: Bar Ilan University Press, 2004
Mm	*Masorah magna*
Mp	*Masorah parva*
MSG	The Message: The Bible in Contemporary Language
MT	The (Tiberian) Masoretic Text, usually referring to Alep
MThZ	*Münchener Theologische Zeitschrift*
NAC	New American Commentary
NASB	New American Standard Bible

NBC	*New Bible Commentary*. 4th ed. Edited by Don A. Carson, R. T. France, J. Alec Motyer, and Gordon J. Wenham. Leicester: InterVarsity, 1994
NBD	*New Bible Dictionary*. 3rd ed. Edited by I. Howard Marshall, A. R. Millard, James I. Packer, and D. J. Wiseman. Leicester: InterVarsity, 1996
NCBC	New Cambridge Bible Commentary
NCV	New Century Version
NEchtB	Neue Echter Bibel. Kommentar zum Alten Testament mit der Einheitsübersetzung
NET	The New English Translation
NETS	A New English Translation of the Septuagint
NIDOTTE	*New International Dictionary of Old Testament Theology and Exegesis*. Edited by Willem VanGemeren. 5 vols. Carlisle: Paternoster, 1997
NIrV	New International Reader's Version
NIV	The New International Version, 1984
NIVAC	New International Version Application Commentary
NJB	New Jerusalem Bible
NKJV	The New King James Version
NLT	New Living Translation
*NPNF*1	*Nicene and Post-Nicene Fathers*, Series 1
*NPNF*2	*Nicene and Post-Nicene Fathers*, Series 2
NRSV	New Revised Standard Version
NSBT	New Studies in Biblical Theology
OBO	Orbis biblicus et orientalis
ÖBS	Österreichische biblische Studien
OTE	*Old Testament Essays*

OtSt	*Oudtestamentische Studiën*
OTL	Old Testament Library
PaVi	*Parole di vita*
PG	Patrologia graeca [= Patrologiae cursus completus: Series graeca]. Edited by J.-P. Migne. 162 vols. Paris, 1857–86
PIBA	Proceedings of the Irish Biblical Association
PL	Patrologia latina [= Patrologiae cursus completus: Series latina]. Edited by J.-P. Migne. 217 vols. Paris, 1844–64
Poole, *Annotations*	Poole, Matthew. *Annotations upon the Holy Bible: Wherein the Sacred Text Is Inserted, and Various Readings Annex'd, together with the Parallel Scriptures, the More Difficult Terms in Each Verse Are Explained, Seeming Contradictions Reconciled, Questions and Doubts Resolved, and the Whole Text Opened.* London, 1683
PRSt	*Perspectives in Religious Studies*
Ravasi	Ravasi, Gianfranco. *I Salmi: Introduzione, testo e commento.* Milano: San Paolo, 2007
Ravasi I/II/II	Ravasi, Gianfranco. *Il libro dei Salmi: commento e attualizzazione.* Vol. I, *1–50.* Lettura pastorale della Bibbia 12. Bologna: Dehoniane, 1981
	———. *Il libro dei Salmi: commento e attualizzazione.* Vol. II, *51–100.* Lettura pastorale della Bibbia 12. Bologna: Dehoniane, 1985
	———. *Il libro dei Salmi: commento e attualizzazione.* Vol. III, *101–150.* Lettura pastorale della Bibbia 12. Bologna: Dehoniane, 1985
RevistB	*Revista bíblica*
Ross 1/2	Ross, Allen P. *A Commentary on the Psalms: Volume 1 (1–41).* Kregel Exegetical Library. Grand Rapids: Kregel, 2011

	———. *A Commentary on the Psalms: Volume 2 (42–89)*. Kregel Exegetical Library. Grand Rapids: Kregel, 2013
RSV	Revised Standard Version
[s]	Some psalms have their superscription as the whole of verse 1; where this happens, English translations begin numbering v. 1 at Hebrew v. 2. Where I refer to Hebrew v. 1 in such cases, I give the English verse reference as [s].
SBAB	Stuttgarter biblische Aufsatzbände
SBB	Stuttgarter biblische Beiträge
SBLAIL	Society of Biblical Literature Ancient Israel and its Literature
SBLDS	Society of Biblical Literature Dissertation Series
SBLMS	Society of Biblical Literature Monograph Series
SBM	Stuttgarter biblische Monographien
SBS	Stuttgarter Bibelstudien
SBT	Studies in Biblical Theology
Schökel I/II	Schökel, Luis Alonso, and Cecilia Carniti. *Salmos I: (Salmos 1–72) Traducción, introducciones y comentario*. 3rd ed. Nueva Biblia Española. Madrid: Cristiandad, 2008
	———. *Salmos II: (Salmos 73–150) Traducción, introducciones y comentario*. 4th ed. Nueva Biblia Española. Madrid: Cristiandad, 2009
Seybold	Seybold, Klaus. *Die Psalmen*. HAT I/15. Tübingen: Mohr Siebeck, 1996
SJOT	*Scandinavian Journal of the Old Testament*
STDJ	*Studies on the Texts of the Desert of Judah*
SubBi	*Subsidia biblica*
SUNY	State University of New York
Syr.	Syriac

TB	Theologische Bücherei: Neudrucke und Berichte aus dem 20. Jahrhundert
TDNT	*Theological Dictionary of the New Testament.* Edited by G. Kittel and G. Friedrich. Translated by G. W. Bromiley. 10 vols. Grand Rapids: Eerdmans, 1964–76
TDOT	*Theological Dictionary of the Old Testament.* Edited by G. J. Botterweck and H. Ringgren. Translated by J. T. Willis, G. W. Bromiley, and D. E. Green. 8 vols. Grand Rapids: Eerdmans, 1974–2006
THAT	*Theologisches Handwörterbuch zum Alten Testament.* Edited by Ernst Jenni, with assistance from Claus Westermann. 2 vols. München: Kaiser, 1971–76
Them	*Themelios*
ThWAT	*Theologisches Wörterbuch zum Alten Testament.* Edited by G. Johannes Botterweck, Helmer Ringgren, and Heinz-Joseph Fabry. Stuttgart: Kohlhammer, 1970–2000
TLOT	*Theological Lexicon of the Old Testament.* Edited by E. Jenni, with assistance from C. Westermann. Translated by M. E. Biddle. 3 vols. Peabody, MA: Hendrickson, 1997
TLZ	*Theologische Literaturzeitung*
TP	*Theologie und Philosophie*
TRE	*Theologische Realenzyklopädie.* Edited by G. Krause and G. Müller. Berlin: de Gruyter, 1977–
TThSt	Trierer Theologische Studien
TWOT	*Theological Wordbook of the Old Testament.* Edited by Robert L. Harris, Gleason L. Archer, and Bruce K. Waltke. 2 vols. Chicago: Moody, 1980
TynBul	*Tyndale Bulletin*
TZ	*Theologische Zeitschrift*

Vesco	Vesco, Jean-Luc. *Le psautier de David: traduit et commenté*. Lectio Divina 211. Paris: Cerf, 2006
VT	*Vetus Testamentum*
VTSup	*Vetus Testamentum* Supplements
Vulg.	Vulgate
WBC	Word Biblical Commentary
Weber	Weber, Beat. *Werkbuch Psalmen*. Stuttgart: Kohlhammer, 2001–3
Westminster Annotations	Certain Learned Divines. *Annotations upon All the Books of the Old and New Testament Wherein the Text Is Explained, Doubts Resolved, Scriptures Parallelled and Various Readings Observed / by the Joynt-Labour of Certain Learned Divines, Thereunto Appointed, and Therein Employed, as Is Expressed in the Preface*. London, 1645
WMANT	Wissenschaftliche Monographien zum Alten und Neuen Testament
WTJ	*Westminster Theological Journal*
WUNT	Wissenschaftliche Untersuchungen zum Neuen Testament
WW	*Word and World*
YLT	Young's Literal Translation
ZAW	*Zeitschrift für die alttestamentliche Wissenschaft*
ZTK	*Zeitschrift für Theologie und Kirche*

1

Introduction

CERTAIN PRAYERS ABOUT ENEMIES in the Psalms have always jarred Christian readers: they appear to be at significant odds with the ethics of the New Testament. The psalmists are full of self-righteousness, blithely unaware of their own sinfulness, and imagining themselves to have earned God's favor against their enemies. They are vengeful and vindictive, wanting nothing more than retribution.

In response, many will grant the cleft between the Psalms and the New Testament, and say that it is only to be expected. The events and teaching of the New Testament *ought* to have improved on the ethics of the psalms. The legalism and exceptionalism of the Old Testament does lead to delusions of self-righteousness, earned merit before God, and superiority over the enemy. They could not have known better this side of the cross of Jesus. Similarly, there was no way for someone like David, born before the age of the gospel, to know that the wicked are redeemable. If he had no notion that the enemy could repent, he had no way of asking for the end of evil than to ask for the destruction of evildoers. Not having seen the example of the Christ, but living in a world where the friend is to be loved but the enemy is to be hated, how could the authors of psalms be expected to love their enemies, or to have known to pray for God to forgive and bless the wicked who troubled them?

A different tack would treat these prayers as only ever appropriate to Jesus, since he is sinless. Their time will come at the end of the age, when there is no more opportunity to repent but judgment finally arrives.

Responses such as these make common assumptions about the Old Testament which need to be investigated. In the Psalms, especially in the most brutal psalms that deal with enemies in very honest ways, we will test these presuppositions about the Old Testament:

1. Do prayers against enemies require perfect righteousness?

2. Alternatively, do such prayers stem from a deluded self-righteousness, which is unaware of the supplicant's own need for mercy and forgiveness?

3. Is suffering a sufficient qualification for praying against enemies?

4. Do the psalms understand that the enemy is able to repent, or do they imagine that they can only ask for the destruction of the enemy?

5. Do the psalms have any notion of loving the enemy, desiring their blessing, or do they simply demand vengeance?

After a brief survey of the responses to these prayers in the Psalms, we will introduce the art of reading a psalm within its context in the Book of Psalms. We will then examine the introduction to the Book of Psalms (Pss 1 and 2) and see that it already begins to overturn some of these assumptions. For example, Ps 2 clearly indicates that the enemy can and must repent. They are redeemable. The psalmist even desires their blessing.

We will see in Ps 3 that David is introduced at the most sinful point of his career and embattled with a wicked enemy. He is presented as a type of Israel in exile, embattled by Babylon. David serves as a model for individuals and for the nation of how to respond in prayer when faced by vindictive, wicked, and murderous enemies. Already in Ps 3, we find that he is well aware of his own guilt and the opposite of self-righteous. He does not presume on God's favor but knows himself to be reliant on God's undeserved mercy to rescue him.

When given victory over his enemies, he foregoes not only vengeance but even justice, and instead desires their blessing. David is presented in the psalms in the aftermath of his disgraceful incident with Bathsheba and Uriah, where David himself understands his sin to be a total apostasy, on a par with Israel turning from Yahweh to the golden calf. As representative king, his sin is equivalent to that of the nation. The same astonishing mercy which Yahweh showed to Israel in Exod 34 is what David has experienced, and psalms which appeal to it are strategically placed in every book of the Psalter.

In Book I, we examine imprecations in Pss 7 and 18, in their context. We find that each of the assumptions above about the pre- and/or sub-Christian Old Testament are ill-founded. David's appeals to righteousness are not the same as claims of perfection and certainly not appeals to merit. In Ps 7, they are an honest confession of "not guilty" in the face of particular false accusations. In Ps 18, they are followed by Ps 19, confessing David's precarious moral standing. As for the enemy, in Ps 7, David warns and desires for them to repent, and if they will not, he is restrained in what he asks for them; he is much harsher with himself than with them. In Ps 18, we see what happens when the enemy will not repent, but the surprising twist at the end of the psalm is that other enemies, kings and nations, come to David submissively. David then promises to tell the enemy kings and nations about Yahweh's forgiveness and relationship with him through his Torah, which he does in Ps 19. Far from living before the gospel age or being ignorant of the repentance of the wicked, we find David as an evangelist to the nations.

David's example in his prayers of Book I and the way that he is introduced by the Book of Psalms is picked up in Book V, which looks back on the brutal experience of the Babylonian invasion and exile. David is enlisted as the representative of the nation, who prayed about enemies in analogous situations, such as his flight from Absalom. Absalom sinfully attacked him, as Babylon did Israel. Absalom and Babylon were God's chosen agents of righteous judgment against sinful David/Israel. A prophetic oracle declared that the sinful agents would be overthrown and that sinful David/Israel would be rescued. How should Israel think and pray about Babylon and about such cobelligerents as Edom? David's prayers will show the way to appropriate Ps 137, where Edom and Babylon are in focus after the end of exile.

We will examine every imprecation in Book V. Book V is artfully divided into three sections, and the devices that signal those divisions make Yahweh's *hesed* prominent: his "steadfast love" which he showed to Israel when Israel deserved the very opposite.

David teaches the nation that their sin makes them entirely reliant on that undeserved mercy. There is no room for self-righteousness. David shows Israel that those who have received mercy must show it to others; why should wicked nations not experience the blessings that wicked Israel enjoyed? In fact, Book V builds up a growing chorus of calls to all the nations to join Israel in celebrating the mercy that Yahweh offers promiscuously to all. Not only can the wicked nations repent and be redeemed, but they also are encouraged to do so. Further, Israel is encouraged to enjoy thanking Yahweh for his mercy alongside their former enemies.

In answer to our five questions, we will see that the gap with the New Testament is much less than often assumed:

1. Prayers against enemies do not require perfect righteousness, but only innocence in the conflict at issue.

2. The supplicants are well aware of their own need for mercy and forgiveness.

3. In any particular conflict, suffering will not supplant innocence: we are not entitled to divine intervention when we are being justly punished for our own wickedness.

4. The supplicants understand that the enemy is able to repent, and sometimes ask for an end to their wicked deeds, as preferable to the destruction of the enemy.

5. These prayers do not simply demand vengeance, but sometimes desire to show mercy to the enemy, even with a hope that the enemy will repent, be forgiven and be blessed.

Such an attitude is not only shown by individual psalmists against their private enemies, but also modelled to the people of God as a whole when faced by their corporate enemies.

While what follows is an exposition of the Hebrew Bible, I have dared to hope that readers from other disciplines will find the topic interesting. In an effort to make the text bearable, I have limited quotations from Hebrew, provided transliterations so that it can be pronounced, and offered translations where appropriate. I have tried to limit technical Hebrew discussion to the footnotes, but those who read below the line are assumed to be Hebraists. (The same goes for the excursus on the textual variants in Ps 2.) I apologize in advance for keeping the Hebrew term *hesed* in transliteration rather than translating it (as in the title!), despite how often it appears. The pregnant ambiguity of many of its uses in the Book of Psalms leaves me no option.

2

A Real, Biblical Problem:
Retribution in the Psalter

[P]eople have frequently told me that they have never been
that angry. I believe them. Most persons who read this book
have never been so completely victimized as the psalmist.[1]

And we cry for deliverance in two directions—either
destruction or conversion. . . . Both are right, and the
results in either direction are up to God.[2]

WHEN CONSIDERING PRAYERS FOR retribution, and the shock they cause
in readers, one approach points to the *Zeitgeist*. Contemporary Western
readers might well have more reason to feel uncomfortable with "break
their teeth in their mouths" than Christians undergoing persecution and
living in less enlightened times. As Jerome Creach points out, modernity "raises the prospect of making human reason the primary guide to
morality and making Enlightenment ideals the judge over the content of
biblical texts."[3]

In this chapter we will briefly illustrate the range of responses to
these texts in the Psalms. We will encounter a range of voices to test the

1. McCann, *Psalms as Torah*, 116.

2. Day, *Crying for Justice*, 121–22.

3. Creach, *Violence in Scripture*, 3.

above assumption. I have included some Jewish and Christian; Patristic, Mediaeval, Reformers, Puritans and Moderns; European (English, Scottish, Welsh, Spanish, German, Swiss, French), US, Canadian, African, Asian; Roman Catholic, Lutheran, Reformed (Anglican, Presbyterian and Independent), Dispensational and Adventist. This breadth cannot be comprehensive, but it broadens the discussion away from contemporary Western concerns.

It is often noted that divine vengeance is the promise of future justice and is a comfort for those oppressed by injustice.[4] This survey includes those who are familiar with oppression and persecution, Early church Fathers, mediaeval Jewish scholars, Protestant exiles fleeing for their lives (Luther, Calvin), dissenting Puritans either side of the Commonwealth (Craddock, Gurnall), Christians under the Nazis (Bonhoeffer, Mowinckel), and troubled parts of Africa (Firth, Okorocha, Ward). We will see the same mixed reactions among them as are found in Western Modernity and for the same reasons. It seems all the more important to investigate what these psalms do say, whether the tension detected with the words of Jesus across cultures is truly there, and to what extent such tension is present.

Without denying that the surrounding culture will have an impact on our readiness to read and appropriate prayers for retribution, we do find that there is an irreducible remnant. In all cultures and circumstances, some authors balk at these texts because of convictions which they deem biblical and not from the world around them. As Eric Peels points out, while modern assumptions may bring problems to the text, there remains a problem for anyone who reads the Bible faithfully.[5] We have before us an exegetical problem, not a worldview problem.

That is not to say that faulty assumptions are not in play, and most of this book is an exegetical test of several common foundational assumptions about the Psalms. We illustrate this need with two contrasting presuppositions about vengeance. On the one hand, Nancy deClaissé-Walford argues explicitly that feelings of anger and desiring vengeance towards oppressors will sap one's energy and make it impossible to get on with providing real solutions.[6]

One the other hand, Peels:

4. So Peels, *Shadow Sides*, 82–83.

5. Peels, *Shadow Sides*, 72–73.

6. deClaissé-Walford, "Imprecatory Psalms," 91–92.

In view of the history of exegesis (Marcion!) it is of great importance to understand the OT preaching of God's "vengeance" correctly. For modern man the word "vengeance" has strongly negative connotations (immorality, arbitrariness, illegitimacy, cruelty); "vengeance" and love are antipodes. In the OT, however, the concept of "vengeance" has a positive connotation, both from a semantic as well as from a theological point of view: "vengeance" has to do with lawfulness, justice, and salvation.[7]

We turn now to survey the major approaches to these problem psalms, in order to identify the claims that need to be tested in the Psalms.

8. What We Mean by "Imprecations"

Terminology in this area is used inconsistently. Some use the term "imprecation."[8] Others object that this term implies calling down a curse and that no such thing is found in any psalm,[9] or only in some of them.[10] "Psalms of cursing," or of vengeance, retribution, imprecation or even of violence, have all been used as monikers in what is often seen as the same discussion. We are not dealing with entire psalms anyway, but sections, sometimes just a hint in half a verse: "in the presence of my enemies" (Ps 23:5).[11] As C. S. Lewis put it, "the bad parts will not 'come away clean'; they may . . . be intertwined with the most exquisite things."[12] A handful of psalms are often singled out as imprecatory, either because of their pervasive tone (109) or particularly shocking content (137), but these are the exception to the rule. Authors select different psalms for the honor of that label, usually choosing three out of: 35, 58, 59, 69, 79, 83, 109, 137.

What is considered problematic varies too: violence or unpleasantness; vengeance; divine judgment; divine justice; self-righteousness. What jumps out at the reader will vary with individual sensitivities. As

---

7. Peels, "נָקָם," 3:154.

8. E.g., Adams, *War Psalms*.

9. E.g., Waltke et al., *Psalms as Christian Worship*, 95.

10. E.g., Bullock, *Psalms 1–72*, 260.

11. The ambiguous terminology can be illustrated by comparing the widely varying lists of problem verses found in: Adams, *War Psalms*, 116; Althann, "Psalms of Vengeance," 1n2; Rodriguez, "Imprecatory Psalms," 65n21; VanGemeren, *Psalms*, 953; Waltke et al., *Psalms as Christian Worship*, 95; Ross 1:115.

12. Lewis, *Reflections on the Psalms*, 21–22.

Carl Laney puts it: "The problem with the imprecatory psalms, or more correctly, *the interpreter's problem* with them."[13]

Our focus is retribution: any kind of punishment or vengeance against an enemy. We will use "imprecation" to refer to any Psalm where that is an issue, for consistency with the wider literature.[14] Less often discussed in this connection, but just as present in the Psalter, we find retrospective celebrations of the kind of thing asked for in imprecations (e.g., Ps 18). We will investigate this problem phenomenon too.

9. Silence

One approach is not to comment on contemporary appropriation. Theodoret of Cyrus, on the dashing of children in 137:9, simply notes that it is a like-for-like judgment.[15] On Ps 109, he quickly dismisses the issue by claiming that it is not a prayer but a plain predictive prophecy, and his exposition is far more concerned with placing the fulfilment with Jesus and Judas, and, even then, his chief concern is the two natures of Christ.[16] From Rashi's commentary on Ps 137, one would not know that vv. 8–9 exist, and in Ps 109, he makes no ethical remarks.[17] David Kimḥi makes none on 5:11; 6:11; 7:7; 9:20–21; 10:2, 15; 17:13.[18]

10. *A Priori* Ethical Rejection—They Have No Place at All

At the most negative end we find the view that these sentiments are, and always have been, wrong. Either they should never have been in the Scriptures, or else the ethical authority of Scripture is deemed irrelevant. Robert Alter tells us that "No moral justification can be given" for Ps 137:9.[19]

Sometimes, the focus is on the "Old Testament," presumed to be inferior to the New Testament. As Margaret Daly-Denton puts it: "The

---

13. Laney, "Imprecatory Psalms," 37; italics added. Similarly, Althann: "The problem . . . does not consist . . . in our not understanding the words but rather in our repugnance for the language of curses" (Althann, "Psalms of Vengeance," 10).

14. Following the lead of Bullock, *Psalms 1–72*, 260.

15. Theodoret of Cyrus, *Psalms, 73–150*, 324–25.

16. Theodoret of Cyrus, *Psalms 73–150*, 200–207.

17. Rashi, *Rashi's Commentary on Psalms*, 727, 640–41.

18. Kimhi, *Psalms*.

19. Alter, *The Book of Psalms*, 475.

Psalter—and the biblical tradition generally—does not excise the embarrassing evidence of earlier, less wise and even foolish attitudes."[20] As
Sue Gillingham points out, the Enlightenment has taken its toll on the
Psalms.[21] It leaves little room for Ps 1, let alone 2 or 137. As Matthew
Schlimm argues, the Hebrew Bible will not comply with the agenda set by
the Enlightenment, and cannot be analyzed using the categories of Modernity.[22] Hassell Bullock observes that some have removed the category
of judgment from their notion of God, leaving no hope for justice.[23]

11. Ethical Rejection, Canonical Acceptance— They Are Evil, but Have a Place in the Bible

Some treat these prayers as sinful yet grant them a function in the
Scriptures.

11.A. Allegories: From Origen to Luther

Many Patristic commentators, while not explicitly rejecting the ethics of
these psalms, allegorize them in such a way that the offense disappears.
Origen offered Ps 137:8–9 as an example of "how the just man 'slays his
enemies,'" and allegorized "land" as lusts of the flesh, and "city" as his soul:

> For "the little ones" of Babylon (which signifies confusion) are
> those troublesome sinful thoughts which arise in the soul; and
> he who subdues them by striking, as it were, their heads against
> the firm and solid strength of reason and truth, is the man who
> "dasheth the little ones against the stones;" and he is therefore
> truly blessed. God may therefore have commanded men to de-
> stroy all their vices utterly, even at their birth, without having
> enjoined anything contrary to the teaching of Christ;[24]

Similar removals of the problem are found in Benedict, Ambrose,
Gregory of Nyssa, Gregory of Nazianzus, and Jerome.[25] With Augustine,

---

20. Daly-Denton, *Psalm-Shaped Prayerfulness*, 173; so also Weiser, *Die Psalmen*,
292.

21. Gillingham, *Psalms*, 195.

22. Schlimm, *From Fratricide to Forgiveness*, 91–113.

23. Bullock, *Psalms 1–72*, 269.

24. Origen, *Cels.* VII.xxii (*ANF* 4:619–20).

25. Benedict, *Rule*, prol. 28 (cited in Schaefer, *Psalms*, xln12); Ambrose, *Paen.*

we find this more extensively, for example, in making every detail of Ps 137 allegorical, and the same conclusion as Origen is finally reached.[26] We find allegorical approaches (among others) in Martin Luther's early lectures, for example on Ps 109.[27] Lewis is explicit in letting his distaste for the literal sense drive him to allegorize, very much in the vein of Origen.[28]

11.B. Walter Brueggemann

Walter Brueggemann illuminates the question by shifting the focus of the perceived problem: "the yearning for vengeance is *here*, among us and within us and with power. It is not only *there* in the Psalms but it is *here* in the human heart and the human community."[29] He therefore will not let us dismiss this as an "Old Testament" problem: "We must not pretend that the New Testament gives a 'higher' view of God in contrast to the Old Testament. . . . [W]e have to do with the same God."[30] He protests against a shallow spirituality that wants nothing negative anywhere near God. Expressions of vengeance are "acts of profound faith."[31] We are free to ask for outrages, because God will not perpetrate them.[32] While these prayers are profoundly sinful, they arise from an uncontrollable psychological state.[33] The Psalter provides a way of expressing these sentiments so that we can then move past them.[34] Human agents are not to be involved in any of the actions described there.[35] In fact, such prayer "saves the social process from bloodletting, which can never be satiated."[36] Similar here are Craigie, Zenger, Althann, Miller, Silva, and Schaefer.[37]

II:xi:cvi (*NPNF2* 10:358); Gregory of Nyssa, *Against Eunomius* I.i (*NPNF2* 5:35–36); Gregory of Nazianzus, *Or. Bas.* XLV.xv (*NPNF2* 7:428); Jerome, *Epist.* 130:8 (*NPNF2* 6:266).

26. Augustine, *Enarrat. Ps.* 137.5 (*NPNF1* 8:630–32).

27. Luther, *Psalms 1–75*, 353–58.

28. Lewis, *Reflections on the Psalms*, 21–22, 136.

29. Brueggemann, *Praying the Psalms*, 64.

30. Brueggemann, *Praying the Psalms*, 78–79.

31. Brueggemann, *Message of the Psalms*, 191n76.

32. Brueggemann, *Message of the Psalms*, 81, 85–86.

33. Brueggemann, *Praying the Psalms*, 34.

34. Brueggemann, *Praying the Psalms*, 36.

35. Brueggemann, *Praying the Psalms*, 67, 70.

36. Brueggemann, *Message of the Psalms*, 86.

37. Craigie, *Psalms 1–50*, 41; Zenger, *God of Vengeance?*, 79; Althann, "Psalms of

12. Rejection Specifically for the Church—They Are Not Evil, but They Have No Place in the Church

12.A. Not Yet "For the New Testament Church"

The next two views are perhaps the most common, owing to the perceived tension between the New Testament and the Old on moral matters.

One view holds that imprecations are fine in themselves, but they are not for the church today. Some see the final judgment as the right time for imprecations, arguing that the church must wait for that day and not use them yet.[38] Others argue that imprecations are rooted in God's promise to bless Abraham's seed and, in particular, to curse whoever curses them. Under a Dispensational scheme, where the Church and Abraham's seed are to be kept distinct, it naturally follows that imprecations continue to be appropriate for Jews, but not for Christians.[39]

Holders of this view do not consider imprecations to be ethically evil, but inappropriate for the church age, where judgment is suspended until the last day. Prayers for judgment are seen as antithetical to forgiveness and love for enemies: "Christ and his apostles who, though they predict judgment upon evildoers, instead instruct the church to love and forgive one's enemies."[40] This is one of the main assumptions which we will test exegetically in the Psalms.

12.B. No Longer "For the New Testament Church"

At its starkest, this view holds that what the Christ could pray then, he can no longer pray.

These authors also do not charge the OT with immorality, but with an incompleteness that is supplemented in the NT. We will spend more time surveying these authors, since they helpfully state what it is about the OT that runs counter to the NT. They will supply us with what we need to test in the Psalms.

Vengeance," 11; Miller, "The Hermeneutics of Imprecation," 201; Silva, "The Cursing Psalms," 220–30; Schaefer, *Psalms*, xliii-xlv.

38. So, e.g., Kline, *Biblical Authority*, 154–62; Waltke et al., *Psalms as Christian Worship*, 95–98.

39. So, e.g., Laney, "Imprecatory Psalms," 41–44.

40. Waltke et al., *Psalms as Christian Worship*, 95.

None of these authors hold to a caricature of the OT as character-ized by wrath, judgment, and retribution, contrasting with the love, for-giveness, and kindness of the NT.[41] Hans-Joachim Kraus saw this dualism assumed by much scholarship, and labelled it a "cliché" ("Klischee") en-tirely devoid of theological sense or content.[42]

Franz Delitzsch explains that David rightly prayed Ps 109, not be-cause the offence of his enemy was against him, but because it was an offence against his office as the anointed of Yahweh. He then makes a distinction: because the persecution was against Christ in the person of David, the prayer takes the Old Testament form. This is a form which is *not* appropriate on the lips of the suffering savior, because they reflect the spirit of Sinai and not Zion, and the NT has sided with Zion and dispensed with Sinai. "This spirit of wrath is overwhelmed by the spirit of love in the NT."[43] Thus, not even Christ himself may pray like this anymore.

Others hold that the cross of Christ brings about a different set of priorities, such as the imperative to proclaim the gospel, which mean that this kind of desire for retribution is at odds with the NT.[44]

For example, Peels not only denies the "cliché" by showing that judg-ment and forgiveness are each found in both testaments. He also reverses the idea: the NT is *more severe*, because of "the possibility of *eternal* ruin (2 Thess. 1:9)," which is hardly known in the OT.[45] It is precisely because this final, eschatological judgment comes into play that Christians can-not appropriate imprecations without modification. The cross of Christ is the decisive act of justice, and the final judgment is now delayed for the purpose of allowing sinners to repent and escape judgment. While impre-cations do appear on the lips of saints in the NT, they are less frequent, and the characteristic (though not exclusive) demeanor of Christians is to entrust judgment to God and pray "for forgiveness and conversion" of the enemy.[46] What cannot remain are specific urgent prayers against particu-lar evils, but instead general prayers for the overcoming of evil in general.[47]

---

41. Rightly lamented by Peels as being a common influence on assessments of im-precatory prayers (Peels, *The Vengeance of God*, 244).

42. Kraus, *Theologie der Psalmen*, 233.

43. Delitzsch 672.

44. Kidner, *Psalms 1–72*, 26, 32; Kirkpatrick 1:lxxxix, xciii.

45. Peels, *The Vengeance of God*, 244–45.

46. Peels, *The Vengeance of God*, 245–46.

47. Peels, *The Vengeance of God*, 246.

Similarly, Puritan William Gurnall, in his famous *Christian in Complete Armour*: "direct thy prayers rather against their plots than person." We are forbidden from praying against our private enemies, only "the implacable enemies of God and his church." The possibility of repentance means that we must never pray against a particular individual.[48] This introduces another assumption that must be tested: is the possibility that enemies might repent a NT innovation, and not expected by the authors of the Psalms?

Dissenting Welsh Puritan Walter Cradock (1606–59) goes further:

> *There is nothing more improper and unbecoming a Saint, than revenge*; and a Saint that hath been a slave, and is redeemed, and kept from the pit by the Lord Iesus Christ, *he should not desire the destruction of any creature*; he hath had mercy by the Gospell, therefore he should have mercy on every creature. . . . And if God will not do this, that they may be bettered, yet That men may know that thou, whose name alone is Iehovah, art the most high, over all the earth.[49]

If Delitzsch, Peels and Cradock assume that the NT has added something, others identify what exactly was missing in the OT. It is often assumed that in OT times one could not love the enemy, and one could not imagine the end of his wickedness apart from the destruction of the whole person:

> the curses can be understood in the sense of exorcizing the *consequences* which result from the actions of such persons. . . . Christian re-reading turns the execration of individuals into a denunciation of the unjust situation provoked by them. While the psalmists sees [*sic*] in the ostracism of persons the solution of the problem, thus purifying the community, the Christian considers the reintegration of them as the only solution.[50]

That the enemy might repent was inconceivable for David:

> And if it be answered that David should have done what we recognize it as duty to do under like conditions, that is to say, that he should have pitied the sinner, even while he condemned the sin, the rejoinder is that this is just what David could not be expected to do, whether as a poet, a Shemite, a king, or an

48. Gurnall, *Christian in Complete Armour*, 2:444–48.
49. Cradock, *Divine Drops*, 103–4; italics added.
50. Althann, "Psalms of Vengeance," 10.

> Old Testament saint . . . this distinction between the sin and the sinner was impossible to David as an Old Testament saint. This impossibility arose out of the fact that the doctrine of Satan, which makes it easy for us to pity the sinner while we hate and condemn the sin, was then very imperfectly revealed.[51]

Likewise, desiring that the enemy be forgiven:

> Jesus prayed for his enemies' forgiveness (Luke 23:34), thus practising his own teaching (Matt. 5:44). The psalmists never did this: their attitude to their enemies is consistently unforgiving.[52]

The total inability of David, and every OT believer, of even grasping the concept of enemy love, or the enemy's repentance, or considering the whole person as redeemable from their wicked behavior, is an assumption which merits examination, since some would argue that these differences are overplayed. Calvin Seerveld argues that both testaments teach that vengeance belongs to the Lord.[53] John Eaton similarly observes that in places imprecations "[jar] against other *Old* and New Testament teachings of forgiving goodwill towards enemies (Gen 5.5f.; 2 Kings 6.22; Prov. 25.21–22; Matt. 5.38–48 etc.)."[54] R.T. France would warn us about misreading Matt 5. The assumption that Jesus in Matt 5 is citing the Law of Moses rather than the errors of his own day is a great debt which we owe to Marcion, who first termed Jesus's teaching there "the antitheses," and does not withstand close scrutiny of the Law.[55] We do not find "love your neighbor and hate your enemy" in the Law, and neither the *lex talionis* nor the Law generally codify grudges and feuds: Exod 23:4–5; Prov 25:21–22. We will see how prayers about enemies in the Psalms fill out this picture.

---

51. Martin, "Imprecations," 547–48; so also Kirkpatrick: "they use the language of the age which was taught to love its neighbour and hate its enemy" (Kirkpatrick 3:lxxxix).

52. Bauckham, *The Bible in Politics*, 65.

53. Seerveld, "Why We Need," 149.

54. Eaton, *The Psalms*, 37; italics added.

55. France, *Matthew*, 194. Wolterstorff identifies Matt 5:38–48 as part of a "reciprocity code" and sees it as widely extended in the Greco-Roman world and in Jewish society. He rightly notes that Jesus repudiates it, but mistakenly identifies the *lex talionis* as an expression of it (Wolterstorff, *Justice in Love*, 122–25).

13. Cautious Appropriation—They Have a Place in the Church

The previous section either rejected appropriation by the church, or else required significant modifications, owing to the difference between the Testaments. We turn to those who argue for a careful ongoing use, which does not assume that imprecations may be "fired at will," but asks when, how, and about whom to pray.

13.A. Reformation and Onwards—Optimistic Appraisals of David's Ethics

The Reformers, while not abandoning the four ancient senses of Scripture, emphasized the priority of the literal sense, from which the others were derived. Allegories that ignored the plain meaning of these prayers (as found in Origen), were excluded. The effective silence we saw with Theodoret's exclusively prophetic interpretation would be equally unsatisfactory. John Calvin's Geneva, for example, was full of Protestant exiles like him, facing the ever-present threat of overwhelming invasion. His daily sermons to such a congregation could hardly be limited to prophetic fulfilment in the life of Christ. Calvin connects David with the believer in his introduction to Ps 109:

> And although David here complains of the injuries which he sustained, yet, as he was a typical character, everything that is expressed in the psalm must properly be applied to Christ, the Head of the Church, and to all the faithful, inasmuch as they are his members; so that when unjustly treated and tormented by their enemies, they may apply to God for help, to whom vengeance belongs.[56]

Calvin dismisses the psychological assumptions on which Brueggemann would later build his case, as we saw above:

> [W]hen David forms such maledictions, or expresses his desires for them, he is not instigated by any immoderate carnal propensity, nor is he actuated by zeal without knowledge, nor is he influenced by any private personal considerations.

---

56. Calvin, *Psalms*, 4:268.

But I return to David, who, free from all inordinate passion, breathed forth his prayers under the influence of the Holy Spirit.[57]

Belonging to the number of the faithful, he would not omit the law of charity, in desiring the salvation of all men. But in this instance God elevated his spirit above all earthly considerations, stript him of all malice, and delivered him from the influence of turbulent passion, so that he might, with holy calmness and spiritual wisdom, doom the reprobate and castaway to destruction.[58]

On the contrary, he warns his congregations against such an inner life, and especially against seeking vengeance against our private enemies, rather than God's enemies.[59] Even then, he further cautions against speedy use of imprecations, and urges one to leave room for repentance and reconciliation.[60] Accordingly, delight in repentance must exceed delight in justice:

[T]he righteous would anxiously desire the conversion of their enemies, and evince much patience under injury, with a view to reclaim them to the way of salvation.[61]

Likewise, as Luther puts it, we should recognize the fact that they are more against Christ than against us, that whatever we might cause to befall them or pray against them is as nothing compared to the judgment of God against them, and therefore we should pity them and pray for their conversion.[62]

This is not to deny that there are grounds for rejoicing if God sends retribution after persistent and unrepentant evil, since that demonstrates God's love to the victim;[63] love of justice gives joy "as pure . . . as his desire for their conversion and salvation was strong and unfeigned."[64] When trust in God is shaken by injustice, and gives way to questioning God's goodness, examples of justice are a comfort.[65]

However, if justice is the issue, David must prove his innocence:

57. Calvin, *Psalms*, 4:275–76.

58. Calvin, *Psalms*, 4:285.

59. Calvin, *Psalms*, 4:276; so also Ames, *Conscience*, 44.

60. Calvin, *Psalms*, 4:276.

61. Calvin, *Psalms*, 2:378.

62. Luther, *Sermon on the Mount*, 123–25; so also Ames, *Conscience*, 44.

63. Calvin, *Psalms*, 2:378.

64. Calvin, *Psalms*, 2:378–79.

65. Calvin, *Psalms*, 2:379; so also Ames, *Conscience*, 44.

> He does not claim the judgment or patronage of God to his cause, until he had, in the first place, asserted his integrity, and stated his complaint against the malicious conduct of his enemies; for God can never be expected to undertake a cause which is unworthy of defense.[66]

Luther goes further, insisting that we cannot pray for the success of those who are about wicked work and injustice, but that we are obliged to pray down curses on their schemes. He shows Jesus cursing and points out that the Lord's Prayer must necessarily lead to imprecation. The "we," however, is not any of us, but those divinely appointed to the task.[67] He carefully applies his Two Kingdoms model to the Christian as a judge and then applies that model to prayers of imprecation in the Psalms.[68] These are later works than those surveyed earlier, which had Luther in a more exclusively Patristic mold.

Finally, Calvin detects in the Psalms the distinction between evil and evildoers: "the hatred in these verses is not directed to the enemies personally but to their deeds or their disposition."[69]

Authors considered in the previous sections are characterized by assuming that David lacked the ethics of the New Testament. By contrast, here we have met authors who assume that by divine inspiration the prayers of the Psalter are full of the very same NT ethics. This includes a concern for justice, rather than vengeance; a present orientation of life in the light of future judgment; a desire for the enemy to repent so that evil actions end while evil persons turn. We have even found the assumption that pleas of innocence are not self-righteous but display an awareness that God cannot be appealed to for favoritism when we are evil against innocent enemies.

These sets of competing assumptions about the Psalms need to be investigated exegetically.

---

66. Calvin, *Psalms*, 2:374.
67. Luther, *Sermon on the Mount*, 101, 124.
68. Luther, *Selected Psalms III*, 245.
69. Peels summarizing Calvin on Ps 139:21–22 (Peels, "'Perfect Hatred,'" 35n2).

13.B. Dietrich Bonhoeffer—Christ at Prayer with His People

Whereas Delitzsch argued that not even Christ can pray these prayers, Bonhoeffer allows that Christ *alone* prays them. However, he is sometimes misrepresented as concluding that we may not pray also.[70]

He states that requests for vengeance require perfect righteousness, which the church lacks. Our sins deserve worse than anything our enemies could dish up: God's wrath. David was preparing the way for the truly innocent Christ. David endured all evil with quietness, and it is Christ's righteousness in David which prays Ps 58.[71]

May we pray it? "Certainly not! . . . No, *we* cannot pray this psalm. Not because we are too good for it (what a superficial idea, what a colossal pride!), but because we are too sinful, too evil for it!"[72] He goes on to show that only Christ is able to pray it. But he does not leave the matter there:

> And now *we too pray* this psalm with him . . . in the fervent plea that God will bring all of *our enemies* under the cross of Christ and grant them grace; in the burning desire that the day may soon come in which Christ visibly triumphs over his enemies . . . Thus we have learned to pray this psalm.[73]

This may seem like special pleading, but it is in fact Bonhoeffer's view of all Psalms and all biblical prayers:

> Thus all prayers of the Bible are such prayers, which we pray together with Jesus Christ, prayers in which Christ includes us, and through which Christ brings us before the face of God. Otherwise there are no true prayers, for only in and with Jesus Christ can we truly pray.[74]

Bonhoeffer's handling of imprecations is the same as his handling of The Lord's Prayer, the Magnificat, and Ps 100.

The central assumption here is that these Psalms state that the supplicant is perfectly righteous, and no-one lacking such righteousness can take them on their lips. A different approach, based on the same premise, sees the church praying simultaneously with Christ (as the one praying

---

70. This seems to be how he is presented in Day, *Crying for Justice*, 33–35.

71. Bonhoeffer, "Psalm 58," 86–87.

72. Bonhoeffer, "Psalm 58," 86–87.

73. Bonhoeffer, "Psalm 58," 96; italics added.

74. Bonhoeffer, *Life Together*, 157.

the psalms) and *as the wicked enemy* about whom the psalms are prayed.[75] We will explore whether such immaculate innocence is a pre-requisite for imprecation in the Psalter.

13.C. Post-Modernism—Prayers of the Oppressed

If Modernity made imprecations more generally unpopular, then more recent moods have given them a plausible way back. What if the supplicant is oppressed, and the enemy is powerful? Scruples against judgmentalism are quickly forgotten in such circumstances. Prayers for vengeance become not only inoffensive, but almost compulsory. Who, in this day and age, would object to imprecations when described like this: "the psalms that pray for vengeance are actually praying for God to address violence done to the poor and lowly"; and "imprecation has its proper setting in the struggle for justice to be done for the powerless."?[76]

For example, Joel LeMon fears that singing such psalms would imply that one can act out their violence.[77] Worse, God might *answer* if we pray them![78] However, not everyone is banned from their use. He notes the importance of the worshipping community regulating imprecations, but assumes that one who is weak and powerless may pray them, whereas anyone with his own resources should be automatically excluded, in case they take matters into their own hands.[79] Similarly, Knut Heim comments on Ps 137: "The psalm has probably been underused by the powerless and overused by the powerful."[80]

We will see whether the mere fact of being poor and lowly entitles one to divine protection.

13.D. Global Church Solidarity—Praying with the Oppressed

The shift in attention to the poor and oppressed as worthy candidates for praying these psalms has coincided with an increased interest in the

75. Jauss, "Fluchpsalmen beten?," 107–15.

76. Creach, *Violence in Scripture*, 194.

77. LeMon, "Psalms," 645.

78. LeMon, "Violent Psalms," 104.

79. LeMon, "Violent Psalms," 108.

80. Heim, "Verbal Violence," 17; I am grateful to Dr. Heim for sharing an advance copy with me.

perspective of Majority World readers as biblical interpreters. The realization that we all bring spectacles to the Bible as readers has raised awareness of the value of comparing notes with readers from other cultures and circumstances. While post-modernism may have given the impetus in the modern academy, this kind of global church cross-fertilization goes back at least as far as Dutch Missiologist Johan Bavinck.[81] (By contrast, in the English translation of Sigmund Mowinckel's 1951 Norwegian *Studies*, a "chapter, which dealt with the use of the psalms in the Church, and which was strongly coloured by having been written during enemy occupation, has been omitted."[82] A use of Psalms produced by one culture is rejected by another.)

The combination of these factors (attention to the poor/oppressed, and an ear to other cultures) has led some recent Western expositors to suggest that it is in persecuted Majority World churches that prayers for retribution have their home. For example, J. Clinton McCann thinks that many Westerners simply have never felt as angry as the author of Ps 109. Victimization that is common in other parts of the world is alien to our experience.[83] He argues that these psalms are cathartic, and suggests (as is often observed) that praying the psalm is an alternative to actual vengeance.[84] Writing in Nigeria, David Adamo explains how the same psalm faces different assumptions: "Western scholars link [Ps 109] to hate, vengeance, cursing, and violence. . . . [T]his psalm is interpreted differently in African Christianity, for example as a psalm of protection, success, healing and, mostly, as a prayer to God to arise and fight for the righteous and the poor rather than leaving them to turn to witchdoctors, herbalists, or evil ones."[85]

Nonetheless, African scholars can have the same misgivings as Western authors. In the *Africa Bible Commentary*, Cyril Okorocha devotes significant space, within his sparse introduction to the entire Psalter, persuading his readers that retaliation is wrong and not "to use these psalms as an excuse for contending with those who contend with us."[86]

81. Bavinck, *Introduction*. Recent examples include: Vanhoozer, "'One Rule to Rule,'" 85–126; Tennent, *Theology*.

82. Mowinckel, *Psalms*, 1:xliii.

83. McCann, *Book of Psalms*, 116–17; cf. Waltke et al., *Psalms as Christian Worship*, 96.

84. McCann, *Psalms as Torah*, 115.

85. Adamo, "Reading Psalm 109," 575.

86. Okorocha, "Psalms," 606.

In Kenya, Martin Ward is similarly keen to play down Ps 109, arguing for the generalized and spiritualized meaning we found above with Peels and Gurnall. Citing a Victorian study to the effect that "with the ancient world it was necessary for the cause to be embodied in a concrete party," we have again the assumption that David was completely *unable* to express hatred of sin other than by hating the sinner. David really wanted the end of sin and prayed according to his limited light.[87]

Culture and circumstances have helped to remove some obstacles to the appropriation of difficult psalms, but they are not the whole picture. Just as some Westerners try to persuade the laity to use these psalms on behalf of African brothers, some African church leaders are afraid that they are being used only too eagerly. Reticence in using imprecations cannot be reduced entirely to cultural stances nor to worldview. There remains a problem across cultures—a perceived clash with the teaching of the NT.

13.E. John N. Day—A Slight Shift in NT Emphasis

John N. Day's *Crying for Justice* deserves special attention because it is both the most recent monograph on the imprecatory psalms and the most positive among modern treatments.[88]

His major original contribution brings to bear comparative material from ANE curses. He first notes that curses are merely prayers which "do not of themselves 'magically' come into force."[89] The one praying leaves all action in the hands of the gods.[90] Second, he finds a distinction between legitimate and illegitimate cursing.[91] Legitimate curses include treaty sanctions to which the vassal signs up and curses on tomb-robbers. Illegitimate ones include "curse for hire" witches attacking innocent parties.[92] This gives rise to another legitimate form: defensive counter-curses.[93]

---

87. Ward, "Psalm 109," 167–68.

88. Day, *Crying for Justice.*

89. Day, *Crying for Justice*, 41–45 (quoting 41).

90. Day, *Crying for Justice*, 38, 41, 109; this more recently confirmed by Kitz, *Cursed Are You!*, 32–33, 61.

91. Day, *Crying for Justice*, 37.

92. Day, *Crying for Justice*, 41–42. Kitz shows that there was also a differentiation between professional, lay, and semi-professional cursers, with the last group being particularly unpopular (Kitz, *Cursed Are You!*, 349–426, 401).

93. Day, *Crying for Justice*, 41–42; Kitz supplies a more general set of counter-curses (Kitz, *Cursed Are You!*, 321–48).

Day, in common with many historical and modern authors, argues that there is no contradiction between curses in the Psalter and the teaching and examples of Christ and his apostles. After outlining unsatisfactory solutions,[94] he concludes with three chapters arguing that the NT data fits with the vengeance texts of the Psalter. They are not in contradiction. The language of "heaping coals of fire" involves divine curse, and the example of Christ, the apostles, and saints in glory includes curses.[95]

He observes, as did the Reformers cited above, a dual prayer for enemies in psalms that contain imprecations.

> And we cry for deliverance in two directions—either destruction or conversion. . . . Either is "okay," for either will accomplish the deliverance of God's people at God's discretion, whether through destruction, frustration, or conversion. . . . Both sides of this request stretch our sensitivities beyond our comfort level. For we who are far from the scene of such severe persecution have a natural aversion to prayers for the destruction of our/ God's enemies. In some sense, we are to love our enemies. And those who may be enmeshed in the midst of such persecution might find it difficult to plead for the conversion of their oppressors. Both stretch us. Both are right, and the results in either direction are up to God.[96]

In keeping with the global focus we identified in the previous section, the book ends with a sermon on Ps 83, beginning: "This Sunday we are participating in the *International* Day of Prayer for the Persecuted Church."[97] However, Day does observe a significant discontinuity between OT and NT use. He qualifies this carefully: "this difference in the progress of the testaments is a difference in degree, rather than a difference in kind."[98] He also insists that we must use the imprecatory psalms in private and public worship.[99] What does the shift in emphasis consist of? In the OT, the special status of Israel as a geographical political entity surrounded by enemy nations but under God's blessing meant that it was legitimate to turn rather soon to prayers of cursing against God's enemies. The church in the New Testament, on the other hand, finds

94. Day, *Crying for Justice*, 21–35.
95. Day, *Crying for Justice*, 85–108.
96. Day, *Crying for Justice*, 121–22.
97. Day, *Crying for Justice*, 117; italics added.
98. Day, *Crying for Justice*, 111.
99. Day, *Crying for Justice*, 116.

herself scattered among the nations. Accordingly, imprecations are no longer our first response but our last resort and only ever used against the recalcitrant enemies of God's people.[100]

We have seen that Luther, Calvin, and others assume that this NT perspective is already true in the Psalms; whether the case can be made from the Psalter or whether NT theology is being read into the texts needs to be investigated.

14. Self-Righteousness—A Further Problem

In our description of various positions above we have focused on the content of these petitions. A quite separate, but very common, objection is the stance of the one making them. Aside from the petitions themselves, some take issue with the psalmist's brazen proclamations of self-righteousness, which are often offered by the psalmist to justify such prayers. For example:

> You might see [Ps 101:1–7] as a prime example of why you don't particularly like many of the psalms. It seems to ooze self-righteousness.

> Who is this fellow [Ps 1] who draws about him the skirts of his own righteousness, carefully avoids the contamination of sinners, and spends all his time gloating in the law? From the moment we hear of him we do not like him.

> It's not difficult to see why someone might find Psalm 1 a quite insufferable Psalm about a quite insufferable fellow. There he sits, day and night, brooding and fretting over the law. What a pedant![101]

Gert Kwakkel argues that this consensus was prominent in the first half of the twentieth century.[102] This time the academic *Zeitgeist*, at least in the German NT academy, may have something to do with it:

> Israel has exemplary significance for [Paul]; in and with Israel *he strikes at the hidden Jew in all of us, at the man who validates rights*

---

100. Day, *Crying for Justice*, 110–11.

101. These quotations are from authors who are anticipating this objection to the Psalms, but do not themselves share it: Daly-Denton, *Psalm-Shaped Prayerfulness*, 64; Mays, "Delight in the Law"; McCann, "The Psalms as Instruction," 118.

102. Kwakkel, *According to My Righteousness*, 2.

and demands over against God on the basis of God's past dealings with him and to this extent is serving not God but an illusion.[103]

If that assumption about Judaism was in the background, protestations of innocence in the Psalms could easily appear as misguidedly self-righteous. All of Kwakkel's examples of this view were published in Germany: Bertholet, Eichrodt, König, Sellin, Staerk. For example:

> In these prayers we find a divide between the piety of the Old Testament and that of the gospel. Nowhere more so than here do we find the naïve self-righteousness, the lack of awareness of the reality of sin as a terrible power within people, and with this the childish claim of reward for good works rendered.[104]

We have seen above that others, with a more positive view of these psalms, agree with the basic claims: Bonhoeffer also sees that the psalmist thinks himself perfectly innocent, is unaware of any sin or sinfulness, and believes himself to have earned rescue as a reward for good works. Whether this leads to reserving the Psalm for Christ's worthy lips or to rejecting it as the product of a deluded naïve OT ignoramus, both approaches agree on what the supplicant claims about himself.

We will test these assumptions exegetically and examine whether self-righteousness is evident in the Psalter.

15. Point of Departure

The above approaches have in common that they seek to explain imprecations by reference to something outside of the Psalter: whether the Abrahamic covenant,[105] ANE background,[106] assumptions about the NT, or theology generally. The point of departure is always that these psalms (or verses) are odd creatures requiring special treatment, and that the

---

103. Käsemann, "Paul and Israel," 186; italics added.

104. "In diesen Gebeten tut sich eine Kluft zwischen alttestamentlicher und evangelischer Frömmigkeit. Nirgends tritt die naive Selbstgerechtigkeit, der Mangel an Erkenntnis vom wahren Wesen der Sünde als furchtbarer Macht im Menschen, und damit der kindliche Anspruch auf Lohn für geleistete gute Werke stärker in die Erscheinung als hier" (Staerk, on Pss 5, 17 and 26, cited in Kwakkel, *According to My Righteousness*, 2).

105. Adams, *War Psalms*, 68; Day, *Crying for Justice*, 80; Peels, *The Vengeance of God*, 240.

106. Day, *Crying for Justice*, 80.

answer lies outside the Book of Psalms. The very book which contains these texts is the one most frequently excluded from the discussion. This is a methodological oddity which we seek to address.

Erich Zenger argues that imprecations are the very heart of the Psalter, if not the whole Bible.[107] McCann makes the same claim specifically about Ps 82, which is a prayer for judgment.[108] Certainly imprecation, retribution and judgment are pervasive in the Psalter. It would therefore be passing strange if the Psalter's own introduction did not begin to prepare us for them.[109]

Patrick Miller has suggested that psalms such as 137 should be read or sung in worship as part of *lectio continua*. The constant exposure to abrasive elements in the psalms in general prepares the congregation for these particular psalms. Sequential reading means that these psalms are not specially singled out for use but arrive when their turn comes.[110] This would use the Psalter context at the level of general impression. Can we go further and ask whether Pss 136 and 138 or the flow of Book V have a more specific role to play in understanding 137?

John Walton concluded his 1991 *Cantata*:

> Certainly dealing with only the macrolevel has the *potential of resolving some of the perennial problems that arise with the book of Psalms, such as imprecatory psalms and the retribution principle.* On the other hand, I cannot justify disregarding the original contexts of the individual psalms. Continued research is needed as we consider the options available.[111]

That is the challenge we now take up. Examining imprecations in the light of the Psalter as a book does give the opportunity to revisit some of the claims about the content of the psalms themselves. Did the psalmists know only to love their neighbor, but not their enemy?[112] Or

---

107. Zenger, *God of Vengeance?*, 12.

108. McCann, "Most Important Text," 63–75.

109. For example, Laney argues convincingly that imprecatory psalms have six purposes ("Imprecatory Psalms," 41). All of these flow from the Psalter's introduction, in my view, though he does not mention this. Laney even goes on to discuss the central importance of David's concept of kingship in the imprecations, but makes no mention of Ps 2 in that regard (Laney, "Imprecatory Psalms," 43).

110. Miller, "The Hermeneutics of Imprecation," 201.

111. Walton, "Psalms," 31; italics added.

112. Bullock, *Psalms 1–72*, 260, who carefully observes that imprecations clash against neighbor-love in *both* testaments, but that Christians additionally need to reckon with enemy-love.

did they know only to love Israelite enemies, with Jesus's new commandment being to love enemies outside of Israel?[113] Could they envisage no
possibility of repentance?[114] Do these psalms involve (delusions of) perfect righteousness? In examining such claims, we will also be testing the
width of the gap between the ethics of the Psalms and the NT.

How do these psalms, and the Psalter as a whole, handle issues of
vengeance, violence, enemies and judgment? Before examining the text,
we need to introduce the idea of readings the Book of Psalms as an organized book with a message.

113. Barbiero, *L'asino del nemico*, 347–52.
114. Althann, "Psalms of Vengeance," 10.

3

Reading the Psalter as Book

A Brief Guide for the Perplexed

The oldest commentary on the meaning of the psalms is
the manner of their arrangement in the Psalter.[1]

[T]he macrolevel has the potential of resolving some of the
perennial problems that arise with the book of Psalms, such
as *imprecatory psalms and the retribution principle.*[2]

WE HAVE SEEN THAT there remain a variety of views over imprecations
in the Psalter and that valuable insights have been gained from Biblical
Theology, OT theology, doctrinal, ethical, pastoral and liturgical considerations, and ANE background. The one context which has not been considered is the one in which they are found: their literary context within
the Book of Psalms.

In this chapter, we briefly introduce the ancient art of reading a
Psalm in the context of the Book of Psalms. How do its neighbors help us
to understand it? How does its place within the whole provide clues to its
intention? What does it contribute to its neighbors and to the flow of the
whole book? We take these questions for granted as an approach to other

---

1. Goulder, *Sons of Korah*, 1.
2. Walton, "Psalms," 31; italics added.

books of the Bible, so we need to begin by explaining why this approach to Psalms even needs an introduction.

1. Psalter Shape: A Venerable Enterprise

There is a mistaken history about the Psalms which has been circulating freely for decades, which tells us that reading Psalms in their context, and treating the Psalter as a coherent book, is an innovation to be dated to 1985.[3] I have shown elsewhere that this is not so.[4]

Understanding individual psalms in context and discerning the message of the whole book is one of the oldest quests in biblical studies. A desire to discover a deliberate message behind the arrangement of the whole collection goes back at least to the third century, with Origen, and blossomed into full-length Christological commentaries in the Victorian era. Bound up with this quest has been the even older idea (beginning no later than Hippolytus in the second century) that the first few psalms are a deliberate introduction to the whole book of Psalms.[5] The basic building block of this model has been the literary context of each psalm: what do the psalms adjacent to a psalm contribute to our reading? Do wider contexts within the Psalms help also? Are there larger structural features designed to guide the reader? Is there even a message behind the arrangement of the whole Book of Psalms?

For much of the twentieth century, the assumed answer to these questions was "no." Put simply by Herman Gunkel, the father of the dominant approach: each Psalm is quite alone and self-contained, and its context within the book tells us nothing.[6] It was not that a psalm had no context, but that it had to be found elsewhere. A psalm was to be understood in the light not of its neighbouring psalms, but of similar psalms.[7] Gunkel bequeathed the world a system for classifying psalms that was based on their *hypothetical* use in the temple cult. This line of enquiry ("cult criticism") gave us "form criticism." A psalm would be compared

---

3. E.g., Willgren, *Formation*, 11.

4. Jenkins, "Antiquity of Psalter," 161–80.

5. For a survey of the history of this quest through the millennia, see Jenkins, "Antiquity of Psalter," 164–76.

6. Gunkel and Begrich, *Einleitung in die Psalmen*, 3–4.

7. For a recent affirmation of this approach, see Longman and Dillard, *Old Testament*, 255.

to various fixed patterns, or "forms," to see whether it was (for example) a psalm used by the king during a festival, or by the whole people at a time of distress. The fit, or lack thereof, to a predetermined form would often then lead to a hypothetical reconstruction of how the original psalm had been edited. This hypothetical editing then explains the delinquent Psalm's failure to conform to hypothetical forms. This approach to the Psalms was in keeping with the general approach to OT books.

It could not last. The latter half of the twentieth century saw a shift away from reconstructing the pre-history behind the text of OT books and towards reading the text as it has come down to us. This sparked a renewal of the quest for meaning behind the arrangement of the whole book of psalms, most famously in the seminal work of Gerald Wilson but including several independent approaches before his.[8] Michael Goulder, a few years ahead of Wilson, put it elegantly: "The oldest commentary on the meaning of the psalms is the manner of their arrangement in the Psalter."[9]

Such an approach to the Psalter has not been without its critics. Some of the skepticism directed to this method stems from its perceived novelty, arising from the mistaken history above. As we shall see, Wilson did indeed set a new tone and breathed new life into the enterprise of finding a coherent message behind the arrangement of the Psalms. However, the quest itself had been ancient.

Neither ancient nor modern authors, now thirty-five years after Wilson's reboot of the enterprise, have considered retribution through the lens of Psalter shape, despite a constant stream of revisiting the problem of imprecations. For example, deClaissé-Walford has produced a deservedly well-known canonical reading of the Psalter, and later an article on imprecatory Psalms. In that article, she offers three contexts for reading imprecations. Yet, even in her treatment of their *canonical* context, she ignores the context within the Psalter.[10]

I hope to show that this is unfortunate, since the Psalter's opening psalms put retribution front and center. I propose to take up Walton's suggestion that attention to "the macrolevel has the potential of resolving some of the perennial problems that arise with the book of Psalms, such as imprecatory psalms and the retribution principle."[11]

---

8. Jenkins, "Antiquity of Psalter," 176–79.

9. Goulder, *Sons of Korah*, 1.

10. deClaissé-Walford, "Imprecatory Psalms," 78–84.

11. Walton, "Psalms," 31.

2. Psalms Have Superscriptions

Wilson's was not the first to attempt a full-length reading of the Psalter attending to its shape and arrangement; however, neither was his work merely one more attempt. He revolutionized the field, by taking advantage of two major bodies of knowledge inaccessible to older generations: comparative work in the ancient Near East (ANE) and the discoveries at the Dead Sea (or Dead Sea Scrolls, DSS). This led him to pay attention to the "superscriptions" of the Psalms, which we must now introduce.

Many Psalms have "superscriptions," which are not part of the poem itself but are part of the text as we have it. In translations, these do not have a verse number and are often set apart from the poem, giving the impression that they are not part of the biblical text. In the Hebrew text, the shorter superscriptions are the beginning of v. 1 and the longer are the whole of v. 1; verse numbers in translation are then out by one or two. For convenience, where this is the case, I give the numbering of translations in square brackets (for example, Ps 18:3 [2]).

Superscriptions can include historical notices and a label associating them with a person, perhaps identifying them as the author (discussed further below). They also often include musical terminology and Hebrew genre markers, such as Ps 19, which labels itself a *mizmor*, usually translated "psalm," or Ps 120, *shir*, "song." We need to clarify the confusing variety of ways that psalms are classified, sometimes relating to these genre markers but most often not.

2.A. Different Ways of Labelling Psalms

The superscriptions may include Hebrew genre classifications, such as *mizmor* and *shir*, but the cult and form criticism of Gunkel was based on an unrelated schema. He hypothesized various fixed patterns into which psalms could fit and gave us labels for describing these patterns. This property of a psalm is often referred to by its German name: *Gattung* ("genre," plural *Gattungen*). These *Gattungen* have no connection to the genre labels which the superscriptions of the psalms themselves carry. Wilson, after considering their possible role in Psalter shaping, dismissed these "categories of the modern form-critics."[12]

12. Wilson, *Editing*, 161.

However, labels that originated as *Gattungen* are often helpful for pointing out something obvious about a Psalm, such as the fact that it is a complaint by one person as opposed to the community, or that it is focussed on the king. This in turn has given rise to a looser use of labels which describe Psalms without being prescriptive. The same psalm can be described as *royal* if that is its subject matter and as a *lament* as opposed to a thanksgiving (such as Ps 3). A psalm can be described as "sapiential" (to do with wisdom) while also being a *Torah* psalm (concerned with the Law), such as Ps 1. These labels don't commit us to locating the psalm within a reconstruction of the Israelite cult. Nor do they require us, if we identify a psalm as "individual," to then splice off any reference to a community beyond the individual. Multiple true perspectives can be described without contradicting each other. We can call a psalm a "Torah" psalm, without claiming that Torah is exclusively central to it, unlike the rigid form critical categories, which were alien to the authors of the psalms anyway.[13]

These different sets of descriptions can cause confusion. Theories about a psalm's use in the temple are often no longer in view, but authors will still use many labels going back to Gunkel, such as "lament" or "royal," as genre designations. The very word "genre" and even the more technical-sounding *Gattung* have become ambiguous: sometimes authors refer to the superscription, other times to the strict form-critical categories, still other times to a looser genre classification.

Unless otherwise indicated, we will use terms such as "genre," "type," or *Gattung* in this loose, descriptive, and non-exclusive sense.

2.B. Descriptive Labels Are Useful

It has been debilitating to Psalms scholarship to let a focus on *Gattung* obscure the connections between adjacent psalms, such as when Pss 1 and 2 are treated 150 pages apart with no mention of each other.[14] As Goulder put it:

> The dazzled student soon suppresses as naive his instinct that it is proper to study 1 before 2, and that there is something curious in beginning a book on the Psalter with the 110th, or 89th

13. Jacobson and Jacobson, *Invitation to the Psalms*, 39; Harrison, *Introduction*, 997.

14. Ewald, *Psalms*, 2:318.

psalm. In time the student suppressing his instincts becomes a professor, teaching what he does understand, and ignoring what he does not. . . . The instinct that the order of the psalms may be important is not however naive, and is far from irrational.[15]

I would like to caution against an over-reaction to form-criticism. We are in danger of missing the significance of psalms as individual, discrete entities. They do not *only* come to us in the canon as part of the Psalter but also as discrete units. Each Psalm is presented to us in two ways: as a stand-alone poem and as a piece of the whole Psalter. Sometimes, superscriptions can pointedly direct us to read a psalm in more than one way. For example, Ps 10 is numbered as an individual psalm and can be read as such. However, it is almost unique within Book I by lacking a superscription, which invites reading it together with Ps 9 as a single composition.[16] A refrain binds 42 and 43 into a single composition, but they are also separate Psalms. Psalm 127 can stand alone, but its superscription marks it as part of the Songs of Ascents (Pss 120–34), while it is also part of the second major section of Book V and of Book V itself. These contexts are presented in the canon.[17]

To ignore the proper sequence of Psalms is, then, debilitating to the reader. However, this dual presentation of each Psalm means that we should also notice how psalms contrast with their neighbors. To ignore the suggestive *differences of type* between adjacent psalms, the way that Psalms of similar type are sometimes grouped, or even chiastic patterns of types (as we will see) would be equally limiting.

One does not have to endorse any particular cult-critical theory to notice that some psalms resemble each other more than others. If Pss 1 and 2 have been closely knit together, that does not change the fact that they are different kinds of speeches (a benediction and a warning) followed by yet a different one (a prayer, Ps 3) or that Ps 1 resembles sections of Proverbs and Pss 37, 19, 73, and 119, while Ps 2 resembles 18 and 110.[18]

---

15. Goulder, *The Sons of Korah*, 8.

16. For one example of each, compare Barbiero, *Das erste Psalmenbuch*, 88–113 with Yefet (the latter cited in Simon, *Four Approaches*, 77).

17. Weber, "Von der Psaltergenese," 738.

18. *Contra*: "Their [Pss 1–2] thorough cohesiveness at various linguistic levels and the resulting coherence of theme and message, in spite of their so-called 'generic' differences, exposes the folly of form-critical categories in any attempt to understand the canonical Psalter" (Cole, *Psalms 1–2*, 45).

Descriptive labels, such as "wisdom Psalm" or "*Torah* psalm" can be helpful even if some of them are borrowed from form criticism.

On a canonical reading of the first three Psalms, the progression
from instruction to prophecy to prayer and the progression in subject
matter from (among other themes) Torah, kingship, and lament should
be attended to; the common theme of the enemies highlights the different relationships in which the enemies stand to the psalmist, the reader,
and Yahweh. I will use terms such as "Torah psalm" and "royal psalm" not
to indicate a hard and fast categorization but to reflect the fact that there
may be editorial intentionality in placing pairs of psalms that deal with
Torah and the king in canonically significant places (Pss 1–2; 18–19 in
Book I).[19] A psalm can fall into more than one category, since these descriptions operate at different levels: subject matter(s), type of speech-act,
tone, or authorship.[20] Psalm 1, for example, could be a Torah psalm (with
a strong emphasis on the Law), without denying that it is sapientially
shaped (resembling passages in the Wisdom Literature).[21]

Our use of such labels will be descriptive, not prescriptive.[22]

2.C. David in the Superscriptions—Applied History

A common feature of superscriptions is a connection with a person, most
often David, but including others: the temple singers David appointed
(Korahites, Asaphites), Solomon, Moses, or "the afflicted." These are pre-
fixed by a Hebrew *lamedh* preposition, with a range of possible meanings.
Thus לְדָוִד (*ledavid*) could mean "about David," composed "for David,"
or commissioned "by David."[23] It is also the most obvious way of saying
"belonging to David." A few of the superscriptions also carry historical
notices pointing to some event. Three questions are commonly asked:
does *ledavid* mean that David is the author? Is this attribution, along with
any historical notice, original, or was it added to the poem later? If the

19. Following Grant, *King*, 213–20, and *contra* Cole's critique of Grant's thesis
(Cole, *Psalms 1–2*, 45).

20. Jacobson and Jacobson, *Invitation to the Psalms*, 39; Harrison, *Introduction*,
997. Even Mowinckel had argued that "royal" is not a *Gattung* but spans all the *Gattungen* (Mowinckel, *Psalms*, 1:47).

21. It has this dual classification in Day, *Psalms*, and in Lucas, *Psalms and Wisdom
Literature*.

22. Firth, *Surrendering*, 143.

23. The range of options is discussed in Kleer, "*Der liebliche Sänger*," 83–86.

latter, is it accurate? This is not the place to set out all sides in these three areas of discussion, but I will briefly present the view that will guide our reading of the Psalter.[24]

To enquire whether *ledavid* means that David wrote a Psalm is to ask too little. We should further ask why we are being given this information. I would argue that *ledavid* does identify David as the author. However, some Psalms written by David deliberately lack such attribution, and this is to help us connect them with their context. For example, Psalms 1 and 2 have no superscription at all, perhaps to highlight their introductory function to the whole book so that Psalms are relevant to anyone, not just to David.[25] Other psalms may have been written by David for general use (as modern hymn writers do), in which case a *ledavid* superscription might be omitted to avoid bringing David's history unnecessarily into the use of the psalm.[26] Conversely, Ps 72 is לִשְׁלֹמֹה (*lishlomoh*); it might be best understood as not *by* Solomon, but by David *about* Solomon.[27] Thus, *ledavid* might not cover all Psalms that David wrote, nor might similar *lamedh* attributions always point us to the author. What then do they tell us, if not always authorship? The presence of *ledavid*, and similar attributions to other characters put us in mind of that person when we read the psalm. It is part of how we are guided to understand the Psalms.

Something similar applies to the historical notices. The notices tell us to bear that event in mind when we read the Psalm. This furthers two ends. Firstly, it helps the individual worshipper at prayer: if a psalm fits on David's lips while he is in a particular situation, then I can take it on my lips when I face similar situations.[28] As Wilson put it: "As David, so every man!"[29] The superscription to such a psalm helps me to know

24. For a sample of opinions, see Childs, "Psalm Titles," 143; Craigie, *Psalms 1–50,* 73; Goulder, *The Prayers of David,* 1–30; Wenham, "The Nations," 165; Zenger, "Was wird anders?," 407–9; Waltke et al., *Psalms as Christian Worship,* 86–92.

25. The argument is made that the superscriptions must have been original, because we have no manuscripts that lack them, including MT, DSS and LXX (Hamilton, *God's Glory,* 276n12). This fails to reckon with the difference in the superscriptions in those sources: DSS and LXX add superscriptions, especially David notices, and some scholars infer a "program of Davidization" behind this (Erbele-Küster, *Lesen,* 86–108).

26. This distinction between author and speaker is drawn out by Brown, "The Psalms and 'I,'" 26–44.

27. Following Tate, *Psalms 51–100,* 225; Kleer, "Der liebliche Sänger," 80.

28. Widely recognized, e.g., Mays, "David," 152; Brueggemann and Bellinger, *Psalms,* 38; Janowski, "Ein Tempel aus Worten," 299; Kleer, "Der liebliche Sänger," 116.

29. Wilson, *Editing,* 172–73.

when to use it. The lack of very concrete details about the situation of most psalms is what allows a broad pastoral application to situations that are not in every respect identical.[30] Derived from that first end follows the second end: David can serve as Israel's ethical tutor when Israel faces situations such as those of David in such a psalm. I see no need to question the accuracy, authenticity, nor originality of the superscriptions in order for them to achieve those ends.[31]

Even if Psalm 1 might introduce the Psalter as a resource for private devotion,[32] David teaches the people as they use his words. Taking a psalm on one's lips implies a commitment to the standpoint of the psalm.[33] David's office as king does not disqualify private individuals from following his example, but encourages it, as he represents the whole people.[34] Similarly, modern hymnody encourages entire congregations to sing as "I" as well as "we" within the same worship service.[35]

Not only the whole people, but the people as a whole. The two most prominent historical events in the Psalms concern the lives of David and of the nation.[36] The king represents corporately: "the king is the one who holds individual and nation together."[37] Through his example, as the nation sings psalms, he is teaching the nation as a nation. After David's days, he teaches the nation as the Levites lead the nation in singing his psalms.[38] The king relates to Yahweh in the same way as the whole nation in the Psalter. The king and the nation are saved by standing in the same relationship to Yahweh in the Psalms.[39] If, with Norman Whybray, the private reader can replace "we" with "I," why should the whole nation

---

30. Grant, "Determining the Indeterminate," 3–5.

31. *Contra* Wilson, *Editing*, 171–73; Zenger, "Was wird anders?," 407–9.

32. Whybray, *Reading the Psalms*, 22.

33. Wenham, *Psalms as Torah*, 57–76.

34. Mays, "David," 154; Allen, *Psalms*, 122–24; Kleer, "*Der liebliche Sänger*," 93; Auwers, *La composition littéraire*, 151; Erbele-Küster, *Lesen*, 53–68; Rendtorff, "The Psalms of David," 63; Nasuti, "Interpretive Significance," 334; Janowski, "Ein Tempel aus Worten," 299; Owens, *Psalms*, 175.

35. Curtis, *Psalms*, xxix.

36. Nasuti, "Interpretive Significance," 313.

37. Firth, "More Than Just Torah," 11.

38. Gillingham, "The Levites," 209.

39. Eaton, *Kingship*, 170.

not be able to replace "I" with "we"?[40] Israel then recites the Psalms "*in persona David*."[41]

Accordingly, we will read the final form by treating the superscriptions as integral parts of their psalms to guide the reader, and as editorial signals for the reader of the Psalter as a whole.

This may help to answer one objection concerning the modern insights gained from Psalter Shape. "[O]ne has to seriously question any new insight like this that has not been recognized over the millennia of previous interpretation."[42] Both the ancient Western tradition of sequential chanting and more modern liturgical uses of the Psalms, such as metrical settings, have consistently ignored the superscriptions. If they are reading guides of the final Psalter, it might explain how various insights have remained unrecognized.

3. One Psalter in Five Books

Wilson analyzed a large body of ANE temple hymn collections and discovered that they have certain organizing principles. Taking his cue from those principles, he focused on the superscriptions of Psalms and sought to establish what logic lay behind the arrangement of the Psalter. He discovered various groupings by authorship and some by genre.[43] However, none of these groups are the "*primary* organizational concern for the final Hebrew Psalter."[44] There is no organization around cultic terms, nor around historical references in the superscriptions.[45] Examining the few "untitled" psalms, he offers an array of evidence that the lack of superscription shows editorial awareness of a tradition that would combine the untitled psalm to its predecessor and therefore is not an organizing feature beyond that.[46] We thus have some false trails (cultic terms and historical notices) and three limited clues (authorship, genre, lack of

---

40. "The 'I' in the psalms can be a particular person, many people, the community" (Mays, "David," 155).

41. Auwers, *La composition littéraire*, 122.

42. Longman, "Messiah," 471.

43. Wilson, *Editing*, 156, 161.

44. Wilson, *Editing*, 156. He uses equivalent phrases later in this chapter, always with "primary" emphasized.

45. Wilson, *Editing*, 170–73.

46. Wilson, *Editing*, 173–81.

superscription). The latter may be *secondary* organizing principles, but Wilson was looking for the *primary* one.

Psalms 41, 72, 89, and 106 conclude with a "doxology," or line of praise, which divides the Psalms into five Books, as has been argued since at least Talmudic times. Wilson argued that these are original parts of their psalms and not editorial insertions to mark the ends of Books. Rather, the presence of the doxologies made these psalms suitable to end the Books.[47] It is by asking further how psalms are arranged within these books and how the books are arranged that the big picture emerges.

Books I–III trace the rise and then fall of the Davidic Monarchy. Royal psalms 2, 72, and 89 are placed at the seams of Books I–III to mark the stages of the Davidic monarchy: from its establishment (2), inheritance by Solomon (72), and downfall in Babylonian Exile (89). There is no royal psalm at the seam between Books I and II, but Psalm 72 is followed by a notice identifying the end of David's prayers, binding Book II with Book I as a unit.[48]

Books IV–V respond to this crisis, and the focus shifts from David as king to Yahweh as king. Part of the shift from David to Yahweh as King can be seen in Ps 90, which opens Book IV as the only psalm "of Moses."[49] Wilson understood this as a pointer away from the covenant with David (the loss of which is lamented in Ps 89, at the end of Book III), and back to the older, overarching covenant made in the days of Moses. David may have fallen, but Torah remains. Torah has pride of place in the introduction (Ps 1) and in Book V through the "massive acrostic" 119.[50]

Psalm 145 is placed to conclude the whole Psalter and to introduce the concluding doxology (Pss 146–50; note 145:21).[51] Thus, the final Psalter has an introduction and a conclusion.[52] It has a basic plot from David as king to Yahweh as King and three plot stages: Davidic monarchy (Books I and II); exile (Book III); response to exile (Books IV and V).

---

47. Wilson, *Editing*, 185–86.

48. Wilson, "King," 391–92.

49. Wilson, "Structure," 240. In his original dissertation, Wilson noted that Moses features prominently in the ensuing Book IV (he writes "Book Five" but clearly means IV; Wilson, *Editing*, 187).

50. Wilson, "Structure," 236.

51. Wilson, "King," 392.

52. Wilson, "Structure," 229.

The notion that the monarchy shifts away from David after Book
III has proved controversial, and we will offer our own detailed proposal
concerning the place of David in Book V in a later chapter.

Wilson's argument that the division into five books is significant for
the placement of each psalm as well as for the overarching message of the
whole has had a decisive impact on much Psalms scholarship. At least two
full-length treatments of the Psalms following Wilson's method arrive at
a similar overarching plot line for the five books.[53] This is an addition to,
not a replacement of, the older tools of the quest for Psalter shape, such as
the introductory function of the first few psalms, a possible conclusion,
the place of adjacent psalms, and longer sequences of psalms.[54]

We have seen that one criticism of this enterprise is its alleged novelty. A more telling problem is the tendency to make claims from large
impressions, rather than the detail of the text. As Whybray (Wilson's first
significant detractor) put it:

> The difficulty with such theories—Wilson's is only one of sever-
> al—is that they paint on a very broad canvas, paying insufficient
> attention to the contents of most individual psalms, whose ap-
> parent randomness of arrangement (for instance the mingling
> of psalms of praise with psalms of lament) remains a stumbling-
> block for those who fail to find any consistency or over-arching
> structure or plan to the book. Any theory of a coherent pattern
> ought surely to provide some explanation of the arrangement of
> the *whole* collection.[55]

Whybray's criterion for "randomness" needs a little explanation: "the
mingling of psalms of praise with psalms of lament." "Psalms of praise"
and "lament" are the form-critical categories of Gunkel discussed earlier.
Wilson had rejected these wholesale, so it is quite a strange criticism.[56]

We might ask why the form-categories of Gunkel should be the *only*
type of arrangement that could be used. All manner of stories can be told
by switching frequently between different genres, as the four Gospels do
(parables, narrative, sermons, poetry). The task is to find the significance
of placing a *particular* hymn after a *particular* lament not simply to wish
that all laments were next to each other. Moreover, whatever the organizing

53. deClaissé-Walford, *Reading from the Beginning*, 34; Robertson, *Flow of the
Psalms*.

54. Jenkins, "Antiquity of Psalter," 172–76.

55. Whybray, *Reading the Psalms*, 120.

56. Wilson, *Editing*, 161.

criterion, why should we look for *sorting*? This is exactly the trap that Gunkel had fallen into and that set scholarship against the older Psalter shape readings: he concluded that since the Psalms had not been filed away by any criterion he could think of, therefore they were not arranged at all.[57]

In hindsight, Whybray's critique of the lack of discerned "arrangement of the *whole* collection" seems premature. Following Wilson, various commentators have undertaken complete commentaries on the Psalter deploying canonical readings of the whole. For example, James Luther Mays suggested: "eventually it may be possible to compose a commentary based on the book itself as the interpretive context of the psalms."[58] McCann then introduced his commentary quoting Mays verbatim, while cautiously acknowledging the limitations of any attempt so close on the heels of Wilson.[59] However, in the following sections, we present some of the various authors who have gone on to do just that.

There is no one unified school of Psalter shape reading, otherwise known as "canonical" readings. Various approaches have developed over recent decades, in many ways similar to the approaches down the centuries of psalms exegesis. We introduce the major planks of our approach in this chapter by choosing authors whose method we will follow more closely than others.

4. From Individual Psalm to Psalter Shape

Contrary to Whybray's critique that the woods are obscuring the trees, Wilson had warned against bringing our own hypotheses of shaping to the text: we should instead focus on detailed rhetorical connections between psalms to discern editorial intent.[60] He may not always have been followed with the same rigor, but his painstaking care over details was evident in his initial thesis. Following his example is the work of Frank-Lothar Hossfeldt and Erich Zenger, who produced a full commentary on the Psalms using Psalter shape and followed it up with a (sadly incomplete) much more detailed technical commentary. Zenger's most recent

---

57. Gunkel and Begrich, *Einleitung in die Psalmen*, 434–36.

58. Mays, *Psalms*, 19.

59. McCann 666.

60. Wilson, "Understanding," 48.

essay on method outlines the following features of the Psalter which must be attended to.[61]

First, connections between sequential psalms can be identified. The end of one psalm can lead to the beginning of the next, such as the end of Ps 7 leading to the beginning of Ps 8. David promises to sing about *Yahweh's name*, Most High. Psalm 8 begins by proclaiming that *Yahweh's name* is splendid; not just "Most High" but over all the earth, which then becomes the theme of Ps 8.

At the level of topic, Ps 50 warns that the worship expressed through sacrifices is displeasing to Yahweh when it is not accompanied by a life-style that honours him. Sacrifices are not there as bribes or penances. Rather, "the one who offers thankfulness is the one who glorifies me" (v. 23). Immediately afterwards, Psalm 51 is the textbook example of the repentance of the inner man being the prerequisite for offering sacrifices:

> [19] God's sacrifices are a shattered spirit, a heart shattered and contrite,
>   God will not despise [it].
>
> . . .
>
> [21] then you will delight in righteous sacrifices.

Adjacent psalms can quote each other, but with significant changes (e.g., 134:1–2; 135:1–3). Psalms can be twinned in a way that suggests that they interpret each other (e.g., 111–12). When a sequence of psalms has been grouped by their *Gattung*, this is known as a "cluster" and can be significant (Pss 3–7 are all individual laments; likewise Pss 25–28). Just as individual psalms can be connected through redactional word-links, clusters can be too. Psalms 55 and 56 are connected by word-links, bringing together the clusters 52–55 and 56–59.

Second, above the level of the individual psalm, we look for Psalm groups and partial-Psalters. These can be identified by compositional structures (25–34) or common superscriptions (David, Asaph, Korah, Ascents); attention should be given to how these groups contrast with each other.

Third, moving beyond collections of adjacent Psalms, we have the macrostructure. This involves features such as the doxologies that divide the Psalter into five Books and the position of *hallelujah*.

At this point we should briefly note the recent caution sounded against canonical methods in the wake of Wilson. David Willgren's exhaustively produced monograph argues that the quest to see how the

---

61. This is a summary of Zenger, "Psalmenexegese *und* Psalterexegese," 31–65.

book of Psalms is more than the sum of its parts has been overplayed. In particular, he notes that psalms might well have been placed together because of features such as similar vocabulary; however, he would deny that there is any intentional message to be gleaned from this. "[T]he 'Book' of Psalms does not primarily provide a literary context for individual psalms."[62] Willgren's proposal fails to reckon with the weight of the evidence. If all we had were pair-wise links of Psalms, and even if those pairs made up the whole of the Psalter (along the lines of Delitzsch's investigation in the nineteenth century), he might have a point. However, as the work of Hossfeld-Zenger illustrates (their work is by no means alone), we are dealing with much more developed features of arrangement, well beyond pairs. Chain-links, as I have shown elsewhere, are an early effort at Psalter-shape readings, which by the Victorian era had grown into much larger-scale observations.[63] We have significant groups with striking internal structure, such as the chiastic arrangement of pairs of psalm types in Pss 15–24 and the transition from laments over national enemies (Pss 3–7) to international enemies (9–14) with Ps 8 pointedly marking the hinge point with its emphasis on God's international sovereignty as judge. The body of evidence for macrostructure and the overall plot line of the five books are among the kind of data that has been worked over in some detail for more than three decades, producing results that are not adequately presented by Willgren.[64]

Fourthly, and finally, for Zenger, the context within the Psalter does not displace the old approach to individual Psalms. As is evident in this essay and in their commentaries, Hossfeld-Zenger are committed to the significance of the final form of the Psalter only through diachronic analysis of its redaction not by synchronic analysis of the final form of the text. For example, Zenger detects redactional insertion of verses or

---

62. Willgren, *Formation*, 389–92.

63. Jenkins, "Antiquity of Psalter," 170–76.

64. For example, Gianni Barbiero's comprehensive (nearly eight hundred pages) study of all the various structures within Book I, backed up by exhaustive evidence of linkage (including extensive lexical links in every case) shows data that cannot be brushed away as simply pair-wise adjacency (Barbiero, *Das erste Psalmenbuch*). The construction of the book consists of larger scale connections forming groups and subgroups. While Willgren cites Barbiero's work, it is only in connection with Pss 1 and 2 (Willgren, *Formation*, 144, 155–58, 162, 169, 197–98) or as a brief description of his overall method (p. 12). Willgren does not attend to the staggering volume of evidence offered by Barbiero, nor to Barbiero's conclusions about the structure of Book I.

psalms to change the original speaker so that 24:6 has been inserted to give 22–25 a national perspective.

Those features of Psalms or of the Psalter which Hossfeld-Zenger identify as redactional are (in my view) significant features of the text, which deserve attention. Nonetheless, not much is gained by attributing them to redactional hands rather than to original authors. There is no contradiction between intentional editorial shaping and such a "synchronic" approach: even the author of a book that is written in a single edition has a plan, edits their own work, and gives the reader clues about the relationship of the parts.

5. A Fully-Fledged Book

Striking among commentators is Jean-Luc Vesco. His commentary is boldly arranged not by individual psalms, but by larger literary units.[65] He does treat each psalm individually, but to find Ps 21 you must first read about Book I, then the unit 15–24, the subunit 20–24, each with their extensive separate introduction, and finally reach the *introduction* to Ps 21, which itself consists largely of comments on its relationship to its context. Only then do you find an exposition of the Psalm text. This is the approach we would expect in any commentary on an epistle, and it is not uncommon among narrative books. For example, Bruce Waltke's Genesis commentary is arranged by Books, Acts, and Scenes.[66] However, among Psalms commentaries, Vesco's approach stands out, even though it is the obvious application of the many books and articles about the shape of the Psalter. As he puts it, he approaches Psalms as a single book, by contrast with classic commentaries, wanting to interpret psalms with reference to their order.[67]

Any investigation of the Book of Psalms in a final, canonical form needs to settle on which of the potential canonical forms to choose. As Wilson found, the DSS contain a variety of collections of texts, some of which include Psalms. The discussion over the status of the DSS as a possible competing canon for the whole OT is beyond this book. The variety of the findings in scrolls that include some of the canonical Psalms may tell us something about the pre-history of the Psalter, or they may tell us

65. Vesco, *Le psautier de David*.

66. Waltke and Fredricks, *Genesis*.

67. Vesco 1:31.

that the canon was not yet settled, or they may represent a competing Psalter; alternatively, they may bear no more relation to a canonical Psalter than a collection of modern church service sheets would to a modern Psalter.[68] I do not consider the DSS to include an alternative candidate for a canonical Psalter.

The Old Greek translation (OG, or Septuagint, LXX), on the other hand, is intended to be at least something close to a translation of the canonical Psalter. It has many more superscriptions than the MT and, naturally, different links in vocabulary. This has been illustrated recently by Alma Brodersen's close study of Pss 146–50 in the OG, DSS and MT, where she argues that it is *only* in the MT that they work together as a conclusion for the Psalter, and not in DSS or OG.[69] We will follow authors such as Vesco and Martin Leuenberger in selecting the MT as the canonical form,[70] while referring to OG and DSS (among other sources) for textual criticism. For convenience, Scripture references will follow *BHS*.[71]

6. From Psalter Context to Canonical Context

Gordon Wenham presses us to treat the Psalter not just as a book but a book within the canon. He enjoins attention to "three canonical contexts." First, we must note the Psalter itself so that placement within the collection and the neighboring psalms are significant. Second, we must give attention to the Hebrew Bible, being aware of connections with the Pentateuch and the person of David; a theology of the Old Testament must account for this. Finally, any biblical theology must account for the context in the Christian canon, especially as the Psalms are the most quoted book in the NT.[72]

---

68. Summaries of the debate, which unfolded as the Scrolls did, can be found in: Flint, *Dead Sea Psalms Scrolls*, 16–18, 135–49; Swanson, "Qumran and the Psalms," 247–62; Flint, "Dead Sea Psalms Scrolls," 16–18.

69. Brodersen, *The End of the Psalter*.

70. Vesco 34; Leuenberger, *Konzeptionen*, 20.

71. Psalm references in *BHS* are not the same as MT. Alep has no chapter numbers for the Psalms (see *AC* despite *MGH*), while L has joined 114 and 115 so that the final Psalm is not 150, קנ, but 149, קמט (*LC*, 804). This is one small example which illustrates that "the MT" must sometimes be considered a family of texts, not a single text (cf. Tov, *Textual Criticism*, 24).

72. Wenham, "Reading the Psalms Canonically," 77.

7. A Thematic Introduction to Guide the Reader

Bringing together all of the above, Beat Weber followed up a full exegetical commentary with a volume on the Psalter as a whole.[73] This not only pays attention to shape, structure, and sequence throughout but also is particularly arranged around three themes that he detects in the three introductory psalms. He argues that their presence in the introduction is intended to guide the reader of the whole Psalter, and he traces these themes all the way through the Psalter and into the concluding doxology (Pss 146–50).

Finding an introductory purpose behind the first few Psalms is one of the oldest forms of enquiry into the overall shape and message of the Psalter, dating back to the second century. This reminds us that while the authors listed above build on the new life that Wilson breathed into the enterprise, we should not imagine that we have here a thing unheard of. Two centuries ago, very similar work was going on in the commentaries of Hengstenberg, Delitzsch, Alexander, Wordsworth and Forbes, among others—including everything from Zenger's close attention to inter-Psalm connections through to Wenham's instinct for the context of the whole canon.[74]

It is to those introductory psalms that we now turn. In the next couple of chapters we will find that the first three psalms are full of guidance for the reader of the Psalter, specifically concerning retribution.

---

73. Weber, *Die Psalmen 1 bis 72*; Weber, *Die Psalmen 73 bis 150*; Weber, *Theologie und Spiritualität*.

74. Jenkins, "Antiquity of Psalter," 173–76.

4

Retribution in the Introduction
to the Psalter

Psalms 1 and 2

Should the ungodly be seen in such absolute, unredeemable terms?[1]

But now, O kings, have insight
let yourselves be disciplined, judges of the earth.
Serve Yahweh in fear
and rejoice with trembling. (Ps 2:9–11)

THE READER DOES NOT have to wade through much of the Psalter before
it contradicts the assumption that the psalms cannot envisage the repentance of the enemy (ch. 2, §5.B, pp. 11–14). Psalm 2 calls on rebellious,
wicked, foreign kings to repent of their high-handed assault on Yahweh's
king and his law, to be instructed in wisdom, to be blessed, and even to
return to their privileged positions as kings.

In this chapter we will see how Psalms 1 and 2 work together as an
introduction to the topic of enemies and retribution. In the following
chapter we will see how Psalm 3 fills out that picture with David in a precarious and ambiguous position. He has sinned, and deserves judgment,

1. Eaton, *Psalms of the Way*, 39.

which God has sent. However, God has sent Absalom to judge him wickedly. What will God do? In the next chapter, we will see how David is introduced as a thoroughgoing sinner yet a recipient of undeserved mercy; in his rescue from sinful Absalom, he is a type of Israel after the exile at the hands of sinful Babylon.

The opening Psalms of the book have been read as an introduction to guide the reader since ancient times.[2] In the following chapters we will consider the effect of placing Psalms 1–3 as the book's opening. In these next three chapters, we first take Pss 1 and 2 together; then Ps 3; and finally we consider how David is introduced to the reader in these psalms, within the context of the whole Book of Psalms and the rest of the Old Testament. The reader of the Psalter first meets David in the context of retribution, the topic of our book.

Divine judgment and a human desire for retribution are obvious themes in Psalms 1–3. Moreover, each psalm makes more concrete what the preceding psalm had left open. If Ps 1 presents a generic man surrounded by enemies, Ps 2 presents the anointed king surrounded by leaders who rebel against his divinely-appointed rule. Psalm 3 is more concrete still, identifying David as the specific king, and pin-pointing Absalom's rebellion among the many such events in David's life. If Ps 1 comforts the man with a future judgment, Ps 2 identifies the king as the agent of judgment. Psalm 3 finds him on the horns of an ambiguity: he faces God's judgment because of his own sin, but God has sent a sinful agent of judgment against him. The judgment is just and unjust; David is innocent of Absalom's accusations, and yet guilty of his sins with Bathsheba and Uriah. If Ps 1 presents condemnation as the fate of the wicked, Ps 2 presents this as a warning, an invitation to repent with the offer of forgiveness and life. Psalm 3 shocks us by presenting the righteous, even David himself, as in need of forgiveness.

1. Retribution in the Introduction to the Book of Psalms

Allowing sequential psalms to shed light on each other is as ancient as Gregory of Nyssa and remains a current concern.[3] Psalms 1 and 2 form a

---

2. Jenkins, "Antiquity of Psalter," 166–68.

3. Gregory of Nyssa, *Inscriptions of the Psalms*, II.XI.138.

joint gateway to the whole Book of Psalms: a double-portal or an introduction proper to themes that can be seen in the rest of the book.[4]

Reading Psalm 1 alone, one could be tempted to see judgment as
the settled fate of the wicked. Reading it alongside Psalm 2, however,
shows that judgment is a warning. The gateway into the Psalms warns
the wicked to repent. Even when they are the personal enemies of the
Messianic king, they are offered blessing. That blessing even involves returning to their exalted positions as judges and national leaders. We will
examine what Psalms 1–2 announce about retribution in this chapter,
and in the next we will consider how Psalm 3 is strategically placed to
help the reader think more deeply about the enemy.

2. Psalm 1: Retribution Expected

[1] O, the blessings[5] of the man who has not walked in the counsel of
wicked ones
and in the way of sinners has not stood
and on the seat of scorners has not sat.
[2] But rather in Yahweh's Torah is his delight
and on his Torah he murmurs day and night.
[3] And he is like a tree transplanted by streams of water
which gives its fruit in its own time
and whose foliage does not wither
and everything that he will do will prosper.
[4] Not so the wicked ones
but rather they are like chaff
which wind drives away!
[5] On account of which, wicked ones will not stand up at the judgment
nor sinners in the council of the righteous ones.
[6] Because Yahweh knows the way of the righteous ones
whereas the way of the wicked ones perishes.

---

4. Throughout the millennia, it has been a matter of debate whether the introduction is only Ps 1, or also Ps 2 (Jenkins, "Antiquity of Psalter," 166–68). Modern
examples of tracing themes from this introduction into the whole Book of Psalms
include Sheppard, *Wisdom*, 136–44; Crutchfield, "Redactional Agenda," 23, 46–47;
Bellinger, "Reading from the Beginning," 125; Janowski, "Ein Tempel aus Worten,"
290–301; Weber, *Theologie*; Wenham, "The Nations," 165–86; Miller, "Who Are the
Bad Guys in the Psalms?," 423–31; Creach, *Yahweh as Refuge*.

5. "אַשְׁרֵי *happy!* . . . has become stereotyped as an interjection," which yields the
translation: "*O the happiness of* the man" (GKC §§91l, 155n(c)). So also Dahood,
Psalms I, 1.

2.A. Torah in Psalm 1

Yahweh's *Torah* is bound up with the identity of the righteous and the wicked in Psalms 1 and 2 and in the Psalter as a whole. Apart from one mention, Psalm 1 alludes to Torah in three ways: via Deuteronomy 6, Joshua 1, and "walk in the way."

Psalms 1 and 2 echo back to two highly prominent Law passages:[6] the *Shemaʿ* in Deut 6, calling Israel to hear and keep the Torah; and Josh 1, where Joshua is promised success in the land if he lives by the Torah.

Deuteronomy 6:7 enjoins reciting *Torah* through four verbs that make up a "merism," where the whole of time is described by the beginnings and ends: from getting up in the morning (קום, *qum*), to lying down at night (שכב, *shakab*); whether walking (הלך, *halak*) or sitting (ישׁב, *yashab*).[7] The same roots describe walking and sitting in the opening verse of Ps 1, while the merism of getting up in the morning and lying down at night is matched in v. 2 by the merism of "day and night." This helps us to identify the evildoers of Ps 1:1. Both Deut 6:7 and Ps 1:2 positively enjoin reciting God's commands.[8] The contrast built between Ps 1:1 and 1:2 suggests that the Torah is what the wicked reject, sinners fall short of, and scorners deride.[9] This contrast between righteous Torah-lovers and wicked Torah-rebels is the subject of the whole Psalm.[10] That contrast continues throughout the Psalter.[11]

The day-and-night meditation on Torah in Ps 1:2, and the ubiquitous prosperity that results in v. 3 allude to Josh 1:8.[12] As in Ps 1:1–3, in Josh 1:7–8 we find that "walk" and "way" have been split across adjacent verses and followed by "prosper" (צלח, *tsalah*). Torah is the key to success in both passages.

"Walking" permeates the Psalter as a metaphor for someone's moral compass, (with the associated ideas of way, path, steps, feet).[13] It high-

---

6. See the literature survey in Grant, *King*, 43–48.

7. As far back as Ibn Ezra (Miller, "Deuteronomy and Psalms," 12).

8. Hossfeld-Zenger I:47.

9. Rashi, *Psalms*, 173.

10. Durlesser, "Poetic Style," 31.

11. McCann, "The Psalms as Instruction," 118.

12. Kraus 1:138; Ḥakham, *Psalms 1–57*, 3; Goldingay 1:86.

13. Brown, *Seeing*, 31–53.

lights Torah in Pss 1 and 2, where "way" (דֶּרֶךְ, *derek*) does a lot of work, as follows.[14]

First, "way" is a bookend in two ways: it appears in the first and last verses of Ps 1 but also in the first and last verses of the pair of psalms (1:1 and 2:12). Secondly, "way" joins with "the blessings of" (אַשְׁרֵי, *ashrey*) to bookend Pss 1 and 2 as a pair. Thirdly, at the end of both psalms, "way" joins with "die" (אבד, *'abad*). Psalm 1 addresses one who is walking in the right way, the way of life, and has kept himself from the wrong way.[15] This way leads to death at the end of both psalms: the way which the wicked of Ps 2 are warned to abandon, lest they end in *Abbadon*.

The metaphor of "walking in the way" is therefore highlighted in these psalms. It has a background in the Torah, for example in Deut 5:33; 6:7; 8:6; 10:12; 11:19; 11:22; 19:9; 26:17; 28:9; 30:16. Joshua 1, which is already brought to mind by Psalm 1, uses walking as a metaphor for obedience to Torah (vv. 3, 11 [*bis*], 14, 15, 16), and Joshua's swansong charges Israel to love Yahweh faithfully, where "walk in all his ways" stresses the need to observe the Torah.

In summary, "walking in the way" is highlighted in Psalms 1 and 2, and is tinged with Torah background. By binding the two psalms together, it brings both psalms into contact with the allusions to Torah (via Deut 6 and Josh 1) that are made by Ps 1.

2.B. Torah and the Expectation of Retaliation

It would seem obvious that Torah should set the standard for retribution. Quite plausibly, many detect the *lex talionis* or "Law of Retaliation" or "eye-for-an-eye" principle as regulating what the psalms ask for against their enemies.[16] We will see in our exposition of various psalms, even the most notoriously vicious imprecatory psalms, that the psalmists ask for much less severe punishments, and sometimes even forego any just retribution altogether.

First we must clarify what is meant by *lex talionis*, since the term is used inconsistently in the literature:

---

14. Cheyne, *The Book of Psalms*, 1:1.

15. Liess, *Der Weg des Lebens*, 17–20; Kirkpatrick 1:2.

16. McCann, *Psalms as Torah*, 113; Day, *Crying for Justice*, 66–69; Firth, *Surrendering*, 142.

1. It is taken to mean that exact retaliation is the way to settle an irreversible injury: loss of eye, limb or life. Once the *lex talionis* has been applied, both parties are at exactly the same disadvantage: both are missing one tooth. This is a ceiling, compassionately designed to prevent disproportionate punishment and end feuds before they start.[17]

2. Others point to ANE parallels. Some take it as designed to prevent unjust leniency. The ANE law codes "routinely provided for fines as satisfying the legal requirement of justice in the case of a superior person's permanently injuring an inferior person."[18] In such a case, the possibility of the victim insisting on exact retribution would provide a strong negotiating position against token compensation. This ensures that the guilty party is seriously punished and not just let off with a minimal fine.[19] A variation of this view argues that (other than for murder) exact retribution was never enacted, and instead judges had discretion to impose imprisonment or fines that would fit the crime; the *lex talionis* in Exod 21:25 is immediately followed by an example where such exact eye-for-eye justice is forbidden, and manumission of the indentured servant is the penalty instead.[20]

3. Some mean a general sense of fittingness, such that the punishment should be appropriate to the crime.[21]

4. Yet others, an even more general sense of poetic justice: "The *lex talionis* expresses the ideal of poetic justice, namely that the punishment should fit the crime."[22]

5. Finally, the Concise OED gives: "the law of retaliation, whereby a punishment resembles the offence committed in kind and degree."[23]

We therefore need to be careful to understand what is meant when an author states that the Psalter regulates retribution according to the *lex*

---

17. Douglas, *Leviticus as Literature*, 213; Wenham, *Story as Torah*, 112.

18. Stuart, *Exodus*, 493.

19. Durham, *Exodus*, 324; Rad, *Theology of Israel's Historical Traditions*, 32, 203n29.

20. Stuart, *Exodus*, 492–94.

21. Wright, *Old Testament Ethics*, 310; see various similar references in Wenham, *Psalms as Torah*, 112–13. Vern Poythress cites the principle in Obad 15; Jer 50:29; Hab 2:8; Joel 3[4]:4, 7 (Poythress, *Shadow of Christ*, 123).

22. Jonathan Burnside, cited in Wenham, *Psalms as Torah*, 112n20.

23. Soanes and Stevenson, *Concise Oxford English Dictionary*, ad. loc.

talionis, since it can have quite a broad range of meanings. When A. F. Kirkpatrick writes: "These imprecations . . . must be estimated from the standpoint of the Law, which was based upon the rule of retaliation,"[24] one needs to ask what exactly he means by "retaliation," and similarly whenever anyone mentions the *lex talionis*.

When considering the Torah, the broad principle of proportionality or "fittingness" could be applied in different specific ways. If a thief is caught stealing a cow, he ends up with one cow fewer than he originally had and the victim with one cow extra (Exod 22:4). If the thief has killed the cow, he pays back five or four-fold (Exod 22:1). Other times restitution is 120 percent (Lev 5:16). These are all applications of the principle of fittingness. However, in the Code of Hammurabi, we find twelve-fold and thirty-fold restitution for various offences (art. 5 and 8). These might all be broadly "fitting" but are quite different from each other; hardly any of them are exact restitution, and some are required by Torah while others are outside it and forbidden.

Additionally, the prophets sometimes have the punishment "fit" the crime rather more poetically or even ironically. David's punishment for the sin with Bathsheba and Uriah fits this pattern (2 Sam 12). Under the Mosaic Law, the only possible punishment for his murder of Uriah was death, but that is lifted (v. 13). Instead, just as he took another's wife in secret, his will be taken publicly, and just as he used the sword to get out of trouble, the sword will be a permanent trouble for him.[25] There are similarities and ironies, but not *exact* correspondence between crime and punishment in vv. 11–14.

Poetic justice can be found in different punishments for similar crimes: breaking the teeth has been suggested as appropriate poetic justice for false accusation. The Code of Shulgi, on the other hand, scrubs out the mouth of an insolent slave with salt (art. 25). Both are crimes of speech. In 2 Sam 24, David is offered a range of punishments, which each apparently fit the same offence.

Related to the principle of restitution is the case of false witnesses to violence. If a scoundrel accuses an innocent man of a crime, the scoundrel ends up with the exact punishment that would have befallen the accused, while the accused walks free (Deut 19:19).[26] For example, writing about the

---

24. Kirkpatrick 3:lxxxix.

25. Rad, *Theology of Israel's Historical Traditions*, 314.

26. We will examine this in more detail below (ch. section (6)4).

individual laments, David Firth detects a consistent pattern. The psalmist asks for the *lex talionis*, or the law of false witnesses. Whatever the enemy was planning to do should befall the enemy instead of the psalmist.[27]

Throughout this book, we will examine the fate of the evildoers, beginning now in Pss 1 and 2. We will notice that the Psalms do not teach us to avenge ourselves on our enemies in a way that reaches the ceiling set by the *lex talionis*.

3. Psalm 1: The Entrance to the Psalms in Light of the Exile

3.A. Exile Motifs from the Wider Canon

As any reader of poetry will testify, simply re-reading the same few psalms will show each in a different light, because they mutually enrich each other.[28] On a first read through the Psalter, one eventually finds exilic content, such as Ps 137. On re-reading the Psalter from the beginning, you can be ready to notice hints of the exile elsewhere, even in Ps 1.[29] Here we will develop that idea and consider some connections that Ps 1 makes within the Book of Psalms but chiefly the connections to the three major portions of the canon: the Law, the Prophets and the Writings.

The tree transplanted by water in Ps 1 appears in a new light, that of temple imagery. David in the house of God is a man like a tree (Ps 52:10 [8]).[30] Even closer, the righteous ones are trees transplanted into the house of God (92:13–14 [12–13]); both this and 1:3 use the same form of the verb שתל (*shatal*, "to plant"; *qal* passive participle). Ezekiel 47 describes the new temple issuing a prodigious river lined with trees whose fruit will not fail (לֹא־יִתֹּם פִּרְיוֹ, *lo'-yittom piryo*, 47:12), rather like Ps 1:3, where we have "its fruit" (פִּרְיוֹ, *piryo*) and its leaves "will not wither" (לֹא־יִבּוֹל, *lo'-yibbol*).[31] The water channels of 1:3 (פֶּלֶג *peleg*) reap-

---

27. Firth, *Surrendering*, 142.

28. Brown, *Psalms*, 116–17; Lohfink, "Psalmengebet," 12.

29. It is common to see a post-exilic final shape of the Psalter, and especially of the placement of Ps 1 (Vesco 1:110; Harman, *Psalms 1–72*, 99).

30. As Hengstenberg observes, "house of God" was applied to the sanctuary long before the temple existed (Hengstenberg, *Psalmen*, 4:339); *contra* Delitzsch 732–33.

31. Creach argues that Ps 1:3 is taken from Jer 17, then edited with these two phrases from Ezek 47:12 and one word from Isa 32:2. Both of the passages from which additions are made into Ps 1 (Ezek 47 and Isa 32) have water flowing from the sanctuary (Creach, "Like a Tree," 40–42).

pear in other texts where water flows from the holy mountain in the same channels: Isa 30:25; 32:2; Pss 46:5; 65:10.[32]

The likeness to a tree, with reference to its foliage, dependability, and fruit, as well as being by a water course, allude to a temple environment.[33] This highlights the lack of temple in Ps 1, suggesting that it has been lost. Significantly, Psalm 137 has trees by the waters of Babylon as an expression of being away from Zion, transplanted through deportation.

The "planting" of the tree in Ps 1 points in the same direction. The tree is described as שָׁתוּל (*shatul* planted). This root is very rare and is always used prophetically of the exile, almost always as a *qal* passive participle, as here. In Ezek 17:8, 10, 22, 23; 19:10, 13, *shatul* symbolizes the exile and restoration of Israel, pictured as a flourishing plant that withers and recovers as it is transplanted back and forth. Hosea 9:13 is similar. In Jer 17:8, the context is very similar to Ps 1: blessings on a man who trusts in Yahweh; he will be like a tree planted by water, whose leaves remain green and who does not stop giving fruit; concomitant curses on evil.[34] The same flourishing tree imagery is applied to individuals there also, but in the context of national exile. The connection with the sanctuary and with royalty is explicit in v. 12. The only other use of *shatal* is in Ps 92, in Book IV, which deals with the crisis of exile and the failure of the monarchy; there it is the righteous individual (v. 13 [12]), of whom more than one is envisaged (v. 14 [13]).

The use of *shatul*, and the related imagery in Ps 1, seems likely to evoke God's care for the righteous throughout the exile and return, anticipating a major theme of Book V.

---

32. Creach, "Like a Tree," 41–43.

33. Creach is followed by Gillingham, "The Zion Tradition," 332–33; Janowski, "Ein Tempel aus Worten," 300.

34. Dependence is argued in various directions (compare the discussions in: Delitzsch 66; Gunkel, *Die Psalmen*, 3; Kirkpatrick 1:1:1–2; Mowinckel, *Segen und Fluch*, 124; Kraus 1:133). Durlesser *contra mundum* denies any dependence in either direction on the grounds that the rhetorical devices, poetic styles and structures of each passage are very different (Durlesser, "Poetic Style," 44). This presumes that an author can only allude to a passage by emulating the style and sentence structures. That would be news to P. G. Wodehouse. He shows no compunction in quoting from the style of an *imprecatory psalm* (Ps 58) and inserting it into the rather different style of his *comic novel* (*Stiff Upper Lip, Jeeves!*). Moreover, he changes the sentence structure: "would stop his ears like the deaf adder, which, as you probably know, made a point of refusing to hear the voice of the charmer, charm he never so wisely" (Wodehouse, *Stiff Upper Lip*, 32).

These exilic connections are strengthened if we consider the location of Ps 1 within the divisions of the canon. The beginning of the Psalter makes connections to the frames of the Prophets and the Pentateuch.[35]

The order of the Writings was not fixed in antiquity, and perhaps only accidentally fixed by the printing press. Most mediaeval MSS have Psalms second, often after Chronicles, despite which the printed tradition settled on Psalms first.[36] In our chosen version, Chronicles ends with the Cyrus decree and Ps 1 follows immediately.[37]

I have shown that the opening of the Psalms emphasizes the importance of "walking in the way" and alludes to important Torah texts. Emphasis on David and his sons, who are kings, walking in the way of Torah runs through Kings and Chronicles. There, David charges his son to walk in his ways, referring to Yahweh (1 Kgs 2:3), but Yahweh repeats the charge in 3:14 as "if you will walk in my ways, in order to keep my statutes and my commandments, just as *David your father walked*." David becomes the exemplary father of the king, by obeying Yahweh's Torah (commands and statutes) and walking in his way. In 11:33, Solomon's sin was failure to walk in Yahweh's way, by keeping Torah, "as David his father," while the offer to Jeroboam (v. 38) requires "walk in my ways" and keeping Torah "as David my servant did." The prophet making this offer becomes an enacted parable of perishing if you depart from the way which Yahweh commanded (vv. 10, 17, 24; Ps 1:6; 2:12). The conduct of kings with regard to Torah and devotion to Yahweh is measured by walking in the way of a wicked archetypal father (1 Kgs 15:26, 34; 16:2, 19, 26; 22:53; 2 Kgs 8:18, 27; 16:3; 21:21, 22) or walking in the way of a righteous father (1 Kgs 22:43; 2 Kgs 22:2). Chronicles also assesses kings as walking in the way of wicked fathers (2 Chr 21:6; 21:13 contrasted with David in the previous verse; 22:3; 28:2); or of father David (2 Chr 11:17; 17:3; 34:2).[38]

Expulsion from the land and absence from the temple are presented to the reader of Psalms 1 and 2 by the themes of walking in the way, Torah, kingship, and royal fatherhood. Kings (the end of the Former

---

35. Weber, "Psalm 1 als Tor," 179–200; Weber, *Theologie*, 242–48.

36. L and Alep have Chronicles first, then Psalms, despite *BHS* and *BHL*, which rearrange L (Dotan, *Biblia Hebraica Leningradensia*, xviii).

37. L has a gap under the end of Chronicles and starts Psalms on a new folio (*LC* 742–43). However, Alep continues straight on (*AC* תפג). For the variations in the order in MSS and in Jewish tradition see Beckwith, *Old Testament Canon*, 452–64.

38. Asa appears once instead of David in 20:32.

Prophets) and Chronicles (adjacent to Ps 1) lead into the Psalter show-ing how the exile came about: successive kings failed to obey Ps 1. The positive presentation of David in Chronicles might set up a hope for the exiles in a son of David who will do as David did, and walk in the way of Ps 1, re-conquering the land in Ps 2. Chronicles places Cyrus's decree of return right before Ps 1, as explicit fulfilment of Jeremiah's prophecy. Psalm 1 cements the imagery of the tree as Israel in exile, awaiting return, by alluding to Jeremiah's "transplanted" (שָׁתוּל, *shatul*) passage.[39]

If Ps 1 follows Chronicles (which began the Writings) and alludes to the start of the Prophets (Josh 1, as we have seen), we might expect the opening of the Torah to complete this picture. The conceptual connec-tions with the tree of life and the temple get us some way there.[40] There is more in the opening of Genesis.[41]

In Gen 1:1—2:3 we find the creation of night and day; they (through evening and morning) become the stage on which God's word is obeyed: "he said . . . and it was so . . . there was evening, morning, the Nth day." Compare Ps 1:2. The final creative day (Gen 1:26–30) sees the creation of man (cf. the man of Ps 1:1), whom he blesses (Ps 1:1, 2:12, 3:9). The blessing involves being fruitful (Gen 1:28) and ownership of trees that bear fruit Gen 1:29), using the vocabulary of Ps 1:3.

In Gen 2, man is surrounded by trees, including the tree of life, that have been planted next to four rivers, just as the metaphor of Ps 1. Man is placed in the garden, by water courses, like the tree of life.[42] Two of the rivers are the "Tigris, which flows east of Assyria," and the Euphra-tes, bringing to mind the two deporting empires and the waters of Ps 137. The garden, by virtue of God's presence with man, is a sanctuary.[43]

39. I find Creach's case for the textual dependence compelling (Creach, "Like a Tree," 37–39). Either way, a prophecy of exile will be most naturally read as prior to the exile.

40. Second Temple sources make the link between the temple and paradise, and Adam and the tree of life (Creach, "Like a Tree," 43–45). Brown discusses the back-ground of the tree metaphor in Ps 1, including the tree of life and the temple (Brown, *Seeing*, 58–61, 74–75).

41. The dependence of the Book of Psalms on the Pentateuch was demonstrated in detail by W. H. Gispen, and has been extended by Wenham (Wenham, *Psalms as Torah*, 99, 120, 127, 129).

42. Aquinas makes a connection between Adam's sleep in 2:21 and David's in Ps 3 (Aquinas, *Commentaire sur les Psaumes*, 58–59) but the context of marriage to which he draws attention is lacking in Ps 3.

43. Kline, *Kingdom Prologue*, 47–48.

Genesis 2–3 may even resemble *the* sanctuary: the tree stylized as the *Menorah*; God's habitation; entrance from the east fenced by a cherub; gold and onyx.[44] The entrance from the East fits with the temple of Ezek 47, whose imagery we have found in Ps 1. In Gen 3:23–24 man is expelled from the sanctuary, eastwards, and kept away by the sword, as with the Assyrian and Babylonian deportations. The cause is association with a scorner of Yahweh's command (Gen 3:1), instead of obedient recitation of his instruction (Gen 3:17). Psalm 1 likens the man to a fruit tree planted next to a river of water, a bitter reminder of a time when another man was placed next to a similar tree. The wisdom that was deceitfully promised in the garden (*hipʿil* of שׂכל, *hiskil*, Gen 3:6) is offered to all the kings of Ps 2:10 (*hiskil* again).

These connections to the wider canon may demonstrate the virtue of opening the Writings with Chronicles, not Psalms. First Chronicles 1 takes us back to the original creation. Psalm 1 picks up the exiles with the decree of Cyrus and emphasizes that obedience to Torah, and not the physical temple, was the true hope of Israel; obedience to Torah is how Yahweh blessed the righteous in exile while they were away from the temple (their "transplanted" experience was Jer 17, not Ezek 17); as Ezra-Nehemiah will make clear, obedience to Torah will remain the *sine qua non*, regardless of how much the temple has been rebuilt. This is applicable in later situations similar to the exile, such as AD 70 and 135:[45] Yahweh's Torah will keep the nation as the tree of Ps 1 even in the absence of a temple.

> Thus, *tôrâ* is implicitly compared to the temple and is perhaps seen as the temple's replacement. . . . It is now meditation on *tôrâ* that makes the righteous steadfast, like a tree planted by the temple stream.[46]

Access to sanctuary blessing is by "murmuring on Torah" (יֶהְגֶּה בְּתוֹרָה, *yehgeh betorah* 1:2). But what does "Torah" refer to?

---

44. Wenham, "Sanctuary Symbolism," 19–25.

45. Curtis, *Psalms*, xxii.

46. Creach, "Like a Tree," 46.

3.B. Torah for Exile: Learn to Pray with David

The righteous individuals will be preserved by Yahweh, while they wait for the end of exile or of similar catastrophes. Taking account this wider canonical sense of Ps 1, what does יֶהְגֶּה בְּתוֹרָה (*yehgeh betorah*, "he murmurs[?] on the *Torah*" 1:2) mean?

For the king, it means obedience to the Torah, reciting it, and judging the nation by it. *Hagah* here is (from context) positive and could be a public reading or a private meditation. We will find the same verb in a negative context in Ps 2, used of rebellious plotting. The ironic antithesis of murmuring on Yahweh's Torah is murmuring against Yahweh's anointed.[47]

"Torah" could mean God's instruction generally,[48] the Pentateuch and its laws,[49] Deuteronomy,[50] "the Mosaic law scroll,"[51] the Psalter (not necessarily exclusively),[52] or the whole Bible (of which Torah is the heart).[53]

We are to some extent weighed down by constant exposure to translations of *Torah*. Some have recently objected that "law" can carry implications of only legislation and offer "instruction" as a corrective.[54] The latter, however, suggests something optional, not bound in covenant obligations.[55] Long ago, Salmon argued that "The very act of committing the Psalms to writing shows that they were viewed as commandments 'just as all the commandments were written down.'"[56] McCann's "God's will" captures the authority beyond legislation.[57] Willem VanGemeren

---

47. On the range of meanings, see Van Pelt and Kaiser, "הָגָה," 1:1006–8.

48. McCann, "The Psalms as Instruction," 118–19.

49. Childs, *Introduction*, 513.

50. Miller, "Deuteronomy and Psalms," 11.

51. Seybold 29.

52. Wilson, *Editing*, 207.

53. Kraus 1:136.

54. McCann, "The Psalms as Instruction," 118.

55. Buber translates as *Weisung* (cited in Kraus, *Theologie der Psalmen*, 40). The objection comes from Grant, *King*, 271–73.

56. Cited in Simon, *Four Approaches*, 63. Willgren's conclusion that Torah here cannot refer to a particularly arranged collection of psalms would end up meaning that it is impossible to have an authoritative collection and order of them (Willgren, *Formation*, 144). Here, we are taking MT, especially as represented in Alep, as a canonical text.

57. McCann, "Psalms," 646. So also Kraus 1:135.

notes that God's *covenant* with Israel is the background for blessing, for distinguishing between righteous and wicked.[58]

> The righteous man is positively identified by his association with "the law of the LORD." The "law" is not to be limited to the Five Books of Moses or even to the OT as a whole. The Hebrew word *torah* ("law") signifies primarily instruction that comes from God. . . . This is the distinctive difference between revelation and religion. . . . Revelation comes from God for the purpose of helping man to live in harmony with God's will.[59]

The connections we saw with the Law of Moses and Josh 1 make it unlikely that it would be understood to exclude the Pentateuch. However, the placement of connections with Ps 1 at the frames of the *Torah* and the Prophets, while opening the Writings or at least the Psalter, and the reliance on Chronicles suggest that the whole Hebrew Bible is in view. The king must live by all of Yahweh's instruction: not only the specific legal codes, but also the history (with its lessons) and the promises, warnings, and teaching of the Prophets and Writings. He must be always reading or reciting the Bible.

For the lay person in exile who awaits the king, access to the whole Bible is unlikely.[60] However, if the Psalter is chanted and memorized in corporate worship it can then be recited during daily activities, as the history of the church shows it to have been.[61] Recent studies argue that the Psalter is arranged with memorization in view.[62] LeMon's suggestion is plausible: הגה (*hagah*) in Ps 1 is "doing the psalms."[63] Yefet and Salmon ben YeruHam saw the Psalter as arranged to meet the needs of the people in exile.[64] It has often been remarked that the Psalter is a complete resource, a whole (Christian) Bible in summary,[65] which would render this understanding

---

58. VanGemeren, *Psalms*, 76. He even allows this covenant background to gloss ידע in 1:6 "covenant commitment" (VanGemeren, *Psalms*, 84).

59. VanGemeren, *Psalms*, 79.

60. This pushes Seybold to conclude a late post-exilic setting, when Torah scrolls were available to read (Seybold 28).

61. Gillingham, *Psalms*, 40. Scottish Presbyterianism abounds with laity who have retained a metrical Psalter memorized in childhood.

62. Lee, "Psalter," 204–22; Robertson, *Flow of the Psalms*, 81.

63. LeMon, "Violent Psalms," 97.

64. Yefet cited in Simon, *Four Approaches*, 88; Salmon cited in Simon, *Four Approaches*, 63.

65. Athanasius, *Ep. Marcell.* xi; Basil, *Exegetic Homilies*; Luther, *Word and*

of *Torah* in Ps 1 plausible. Salmon again: "there is no root or branch of the Torah that is not included in this book. . . . [I]t also contains most of the consolations that were written by the prophets in all their aspects and particulars."[66] Luther envisages precisely this use of the Psalter "in order that they who are unable to read the whole Bible may nevertheless find almost the whole sum comprehended in one little book."[67]

Psalm 1, in introducing the book, points to the whole book as necessary instruction for coping with a crisis such as exile. As we will see next, the opening to the book quickly points to David as a teacher. As a representative Israelite, and also as a representative of the whole nation, his prayers are worked examples of how to pray, individually and nationally.

4. Psalm 2: The Enemies Are Invited to Repent and Be Blessed

1 Why have the nations raged
    and the peoples are murmuring vainly?
2 The kings of the earth are taking a stand
    and the dignitaries have conspired together
        against Yahweh
            and against his anointed one.
3 "Let us burst their bonds
    and throw off their fetters from us!"
4 The one sitting in heaven laughs!
    The Master derides them.
5 Suddenly he is speaking to them in his ire
    and in his fury terrifying them.
6 "It is I who has appointed my king
    on Zion, my holy hill."
7 "Let me recount Yahweh's statute
    he said to me:
  'My son is who you are
    this day I have begotten you.
8 Petition me so that I will give you nations—your inheritance
    and your domain—the ends of the earth.

Sacrament I, 254; Calvin, *Psalms*, 1:xxxvii; Ravasi 27, the latter citing Bellarmine. Augustine and Thomas Aquinas are sometimes quoted to the same effect.

66. Cited in Simon, *Four Approaches*, 61; see also his assertion of the complete sufficiency of the Psalter (cited in Simon, *Four Approaches*, 63).

67. Luther, *Word and Sacrament I*, 254.

[9] You shall crush[68] them with an iron staff
     like a vessel from the potter, smash them.'
[10] Now then, O kings, get wisdom;
     submit to retraining, O judges of the earth.
[11] Serve Yahweh fearfully,
     rejoice and tremble.[69]
[12] Kiss the *Sohn*[70]
     lest he anger so that you perish while on the way
     because suddenly kindled is his ire.
     O, the blessings of all who take refuge in him!

Psalm 1 has the righteous individual passively besieged by his enemies. Psalm 2 shows the king, active and as the agent of judgment. We might expect him to judge according to the Torah, exacting retribution. We find the opposite.

4.A. *Excursus*: Textual Criticism of the Crushing Son and Fearful Rejoicing

There are three significant textual questions in Ps 2. I will argue that they are interrelated, and it seems clearest to offer a solution to all three up-front. As promised in the introduction, I have tried to keep any material that requires knowledge of Hebrew to the footnotes of this book, with the exception of this brief and necessarily technical *excursus*.

4.A.1. *Crush or Shepherd?*

Four Hebrew roots are relevant to תְּרֹעֵם (2:9): רעה, רעע, רעע, רצץ.

1. LXX translates as ποιμανεῖς,[71] which implies revocalizing as תִּרְעֵם, from רעה, 'to shepherd.'

2. MT is a form of רעע, which represents two roots. One is related to רע, but is never transitive in the *qal*,[72] and can be excluded.

---

68. See the *excursus* below.
69. On this phrase and the next, see the *excursus* below.
70. See the *excursus* below on this translation.
71. Rahlfs, *Psalmi*, 82, offers no exceptions.
72. *HALOT* 1269–71; *BDB* 949.

3. The homonym is a loan-word from Aramaic רעע,[73] which also means "to shatter."[74] The use of רעע in Hebrew is rare, and mostly textually conjectural.[75]

4. That Aramaic root has transferred more normally to Hebrew as the root רצץ, which occurs nineteen times.[76]

Gerhard Wilhelmi, after surveying the literature, lamented the paucity of weighty arguments offered on either side of this decision.[77] He asks why an author would have used a (disputed) Aramaic root (רעע) when a perfectly serviceable Hebrew one (רצץ) was available.[78] I believe that I have an adequate answer.

First, there is no *Hebrew* manuscript evidence against רעע.[79] We explain the LXX translation below.

Second, I suggest that the author used an Aramaism because he specifically wanted to introduce an Aramaism, according to the device recently labelled as "Addressee Switching." This technique is used by Biblical Hebrew writers when their topic concerns foreigners: they create a foreign ambience through non-standard language.[80] Here it would seem fitting to follow the reference to the nations and "the ends of the earth" with a foreign word, from a recognizable language.

Peter Craigie offers a similar argument, noting simply that it seems appropriate to address foreign nations, whose kings might even have spoken Aramaic, in such a way: "It is possible that the poet deliberately uses a foreign word (loan-word) to dramatize his poetic intent at this

73. *HALOT* 1270–71; *BDB* 949–50.

74. Jastrow 1488.

75. *HALOT* 1269–71, but note that "Jer 15:2" should be Jer 15:12 and that many take Prov 18:24 as an instance of the more common homonym. Job 34:24 is the only undisputed use of this root.

76. *HALOT* 1285–86; *BDB* 954.

77. Wilhelmi, "Der Hirt," 196.

78. Wilhelmi, "Der Hirt," 197.

79. Alep and L have the same form here and both mark this form as a hapax. The Masoretes were clear on the reading and aware of the temptation to change it (*Mp* only marked readings when there was a danger of losing an unusual or surprising spelling: Kelley et al., *The Masorah*, 46–47). The verse does not survive among DSS (see Ulrich, *The Biblical Qumran Scrolls*, 793).

80. Work in this field is summarized by Rendsburg, "Addressee-Switching," 1:34–35; Rendsburg, "Style-Switching," 3:633–36.

point."[81] Allen Ross is slightly different: "In addressing leaders of other countries where Aramaic was spoken, using the Aramaic word made sense."[82] However, we would then expect the entire speech to be in Aramaic. It seems more likely that the occasional Aramaism aims to evoke a foreign ambience, and a mockery of how a foreigner might mis-speak Hebrew. It is far from clear, in any case, that the psalm was to be heard by the foreigners rather than performed by natives.[83]

The context of Job 34:24 (the only undisputed use of this Aramaism) may point in the same direction (vv. 13, 18–19).

This might also explain why before Ps 2:8 the "decree" includes the Hebrew בֵּן (2:7) since that is addressed to the Jewish king, while after 2:8 the Aramaic בַּר is used, addressing the nations directly. This would fit the description of "addressee-switching" given by its first exponent, Chaim Rabin:

> It is a feature of the First Isaiah's style that, when speaking of or addressing a foreign nation, he creates "atmosphere" by using some word or words in that nation's language. Of course such phrases must not be expected to be correct expressions in the foreign language in all respects. Over-correctness in such "stage" use of a foreign language would defeat its purpose. The point is to give the listener some feature which strongly suggests the other language, but which is sufficiently familiar to be understood.[84]

His final point about sufficient familiarity should answer Wilhelmi's question of why, of all things, an Aramaism (רעע) that *has a more common Hebrew equivalent* (רצץ) was chosen.[85] Rabin again: "For instance, an English narrator trying to suggest an Italian speaker to his audience

---

81. Craigie, *Psalms 1–50*, 64.

82. Ross 1:198n6.

83. See the discussion in Craigie over the plausibility of such an audience (Craigie, *Psalms 1–50*, 64), and see Rabin concerning the point of the device for an Israelite audience ("Isaiah," 305).

84. Rabin, "Isaiah," 304–5. In this article, he discusses Isa 21:11–12 and suggests that it should be understood in those terms, but he does not offer other examples to establish the point about style. These are offered by Rendsburg and include: Isa 17:10, 12; 33:12; Jer 48:36; 49:25; Ezek 32:19; Joel 4:5 (Rendsburg, "Biblical Hebrew," 96–97) and Isa 23:13; Jer 50:15; Ezek 26:11; Amos 1:5; Zech 9:3 (Rendsburg, "Linguistic Variation and the 'Foreign' Factor in the Hebrew Bible," 184–87, cited in Rendsburg, "Addressee-Switching," 1:35); Gen 24 and 30–31 (Rendsburg, "Style-Switching," 3:634).

85. On this point of avoiding unintelligibility, see also the recent proposal of similar devices in the Book of Ruth (Holmstedt, *Ruth*, 45–46).

would make him use phrases like 'bellissima' and pseudo-Italianized English such as 'I no go', but not real Italian."[86] If one were trying to create a foreign atmosphere in English, and selected German, one would choose *Sohn* over *Kind*, because of its similarity with "son."

I would therefore suggest that the LXX *Vorlage* was supposed to be pronounced as the MT has it. It is easy to explain how the LXX change came about.[87] The only two places in this psalm where LXX differs are precisely where Aramaisms (רעע, בַּר) are employed in Hebrew, and that may have been too much for a translator of the unvocalized text.[88]

4.A.II. You Can Rejoice and Tremble

I agree with Alter's summary, on this phrase in v. 11 and the next (in v. 12): "the most elaborate efforts have been undertaken—none very convincing—to make the text mean something by extensive reconstructive surgery."[89] For example, a suggested emendation involves rearranging the last two words of v. 11 and the first two of v. 12, and then ignoring all pointing, *matres lectionis* and even word divisions, to yield: בִּרְעָדָה נַשְּׁקוּ בְרַגְלָיו "küsset seine Füße mit Zittern!" ("kiss his feet with trembling!").[90] This is meant to resolve the "incomprehensible" בַּר, the problem of trembling while rejoicing, and "does justice to the *parallelismus membrorum*."[91]

We have begun to see the rationale for בַּ in the previous section. I discuss the perceived tension between trembling and rejoicing in the exposition below. This leaves the question of parallelism.

The presumption that the line as it stands fails to exercise *parallelismus membrorum* is unjustified (Kraus does not explain it). At the syntactic and morphological level, there is a parallelism in the use of

86. Rabin, "Isaiah," 305.

87. Cf. Ross 1:198n5.

88. Kraus follows Duhm in keeping the MT, making an argument from parallelism (Kraus 1:144) which Wilhelmi rightly counters as insufficient (Wilhelmi, "Der Hirt," 196–97). MT is also kept by Vesco 63–64; Hossfeld-Zenger I:54; Ravasi 32; Kirkpatrick 1:11n9; Ross 1:198; Weber I:52; Seybold 30n9a. Schökel is spectacular: "los triturarás" (blend/mince them; Schökel I:142, 160). Goldingay exegetes both options (Goldingay 1:101).

89. Alter, *The Book of Psalms*, 7n12. He goes on to claim that the text makes little sense, so he revocalizes בר.

90. This emendation originates with Bertholet and is reported by Kraus 1:144, and followed by Schökel I:141, 147; Ravasi 32.

91. Kraus 1:144.

qatal plural imperatives with modifying feminine nouns introduced with ב prepositions. Not all parallelism must be semantic.[92]

There is no textual evidence for emendation here, except one single Hebrew text that replaces בְּיִרְאָה with בְּשִׂמְחָה (so *BHS*), which is a natural *lectio facilior*.[93] LXX sometimes adds "in him" (επ αυτω / επ αυτον) after "rejoice."[94] The Masoretes have taken the trouble to mark each of the four words that scholars want to emend with a circucellum, giving a word count of four for "rejoicing," and marking trembling and kissing as hapaxes.[95]

4.A.III. Son

Kraus speaks for many on בַּר in a parenthetical remark: "בר (unverständlicher Aramaismus! In v7 steht בֵּן)."[96] No justification is given for rejecting the Aramaism, and the text criticism begins.[97]

Kirkpatrick rejects the MT: "We should not expect a poet to borrow a foreign word for *son* here either for 'emphasis' or for 'euphony.'"[98] Indeed, but a better explanation exists. He notes that the only other Hebrew use of בַּר is in Prov 31, "which contains other marked Aramaisms." Quite so, as Ps 2 does.

No Hebrew MS has anything different here.[99] We saw in the previous section that each word at issue is emphatically marked by the Masoretes. On בר, the *Mp* of L go so far as to warn us דמטע, which is "Applied to textual readings that might logically seem to need to be corrected, but

---

92. Alter, *Biblical Poetry*, 19; Berlin, *Dynamics*, 3.

93. The two roots occur together in Isa 9:2; 29:19; Zeph 3:17; Ps 51:10.

94. Rahlfs, *Psalmi*, 82.

95. So L. Alep only marks "trembling" and "kiss" as hapaxes. See the next section for the masoretic note on "son."

96. Kraus 1:144.

97. While Alter rejects textual emendations, he still revocalizes this to remove the Aramaism (Alter, *The Book of Psalms*, 7n12; so also Vesco 63, 65).

98. Kirkpatrick 1:11–12. His comment about euphony is probably aimed at Delitzsch 75, who thought the point was to avoid a clash with פֶּן. That said, Cole offers a compelling poetic analysis of בר, based on alliteration within 9–12 "... בְּיִרְאָה ... בָּרֶל ... בַּר ... בַּרְעָדָה ... יְבַעֵר" (Cole, *Psalms 1–2*, 131–32, underlining his) and to highlight the contrast between אַפּוֹ, vv. 5, 12, and בוֹ, v. 12 (Cole, *Psalms 1–2*, 140).

99. So *BHS*, which suggests the above emendation and makes its complexity apparent. Alep is in clear agreement with L.

where such correction would lead to error."[100] LXX has some changes here, mostly giving δράξασθε παιδείας, "seize upon instruction."[101] This means that the only two places where LXX disagrees significantly with MT are where there are Aramaisms to stumble over: בַּר and רעע.

As Craigie puts it: "The dissatisfaction created by the multitude of solutions prompts a reexamination of the initial (supposed) problems, which gave rise to the identification of the *crux* in the first place."[102]

To conclude this *Excursus*, the MT, including its pointing, is to be retained in these three places.

4.B. The King Is the Judge

The king and the Torah belong together. It makes good sense for Pss 1 and 2 to bring both together. Two prominent royal duties are to rule the land, and to adjudicate as the highest court, and both are under Torah.[103] Unlike other nations, the kings of Israel were only the highest court in the land *under* Torah: the king neither creates nor promulgates laws.[104] The kings of Israel were not to be law-makers, but model law-keepers. He is

---

100. Kelley et al., *The Masorah*, 94–95.

101. Since the removal of the 'son' leaves no subject for 'ὀργισθῇ' they also insert 'κύριος.'

102. Craigie, *Psalms 1–50*, 64. The various solutions include: Goldingay reads בר as "sincerely" and נַשְּׁקוּ as "submit," and sees the phrase as part of the previous verse (Goldingay 1:93n). "'Serve' and 'submit' form a pair, as do 'reverence' and 'trembling,' each time a less-common word reinforcing the more-common one" (Goldingay 1:103). This is a general principle of parallelism: "The predominant pattern of biblical poetry is to move from a standard term in the first verset to a more literary or high-falutin term in the second verset" (Alter, *Biblical Poetry*, 13). It works just as well, or better, with the rare Aramaism and with 'kiss.' Nor does the phrase need to be moved: the parallelism is established by the first phrase being followed by a positive outcome and the second with a negative warning. As Goldingay has appealed to a homonym, so Rashi, who takes it as "fight," i.e., "arm yourselves" (Rashi, *Psalms*, 182n26). Many others have offered explanations of the problem, but if the above shows that there is no actual problem, we need not consider each of them. See the references in Goldingay 1:93n. MT is followed by Ross 1:198; Weber I:52; Hossfeld-Zenger I:52n11–12a; Delitzsch 69, 75; Calvin, *Psalms*, 1:24.

103. Rad, *Theology of Israel's Prophetic Traditions*, 322.

104. Vaux, *Ancient Israel*, 150–51.

not entitled to change the law, but must enforce it. "[T]he rule of that king is utterly determined by obedience to the law of the Lord."[105]

The image sitting in the seat of scorners is applicable to both of these royal duties. To "sit" is a common frozen metaphor for acting as judge (even as today a court "sits") and for sitting on the throne as king.[106] Unlike the king's devotion to Torah in v. 2, the scorners of v. 1 could be *sitting* as a court, setting aside God's law as the standard of judgment. The righteous king is not to turn aside and join them, but to retain the Torah as the standard for judgment. He must reject their rejection of Torah. Psalm 1 slated such scorners for death at the judgment. Consistent with the duty of kings, Psalm 2 ends by identifying the anointed king as the agent of their judgment, whose wrath the wicked must flee.

4.C. The Enemy Are Rebellious Kings and Judges

Various links across Pss 1 and 2 make it easy to identify the protagonists and antagonists with each other, so that Ps 2 becomes a concrete example of Ps 1.[107] We have seen above how the protagonist is the Messianic king in Ps 2. The antagonists very pointedly do the opposite of what makes the king righteous in Psalm 1. He meditates on the Torah, murmuring (הגה, *hagah*) it. They also murmur (הגה, *hagah*) as they plot.

They oppose Yahweh in both Psalms: his Torah in Ps 1 and his anointed agent of Torah in 2:2. They are kings and judges in v. 10. The fetters and yoke that the vassal rebellion throws off in v. 3 are his covenant with its law.

Psalm 1 threatened such Torah-scorners with death at the judgment. Psalm 2 offers a concrete example of such scorners, and identifies the king as their judge in all his wrath. Surprisingly, Ps 2 offers them an alternative: restoration and blessing.

4.D. Rebel Judges Are Invited to Repent and Be Blessed

Judgment is a common theme in these psalms: the winnowing of the chaff in Ps 1 corresponds to the terrifying of the rebels in Ps 2.[108] Each

105. Miller, "Deuteronomy and Psalms," 12.

106. Kaiser, "ישׁב," 412; Wilson, "ישׁב," 2:550–51.

107. Botha, "Ideological Interface," 202.

108. Botha, "Ideological Interface," 202.

psalm ends with the threat of "perishing" in the "way," (italicized below) contrasted with an alternative (underlined below).

> **1:6** <u>Because Yahweh knows the way of the righteous ones</u>
> whereas *the way* of the wicked ones *perishes.*
> **2:12** <u>Kiss the son</u>
> lest he anger so that *you perish while on the way*
> because suddenly kindled is his ire.
> <u>O, the blessings of all who take refuge in him!</u>

In Ps 1, the alternative could be construed as already decided: the righteous will live, the wicked will perish (v. 6). Not so in Ps 2, where only the wicked are addressed, and given the choice between perishing, or kissing the son; between suffering the son's wrath, or being blessed. Psalm 2 guards against misreading Psalm 1 with any sense of grim fatalism or gleeful one-upmanship. Some even view Ps 1 as a model of confession for sinners. Far from setting an ethical bar that only the moral can clear, it invites the reader to enter the Psalter by rejecting their own wickedness.[109] This would be consistent with predictions of judgment generally in the OT: not fatalistic clairvoyance, but are exhortations to turn away from the behavior that brings judgment.[110] Psalm 2 would reinforce such an understanding of Ps 1. The whole final stanza of the poem is given over to this.

> **10** Now then, O kings, get wisdom;
> submit to retraining, O judges of the earth.

The climactic final stanza opens in v. 10 by addressing these rebels as kings and judges. These who had departed from the way of murmuring (הגה, *hagah*) Torah in contemplation (1:1–2) and instead murmur (also הגה, *hagah*) their plot vainly (2:1), are now enjoined to meditate accurately and profitably, as the righteous one of Ps 1 had done: "get wisdom; submit to retraining" (הַשְׂכִּילוּ הִוָּסְרוּ, *haskilu hiwwaseru*).[111]

The first verb, שׂכל (*sakal* in the *hipʻil* stem), gathers two ideas from Ps 1: the idea of meditating with understanding, and of success or

---

109. Boda, *A Severe Mercy*, 396.

110. Eissfeldt, *The Old Testament*, 78–79; Rad, *Theology of Israel's Prophetic Traditions*, 230–32; Schökel, *Hermenéutica de la palabra*, 106.

111. "The call to respond wisely by dissociation from sinners (1:1) parallels the rebuke to kings and nations to submit themselves to the Lord and his Messiah (2:10)" (VanGemeren, *Psalms*, 78).

prosperity.[112] The kings are being urged to acquire wisdom. This wisdom would allow them to assess the likely outcome of their present rebellion and weigh the alternative. They should become wise enough both to seek Yahweh and then to prosper,[113] just as the righteous in Ps 1 pays attention to Torah and then prospers in all his endeavors (1:2–3).

The second verb, יסר (yasar in the nipʿal stem), more neutrally implies allowing oneself to be instructed through corrective discipline.[114] This is a fresh start, a second chance to learn from the Torah that they had rejected.

Most strikingly, the rebels are not only to reassess and wisely abandon their rebellion, in favor of serving Yahweh (2:11) and kissing the son (v. 12). They are called back to their offices of kings and judges, to judge justly and rule wisely under Torah. Being invited to serve (עבד,

---

112. The verb is very common and has both of these senses in the hipʿil. It occurs notably in Gen 3:6 of the tree that makes one wise, and of the shepherds after Yahweh's own heart who will tend his flock with knowledge and with *understanding*. In Deut 29:8 and in 1 Kgs 2:3 it refers to the prosperity that follows keeping the covenant (similarly, 1 Sam 18:5; 2 Kgs 18:7). One of the connections between Ps 1 and Josh 1:7, 8 is a different root for prospering (צלח, tsalach), and we find the hipʿil of this verb (שׂכל) there in parallel with it, and repeated throughout Josh 1. In Deut 32:29 it especially refers to having insight to foresee the consequences of one's actions (also Isa 41:20; 44:18; Jer 9:23). Isa 52:13 perhaps brings insight and prosperity together, while Jer 10:21 contrasts lack of insight with lack of prosperity. In Psalms it is often ethical and connected with seeking after God and doing good: e.g., 14:2, 32:8; 36:4.

113. The process in view here is described well by Zenger (Hossfeld-Zenger I:54), but not quite captured by such translations as "act wisely" (Kraus 1:143 is similar); "pay mind" (Alter, *The Book of Psalms*, 6); "prêtez attention" (Vesco 63–64); "be sensible" (Goldingay 1:93); "sed sensatos" (Schökel I:142).

114. יסר is rare in the nipʿal. The qal meaning of "instruct" is almost only found in emendation (HALOT 418) but the piʿel is common (twenty-nine times) and seems to mean to instruct (e.g., Isa 28:26), often as discipline (Deut 8:5; 21:18), often punitive (Lev 26:18, 28; Deut 4:36), and sometimes penal *without* instruction (Deut 22:18) or even oppressive (1 Kgs 12:11, 14). In context, I take it here as corrective, instructive discipline, in line with the parallel use of שׂכל in this verse, and in the later offer of refuge, but with an ambiguity that suits their status as *judges* who would be the ones meeting out punishment. They may expect a scourging, but the offer will in fact be one of pardon. (Few Targum MSS suggest the variant הוסדו. This would be a form of יסד and involve a simple misreading of ר for ד. It is used in v. 2 of the conspiring and could fit the sense. However, the textual weight remains on the Hebrew form we have.) "Be warned" and the like (Kraus 1:143) is too neutral. Better are "be chastened" (Alter, *The Book of Psalms*, 6); "Laissez-vous corriger" (Vesco 63); "allow yourselves to be put right" (Goldingay 1:102); "escarmentad" (Schökel I:160: "to be tutored by experience" or "to heed a warning" which he contrasts with the nations planning a failure earlier in the Psalm).

'abad) does not deny that they are leaders: king David in 132:10 is not only "your anointed" (מְשִׁיחֶךָ, *meshiheka*) but also "your *servant*" (עַבְדְּךָ, 'abdeka); Moses is Yahweh's servant (עֶבֶד, 'ebed) in Exod 14:31 and Num 12:7, 8. The verb applies to vassal kings.[115] These rebellious kings are not being dethroned, but offered back the very jobs they had rejected. They are being offered instruction in the art of kingship.[116] They are promised *restoration.* "The unexpected and generous positive invitation to rejoice stands out as the central word in the line."[117] Had they merely been told to "save your skins from the punishment to come," that would already have been an abundantly gracious offer in the light of Ps 1, and out of keeping with any inflexible principle of retribution. In fact, they are offered even more: "return to your positions of honor as servants of Yahweh, vassal kings."[118] The choice is a simple assonance 'ibedu (עִבְדוּ, serve, 2:11) or to'bedu (תֹּאבְדוּ, perish 2:12). "Abandon, or Abaddon."

Instead of finding what some expect, a rigid principle of just retribution against sinners, we find the very thing that some claim the Psalms had no concept of: a desire that the wicked, even the personal enemy, should repent and fair well.

> 11 Serve Yahweh fearfully,
>   rejoice and tremble.

The following verse reinforces the two ideas of wisdom and success:[119] Fear (יְרָאָה, *yir'ah*) is connected with wisdom and right living, in the Psalms and elsewhere.[120] Throughout the Psalms, Isaiah, and the Twelve, rejoice (גִּיל, *gyl*) is associated with salvation and judgment which bring renewed prosperity to the people.

This connection between fear and rejoicing, because of both salvation and judgment, is developed in Psalm 67. Verse 4 calls for praise from all the peoples because of the salvation of v. 3b. Verse 4 is repeated in v. 6, bracketing a further call to the nations. The nations are to be joyful and glad, but this time because Yahweh *judges* them justly. The psalm ends by

115. Craigie, *Psalms 1–50*, 68.

116. Hossfeld-Zenger I:54.

117. Goldingay 1:103.

118. Goldingay notes that the warning about flaring wrath is specific to these rebels in this instance, and not gnomic (Goldingay 1:94n).

119. Goldingay sees v. 11 as epexegetical of v. 10: how the kings are to be instructed (Goldingay 1:102).

120. We will see this in the following chapter, section (6)2.

declaring twice that God will bless, and that the ends of the earth will *fear* him, in fulfilment of Yahweh's promise to the Son in Psalm 2:8b.

The use of trembling (רְעָדָה, re'adah) will not allow "fear and tremble" to be taken purely as an expression of trust and obedience (see its uses in Isa 33:14; Ps 48:7; Job 4:14). Nonetheless, rejoicing in true service rightly coexists with a proper fear of transgression and punishment. As Deut 28:47 puts it, while serving joyfully and gladly is what Yahweh wants, the alternative is punishment.[121] The officers rejoice at a second chance and fear the judgment which would follow any further transgression. As Phil Botha puts it: "the prospect of happiness and honour for those who choose to *dissociate* themselves from the wicked (Psalm 1) corresponds to the promise of happiness for those who choose to *associate* with the anointed of Yahweh in Psalm 2."[122] Note the implication: the wicked are not to be shunned personally, but only as long as they remain unrepentant.

4.E. The Restored Leaders Are a Cause for Rejoicing among Their People

Righteous rulers are a cause of celebration for their people: Ps 48:11; 63:11; Prov 11:10; 29:2; Deut 4:6. It is not hard to see why; the concluding "prayer of David" (Ps 72) prays for the king and explicitly prays for him to be the cause of justice and prosperity for his people. "The human king is accountable for the welfare of the entire people, for the entire land, and for all of the creatures that live in the land."[123] "The fundamental duty of kings is to judge their people justly and deliver the oppressed."[124] Those who are ruled by these repentant and restored kings would therefore welcome their masters' new-found fear of Yahweh.[125]

---

121. There is thus no need for conjectural emendations that do away with the contradiction of fear and joy here, since no such contradiction exists: see Kirkpatrick 1:11; Alexander, *Psalms*, 18.

122. Botha, "Ideological Interface," 202.

123. Jacobson and Jacobson, *Invitation to the Psalms*, 170.

124. Wenham, *Psalms as Torah*, 113; so also McCann, "Psalms," 647.

125. Clines does not do justice to the third person pronouns in 2:3 when he collapses the leaders and nations into one group that "represent themselves . . . as slaves" (Clines, "Psalm 2," 247). He assumes too quickly that the *demoi* share their leaders' "aspiration to independence," that justice and power are mutually-exclusive choices (Clines, "Psalm 2," 257), and that the "crushing" of the Messiah is aimed at the nations and not the leaders (Clines, "Psalm 2," 258).

Yahweh's good, prospering Torah of Ps 1:2–3 had been removed from them with populist rhetoric in 2:3, but throwing off *righteous* kingship is no blessing at all. Removing Yahweh's Torah from their rule leaves the people exposed to judicial injustice and the judgments that follow lawlessness (1:4–5). When wicked rulers repent and fear Yahweh, it is good news for the righteous who are under them (58:11–12; 72:1–7), because Yahweh restores his good Torah judgments.[126] "God is a protector and vindicator. . . . God's concern for order . . . is mirrored by a concern for order in human society."[127] This connection between a people rescued (ישע, *yasha'*) from godless, unjust rule,[128] and that people being judged (שפט, *shaphat*) rightly is axiomatic to the aptly named Book of Judges.

> The judges (*shophetim*) were men who procured justice or right for the people of Israel, not only by delivering them out of the power of their foes, but also by administering the laws and rights of the Lord (Judg. 2:16–19). *Judging* in this sense was different from the administration of civil jurisprudence, and included the idea of government such as would be expected from a king.[129]

In Ps 2, the renewed kings and judges get to join in the joy of their people, who are rejoicing at their renewed officers. The assumptions that are brought to the Psalms might expect the people to rejoice because the wicked kings are judged and replaced. The opposite is true.

Furthermore, in Deut 6, if Israel serves the Lord with fear (6:13, cf. vv. 2, 24), they dispossess the enemy nations. The judgment of the enemy nations in Deut 6 and Josh 1, which is alluded to in Ps 1, has become the offer of repentance, refuge and blessing in Ps 2. The close of the psalm

---

126. *Contra* Brown: "The encompassing power of the 'refuge' motif is strained when pressed to give account of *tôrâ*, in particular, and the Psalter's overall shape, more broadly" (Brown, *Seeing*, 32).

127. Curtis, *Psalms*, xxxvi.

128. Throughout, I'm following Robert Alter's rendering of ישע words as "rescue" rather than "salvation" (Alter, *The Book of Psalms*, xxxii). See also Kirkpatrick who translates it as "help" in 3:2 and suggests "victory" in 3:8, explaining the earthy, physical and sometimes military use of "salvation" which is always on the lips of the psalmists (Kirkpatrick 1:16). Rescue does correspond to "salvation" as properly understood in Christian theology, but it is popularly construed more narrowly, in a way that excludes God's intervention in earthly troubles.

129. K&D 2:177; *contra* Block, *Judges, Ruth*, 22–23, who sees the delivering function of שפט in Judges as evidence that the lexeme has an alternative, non-judicial meaning.

invites not only the kings and rulers, but also the peoples, to take refuge in the son, including the rebel kings and nations.[130]

I have rejected the softening emendation of "crush" (2:9) to "shepherd." Other efforts to soften are special pleading: "crush" is not merely a picture of dominion, nor of ease of conquest.[131] The dominion and conquest that "crush" represents will involve violence to those who do not submit (2:12). Nonetheless, the aim of Ps 2 is the rejoicing of the rebels, not their destruction: they are invited, urged and motivated to repent, serve, rejoice, and take refuge in the son. Even this is too much for David Clines: the mere fact that the Moabites (for example) are given no option between serving the Israelite God and king or destruction is scandalous "from any point of view that does not identify with the text."[132] Clines does not substantiate this claim or show that no other points of view would fail to be scandalized. It might be true among Modern Western authors (though perhaps less so now than when Clines penned this comment), but surely not much imagination is needed to think of historical worldviews that would applaud the text: Viking, Roman, Babylonian, most empires. The universe of points of view will not arise to condemn this text with one voice. More importantly, then, Clines gives no reason why we should fail to identify with the text other than his idea of what is scandalous. Why should he offer his readers no choice between serving *his* world-view or facing *his* opprobrium? That is scandalous from any point of view that does not identify with Clines. Why not choose the reproach of the text over the pleasure of Clines? As we have seen above, the Torah which is being thrown off is life-giving, the source of blessing, which is the *telos* of the Psalter. The rebel kings are leading their peoples to death unless the son rescues them from the way of the wicked.

Clines assumes that all dominion is equally illegitimate. "So, we must conclude, for the Christian interpreter the theology of Egypt was in the right after all, and we may be grateful that the Hebrew poet had the breadth of vision to lay under tribute the wisdom of his erstwhile national oppressor."[133] But this is not the same *theology* because it is not the same *theos*. The "gods" of Egypt and Israel had a showdown, and Yahweh won, as the Psalms will make abundantly clear in their celebration

---

130. Goldingay 1:106; Miller, "Deuteronomy and Psalms," 12.

131. In agreement with Clines, "Psalm 2," 258.

132. Clines, "Psalm 2," 274–75.

133. Clines, "Psalm 2," 263–65.

of the exodus in Book V. Egypt's nobles will join in Yahweh's praise (e.g., 68:31) and it will not be oppressive: we will show this in our exposition of Book V. Clines needs to justify his *assumption* that life cannot be better as a subject of David and his God, than under Pharaoh and his gods (especially when the Psalter claims as much).

Eaton asks of Psalm 1, "Should the ungodly be seen in such absolute, unredeemable terms?"[134] Psalm 2 suggests not: it offers them restoration. In fact, Eaton himself acknowledges as much, and sees that Ps 2 is one of a series of texts that show that the king not only teaches, but also admonishes against rebellion and invites repentance, and does so to all nations.[135] This is a good example of the value of canonical readings; Eaton's monograph on kingship never cites Ps 1, while his monograph on "psalms of the way" fails to notice what his own earlier monograph saw in Ps 2, and the significance of their sequence to his own question.

5. The Introduction to the Psalter in Summary

Psalm 1 does not describe one who never sins, but rather a man who loves Yahweh, delights in his Torah, and shuns the gatherings and schemes of those who hate Yahweh. Righteousness and wickedness are here (as often in the rest of Scripture) matters of allegiance and of the orientation of life, not a claim to have lived without spot or blemish.[136] Calvin and Kirkpatrick deserve quoting here:

> From his characterising the godly as delighting in the law of the Lord, we may learn that forced or servile obedience is not at all acceptable to God, and that those only are worthy students of the law who come to it with a cheerful mind, and are so delighted with its instructions, as to account nothing more desirable or delicious than to make progress therein. From this love of the law proceeds constant meditation upon it, which the prophet mentions on the last clause of the verse; for all who are truly actuated by love to the law must feel pleasure in the diligent study of it.[137]

134. Eaton, *Psalms of the Way*, 39.

135. Eaton, *Kingship*, 181.

136. Kraus dispels Modern (especially Gunkel's) views of nomism (Kraus 1:135–41). Similarly, Mowinckel points to the covenantal importance of righteousness, rooted in a relationship with Yahweh and his people (Mowinckel, *Psalms*, 1:208–10).

137. Calvin, *Psalms*, 1:4–5.

The law of the Lord is his rule of conduct. It is no irksome restriction of his liberty but the object of his love and constant study (Deut. vi. 6–9). True happiness is to be found not in ways of man's own devising, but in the revealed will of God. 'The purpose of the Law was to make men happy.'[138]

Unlike the wicked, he will withstand judgment. Psalm 2 introduces a twist to the plot of Ps 1: the unrighteous will not necessarily fall at the judgment either. They are invited to repent. Even foreign rebel kings and judges are offered full restoration to their exalted positions as servants of Yahweh who rule and judge justly under Torah. This possibility means that those who are unjustly ruled, who would benefit from the removal of the wicked, must wait like the man of Ps 1 while the wicked are given time to turn, before the wrath of the son turns on them.

We will now see that Ps 3 applies this, using the life of David as an example for Israel.

138. Kirkpatrick 1:3n2.

5

Retribution in the Introduction to David

Psalm 3

Psalm 1 described the conduct of the righteous, and the blessing that God gives him. Psalm 2 presented the messianic king
confronted by the wicked, yet assured of victory. Psalm 3 identifies
that righteous one and that messianic king confronted by wicked
people and by adversaries: it is David fleeing from Absalom.[1]

In these three psalms there is a sensible gradation or progressive develop-
ment of one great idea. The general contrast, which the first exhibits, of the
righteous and the wicked, is reproduced, in the second, as a war against the
Lord and his Anointed. In the third, it is still further individualized as a conflict between David, the great historical type of the Messiah, and his enemies.[2]

PSALM 3 OVERTURNS THE assumptions about David and the Old Testament
that we have set out to examine. David shows a very practical awareness

1. "Le Ps 1 décrivait la conduite du juste et le bonheur que Dieu lui donne. Le Ps 2
montrait le roi-messie affronté aux impies, mais assuré de la victoire. Le Ps 3 identifie
ce juste et ce roi-messie affronté aux impies et aux adversaires, c'est David fuyant Absalom" (Vesco 100).

2. Alexander, *Psalms*, 19.

of his own sinfulness, the very opposite of self-righteousness. He shows mercy to his enemies and even prays that they would be blessed.

Psalm 3 joins Psalms 1–2 in opening the Book of Psalms.[3] Of all the similar David psalms that could have been chosen, Ps 3 is presented to the reader first, and is the first mention of David. By placing Ps 3 strategically at the opening, we are helped to see David in its light before reading on in the Psalms.

Psalm 3 points us to the Absalom narrative in Samuel. It also develops the theme of retribution introduced by Psalms 1 and 2. Moreover, Psalms 1, 2, and 3 make some important connections with the way that the whole of the Absalom narrative is told in 2 Samuel. These highlight David's approach to retribution.

1. Psalm 3

3:1 [s] *A psalm for stringed accompaniment. David's, when he was fleeing from Absalom, his son.*

2 [1] O Yahweh: what a multitude my foes have become!
    Multitudes are rising up against me!
3 [2] The multitudes are saying about my life:
    "There will be no rescue for him from God"!

                                          Selah.

4 [3] Yet you, O Yahweh, are a shield around me my glory
    and the one who raises my head.
5 [4] With my voice I had been calling to Yahweh,
    and he answered me from his holy hill.

                                          Selah.

6 [5] As for me, I lay down and fell asleep
    I did wake up because Yahweh had been sustaining me.
7 [6] I do not fear the myriads of a nation,
    who have surrounded me and set themselves against me.
8 [7] Rise up, Yahweh!
    Rescue me, my God!
        Because you have struck all my enemies on the cheek,
        you have broken the teeth of the wicked.

---

3. Including Ps 3 in the introduction has been considered since antiquity (for example Gregory of Nyssa, *Inscriptions of the Psalms*, II.XI.138). While it has always been a minority report, it remains an active concern (for example Lohfink, "Psalmengebet," 12). Recently, Weber has championed the inclusion of Ps 3 into a three-fold introduction to the Psalter so that each of Pss 1–3 introduce a theme that becomes programmatic for the Psalter (developed fully in Weber, *Theologie*).

9 [8] It is to Yahweh that rescue belongs!
May there be a blessing upon *your* nation!

Selah.

2. The Backstory to Psalm 3: Absalom (David Is Innocent); Bathsheba (David Is Guilty)

The superscription points us to David's flight from his son, Absalom. The superscriptions seem to refer predominantly to events of David's distress which are portrayed in Samuel.[4] We will present the backstory here in summary, since Ps 3 takes it as read.

Some object that the superscription does not fit, because the body of Psalm 3 does not specify the situation, for example, by not mentioning that David is fleeing.[5] This misunderstands the Psalter's approach to historiography: even historical Psalms (such as Pss 78, 105, 106) *assume*, rather than restate, knowledge of the histories which they comment on. They assume the reader's detailed familiarity and present the events afresh.[6] One could just as well object that the body of Ps 3 does not fit the superscription because it does not tell us who David or Absalom are. With the Absalom narrative fresh in our minds, the plot of Ps 3 becomes clear.

We find David fleeing from Absalom in 2 Sam 15:13 onwards. David flees because Absalom has successfully stirred up an overwhelming rebellion against David, by recruiting the Northern tribes of Israel to topple David in Absalom's favor. However, we must first see where Absalom's rebellion comes from in Samuel.

The background to the Absalom narrative seems to be overlooked by exegetes of Ps 3.[7] The root cause is David's sin with Bathsheba, causing the death of his firstborn, the sword never to depart from his dynasty, and specifically Absalom's usurpation, as prophesied by Nathan (2 Sam

---

4. Kleer, "*Der liebliche Sänger*," 116.

5. Goldingay 1:109.

6. Alter, *Biblical Poetry*, 27.

7. Erbele-Küster, *Lesen*, 66–68, joins many others in seeing the connection with 2 Sam 15–19 without observing the relevance of David's sin with Bathsheba, which precipitates that entire narrative. Sumpter's analysis of the transition between Pss 1–2 and 3 likewise misses the entire dimension of David's sin by beginning at 2 Sam 15 as the parallel with Ps 2 (Sumpter, "The Canonical Shape," 518–19).

12:10–14).[8] I will show that this is significant for the Psalter's theology of
retribution.

2.A. From Bathsheba to Absalom

It all begins with David's sin with Bathsheba and murder of her husband
Uriah (2 Sam 11). Yahweh issues a prophetic oracle via Nathan, that "the
sword will never turn away from his dynasty" (12:10). More immediately,
Yahweh tells him: "I am about to raise up trouble against you from within
your own dynasty." Yahweh will bring about poetic justice, with David's
wives taken adulterously from him in public, exposing David for taking
Uriah's wife in secret (vv. 11–12).

The reader of Samuel does not wait long for the "sword" to appear
within David's dynasty: 2 Sam 13. His son Amnon rapes David's daughter
Tamar. Tamar is avenged by David's son Absalom, who kills Amnon and
flees from justice. One daughter raped, one son killed and one son fleeing
from justice, but that is just the beginning.

Absalom is allowed to return to Jerusalem (2 Sam 14), and it soon
becomes clear who is going to take David's wives, and much more be-
sides, from him. Absalom conspires to raise up a rebellion against his
father by persuading all of the Northern tribes that king David only dis-
penses justice to members of his own tribe (15:1–4), and points out how
much better and impartial a king he himself would be in David's stead.

After four years of this plot, Absalom has won over the Northern
tribes and has himself crowned king, and increases in manpower (2 Sam
15:7–12).

It is at this point that David hears of the conspiracy and flees Jerusalem, and the plot of 2 Samuel maps neatly onto Psalm 3. Before we
see this in more detail, we must notice that David is simultaneously the
innocent party and yet receiving just retribution from Yahweh.

2.B. David Is Simultaneously Innocent and Guilty

David faces a rebellion from the Northern Tribes which is stirred up by
slander. Absalom has lied about David's impartiality as judge and won
the people over by a sustained campaign of misinformation. If the Northern Tribes are motivated by David's unrighteousness as judge, David is

8. Briefly noted by Althann, "Atonement and Reconciliation," 76.

innocent of all charges. He is being pursued by an unjust usurping son with no righteous cause behind him. David is innocent.

David is guilty. David faces the judgment that Yahweh prophesied through Nathan. The sword has not turned away from his dynasty (12:10), but is now in the hand of Absalom. Even more specifically, Yahweh fulfils the further punishment. Absalom will go on to do the very act of poetic justice that Yahweh had promised in 12:11—Absalom will be the trouble that is raised up from David's dynasty, indeed from his immediate family. Later, as promised, Absalom will be the one to take his wives publicly (16:20–22) just as much as David had taken Uriah's wife secretly. The human agent who advises Absalom to do this is David's most trusted counsellor, Ahithophel. Ahithophel goes over to Absalom in 15:12, and it is immediately after this that David gets wind of the conspiracy and flees. David is fleeing because of Yahweh's judgment on him for his sin with Bathsheba and Uriah, exactly as prophesied. David is guilty.

He is innocent and guilty, but not in the same way, not regarding the same charges. When faced with Absalom, he is both justly facing Yahweh's righteous condemnation, and yet also facing a wicked and undeserved plot by an unrighteous slanderer who wants to steal Yahweh's throne. How will this turn out?

2.C. The Flight from Absalom: David as Innocent and Guilty in Psalm 3

In 2 Sam 15:13, David suddenly realizes that the Northern Tribes are following Absalom against him, so he flees Jerusalem with those loyal to him. As he leaves the city, he meets with a mixture of support and scorn; he does not accept all the support, nor react against the opposition.

Most tellingly, he refuses to allow Zadok, the high priest, to bring the ark of the covenant with him (2 Sam 15:25). The ark goes on the march with Israel so that Yahweh scatters his enemies (Num 10:35). David's unwillingness to assume that his personal enemies are Yahweh's enemies is evidence that he understands his own guilt.[9] As he puts it to Zadok in 2 Sam 15:25–26: "Return the ark of God to the city. If I find grace in Yahweh's eyes, he will return me so that I will see it and where

---

9. "Until David has evidence of Yahweh's actions, he will not act"; and "submission to Yahweh involves accepting legitimate punishment for iniquity" (Firth, *1 & 2 Samuel*, 459, 461).

it dwells. On the other hand, if he says, 'I do not delight in you,' look, here I am, let him deal with me as seems good in his eyes."[10] We will see that, when David perceives clearly that Yahweh has shown him grace and intends to rescue him from Absalom, David will summon his help using the precise language of Num 10:35, as though he had the ark with him. At this point, though, David knows that just as much as Absalom is guilty, so David himself is guilty, and does not deserve Yahweh's support.

Very pointedly, David's advice to Ittai not to throw his lot in with David contrasts David's lack of knowledge about his fate, with his confident prayer that Yahweh would show steadfast love and faithfulness to Ittai if he leaves David (15:20). Ittai's choice to follow David underlines the point: rather than relying on Yahweh's favor, he will stand by David, but does not know whether David is facing death or life (v. 21).

David tells Zadok that he will wait in the fords, this side of the Jordan, until he hears word. The next news he hears is that Ahithophel, his most trusted counsellor, has joined the conspiracy, causing David to pray that "Yahweh would frustrate Ahithophel's counsel" (v. 31). His location at the fords, and the prayer against Ahithophel's counsel will be central to the plot and to Ps 3.

David is aware of his ambiguous standing: his *rightful* punishment from Yahweh is to be *wrongly* attacked by Absalom. Therefore, David is willing to act in self-defense against Absalom, but not to presume on Yahweh's support (for example with the ark of the covenant), and instead see his chastising hand against David's sin. So, he sends Hushai to pretend to be a turncoat to Absalom's side (v. 34) and spy for David. However, on being cursed by Shimei, and being offered vengeance by his retinue, "Leave him be, let him curse, since it is Yahweh who has told him to" (16:11). David is certain that Shimei's curses are of divine origin, but only hopes (without prejudice) in divine protection for himself: "Maybe Yahweh will notice my affliction and repay me with good in exchange for his cursing today."[11]

---

10. Firth sees this as an example of David repenting of the behavior for which he is being punished; he had grasped after power and control, like the kings of the nations; now he is no longer certain that Yahweh is with him, but he accepts Yahweh's right to decide the issue, as one who installs and removes kings (Firth, "Shining the Lamp," 222–23; so also Smith, *The Fate of Justice*, 95).

11. Smith sees this refusal as evidence that David is aware that he is being punished in line with Nathan's oracle (Smith, *The Fate of Justice*, 96; so also Kleer, "Der liebliche Sänger," 91; Johnson, *David in Distress*, 24; Firth, *1 & 2 Samuel*, 459). Smith assesses numerous lines of possible evidence that David and the narrator were aware of this throughout 13:1—20:26 (Smith, *The Fate of Justice*, 94–101).

This makes sense of a strange feature of Ps 3. While Ps 3 obviously contains a lament, and even contains an imprecation (vv. 8–9 [7–8]), it breaks the pattern of laments. We expect laments to open with a prayer to God, asking him to hear, or at least complaining that he is not hearing. We find nothing like this in Ps 3 until the psalm is almost over. Verses 2–3 [1–2] simply describe the situation, but do not ask for relief. The psalm simply opens with a description of the myriads of foes rising against him, which is what Absalom and his army were doing. His lack of prayer at that point is explained by his unwillingness to presume that Yahweh will be on his side, because of his own sin.

His journey ends at the near side of the Jordan, where his army settles for the night, awaiting word from Hushai (cf. 15:28), having prayed against Ahithophel's counsel (cf. 15:31) in 16:14. That counsel is offered immediately.

In the next verse, Ahithophel is singled out among "all the people" who accompany Absalom to Jerusalem (v. 15). As soon as David's spy Hushai inveigles his way into Absalom's court (vv. 16–19), he seeks advice on how to proceed. Absalom begins by doing exactly what Ahithophel suggests (vv. 20–22). This is explained because: "Ahithophel's counsel was like when a man enquires after the word of God; so was *all* of Ahithophel's counsel, both when offered to David and just as much when offered to Absalom" (16:23). David's prayer that his counsel be frustrated, or received as folly, is as asking for nothing short of a miracle.

In Ps 3:3 [2] David complains that his foes are saying that God will not save him, in an oft-noted denial of the divine promise of Ps 2:7–9. We have seen Shimei tell David that it is Yahweh who has taken the kingdom from him and given it to Absalom (16:8), while here there is no doubt in the mind of Ahithophel that David can easily be killed (17:3).

The turning point comes when Ahithophel gives direct advice on how to finish David off. He asks for a small force with which to deal with David's haggard forces by a surgical strike in the night. He will kill only king David, and his exhausted and disheartened army will disband. Absalom will have won over the whole people (17:1–3). Not only Absalom, but also all Israel's elders approve of the plan, as expected, since it is Ahithophel's counsel.

Absalom, surprisingly, asks Hushai (David's spy) to give his advice. Hushai artfully plays for time by exaggerating the threat of David's men and encouraging Absalom to wait until he can muster an overwhelming force from all Israel and wipe out not only David, but all his fierce and fiercely-loyal troops (vv. 6–13).

Contrary to all expectations, the counsel which was always treated, even by Absalom, as God's own oracles, did not prevail. Hushai's plan won the court over. We are told why: "Absalom and all the men of Israel said, 'Hushai the Archite's counsel is better than Ahithophel's counsel.' Yahweh had determined to nullify Ahithophel's *good* counsel, with the express purpose that Yahweh should bring harm against Absalom." (v. 14). Having gained time, Hushai clandestinely sends word to David: "Get up and hurry across the water, for Ahithophel has counselled against you as follows" (17:20). We then discover that Ahithophel was so confident in the wisdom of his plan, and the folly of Hushai's, that he committed suicide rather than live to see David's certain victory and revenge against him (17:23).[12] The whole tale emphasizes that, not only was Ahithophel's counsel expected to be followed, but it was also undeniably the correct course of action for Absalom. Yahweh answered David's prayer of 15:31, to frustrate Ahithophel's counsel.

The turning point in Samuel explains the turning point in the psalm. Up to Ps 3:3 [2] David had merely been lamenting the overwhelming forces that were assembling against him, with no apparent confidence. In v. 4 [3], David is suddenly confident that Yahweh protects him, and he explains what has happened to show him that in vv. 5–6 [4–5].

David had cried out to Yahweh, and Yahweh answered "from his holy mountain" (v. 5 [4]). This is because David had fled Jerusalem and the tabernacle. His lack of presumption, by not taking the ark of the covenant with him, has not proved an obstacle to God, who has answered at a distance. How does David know that Yahweh answered him? David's sole prayer had been to confound Ahithophel's counsel.[13] Ahithophel counselled catching David by surprise in the night.[14] David knows that he had lain down to sleep (v. 6 [5]) and would therefore have been ripe for the taking.[15] However, instead of being caught and killed, *he woke*

---

12. On this point, Alter, *Prophets*, 382.

13. *Contra* Schökel I:167, who identifies the prayer of v. 5 with v. 8.

14. Vivian Johnson suggests that Absalom's counsellors clashed because Ahithophel wanted David caught asleep (Johnson, *David in Distress*, 26–27).

15. So, representing the majority, Curtis, *Psalms*, 7; David is not overcome with vexation and fear, *contra* Rashi, *Psalms*, 183. David was unaware of the danger of which Hushai would only warn him later, when he woke him.

up because Yahweh had been sustaining him.[16] How did he physically wake up? When messengers came from Jerusalem. Yet, they only had time to come and warn David because Ahithophel's counsel of haste was disregarded. David has opportunity to *rise* again after lying down to rest (2 Sam 17:21–22; Ps 3:6 [5]).[17] Yahweh has literally lifted his head (Ps 3:4 [3]). We are pointedly told that *by daybreak*, not a single one of David's men was left on the wrong side of the Jordan (2 Sam 17:22). David's short nocturnal respite (16:14) followed by his rising to flee (17:22) is only possible because God has answered his prayer of 15:31; had Ahithophel's counsel been heeded, David would not have been able to rise again.[18]

Notice how it is immediately after David refuses to take the ark with him (15:25–28) and we find the ark on one mount, and David on another (vv. 29–30) that David hears about Ahithophel and prays from the mount of Olives to God's holy mountain (v. 31).

David's one prayer has been answered in ways that he had not foreseen: Yahweh has simultaneously saved his life and shown that he is on his side. The answer to prayer is proved not by David sleeping unconcerned, but the rising from sleep, becoming concerned and evading death.[19]

As a result, his lament about the enemies in Ps 3:2–3 [1–2] is turned into confidence in the face of the exact same enemy: he will not fear the myriads (v. 7 [6]). In the Samuel narrative, we note that the number he is faced with at this point is much greater than the number he faced at

---

16. ישן can mean to sleep in death (e.g., Ps 13:4). Nonetheless, Cole's argument that "the lying down, sleeping and arising of 3.6 is tantamount to death and resurrection, as the only parallel to this threefold combination of verbs in the Hebrew Bible, Job 14.12, reveals" (Cole, *Psalms 1–2*, 145) is unconvincing. While Cole rightly sees שכב as lying in death there, this is not because the negation of the following three verbs (עור, קום as well as ישן) implies resurrection (*I will die and not be resurrected*). Much more mundanely, they mean to arise, and failure to arise after lying down implies death (*I will lie down and never get up again*). ישן and שכב appear as natural sleeping-then-waking in 1 Kgs 19:5, Ps 4:9, and Job 3:13 without hint of death. Cole's statistics show that death is a minority for each lexeme (Cole, *Psalms 1–2*, 148). The parallel in Ps 4, with its many linkages to Ps 3 (Barbiero, *Das erste Psalmenbuch*, 69–71) but no mention of קיץ particularly mitigates against reading resurrection into this combination. By contrast with Job, David will lie down and *instead of dying* he will rise again. The Psalter is full of deliverance from death's very door, and Cole is importing texts such as 7:6 without proving that death has been accomplished (Cole, *Psalms 1–2*, 149).

17. Auwers, *La composition littéraire*, 138.

18. Auwers, *La composition littéraire*, 138.

19. Cole's further protest that a good night's sleep is hardly an answer to the prayer of v. 5 (Cole, *Psalms 1–2*, 148) misses the point.

the start of the Psalm: Shimei's playing for time allowed Absalom to enlarge his forces massively. No matter, the key for David is that Yahweh has made his choice.

2.D. The Aftermath: David in Victory

Accordingly, David prepares his army for battle, and sends them into the fray. Psalm 3 shows this through the summons to Yahweh to fight, as though David had the ark with him (v. 8 [7]), and 2 Sam 18:1–4 shows the action. Even as his troops set off, he asks for Absalom to be dealt with gently, for his own sake (v. 5) and is disconsolate when Absalom does die (v. 33 and into ch. 19).

Steven Mann shows that David's departure from the city, and the removal of all those who might be loyal to him, had been designed to avoid military confrontation and that the overarching aim was to spare Absalom's life.[20] Similarly, Richard Smith argues that David's plot never intended the death of Absalom. He thinks David sent Hushai as a mere spy, and that Hushai was forced into action by Ahithophel's advice, so that David's plan ran away from him (in accordance with Yahweh's decree, 17:14), leading to Absalom's death.[21] David's grief, far from insincere, is concealed and accidentally revealed.[22]

In dealing with his children, David had shown himself to be emotional, unreliable and open to manipulation. His anger on the rape of his daughter Tamar is not matched by any action at all from the king who is supposed to be the judge in Israel; two full years pass before Absalom takes matters into his own hands (13:21–23). Grief over the wrongly-reported death of all his sons (v. 33) is again not matched by action when he establishes that Absalom has murdered Amnon (v. 34). Instead of bringing fugitive Absalom to justice, David pines away for him once he gets over the emotion of losing Amnon (v. 39). Thus, after some more trickery, Absalom had been allowed to return to Jerusalem, evade accountability, and plot to overthrow David.

---

20. Mann, "Run, David, Run!," 121, 200; *contra* Johnson's view that David's grief was insincere, on the grounds Absalom's death was politically expedient for him, and that he did not punish Joab for killing him (Johnson, *David in Distress*, 25).

21. Smith, *The Fate of Justice*, 185–88.

22. Smith, *The Fate of Justice*, 198.

We would be forgiven for doubting that David's concern for Absalom's life is a matter of high principle. Nonetheless, what we cannot say is that David's actions are consistent with revenge. He clearly did not desire the death of his named enemy. More to the point, Joab rebukes him in 19:7 [6] not for loving "the one who hates you" but "those who hate you," plural.

Accordingly, even more telling than his treatment of Absalom, is his treatment of the enemy army. Following the victory, the Northern army scatters and flee to their homes. David enlists his own tribe, Judah, to restore him to the throne (19:16 [15]).

He meets none other than Shimei, who had cursed him as he left Jerusalem, now confessing his sin and asking for mercy (vv. 20–21 [19–20]). Abishai offers to provide him with justice instead of mercy. David, without denying that Shimei is guilty as charged by Abishai and even having confessed to deserving the death penalty,[23] is outraged at the thought of killing a fellow Israelite and insists that he live (vv. 22–24 [21–23]). As far as David is concerned, he and Shimei are brother members of God's nation, not on opposite sides of a war that is now to be forgotten.

David's lack of vengeance is hidden between the lines of the tragicomical complaint of his enemy army. Judah, and half of formerly-enemy Israel, install David as king. Straight away (v. 42 [41]) all the rest of Israel complain that they have been left out. So quick has David been to forgive them, that they do not even notice how incongruous it would be to invite the defeated enemy to partake of the victory celebration. Yet here they are, most indignant, because they have been left out. They think of themselves as snubbed relatives, not as freshly-defeated enemies who had been about to kill David.

Already from Ps 2, this should not surprise us. Rebel leaders, even kings, and the people they lead, are offered restoration following repentance, not punishment. As we will see below, David's treatment of Absalom, Shimei and the Northern tribes is in keeping with his prayer for blessing on God's people, rather than only on those who had been with David.

---

23. Bergen, *1, 2 Samuel*, 429.

3. David and Retribution in the Background of Psalm 3: Psalms 1–2 and 2 Samuel

In our previous chapter, we reviewed the well-known literary connections between Pss 1 and 2, and noted that the king in Ps 2 can be read as a specific example of the man of Ps 1: a righteous king facing international enemies who rebel against Yahweh and the king as judge. Retribution is a significant theme in both psalms. Because there are so many well-recognized links between Pss 1 and 2, it is tempting to ask whether those connections stretch into Ps 3 also.[24] It turns out that they do. Not only Ps 3: its backstory in Samuel also makes literary connections to Pss 1 and 2, and highlight the theme of judgment.

We will now see that the king and his enemies are made more specific still in Ps 3. David flees from Absalom and his rebel army. Of all the prayers in the Psalter, and even of all the similar laments of David in Books I–II, Ps 3 has been placed in pole position to introduce them. What makes Ps 3 so distinctive, that it deserves to join Psalms 1 and 2 in guiding the reader into the Psalms? It is precisely the way that it presents retribution within a context of guilt (rather than self-righteousness), of facing down unrighteous enemies who are sent by Yahweh because of our guilt, and demonstrating the evangelical outworking of that awareness.

As we will examine in the next chapter, this will be vital for users of later psalms following the brutality of the Babylonian conquest and exile, and all readers down the ages recovering from enemy action.

3.A. The Theme of Retribution Extends into Psalm 3

We have seen that the expectation of judgment in Ps 1 is developed in Ps 2; it is now developed further in Ps 3. The characters in Ps 3 are more specific examples of the king and the rebellion in Ps 2, which in turn are more specific examples of the righteous man and the wicked in Ps 1.[25] The Northern tribes, led by a usurping, rebel king (Absalom), rise against the anointed king.

As in Ps 1, David was righteous under suffering and opposition from the wicked, and Yahweh preserved him (1 Sam 19—2 Sam 5). As in

---

24. Cole, *Psalms 1–2*, 142.

25. The antagonists of Pss 1, 2 and 3 are identified as the same by, e.g., Miller, "Beginning of the Psalter," 88–89; VanGemeren, *Psalms*, 90; Brown, *Psalms*, 117.

Ps 2, he was rewarded with the crown and, when faced with a string of rebellions, had Yahweh's full support (2 Sam 6–10).

As the wicked try to do in Ps 1:1, Absalom *stands* and waylays people on their *way* to the gate. The gate is the place of judgment, and Absalom is offering his own judgment instead (2 Sam 15:2). He is a wicked ruler who usurps the throne by rebelling against Yahweh's anointed (Ps 2).

In Ps 1, any man (אִישׁ, *'ish*) who does not stand (עָמַד, *'amad*) in the way (דֶּרֶךְ, *derek*) of sinners, is able to face the judgment (מִשְׁפָּט, *mishpat*), because he is walking in the right way (דֶּרֶךְ, *derek*). Absalom stands (עָמַד, *'amad*) by the way (דֶּרֶךְ, *derek*) on which any man (אִישׁ, *'ish*) approaches the king for judgment (מִשְׁפָּט, *mishpat*), 2 Sam 15:2. Psalms 1 and 2 would declare such a man blessed, but Absalom waylays him and subverts the judge whom God has appointed. Instead of God's **judg**ment (מִשְׁפָּט, *mishpat*) which vindicates the **just** (צַדִּיקִים, *tsadiqim*) in Ps 1:5, Absalom in 2 Sam 15:4 wants to be the **judge** (שֹׁפֵט, *shophet*) and hand out **just**ice (*hip'il* of צדק, *hitsdiq*) to anyone who has a cause for **judg**ment (מִשְׁפָּט, *mishpat*). In Ps 2, the appointed judge is God's own son, and he is to be kissed (נָשַׁק, *nashaq*) in homage. In 2 Sam 15:5, the usurping son redirects the homage due, and does the kissing (נָשַׁק, *nashaq*) as part of subverting God's son as judge and king.

Related to the enemies and retribution against them, the metaphor of rising/standing is a theme through Psalms 1–3.[26] In Ps 1, we find this with the verbs "stand" (עָמַד, *'amad*) and "rise up" (קוֹם, *qum*). Because the wicked (חַטָּאִים, *hatta'im*) stand (עָמַד, *'amad*) in their own way in v. 1, the same wicked (חַטָּאִים, *hatta'im*) will not be able to stand up (קוֹם, *qum*) after the judgment (v. 5).

Psalm 2 takes up the idea of standing and rising in rebellion. The kings take their stand belligerently in v. 2.[27] Instead of standing ready to

26. This is missed if only individual key-word linkage is observed; there is no individual word for this theme that links all three psalms.

27. *Hitpa'el* of יצב. It is likely to be a verb of standing physically, not just metaphorically. Paul Gilchrist considers it synonymous with עמד (Gilchrist, "יצב," 394). Its various uses suggest a sense of alert and resolute readiness, which include (1) being before kings; (2) awaiting Yahweh before the tent of meeting or at the foot of Sinai; (3) being ready for battle or successfully withstanding enemy assault (Gilchrist, "יצב," 394; Martens, "יצב," 2:500). That makes it particularly suitable here, since senses 2 and 1 would be appropriate before Yahweh and his anointed king, respectively, whereas the sense ironically is 3, of waging war against them. Being before kings, awaiting Yahweh before the tent of meeting or at the foot of Sinai, being ready for battle, and successfully withstanding enemy assault, all probably require standing. The suggested emendation to יִתְיָעֲצוּ (*HALOT* 427) is to be rejected. MT is kept by Kraus 1:143, who takes the military sense as operative here, and Kirkpatrick 1:8.

serve Yahweh and dispense justice, these kings have taken their stand
against him (2:2),[28] and against his anointed, which is how David describes the situation in 3:2, "they have risen against me" (קָמִים עָלָי, *qamim
'alay*). By contrast with the enemies who rise, David lies down (v. 6 [5]).
In v. 8 [7], he calls on Yahweh to rise up (קוּם, *qum*). This verb describes
what the wicked cannot do at the judgment (Ps 1), what they try to do
in rebellion (Ps 3), and the intrusion of judgment against them (Ps 3).[29]
Judgment rescues David and *raises* his head (v. 4 [3]).

We have seen that judgment themes connect Ps 3 with Pss 1 and 2.
The link with Absalom in the superscription strengthens that connection.

3.B. Literary Connections Within Psalms 1–3

There are strong connections between Ps 3 and the introductory Pss 1
and 2.

First, despite their very different genres, their plot is similar.[30] Each
Psalm begins with a threat, declares the security of the psalmist, and concludes with divine judgment ending the threat.[31]

Second, as we have seen above, connections between adjacent
Psalms can be highlighted when reuse of words becomes significant
enough. The following link Ps 3 with Pss 1–2.[32] Some of the links are quite
common words, which would by themselves prove little. However, these
are significant within the plot of each Psalm. The key declaration about
the king in 2:7, and his bane in 3:1 [s] is בֵּן (*ben*, "son"). The rebels are
invited, in 2:11, to fear (ירא, *yara'*), as a result of which David does not
fear them in 3:7. Yahweh installs the king, in 2:6, on "my holy mountain"

---

28. The issue of justice and of their duty as judges may be further ironically brought
out by the use of עָמַד and *hitpa' el* of יצב in these psalms, which are used in courtroom
contexts in the OT (Bovati, *Ristabilire la Giustizia*, 210–19). On the pervasive legal
language in an ANE context of Ps 2 in particular, see Lam, "Psalm 2," 34–46.

29. Vesco sees קוּם as an inclusio around the Psalm, contrasting the rising of the enemy with God's (Vesco 101). Weber suggests juridical overtones of קוּם in Ps 3 (Botha
and Weber, "'Killing Them,'" 286n28).

30. On analyzing the way psalms are structured as poems, rather than through the
lens of *Gattung* see Schökel, "Poética hebrea," 216.

31. Ironically, the focus on exegeting psalms based on the similarity of their forms
led Gunkel to hide this telling repetition: Gunkel and Begrich, *Einleitung in die Psalm-
en*, 385, 140, 172–73 (on Pss 1, 2 and 3 respectively; notice the distance between them
and their order).

32. The lexical links are listed by Barbiero, *Das erste Psalmenbuch*, 66.

(הַר־קָדְשִׁי, *har qodshi*), and from there he answers the prayers of the king in 3:5 [4]. The enemy trouble in 2:2 and 3:2 [1], as well as the turning point of David's confidence in the face of trouble in 3:7 [6], are all described as *'al* (עַל, "on/against"). The enemy in 3:3 [2] is denying Yahweh's promise in 2:7, and these contradictory speeches are drawn to our attention by "speak" (אמר, *'amar*). On the other hand, the same promise to David in 2:7 is contrasted with David's confidence in that promise in 3:4 [3], by the very pointed use of "you" (אתה, *'atah*) which is redundant in Hebrew. The equally redundant and pointed "I" marks the turning point that gives confidence to the king in both Psalms: Yahweh's begetting of him in 2:6, and David not only lying down, but also waking up again by Yahweh's intervention in 3:6 [5]. The problem in Ps 1:1, whom Yahweh judges in vv. 5, 6, are "the wicked" (רשעים, *resha'im*); David's grounds for confidence in 3:8 is that same judgment on them. As a result, the wicked cannot arise (קום, *qum*) when Yahweh intervenes in judgment in 1:5; they are arising against David in 3:2 [1], which is how Yahweh will judge them in 3:8 [7].

Third, the envelopes which connect Pss 1 and 2 extend to Ps 3. Psalms 1 and 2 were book-ended by "O, the blessings" (אַשְׁרֵי, *'ashrey*), and the same idea ends Ps 3 with "blessing" (בְּרָכָה, *berakah*).[33] The other half of 3:9 ("It is to Yahweh that rescue belongs!") reinforces that frame. The choice that ends Ps 1 is Yahweh knowing the way of the righteous, while the way of the wicked perishes. Psalm 2 ends by developing both halves of this choice as an invitation: perish or be blessed by the son. Psalm 3 ends by developing the two positive sides of the choices from Pss 1 and 2. Yahweh who knows the way (Ps 1) is Yahweh to whom rescue belongs (3:9a); the son (Ps 2) is the one whose people are blessed (3:9b). Connected with that "O, the blessings" frame, Pss 1, 2, and 3 are unusual in each opening with an exclamation.[34]

Fourth, each of the first three psalms introduces new features that are central to the Psalter.[35] They introduce characters and themes that are developed throughout the Psalter. Perhaps most surprising of all, a book full of prayers opens with two psalms which are not, highlighting Psalm 3 as the first prayer.[36] The speech in Ps 1 is inter-personal (introducing the

33. Vesco 100.
34. Cole, *Psalms 1–2*, 145; Vesco 100.
35. This is the foundational observation of Weber, *Theologie*.
36. Erbele-Küster, *Lesen*, 66.

theme of instruction) and in Ps 2 the speech is from God (introducing prophecy); only in Ps 3 is the most common direction of speech introduced: God addressed in prayer.[37]

3.C. David's Flight from Absalom within Psalms 1–3

If Ps 1 promises justice and Ps 2 establishes the king as the agent of justice, then Ps 3 sees the king unable to dispense justice. This struggle for justice is a significant theme of the Absalom narrative.[38] Judgment connects the man of Ps 1 with the king of Ps 2 and the king of Ps 3. Similarly, Absalom usurped David's throne as *king* by pretending to be a better *judge*. Anyone coming "to the king for judgment" would be greeted with the assurance that there will be no justice, but "if only I were made judge over the land" (2 Sam 15:2, 4). David as the judge and king who puts down the rebels who *rise/stand* against him is a theme connecting Pss 1–3, also connecting these to the Absalom narrative, following the superscription of Ps 3.[39] The Cushite declares rescue from Yahweh from all who *rose* or will *rise* against David (2 Sam 18:31–32; Ps 3:9).[40] Conversely, the use of קוּם (*qum* "rising") and עַל (*'al* "against/over") in Pss 1 and 3 are links with Nathan's oracle in 2 Sam 12:11.[41] The judgment motif of Psalms 1–3 is connected to the judgment motif of the Absalom narrative as David's punishment.

Psalm 1:1 talks of "walking in the counsel [עֵצָה *etsah*]," which makes a striking link with the Absalom narrative. "Counsel" (עֵצָה, *'etsah*) appears in 2 Sam 15:31, 34, 16:20, 23 (*bis*), 17:7, 14 (*3x*), 23. It is a *Leitwort* in the Absalom narrative, but does not occur anywhere else in Samuel. It occurs more often in the Absalom narrative alone than in any, entire book of the Bible except Isaiah. We meet this *Leitwort* in the very first verse of the Psalter, in the first phrase of the tricolon. Ahithophel takes the place of the "wicked" of Ps 1:1 whose counsel was to rise against Yahweh's anointed (Ps 2:2) as though God would not rescue David (3:3), leading to his own perishing as well as Absalom's who walked in his

37. Miller, "Beginning of the Psalter," 88; *contra* Auwers, *La composition littéraire,* 136, who sees prayer in Ps 2.

38. Smith, *The Fate of Justice,* 78.

39. As Craigie puts it: "the *substance* of the Psalm" shares significant parallels with "the historical event" (Craigie, *Psalms 1–50,* 72).

40. The connection between v. 2 and 2 Sam 15:13–18 via הַקָּמִים עָלֶיךָ is often seen (Auwers, *La composition littéraire,* 138).

41. Johnson, *David in Distress,* 24.

counsel (1:6; 2:12), because Yahweh preserved David (Ps 1:3, 6; 2:6–9; 2 Sam 17:14). David's prayer in Ps 3:5 corresponds to 2 Sam 15:31. It is answered, since the plot of 2 Sam 15–17 is the overthrow of a counsel that rivals Yahweh's word (2 Sam 16:23)[42] and contradicts his decree (2 Sam 7:14; Ps 2:7; 3:3). This connection with the opening of the introduction to the Psalter (1:1) suggests that the superscription of Ps 3 invites us to read Ps 3 in connection with that introduction.[43]

We turn now to examine in more detail what and how David prays for his enemies in Psalm 3.

4. Retribution in Psalm 3

If Ps 3 can naturally be read on the lips of the king of Ps 2, so can almost the whole of Book I.[44] Even with the enemies in mind, the enemies of several Psalms could loosely fit with Ps 2. Why, then, has Ps 3 been chosen specially to be the first David Psalm we encounter? What does it teach us about retribution and enemies?

With the backstory fresh in our minds, and knowing that retribution is significant in the opening three psalms, we can look more closely at what David prays here.

4.A. The Imprecation in Psalm 3 Did Not Require Innocence

As we have seen, Bonhoeffer, James Adams, and others argue that only the impeccable Christ has a right to pray imprecations. David had no right to pray like this: these were always the prayers of a perfect man, unlike David or anyone other than Christ (see ch 2, §6.B, pp. 18–19). This rests on an assumption about what is being claimed by protestations of innocence in some such psalms.

We would expect, from what we have seen in Ps 2, that the distinction between the righteous and the wicked is not based on perfect

42. The narrator expressly restates that both David and Absalom esteemed his counsel equally highly (Mann, "Run, David, Run!," 203).

43. Contrary to Childs' claim that there are no linguistic connections between Ps 3 and the Absalom narrative (Childs, "Psalm Titles," 143), see Auwers, *La composition littéraire*, 138; Erbele-Küster, *Lesen*, 67; Vesco 99–100; Botha and Weber, "'Killing Them,'" 286–87).

44. Miller, "Beginning of the Psalter," 88–89.

sinlessness. The rebels of Ps 2 are invited to repent; they will find refuge and blessing despite their track record.

In Ps 3 David prays, even though he is thoroughly aware of his own guilt, as shown above in 2 Samuel. Perfection is not the standard for praying for divine intervention against enemies. The opening psalm of David would not let that notion stand.

Psalm 3 introduces David by pointing out that he is reaping the punishment for his sin with Bathsheba and Uriah. David perpetrated a complete aberration of integrity and justice: a premeditated perversion of his duty as judge. David's murder of Uriah displays callous disregard for the lives of Israelite soldiers in Uriah's vicinity (2 Sam 11:17–25). Hebrew narrative normally eschews explicit moral judgment, leaving the reader to make inferences.[45] This sin is a notable exception: 2 Sam 11:27; 1 Kgs 15:5. David, in Ps 3, is far from innocent, much less impeccable. Yahweh's decision to save him from Absalom does not change that fact. Yet David can pray for divine protection, in the imprecation that we will analyze below.

Imprecations are not the prayers of one who is innocent without qualification.

4.B. A Sinner Awaits a Merciful Verdict: vv. 5–6 [4–5]

As we have seen, protestations of innocence in the Psalms strike many as self-righteous, in a way that is antithetical to the Christian gospel. They presume that vindication against enemies is a right earned legalistically (see ch. 2, §7, pp. 23–24).

As we have seen in the Absalom narrative, David's approach in Ps 3 is the opposite. He knows that he is entirely reliant on God's mercy and will not presume on God's favor. Even when God has taken his side, this does not mean that David is praying from a position of being in the right. He is one who has received mercy, and has been spared despite his sins that led to Absalom's revolt.

Neither Ps 3 nor the Absalom narrative presents David's temporary suffering as atoning for his sin, nor his repentance as automatically putting him in God's favor against Absalom.[46] David does not know why

---

45. Alter, *The Art of Biblical Narrative*, 44, 97, 158–59, 184.

46. *Contra* Althann, "Atonement and Reconciliation," 76–77, who assumes that David's repentance causes him not to be alienated from God (while further atonement was also necessary).

God has chosen to defend him against Absalom; he receives that rescue as a mystery, in the same way that God spared his life, putting away his sin with Bathsheba and Uriah, without explanation (2 Sam 12:13).

David, in Ps 3:6 [5] simply attributes his salvation to Yahweh sustaining him. This in answer to his prayer (v. 5 [4]), which we have seen to be one that David was far from confident would be answered. It is pointedly presented as answered "from his holy mountain," highlighting David's distance from Yahweh's ark, which he knew he did not deserve to take into battle. David's imprecation in the rest of the Psalm is offered because he received mercy, not because he believed that he had earned anything. As Firth observes regarding this incident in Samuel: "forgiveness is always unfair; that is what makes it grace."[47]

4.C. What Is David Asking For?: v. 8 [7]

8 [7] Rise up, Yahweh!
    Rescue me, my God!
        Because you have struck all my enemies on the cheek,
            you have broken the teeth of the wicked.

The second line of this verse is understood in different ways, and the first question is whether there is a request here or not.

Grammatically, the verbs are indicative, not an expression of desire. Some would argue that there is a special "precative" use of such verbs, so that indicatives function as requests.[48] On balance, it seems unlikely.[49] These are statements, not requests.[50] Nonetheless, these statements of Yahweh's past actions are the ground for asking him to *arise* in the first half of the verse, implying a desire for similar action. Wenham observes that the Psalms promise the destruction of the wicked almost as

---

47. Firth, *1 & 2 Samuel*, 431.

48. E.g., Buttenwieser, *Psalms*, 397.

49. VanGemeren cites Joüon 119l, to say that these *qatals* must be taken as imperatives (VanGemeren, *Psalms*, 105). However, Joüon is there discussing the *w-qataltí* form when it continues a volitive sequence, whereas here we have straight-forward *qatals*, not continuation forms. In fact, Joüon explicitly translates this text as preterite, as does Gesenius (Joüon §126g; GKC §117ll).

50. It is taken as indicative by ASV, Darby, ESV, EÜ, GNB, HCSB, KJV, LEB, NASB, NCV, NET, NETS, NKJV, NRSV, RSV, YLT; volitive: MSG, NIV, NLT.

frequently as they ask for it, and therefore petitions and promises often appear together, as in this verse.[51]

The violence that they describe belongs with the prayer for Yahweh to arise for battle, and it belongs in any list of imprecations. As Kraus puts it from the allusion to Num 10:35 in the first half of the verse: "As a ruler arises from his throne and attacks, so may Yahweh stand up and come to the rescue."[52]

What is David asking for?

One option is that a literal striking of the face and breaking of teeth is in view, as an act of poetic justice. This would silence those who were speaking against David.[53] While this justice might be poetic, it would be both too lenient for treason and attempted murder of the king, and also far more severe than the *lack* of punishment that David metes out in Samuel. A better view accounts for the close connection between slanderous words and murder in the Psalms. Such murderous enemies are portrayed with animal metaphors.[54] Their lying words are therefore presented as the weapons of such animals, such as teeth.

There is a fascination with animals in ANE iconography.[55] Whenever Psalms use animal metaphors for enemies, the enemy seeks the *life* of the psalmist.[56] Lions are especially common depictions for enemies in similar individual laments: Ps 7:3 [2]; 10:9–10; 17:12; 22:14–22 [13–21]; 35:17; 58:7 [6].[57] We can see how fitting it is for Ps 57:5 [4] to present the weapons of David's enemies as the teeth of lions. Whereas the lion was depicted as invincible in ANE.[58] David, by contrast, is the king who had defeated lions as a shepherd.[59] When the next psalm asks for their teeth to be broken (58:7 [6]) the lion metaphor represents the wicked of v. 4 [3]. Verse 7 [6] reads:

51. Wenham, *Psalms as Torah*, 144.

52. "Wie ein Herrscher sich von seinem Thronsitz erhebt und eingreift, so möge Jahwe aufstehen und zur Hilfe kommen" (Kraus 1:163).

53. Hossfeld-Zenger I:58; Ravasi 39; Hackett and Huehnergard, "On Breaking Teeth," 262; Riede, *Im Netz des Jägers*, 121.

54. Seybold 36; Brown, *Seeing*, 136–44; Riede, *Im Netz des Jägers*, 150–338; Basson, "'Rescue Me,'" 9–17.

55. Schroer and Keel, *Mesolithikum*, 58–59, 109–10, 179, 182–83, 187–88, 190–93.

56. Keel, *Die Welt*, 76–78.

57. Keel, *Die Welt der altorientalischen Bildsymbolik*, 75–78.

58. Keel and Uehlinger, *Göttinnen, Götter und Gottessymbole*, 26.

59. Keel, "Tiere als Gefährten und Feinde," 25.

O God, tear down [הֲרָס, *haros*] their teeth in their mouths,
tear down [נְתֹץ, *netots*] the young lions' fangs, O Yahweh.

Translations such as "*break* their teeth" and "*tear out* their fangs" obscure how unusual these metaphors are. הרס (*haras*) nowhere else has a sense that fits with dentistry, but generally means to tear something *down* (not *out*), overpower, or ruin. The context is usually military and/or architectural.[60] The architectural destruction is even more obvious with נתץ (*natats*).[61] In both cases, *HALOT* creates a separate meaning to accommodate purely this verse, and translations change the metaphor to something more natural (break, tear out). However, when the teeth of animals, especially lions, represent the deadly weapons of human enemies, military metaphors make good sense: disarmament is in view which need not involve hurting people's body parts.[62]

Similarly, in Ps 3 we find:

you have broken [שִׁבַּרְתָּ, *shibbarta*] the teeth of the wicked.

שבר [*shabar*] is commonly used of lions devouring people and *crushing their bones* in the process.[63] David is then asking for much less than a proportional response: he asks for disarmament, not retribution.

[T]hese expressions . . . are, further, tied to metaphors involving wild animals, presumably because the teeth of wild animals are among their weapons for destroying or capturing prey, and because injuring those teeth is an effective *defense*.[64]

Not the wicked themselves, but only the weapons (teeth) with which they seek to kill him are to be destroyed (שבר *shabar*).[65] This would fit perfectly with David's desire for Absalom to be unharmed, and his failure to pursue the enemy once the battle is won.

We are seeing here an example of a wider phenomenon in the Psalms: the emphasis on the speech of the enemy. In Ps 58 the ones whose

---

60. *HALOT* 256–57.

61. *HALOT* 736.

62. So Theodoret of Cyrus, *Psalms 1–72*, 62; Rashi, *Psalms*, 183; *Westminster Annotations*, ad loc.; Kirkpatrick 1:16; Wilson, *Psalms*, 134; Harman, *Psalms 1–72*, 112.

63. Riede, *Im Netz des Jägers*, 191–92.

64. Hackett and Huehnergard, "On Breaking Teeth," 273–74; italics added.

65. Riede notes that שבר appears as a technical term for destroying arsenals of armaments in 46:10; 48:8; 76:4, even though he dismisses the interpretation I offer here of this verse (Riede, *Im Netz des Jägers*, 121).

weapons are to be destroyed by having their teeth broken are both dealing out violence (v. 3 [2]) and speaking lies (v. 4 [3]). The connection in
many cases is *slander*, especially if it leads to judicial murder or otherwise
threatens the life of the victim: Absalom's attack on David in Ps 3 is a
case in point, and it is no surprise to find David complaining about the
enemy's speech alongside their actions (vv. 2–3 [1–2]).[66]

If the crushing of the teeth points to disarmament, the striking of
the cheek, in the first half of the line, is even easier to understand. Striking on the cheek has long been recognized as an act of ritual and legal
humiliation, which would not involve the level of force required literally
to break teeth.[67] Nahum Sarna considers 1 Kgs 22:24; 2 Chr 18:23; Mic
4:14; Job 16:10 and Lam 3:30, where the cheek is struck, and concludes
that this is "an intolerable insult, a deep humiliation, not a mere slight
to be forgotten," and the psalmist is asking for "a humiliating, crushing
defeat on the enemy."[68]

The two metaphors go together nicely: Absalom and his army is to
be shamed with an overwhelming defeat, which leaves them disarmed
and posing no further threat to David. That is what happened in 2 Samuel. The backstory also explains why the crushing of teeth and striking of
the cheek of all his enemies is in the past. David had, before the time of
Absalom, seen off Saul and all his other foreign enemies. David did not
desire the destruction of Saul, even though Saul had tried to murder him
repeatedly, and even though David was chosen by Yahweh. He did not
lift a finger against him (1 Sam 24:6), and when Saul died, David taught
all Israel to mourn him (2 Sam 1). So with Absalom: David did not want
him to die and mourned him. David does not here want his enemies to
be punished, but to be disarmed and defeated. Their taunts that he would
not be rescued by God are to be replaced by their public humiliation.

The first prayer for divine action against the enemy in the psalter is
therefore not based on *lex talionis*, nor is it retributive at all. It is a desire
for the minimal necessary force to disarm the enemy.

---

66. See the following section on the importance of innocence.

67. Rashi, *Psalms*, 183–84; Dickson, *Commentary*, 1:13; Delitzsch 82; Kirkpatrick
1:16; Craigie, *Psalms 1–50*, 75; Hossfeld-Zenger I:58; Seybold 36; Wilson, *Psalms*, 134;
Kraus 1:163.

68. Sarna, "Legal Terminology," 176–77; so also Kraus 1:163. To these, Hackett and
Huehnergard add a number of ANE examples where being struck in the face is an act
of legal humiliation (Hackett and Huehnergard, "On Breaking Teeth," 273n73).

When we analyze what David asks for, we should bear in mind some distinctions. Zenger distinguished between what we culturally view as "vengeance," an uncontrolled spiteful vendetta, and the righteous, Torah-regulated, *justice* which the Psalter promises.[69] Another common candidate when considering "imprecations" is "cursing," which is rightly rejected as not found in such psalms.[70] Despite the pervasive theme of retributive judgment, we do not find any of the lexemes for cursing[71] in Psalms 1–3, which are instead framed by words of blessing. We do not even find vengeance in Ps 3: Absalom's army, upon being defeated, are left to go free and there is no punishment against them.

4.D. Blessing the Enemies: vv. 8–9 [7–8]

It is easy to assume that the Psalter and OT know nothing of enemy love. We saw this view among Psalms scholars through the ages (ch. 2, §5.B, pp. 11–14). They assume that David could not have *imagined*: (a) the repentance of the enemy; (b) the end of evil deeds apart from the destruction of the evildoer; (c) love for enemies. We saw that this has a mixed pedigree, since other authors *assume* that David did not lack any "New Testament virtue" (ch. 2, §6.A, pp. 15–17). The question must be decided by exegesis of the Psalter.

Already in the introduction to the Psalter, we have seen enemy repentance in the staggering offer of Ps 2. The time which Yahweh allows to pass before intervening in judgment, while uncomfortable for the righteous (e.g., 6:3; 13:1–2; 35:17), is an act of mercy towards the wicked; it is driven by a desire for their repentance. This theme develops in Ps 3, as we will see in the contrasting roles of the "people" in vv. 7 and 9 [6 and 8].

English idiom struggles with v. 7 [6], "I do not fear the myriads[72] of a nation" (לֹא־אִירָא מֵרִבְבוֹת עָם, *lo' 'ira' meribbot 'am*).[73] Rendering עָם (*'am*) as

---

69. Zenger, *God of Vengeance?*, 70.

70. Zenger, *God of Vengeance?*, viii; Waltke et al., *Psalms as Christian Worship*, 95.

71. תאלה, שבועה, קרא, קלל, קבב, מבטה, מארה, זעם, ארר, אלה, and הוי.

72. Targum has ממצותא (though Diez Merino reports a variant מרבבון). BHS only reports the former and thinks this implies מֵרִיבוֹת, while Kraus thinks it implies the construct מֵרִיבֵי, either way from ריב "strife." Stec argues that this is a double translation of the form preserved in MT (Stec, *The Targum of Psalms*, 31n9), itself a common technique (Stec, *The Targum of Psalms*, 11). We therefore keep MT, as do Goldingay 1:108; Schökel I:165.

73. Similarly, Goldingay 1:108. It is not clear why Vesco makes עָם plural (Vesco

"people" in this context gives the unfortunate impression that David is describing "myriads of *human beings*."[74] This is, however, a concrete people, from which tens of thousands have arisen: the nation that has rebelled against him in following Absalom. David is beset by myriads from the nation of Israel, as 2 Sam 17:2 reports, when Ahithophel asked to choose twelve thousand from among the available multitude, and that was before all Israel were gathered to Absalom as the sand of the sea (v. 11). By contrast, David could only set commanders over hundreds and thousands (2 Sam 18:1). This makes the use of "myriads" particularly ironic because it is famously used in the song about Saul and David "but David [has killed] his myriads" (1 Sam 18:7, 8; 21:12; 29:5) and nowhere else in 1–2 Samuel.

However, in Ps 3:9 [8] David makes a surprising turn. His concern with the whole nation causes such confusion among some scholars that they dismiss this whole line. Alter is disappointing in his judgment that "the sudden appearance of a national perspective at the conclusion of an exclusively first-person poem looks odd."[75] However, the national character of Ps 3 does not appear suddenly in the final line. The superscription associates it with David, the king of the nation, and places it during the national crisis of civil war. Verse 9 [8] does not introduce the nation, but repeats the use of עַם (*'am*, "people") from v. 7 [6].[76] David as king is the interface between the individual and the national; we need not reach for diachronic solutions to what is not incongruous. David prays as an individual but seeks some application to the whole nation, as here and at the end of Pss 25, 51, and as imitated in Ps 130 (which we discuss below).

He ascribes rescue to Yahweh, and in the context one would assume that this is Yahweh's act of rescuing David (and his band) *from* the rebellious nation (עַם, *'am*). Not so, since he continues: "May there be a blessing upon *your* nation" (עַל־עַמְּךָ בִרְכָתֶךָ, *'al-'ammeka birkateka*). David is mindful that his enemies, who are also Yahweh's enemies, are nonetheless

---

1:101); Seybold likewise, which leads him to see it as an implausible exaggeration (which myriads of nations would be). He offers textual emendations (Seybold 34, 36) that have no MS support, except arguably the sense of strife in the Targum. We have seen that Targum is a double translation that does not reflect a different *Vorlage*; taking "nation" as a singular removes the exaggeration.

74. See, e.g., the use of "people" in ESV, NET, LEB, YLT.

75. Alter, *The Book of Psalms*, 9n9; similarly Kraus, who sees the blessing as a later addition enlarging the original individual rescue (Kraus 1:163).

76. Vesco is half right to see that the original psalm enlarges an individual perspective to a national one in the final verse (Vesco 100); the national perspective is there throughout.

Yahweh's people and he prays a blessing on them. It may be tempting to imagine that David is pointedly declaring that Absalom's forces in v. 7 [6] are merely "a people" while in v. 9 [8] his own associates are the *true* people of Yahweh,[77] but that would sit awkwardly with David's un-presumptuous demeanor in the Absalom narrative. As far as David is concerned, the city and the ark belong to Yahweh's people (2 Sam 15:24–29), while Yahweh's pleasure in David is less certain (v. 25–26). The question is not how many people are in David's and Absalom's respective kingdoms, but who will be king over the *whole* people. His response to Shimei's cursing indicates the same thing: Yahweh may have rejected David (16:10). This all makes sense in the light of David's consciousness that the sword besetting his family is the result of his own sin. Most starkly, David did not want the death of the named enemy: Absalom, his son (Ps 3:1, 2 Sam 18:5, 33).

I suggest that the "nation" of Ps 3:9 [8] includes the "nation" of v. 7 [6].[78] David's prayer for blessing includes his enemies.[79] In Joab's words to David: "you love those who hate you" (לְאַהֲבָה אֶת־שֹׂנְאֶיךָ, *l'ehabah 'et-son'eka* 2 Sam 19:7 [6]). In the light of the preceding two psalms, we can suggest that David prays in Ps 3:9 [8] for his enemies to be blessed by repenting, taking refuge, and being restored. This has been expressed clearly through the ages:

> [T]he welfare of his people is more than his own personal safety. Like Him of whom he was the type, he intercedes on behalf of the rebels, for 'thy people' cannot be limited to the loyal few. (Kirkpatrick)

> [David in 3:9 seeks salvation and blessing] not on himself alone, but on the church of which he was the visible and temporary head. (Alexander)

> . . . who are fighting with me. Yet I am distressed also for those who are fighting; after all they bear the name of your people. So grant the blessing of peace, Lord, to both sides. He intimated

---

77. Eaton, *Psalms*, 69.

78. Expositors seldom identify these two uses of עַם. If the context of Absalom is ignored, the link is missed. Kimhi is the rare exception: he identifies the people with the whole nation (Kimhi, *Psalms*, 25).

79. Vesco directly connects v. 9 with blessing his enemies, specifically Shimei (Vesco 99–100).

as much, in fact, with the words, *May your blessing be on your people*. (Theodoret)[80]

Delitzsch thinks that he is praying for the northern people as led astray, and the imprecations are only aimed at the leaders. As king he cannot ask for salvation without the salvation of all his people.[81] I think even that is an insufficiently generous view. After all, Absalom is the ringleader and David mourned him.

The placement of the blessing at the very end of the Psalm extends the similar endings of Pss 1 and 2, as we saw above, and it would be natural if it served the same function: offering blessing through repentance to the unrighteous.

In v. 8 [7], once he knows that Yahweh has sided with him against Absalom, David asks Yahweh to "arise." This reverses David's earlier decision not to assume that the ark (and Yahweh) is on his side. Israel would speak this same imprecation against Yahweh's enemies when the ark set out (Num 10:35).[82] David asks Yahweh to arise as kings arise to go to war. Now that David is confident that the power behind the ark is with him, is he asking for revenge? We should first consider that the Psalm probably alludes to Num 10:35 *and* 36.[83]

> When the ark would set out, Moses would say: "*Rise up, Yahweh* [קוּמָה יְהוָה, *qumah Adonai*], and let *your enemies* [אֹיְבֶיךָ, *oyveka*] be scattered, and let those who hate you flee from your presence." But when it would come to rest, he would say: "Return, Yahweh, *to the myriads of thousands of Israel* [רִבְבוֹת אַלְפֵי יִשְׂרָאֵל, *rivvot alfey yisrael*]."

In Ps 3:8 [7], the call for Yahweh to rise is followed by David's ("my") enemies (אֹיְבַי, *'oybay*), and the same call for Yahweh to rise in Num 10:35 is followed by Yahweh's enemies (אֹיְבֶיךָ, *'oybeka*). In Ps 3, these enemies are the "myriads of a people" (רִבְבוֹת עָם, *ribbot 'am*) of 3:7 [6]. Israel is described similarly in Num 10:36, as the "myriads of thousands of Israel." Thus in Num 10 the call for Yahweh to arise concerns *his* (Yahweh's) enemies and the people of Israel. In Ps 3, it is David's enemies, but they

---

80. Kirkpatrick 1:16; Alexander, *Psalms*, 22; Theodoret of Cyrus, *Psalms 1–72*, 62; so also Hengstenberg, *Psalmen*, 1:70; and among contemporary authors: Harman, *Psalms 1–72*, 112; Waltke et al., *Psalms as Christian Worship*, 207.

81. Delitzsch 82.

82. Kraus 1:162–63.

83. Kirkpatrick 1:16; Craigie, *Psalms 1–50*, 74; Schökel I:168.

are *Yahweh's* ("your") people (עַמְּךָ 'ammeka) in v. 9 [8]. Just as Yahweh in Num 10 is to arise against his enemies and then return to his people, so in Ps 3 he is to arise against enemies, but then return to *his* people, by blessing all Israel.

Some think that David acts spitefully towards Israel, when he thwarts their desire to be involved in his return to the throne (2 Sam 19:10–16).[84] However, the complaint of the Northern Tribes is a comical demonstration of David's leniency. They have attempted to kill David; he has defeated them in war. No sooner do they cease their hostilities, than he ceases from his. Put alongside Ps 2 and others (such as Ps 18), the fact that they are around to complain about seating arrangements is a sign that David has set retribution aside.

> Amasa's appointment . . . held out an olive branch to the rebels. It showed not retribution but David's concern with reconciliation. Reconciliation also holds together the three subsequent encounters. . . . David reached out to a known enemy [Shimei]. . . . David still sought reconciliation [with Mephibosheth]. . . . David wanted to retain reconciliation [with Barzillai].[85]

Notably, David refuses—for a second time—to allow Shimei to be killed. Even after Yahweh has chosen to take David's side (2 Sam 19:17–24 [16–23]), in a passage where Shimei presents the kind of repentant obeisance that Ps 2 commends to the king's enemies: "I have sinned, . . . your servant went astray" (vv. 20–21 [19–20]). Earlier, David had been unsure whether he would receive mercy; now he himself shows mercy to his enemies.

The same redefinition of "people" and "enemies" that we see in Ps 3 is brought out in 2 Samuel by David's handling of Abishai. When Shimei confesses his sins and asks for forgiveness, "Abishai, son of Zeruiah" calls for David to have Shimei executed. Astonishingly, David does not merely commute Shimei's sentence, but answers Abishai in terms of who his enemies are, and who his people are. Not one man is to die *in Israel* today, because David is king over Israel (2 Sam 19:23 [22]). Israel, the former enemy, are David's people. However, not only Abishai, but his whole house ("sons of Zeruiah") are David's adversaries, by virtue of calling for

---

84. Smith, *The Fate of Justice*, 208–12.

85. Firth, *1 & 2 Samuel*, 490–91. He views all this as "a consummate politician" securing peace with the North. Even if so, David is setting aside retribution in favor of peace.

the death of a single Israelite (v. 23 [22]). David is for all Israel, and if anyone suggests hurting anyone in all the people, they are against David.[86]

Many have claimed that David's character and actions in this psalm are incongruous with the David of the Absalom narrative.[87] In particular, Ps 3 has an imprecation in v. 8 [7] and calls the people his foes, while David never calls them foes in Samuel, and even tries to save Absalom. As we have seen, this misunderstands how the Psalter comments on assumed knowledge of history. Psalm 3 assumes that we know the events of Samuel: we should not look for trivial restatement.[88] The two portrayals of David mesh well.[89] The two objections concerning Absalom and the foes are resolved if I am correct in seeing the repetition of "people" (עַם, ‘am) in vv. 7, 9 [6, 8] as an awareness that the foes are also God's people and a desire for God to bless them.[90]

In fact, the mercy which this psalmist shows is so obvious in the text, that Moses Buttenwieser sees it as certain proof that the psalm cannot have been penned by David. He rests this on the assumption that divine forgiveness, even in the face of evil, only originated with the post-exilic prophets and flies in the face of the ethos of earlier books, such as 2 Samuel.[91] Buttenwieser sees clearly that Ps 3 presents a David who intends to bless the whole people. There is, in fact, no contradiction between this psalm and Samuel. The narrative in Samuel shows us David imitating Yahweh, as the one who sets aside retribution in favor of grace.[92]

---

86. It could be that David is calling Abishai an accuser (שָׂטָן) of Shimei, rather than an adversary of David (so Anderson, 2 *Samuel*, 237). The point stands: David is for Israel and will not hear accusations against them today.

87. Gunkel, *Psalmen*, 13; Kraus 1:160; Buttenwieser, *Psalms*, 399.

88. For instance, to object that Ps 3 has no mention of flight (Goldingay 1:109) is to assume that the Psalm has to restate everything; but the Psalm also does not tell you who Absalom is, what he has done or why David is fleeing from him. As Millard points out, nothing about Ps 3 contradicts the notion that David is fleeing from Absalom (Millard, *Die Komposition des Psalters*, 131).

89. Millard considers the psalm a Midrash on Samuel (Millard, *Die Komposition des Psalters*, 131).

90. Goldingay thinks the mention of God's people in v. 9 contradicts the civil war of the Absalom setting and points to a national crisis instead (Goldingay 1:109); detecting a contradiction too hastily is a way of missing what the editors are conveying.

91. Buttenwieser, *Psalms*, 399–400.

92. Mann, *Run, David, Run!*, 157.

5. Conclusion

The first David psalm presented to us by the Psalter calls into question some of the assumptions that are brought to the psalms, concerning the attitude of the psalmists to themselves and to their enemies. We find David to be aware of his guilt and acting accordingly; we certainly do not find that perfection is a criterion for praying an imprecation, as he does. In his view of the enemy, David asks for respite from the enemy attack, not for vengeance nor even for justice. In keeping with Ps 2, David asks for the enemy to be blessed once they have turned from their attack, and we see him acting magnanimously in victory.

In chapter 7, we will see how this opening to the Psalms is placed within the OT as a whole and the connections it makes to other significantly-placed David Psalms. It presents David's prayers for enemies as a model for the nation of Israel to pray in the light of the exile; this will prove particularly important when we come to Psalm 137 later.

6

Because of My Innocence

Self-Righteous or "Not Guilty"?

To be righteous is to be forgiven, to be open to God's instruction, to live in dependence upon God rather than self.[1]

PRAYERS CONCERNING ENEMIES ARE often seen as self-righteous. As we
saw above, this has led some to reject them as deluded and legalistic,
pregnant with a moral superiority which proves that the Old Testament
mindset was far from the Christian gospel. Others conclude that these
prayers are only ever appropriate on the lips of Jesus, the perfectly sinless human being, on the assumption that the Psalms in question are
claiming complete and impeccable righteousness. Either way, the Psalms
are understood as relying on a merit which has been earned and which
deserves Yahweh's favor. In this chapter, we clear some misunderstand-
ings out of the way. We show why a protestation of innocence is not a
self-righteous claim to perfect sinlessness, nor even necessarily a claim
to moral superiority.

---

1. McCann, *Psalms as Torah*, 110–11.

1. A Flawed Assumption: Innocence vs. Sinlessness

Before explaining why this assumption is flawed, we will illustrate a simple but overlooked fact. A psalmist can simultaneously claim to be innocent, and yet confess that they are guilty of sin. Here is Psalm 41, for example.

An explicit confession of sin:

5 [4] But I, I said to Yahweh: "Be gracious to me.
   Heal my life, even though I have sinned [חטא *hata'*] against you."

This is followed by the psalmist explaining why he has been kept safe:

13 [12] As for me, it is because of my perfection [תֹם *tom*] that you have upheld me.

This is not a lone example, and it shows that a claim to righteousness, even using the lofty language of "perfection," does not mean that the supplicant believes himself to be free from sin. In fact, they will sometimes combine their protestation of innocence with a confession of sin, as here.

2. The Righteous vs. the Wicked in the Psalms

Righteous (צַדִּיק *tsadiq*) and wicked (רָשָׁע *rashaq*) are opposites which describe two distinct groups of people. The division of humanity into these two groups is basic to the OT,[2] and permeates the Psalms.[3] By contrast with the wicked, the righteous are marked out by their fear of, and trust in, Yahweh.[4] The orientation of their affections towards God and his law means that they hate sin (including their own sin) in principle. However, this does not mean that sin is absent from their lives, and they know this. Membership of the righteous goes hand in hand with indwelling sin, and they often coexist in the same psalm.

As we have seen, Psalms 1–3 announce, at the very entrance to the Psalter, that the distinction between "righteous" and "wicked" is complicated by forgiveness.

If a psalmist claims the label of "righteous," he does not deny the presence of individual sins, past or present. The category of those who

2. Von Rad, "'Gerechtigkeit' und 'Leben,'" 231.
3. Ruppert, *Jesus als der leidende Gerechte?*, 18–19.
4. Miller, "Psalms as a Meditation," 109.

fear and trust God includes sinners who have repented and sought forgiveness, following the invitation of Ps 2 (*kiss the son*). The category of
righteous includes those who, like David in Ps 3, are guilty of the most
grievous sins. The superscription there points us to his fleeing from Absalom, which in turn is the result of the episode involving Bathsheba and
Uriah, where he breaks five of the Ten Commandments.[5] He is nonetheless innocent of the slanderous accusations which Absalom has used to
usurp the throne.

Surprisingly, he even remains "righteous" as a general description
of his orientation to Yahweh: "David did what was upright in Yahweh's
sight, and did not turn away from anything that he commanded him—all
the days of his life—apart from that business with Uriah the Hittite" (1
Kgs 15:5). This summary overlooks other sins committed by David and is
quite a stark contrast with David's own self-assessment as a thoroughgoing sinner in Ps 51.

Despite his general sinfulness and wicked disposition, and despite
many actual sins, he was innocent of the matter at issue in Ps 3 and is in a
relationship with Yahweh characterized as "righteous." To call oneself one
of the righteous is not a denial that one is sinful.

As we have seen, the Psalms, and especially Books I and II, guide
us to see David as a sinner, and in fact at his very worst, with Uriah and
Bathsheba in view in the two psalms that introduce him: Pss 3 and 51.
As an example of the "man" of Ps 1, he is a model for the reader of the
Psalter, and in the next chapter we will see that he is especially positioned
to be a model for the whole nation as they look back on the guilt that
led them to exile. This should already give us pause before concluding
that the prayers in these books are expressing self-righteous claims to
moral impeccability. The Psalter moves us seamlessly from righteousness
to guilt: "the David who in Psalm 26 confesses his innocence is the same
David who just confessed his sin in Psalm 25."[6]

The point is put surprisingly in Pss 32, 33. The lack of superscription
of the latter invites us to read them as a pair. Psalm 33:1 opens where
32 ended, commanding the righteous to rejoice. However, the pair opens
by identifying the blessings of a man, using אַשְׁרֵי (*ashrey*) which framed
Psalms 1 and 2. He is blessed not by self-righteousness, but by forgiveness.
The psalm closes by expressing trust in Yahweh. McCann puts it well:

---

5. McCann, *Psalms as Torah*, 102.

6. Futato, *Interpreting the Psalms*, 154.

Psalm 32 reinforces the understanding of righteousness which we reached on the basis of Psalm 1. To be righteous is not to manage somehow to obey all the rules, to be sinless, to be morally perfect. In fact, as Psalms 32 and 51 suggest, the life of the righteous is pervaded by sin and its consequences. To be righteous is to be forgiven, to be open to God's instruction, to live in dependence upon God rather than self.[7]

This is what the first three Psalms have led us to expect: any impression of self-righteousness in Ps 1 is immediately qualified in Ps 2 and refuted by Ps 3. To be "pervaded by sin and its consequences" is how the superscription of Ps 3 introduces David. "To be forgiven" is the offer of Ps 2 and is contingent precisely on the commands "to be open to God's instruction" (*let yourselves be made wise*, 2:10) and "to live in dependence upon God" (*blessed are all who take refuge in him*, 2:12).

Righteousness does stand in sharp contrast with membership of the "wicked,"[8] but to claim not to belong to the wicked is not to think that one is sinless. This is not a special function of some psalms. Generally in the OT, "righteous" and "wicked" do not mean that someone protesting one's own righteousness is laboring under delusions of perfection nor guilty of "self-righteousness."[9]

3. Confessions of Sin Coexist with Protestations of Innocence

We will illustrate this with a couple of psalms where a protestation of innocence sits alongside a confession of sin.

In Psalm 40, among the kinds of claim to trust in Yahweh which we expect from the righteous, we find a claim to righteousness:

9 [8] To do your will, my God, is my delight,
    and your law is in my inmost being.
10 [9] I have announced the good news of righteousness [צֶדֶק *tsedeq*] in the
    great assembly.

---

7. McCann, *Psalms as Torah*, 110–11.

8. Weijden, *Die 'Gerechtigkeit' in den Psalmen*, 81.

9. Kwakkel, *According to My Righteousness*, 297–303.

Yet:

13 [12] evils have encompassed me, which are beyond number,
       and the things of which I am guilty have overtaken me.

There follows a description of woe and an appeal for God to rescue David. David's actual misdeeds are in view: his request for divine mercy is presented as undeserved.

We can now explain the contrast we found in Ps 41 at the start of this chapter: "I have sinned against you" vs. "because of my perfection." Psalm 41 holds together a life of righteousness in principle, with actual sins. David expects Yahweh to rescue him, and to help him overcome foes who are enjoying his affliction. Those who consider the poor can expect protection (vv. 2–4 [1–3]), and David's perfection will result in Yahweh's delight and rescue (vv. 11–13 [10–12]). Yet all of this is insufficient. David *has* sinned against Yahweh in some way: v. 5 [4]. He deserves what is befalling him, even though the enemies are speaking evil, and are as worthless a bunch as are found in any of David's prayers (vv. 6–10 [5–9]). David's generally righteous disposition towards Yahweh is not sufficient for him to appeal to justice; he needs mercy and forgiveness to cover this specific sin. Psalm 41 is significantly placed at the close of Book I. David is introduced to Book I as a sinner, and he is a sinner in each of its final four psalms.[10] In fact, throughout Book I, righteousness is marked out by confessing sin and appealing for forgiveness: the opposite of self-righteousness.[11]

4. A Plea of "Not Guilty" Is Not Self-Righteousness

It is one thing to claim to be righteous in general, but quite another to claim to be the innocent party in a dispute with evildoers. The term "righteous" (צַדִּיק, *tsadiq*) in the OT generally does not mean sinless. It has different uses in different genres, but is hardly ever found in legal material. When it is found in legal contexts, "righteous" is not an evaluation of sinless righteousness; it is the equivalent of "not guilty" with respect to a particular charge (Exod 23:7–8; Deut 16:19; 25:1).[12]

---

10. Robertson, *Flow of the Psalms*, 19.

11. McCann, "The Shape of Book I of the Psalter," 344.

12. Schultz, "Old Testament Theology and Exegesis," 1:192.

Often, a protestation of innocence will involve pleading "not guilty" to a particular accusation, without denying the presence of other sins. In the Psalter, to be the "righteous" often means to be oppressed by the "wicked" (רְשָׁעִים, *resha'im*) despite being innocent of anything that would deserve their actions, and sometimes even through false accusation.[13]

Such false accusation is often the key to understanding apparent pleas of righteousness. The term behind "false witness" in the Decalogue (שֶׁקֶר, *sheqer*) indicates a breach of law, especially by lying witnesses.[14] It has three shades of meaning in the Psalms: breach of covenant against God's law, breach of covenant against norms of neighborliness, and false witness in court.[15] Where an individual is pleading in a psalm, it always concerns *perjury* in court.[16] In the Decalogue it qualifies false testimony (Exod 20:16), and several times in the Pentateuch it indicates lies, especially in court (Exod 5:9; 23:7; Lev 5:22, 24; 19:12; Deut 19:18). Notice that these include passages cited above, where "righteous" is a technical term for "not guilty," which would fit a person *falsely* accused.

Particularly interesting is Deut 19, which handles a *single*, uncorroborated witness who is bent on violence: the "violence witness" (עֵד־חָמָס, *'ed-hamas*) of v. 16. The court cannot know in advance whether the witness is truthful, so "violence witness" means that he claims to have witnessed violence, and therefore must ask for a violent sentence as just retribution from the court. He is a "witness *to* violence." The court must establish whether he is truthful, and legislate for his punishment if he is a false witness (עֵד־שֶׁקֶר, *'ed-sheqer*,) who has testified falsely (שֶׁקֶר, *sheqer*).[17] In such a case, accuser and accused appear *before the face of Yahweh, before the faces of the priests and judges*. The outcome is that either the guilty accused is punished, or the false witness receives the exact same punishment. The only way that the perjuriously accused, innocent victim can be vindicated is by Yahweh's issue of a righteous judgment through the court.

This means that, where false accusations of violence are brought to court, someone is going to be condemned. Someone falsely accused has

13. Miller, "Beginning of the Psalter," 85–86.

14. Wagner, "Beiträge zur Aramaismenfrage," 364–65; Christensen, *Deuteronomy*, 430.

15. Klopfenstein, *Die Lüge*, 78.

16. Klopfenstein, *Die Lüge*, 45, 80.

17. Merrill, *Deuteronomy*, 280.

only one thing he can ask for: the punishment of his accusers. There is no neutral way out.

The immediately preceding verse, Deut 19:17, shows that while it is priests and judges who are the agents of judgment, the whole process takes place in Yahweh's presence. In situations such as Ps 3, where David is away from Yahweh's court, he can still appeal directly to Yahweh and be heard (v. 5 [4]). Accordingly, in situations where such false accusations are happening outside of court, and the psalmist is in mortal danger owing to false accusations which are not being handled in court (for example, Absalom's rebellion), the psalmist can still appeal to Yahweh as though a regular court were in session. All cases are ultimately tried by Yahweh.

So much for false accusation. The flip side is that a psalmist cannot expect divine protection from *accurate* accusation. He must show that he has not earned the trouble that he is in. A murderer being punished for the murder he has committed has no claim on Yahweh's protection against those punishing him. Mowinckel captures the idea by suggesting that a protestation of righteousness is made in the context of being treated *as though* one were unrighteous, when one is not.[18]

> He does not claim the judgment or patronage of God to his cause, until he had, in the first place, asserted his integrity, and stated his complaint against the malicious conduct of his enemies; for God can never be expected to undertake a cause which is unworthy of defense.[19]

When falsely accused, to call oneself "righteous" is to make no claim at all about one's life in general: it is a specific counter-claim to a particular accusation. Even to call oneself "righteous" by contrast to the "wicked" is not a claim to moral superiority, but part of the claim that the accuser is (on this occasion) a false witness.

For example, in Ps 31 the wicked bear false witness, and in v. 19 [18] David asks for perjurious (שֶׁקֶר, *sheqer*) mouths, which speak against the "righteous," to be silenced. David is innocent of their specific charges. However, David confesses his sinfulness explicitly in v. 11 [10]: "My strength has tottered because of my iniquity."

---

18. Mowinckel, *Psalms*, 2:112.

19. Calvin, *Psalms*, 2:374.

Similarly, David admits his guilt in Ps 38:2, 4–6, 19 [1, 3–5, 18], but in the very next verse follows it up with a protestation of innocence.[20] In v. 20 [19], once again the enemies hate the psalmist perjuriously (שֶׁקֶר, *sheqer*). He is facing strife and hatred on the basis of falsehood.[21] In fact, he is being repaid evil for good (v. 21 [20]).

As we see in these two examples, even in situations where the psalmist is accurately claiming that they are in the right over against wicked accusers, they are still aware of their wider guilt before God and confess their sins accordingly.

In short, innocence in the matters at issue is essential to prayer for retribution. This may be why the one who prays often laments lying lips and slander: Pss 12:3; 58:4; 120:3. In a courtroom, lying lips, tongues and throats are deadly weapons.[22] It is no surprise that these feature frequently in imprecatory psalms, which are themselves words: truthful speech to Yahweh is a fitting response when the enemy's weapon is false speech before Yahweh.

The gap with the ethics of the New Testament will be hard to find. First Peter 2:19–23 warns Christians that suffering at the hands of the authorities when they have in fact been guilty of something is hardly commendable. On the other hand, if suffering when they are innocent, they are to follow Christ's example of not retaliating or rebelling, but instead entrusting judgment to God. That is precisely what David shows us in such psalms: under false accusation, even threat of death, he appeals to Yahweh for just judgment.

5. A Word of Caution about "Grace" and "Salvation"

In examining whether a psalmist is aware of their sinfulness, it would be tempting for readers, especially Christian readers, to read such awareness into the language of mercy and salvation. If he calls God his redeemer in Ps 19:15 [14], or the God of his salvation in 18:47 [46], does that not mean that he is a sinner in need of forgiveness?

In a word, "no." We will look at various terms for mercy in the next chapter, but here we need to be aware that all manner of Hebrew words

---

20. Kraus 1:449–50.

21. Seybold 158.

22. Wenham notes that the ninth commandment is the most prominent in the Psalter (Wenham, "Ethics of the Psalms," 114–15).

that are thoroughly applicable and appropriate for sinners, do not necessarily establish that sin is the issue. An English reader of the psalms can be saved, delivered, or redeemed from all manner of troubles which are unconnected with sin. They can find mercy, grace, and compassion without sin being the issue.

6. The Limits of "Template" Criticism

The system of classification which form criticism has given us teaches that a "lament" psalm will often include *either* a "protestation of innocence" *or* a "confession of sin."[23] Gunkel was adamant that it could not contain both: you can be penitent and confess sin, or you can appeal for help from a position of innocence, but they are antithetical.[24] Gunkel acknowledged that laments of the righteous could include requests for greater righteousness. However, the rigidity of his classification caused him to look at Psalm 51, which is a paradigm of confession of sin, and classify it as a lament of the *innocent*.[25] This inflexible choice between confession and innocence is not borne out by the evidence, as we have seen. Nonetheless, unfortunately this sharp dichotomy between confessing sin *or else* claiming to be "not guilty" has proved resilient against the evidence, and primed generations of readers to see "innocence" as self-righteousness.

7. Conclusion: Not Self-Righteousness, but Specific Righteousness

Yes, David protests his innocence of particular charges. True, he may even plead that his life in general is upright. That does *not* mean that he feels that he has *earned* God's favor, *merited* grace, or *deserves* rescue.

Misunderstanding this point leads to the common observation that these are prayers of someone perfectly sinless, which is applied to discussions of the proper use of imprecations in the Psalms. "'Did David not recognize his sin? These sound like the words of a perfect man.' The fact

---

23. E.g., Longman, *Psalms*, 27.

24. Gunkel and Begrich, *Einleitung in die Psalmen*, 223.

25. Gunkel and Begrich, *Einleitung in die Psalmen*, 224.

jumps off the page at us as we read this psalm."[26] It only "jumps off the page" when sin and righteousness are misconstrued.

Many of the psalms at issue are included in the *Prayers of David* (the collection that ends at 72:20), and are marked with superscriptions that identify him with them. These invite the community to use and imitate them as prayers. It would contradict the nature of the Psalter if they were off limits even for David, let alone for the rest of God's people. To detect claims of sinless perfection is to fail to read them in the context of the Psalter, which presents David as guilty of many and grievous sins.

We will now see that David's sinful, forgiven persona is a model for readers of the Psalter, and especially for God's people as a whole.

---

26. Adams, *War Psalms*, 21–22.

7

David and Israel in the Psalter

[W]hen David fled Jerusalem, "Israel" went into exile. . . . David's life as
the representative Israelite foreshadowed the future history of Israel.[1]

David's story becomes a paradigm for the nation as a whole as
they are assured that . . . [they] will see their current suffering
come to an end. Moreover, because the promise to David was still
valid, then the people could still look forward to restoration.[2]

DAVID IS PRESENTED IN the Psalter as a model for the whole nation to
follow in praying about their exilic enemies. First, there is a typological
correspondence between David in his flight from Absalom, and Israel's
exile at the hands of Babylon. Second, the Psalter re-introduces David
in Ps 51, establishing a correspondence between his sin and the national
apostasy at the golden calf. Thus, the mercy that David needed in order
to escape Absalom is instructive for a nation reaping the punishment for
apostasy, in exile. Finally, Ps 1 makes connections to the wider canon, and
especially to the frames of the three main divisions of the canon, which
present the Psalms as facing the exile. The instruction to the righteous

1. Leithart, *A Son to Me*, 267.
2. Firth, "Shining the Lamp," 224.

in Ps 1 is then instruction on how to live and be blessed through exile, as David was in Ps 3. That instruction is to meditate on *Torah*, which includes David's prayers in the Psalms. When the nation faces a crisis such as the exile, David's prayers will be models.

1. David and Absalom as Types of Israel and Babylon

1.A. Typology in the Absalom Incident

We have seen that Ps 3, by its position, content, literary connections and superscription, invites us to read it in the light of the first two Psalms, and yet the correspondence is not exact.

In Ps 3 David could be a concrete example of the king of Ps 2, himself an example of the man of Ps 1, which would encourage the reader to identify Absalom as the enemy.[3] However, the fit is awkward, since Absalom is no foreign vassal king. The use of גוֹיִם וּלְאֻמִּים (*goyim ule'ummim* "nations and peoples") and מְלָכִים (*melakim* "kings") in vv. 1–2, probably implies foreign nations, even though אֶרֶץ (*'erets*) could be anything from "country" to "world."[4] On the other hand, in v. 8 "heritage" (אֲחֻזָּה, *'ahuzah*) is almost exclusively used of the promised land.[5] This could suggest that אֶרֶץ (*'erets*) in מַלְכֵי־אֶרֶץ (*malkey-'erets*, v. 2) be limited to something like "kings of the land." Even so, it can certainly include such vassal states as Edom, Moab, Ammon, Philistia, and Amalek (2 Sam 8:12).

Then again, Ish-Bosheth and Sheba (2 Sam 2, 20) are described as *kings* of Israel: Abner makes Ish-Bosheth king in 2 Sam 2:9. So a rebellion can come from a king over Israel (rather than Judah) who challenges David's heritage. Absalom is very similar to both of them, leading Israel to challenge David. He and his followers are scorning (Ps 1:1) Yahweh's decree of 2:7 in 3:3 [2], and throwing off the fetters of David's rule and jurisprudence (2:3). Nonetheless, it would be too much of a stretch to consider Ish-Bosheth and Sheba to be kings over "nations and peoples," as in Ps 2. For example, in 2 Sam 22:44 (= Ps 18:44) David contrasts the "nations" (גּוֹיִם *goyim*) with his own "people" (עַם *'am*). It is that latter term, as we have seen, that David used for Israel in Ps 3.

---

3. Erbele-Küster, *Lesen*, 67.

4. רוֹזְנִים is rare and always appears as a parallel term in poetry, presumably because of its rarity; we can conclude little from it use here.

5. Wolf, "אָחַז," 32–33; Koopmans, "אֲחֻזָּה," 1:358–59.

Despite the mismatch, *this* psalm has been selected to introduce David in the Psalter. Several psalms could have been chosen which fit the international conflict of Ps 2, and the innocence of Ps 1, much better, e.g., Pss 9, 18. If a Psalm was needed that connected with an event in David's life via the superscription, thirteen were available.[6] Choosing Ps 3 creates two further anomalies. First, almost all the rest are in the early stages of David's persecution by Saul.[7] The Absalom incident is much later, making it a curious choice for an opening psalm of David: this puzzle has exercised readers since at least Mediaeval Jewish scholarship.[8] James Hamilton offers a solution, whereby the reversal in order between Saul and Absalom in the Psalter, coupled with the similarities between the two characters in Samuel (their beauty and their winning over of Israel), would "forge a link between David's enemies, as though they are all the same."[9] We are not being given a mere history lesson about David, but invited to see his psalms in a certain light and learn from him typologically.

The second oddity in choosing Psalm 3 out of the other psalms with historical notices is curiouser still. In those psalms, David is innocent, which would be a splendid way to follow Pss 1 and 2: the righteous beleaguered by the unrighteous. There are only two psalms which would not fit the innocent man of Pss 1 and 2, yet one of them has been chosen to introduce David in the Psalter. As we will see, the other one reintroduces him in Book II: Ps 51.[10] David is introduced to the reader as a sinner.

Psalm 3 has been placed to introduce David to the reader of the Psalter for two reasons. First, Ps 1 presented the righteous and the wicked in simple terms. Psalm 2 has muddied the waters as far as the wicked go: they have a chance to repent. Psalm 3 invites us to ask: what if the protagonist, the anointed, the judge himself, is unrighteous? David is innocent in the Absalom narrative, where Absalom falsely accuses him of being an unrighteous judge towards the northern tribes. However, he

6. Pss 3; 7; 18; 34; 51; 52; 54; 56; 57; 59; 60; 63; 142.

7. Auwers, *La composition littéraire*, 122.

8. This led Ibn Ezra to reject Saadiah Gaon's canonical approach to the Psalms (Simon, *Four Approaches*, 316–18).

9. Hamilton, *God's Glory*, 281n27.

10. Arguably, Ps 63 might also relate to the Absalom incident (Hossfeld-Zenger 2:195). Psalm 63 is the last David Psalm in Books I–II that has a historical note in its superscription. If Ps 63:1 does relate to Absalom, then it strengthens the presentation of David as a sinner. His unrighteousness in Pss 3, 51, and 63 would bracket his history in Book II and in the *Prayers of David*.

is reaping the punishment prophesied by Nathan following his sin with Bathsheba and Uriah, which entailed the fratricide that led to Absalom's expulsion and the ensuing events. We therefore find David's standing as less than clear-cut. He is innocent of the crime at issue (Absalom's accusation against him is false). Yahweh is punishing him for his guilt, using Absalom as an unrighteous instrument of punishment. This moral ambiguity makes the Psalter a more realistic prayer book.

1.B. Typology of Exile

The second reason for putting Ps 3 in pole position is that David typologically resembles post-exilic Israel. David has been exiled from Zion, as part of a punishment for his sin, prophesied in a divine oracle: like Israel in Babylon.

In Ps 2, Yahweh sat in Heaven while the king was on Zion. In Ps 3, Yahweh (and his ark, 2 Sam 15:29) remain in Jerusalem, so that Yahweh's rescue is far from the Davidic king. However, even if the king is no longer installed on "Zion, my holy mountain" (צִיּוֹן הַר־קָדְשִׁי, *tsiyon har-qodshi* Ps 2:6), Yahweh does answer "*from* his holy mountain" (מֵהַר קָדְשׁוֹ, *mehar qodsho* 3:5 [4]).[11] Within David's life, only the Absalom narrative fits the prayer of 3:5. Before 2 Sam 6, the ark was not in Zion. After that, at no other point was David separated from the ark in battle, except in his flight from Absalom.

However, the agents of punishment are unrighteous and will be punished by Yahweh, leading to David's restoration to Zion. Absalom is Yahweh's chosen means of chastising David, but behaves unrighteously in doing so, and is overthrown by Yahweh: like Babylon. Just as Israel received a prophetic oracle in advance of Babylon's overthrow (Isa 13), so David receives word from Zadok that Ahithophel's counsel is overthrown, which is how David knows that Yahweh is with him.

Mann argues that both Ps 3 and the Absalom incident as told in 2 Sam 15:1—17:24 are written in a way that would particularly encourage exiled Israel. He does not limit the application to exilic Israel, but to any group in a comparable situation.[12] This supports my claim that Ps 3 presents David as a type for future times of national distress, which we will develop in Book V. As I have argued above, Ps 3 and the incident in

---

11. So also Vesco 100.

12. Mann, "Run, David, Run!," 205–8.

Samuel are connected more closely to the exile than Mann allows, and also to the *return* from exile.[13] As Firth puts it, the application to the *exiles* is that: "David's story becomes a paradigm for the nation as a whole as they are assured that . . . [they] will see their current suffering come to an end. Moreover, because the promise to David was still valid, then the people could still look forward to restoration."[14]

David returns from exile within Ps 3, so his prayer in this situation is a model for Israel on being returned to the land, and will be important for understanding such difficult prayers as Ps 137. David's prayer concerning his enemies should be instructive for post-exilic Israel when they consider their Babylonian captors. As we have seen, the Psalter introduces him as both not deserving rescue from his foes, and showing them mercy.

As we saw in our guide to using the superscriptions (ch. 3, §2.C, pp. 30–36), Ps 3 is often taken to establish a typological correspondence between David and any supplicant, and with the whole nation. The national note on which the Psalm finishes is so marked, that some do not believe it was part of the Psalm originally. On the contrary, this "unexpected" verse is what we should expect, if David as king connects his life as an individual with the whole nation which he represents. As Peter Leithart puts it, "when David fled Jerusalem, 'Israel' went into exile. . . . David's life as the representative Israelite foreshadowed the future history of Israel."[15] As Bernd Janowski points out, to apply pre-exilic texts such as Pss 44 or 51 to the exile does not require that they be read against the grain, but that some points in history have a paradigmatic significance.[16]

We will now see that David's second introduction within the Psalter strengthens this connection between his own life and the exiled and restored nation. He presents sin with Bathsheba as equivalent to a time of national apostasy: the golden calf.

13. Mann moves a little in that direction in his revised thesis: "To tell his story in this way is to present David's conviction that Yhwh is someone who intervenes in the lives of his people and can be expected to bring his banished ones back to Jerusalem" (Mann, *Run, David, Run!*, 158).

14. Firth, "Shining the Lamp," 224.

15. Leithart, *A Son to Me*, 267.

16. Janowski, "Ein Tempel aus Worten," 298.

2. David's Sin as a National Apostasy in the Psalter

2.A. David's Second Introduction: Psalm 51 and the Golden Calf

Books I and II are largely composed of the first two David Psalters, as suggested by the concluding verse of Book II: "The prayers of David, son of Jesse, are completed" (72:20). More precisely, the whole of Book I consists of David Psalms.[17] Book II begins with a run of Korah psalms,[18] one of Asaph, and then consists entirely of David Psalms, until the final Solomon Psalm. After David's temple singers (Korah and Asaph) open the book, how does David reappear in the Psalter? It is in the penitential psalm *par excellence*: Ps 51.[19]

Both psalms that introduce and re-introduce David to the reader of the Psalter have historical notices connected with David's great sin with Bathsheba and Uriah: Psalms 3 and 51. David is introduced to us as David who sinned greatly, yet throughout Books I and II he pleads for and expects God's mercy.[20] The failure of the monarchy in Book III may be less of a surprise in the flow of the Psalter, if the way David is introduced in Books I and II is attended to.[21]

We have already seen that Ps 3, by pointing to the backstory in 2 Samuel, introduces David in the light of his most notorious and egregious collection of sins. We will now see that Ps 51 presents him as the king who represents the nation. His sin is the equivalent of the national apostasy at the golden calf, and so David's prayers serve as models for the nation.[22]

17. Apart from four that which lack all superscription: Pss 1 and 2 (which are introductory) and two which should probably be read together with their preceding psalm (Pss 10 and 33).

18. Again, taking 43 together with 42, guided by the refrain that binds them.

19. Goulder also sees this as significantly placed (Goulder, *The Prayers of David*, 28).

20. Zenger argues that part of the Davidization of the Psalter involved adding 51 to the beginning of the pre-existing collection of 52–68*, precisely to begin a David section with an exemplary David. He does not hide his sin, but confesses it to God in true repentance and receives forgiveness (Hossfeld-Zenger 2:56).

21. Analyses of the "Messianic Psalter" of Pss 2–89* usually notice the significance of Pss 2 (the son promised) and 72 (the son apparent) for the concluding Ps 89 (the promise apparently failed). E.g., Zenger, "Zion als Mutter," 149.

22. As Häner points out, while the final verses of Ps 51 clearly go beyond the exact situation that the superscription describes, they are nonetheless an excellent fit for the character of David in Samuel and Chronicles, and these verses cement what the placement of the Psalm has achieved: David at prayer is a model for the whole nation, not just for individuals (Häner, "David als Vorbeter," 22–23).

Psalm 51 develops the link between David and Israel further. David prefaces his plea for forgiveness by piling up mercy terms from Yahweh's self-disclosure following Moses's successful intercession after the golden calf (Exod 33:19; 34:6–7).[23] Similarly strong uses of these mercy terms, alluding to Exod 34, are found in very significant places in Books III–IV, as we will see. Therefore, we need to invest a little time to understand what these terms do and do not mean, especially *hesed* and *emet*. We will then see the significance of David alluding to Exod 34 in Ps 51.

2.B. Divine Mercy: The Meaning of Exod 34:6–7

2.B.1. The Meaning of חֶסֶד (hesed)

Hesed is particularly frequent in the Psalter, with 127 out of 249 OT occurrences, while no other book contains more than twelve. Its meaning has been debated in the last century. Does *hesed* imply handing out just deserts, or does it mean something like mercy?

Traditionally, *hesed* had been understood as roughly synonymous with love, and very much consistent with mercy and sin, hence KJV's "lovingkindness." One of the earliest Hebrew lexica (early eleventh century) simply glossed it as טוב (*tov*, "goodness").[24] A sense of undeserved mercy was assumed by translators, versions and lexica, before the 1958 edition of Koehler and Baumgartner, *Lexicon in Veteris Testamenti Libros*.[25]

The prior consensus had been questioned by Nelson Glueck's thesis in 1927 that it is a covenant treaty term, and implies acts of kindness which are the obligation of the covenant partner. Divine rescue would therefore be rescue fitting the stipulations of a covenant; *hesed* could not describe God's merciful rescue of sinners who deserve the peril that has befallen them when they breach the terms of the covenant treaty. It can only apply to just rewards that have been deserved. Glueck's thesis was widely followed, but has also been challenged.[26] The central question in

---

23. Wenham, "The Golden Calf," 175–76.

24. Ibn Ǧanâḥ, *Sepher Haschoraschim*, 162–63; he also considers a completely separate meaning of "disgrace" (on which see Stoebe, "חֶסֶד," 1:600).

25. Harris, "חסד," 305. An analysis of translations of חֶסֶד and of אֱמֶת in Targums, Peshitta and LXX is given by Kellenberger, *ḥäsäd wä' ämät*, 23–32.

26. For a summary of the debate and conclusions similar to those I offer below, see Stoebe, "חֶסֶד," 1:600–21; Harris, "חסד," 305–7; Zobel, "חֶסֶד," 5:48–71; Baer and Gordon, "חֶסֶד," 2:211–18.

the ensuing debate was whether the love is freely given or is an obligation from a covenant (either a covenant which is explicitly made or one
implied by social norms).

Glueck first argues that, in secular inter-personal contexts, *hesed* is
only possible between parties that are in a relationship, and identifies six
such relationships.[27] Second, he argues that *hesed* is always a matter of
fulfilling obligations within each of those six sets of relationships: "*Hesed*
is the behavior for relationships governed by rights and obligations."[28] It
is never gratuitous: "In the older sources of profane usage, *hesed* is never
an act of mercy, goodness, grace or love that are arbitrarily given as gifts."[29]
Glueck therefore sees *hesed* as synonymous with strict faithfulness to an
explicit or implicit covenant, so that the term אֱמֶת (*'emet*, the meaning of
which is discussed below) appears with it epexegetically; *hesed* and *'emet*
should be seen as a hendiadys.[30]

Third, he examines the religious sphere, and how it applies to in-
terpersonal relationships. Strict obligation is key again, even though the
outworking of that obligation will involve kindness and love. Glueck argues that *hesed* is synonymous with fearing God.[31]

Finally, Glueck examines the term as applied to God. Once more,
strict merit operates. It is synonymous with faithfulness. Covenant
precedes *hesed*: "God's *hesed* is the consequence of his covenant, or his
promise, or his oath."[32] It is distinguished from רַחֲמִים (*rahamim*, "compassion") precisely by being faithful to the covenant, for good or ill. *Hesed*,
does not mean graciously exceeding the blessings deserved under the
covenant, neither does it mean mercifully reducing the penalties that are
due. However, Glueck notes that grace is clearly in view in divine *hesed*,
because the covenant itself is the result of God's gracious act of election.[33]

27. Glueck, *Das Wort hesed*, 3.

28. "חסד ist die einem Rechts-Pflicht-Verhältnis entsprechende Verhaltungsweise."
Glueck, *Das Wort hesed*, 20.

29. "חסד im profanen Sprachgebrauch in den älteren Quellen ist nie willkürlich
geschenkte Gnade oder Güte oder Huld oder Liebe." Glueck, *Das Wort hesed*, 21.

30. Glueck, *Das Wort hesed*, 20–21.

31. Glueck, *Das Wort hesed*, 34.

32. "Gottes חסד ist die Folge seines Bundes oder seiner Verheißung oder seines
Eides." Glueck, *Das Wort hesed*, 66–67.

33. Glueck, *Das Wort hesed*, 66–67.

In other words, *hesed* itself is gracelessly legalistic, but the existence of a contract to be legalistically applied is itself a gracious context. Is this how God administers a covenant when he uses the term *hesed*?

Before turning to particular texts, we must note David Baer and Robert Gordon's warning "that the instances of חֶסֶד as a divine characteristic greatly outnumber the rest and that attempts at comprehensive definition can therefore easily become unbalanced."[34] Indeed, some of the studies begin with the secular and then argue to the religious or treat them separately at first and then try to relate them. Given the weight of the data on the divine side and since our concern is to establish whether the presence of God's *hesed* in a Psalm implies forbearance of sin I think it more prudent to concentrate on divine *hesed*.

Now we turn to some striking and significantly formative uses of *hesed*. In the Decalogue we read the prohibition of graven images enforced by these sanctions, grounded in God's own nature, Exod 20:5–6:

לֹא־תִשְׁתַּחֲוֶה לָהֶם וְלֹא תָעָבְדֵם
כִּי אָנֹכִי יְהוָה אֱלֹהֶיךָ אֵל קַנָּא פֹּקֵד עֲוֺן אָבֹת עַל־בָּנִים עַל־שִׁלֵּשִׁים וְעַל־
רִבֵּעִים לְשֹׂנְאָי׃
וְעֹשֶׂה חֶסֶד לַאֲלָפִים לְאֹהֲבַי וּלְשֹׁמְרֵי מִצְוֺתָי׃

Do not worship them, neither serve them,
for I, Yahweh your God, am a jealous God, who will monitor[35] the fathers' wrongdoing ['*avon*] among the sons, up to the third and fourth generation of those who hate me,
but who acts in hesed to thousands who love me and keep my commandments.

There is a gracious asymmetry numerically: "the greatest numerical contrast in the Bible (three//four to thousands)."[36] The extent of punishment is strictly limited, but the *hesed* seems to be unlimited.[37] Hatred for God will be dealt with to the third and fourth generation, while love for God will result in *hesed* to thousands, or thousands of descendants or of generations.[38]

34. Baer and Gordon, "חֶסֶד," 2:212.

35. Following Rose, "How Will God Deal?," 22. Nonetheless, even if פקד had the sense of "visiting punishment on the sons," it still contrasts with the much more extensive display of *hesed*.

36. Stuart, *Exodus*, 454.

37. Durham, *Exodus*, 287.

38. On the options, see Childs, *Exodus*, 388.

That conversation with Moses is cut short by the national apostasy of the golden calf, breaching that very commandment. God announces that he will destroy the nation: Exod 32:7–10. Moses's intercession results in the nation being spared. While there is serious punishment from God's hand, it is mercifully lighter than national destruction. That is the context in which God reveals his name and character in 34:6–7. Walter Moberly brings out the special status of this passage:

> The most important OT passage in this regard is Exod 34:5–7, which is the most extensive statement about the name, i.e., character, of God in the whole Bible—a statement found, moreover, on the lips of God himself—and thus representing the very heart of God's self-revelation within Israel.[39]

Exod 34:6–7:

וַיַּעֲבֹ֨ר יְהוָ֥ה ׀ עַל־פָּנָיו֮ וַיִּקְרָא֒
יְהוָ֣ה ׀ יְהוָ֔ה אֵ֥ל רַח֖וּם וְחַנּ֑וּן אֶ֥רֶךְ אַפַּ֖יִם וְרַב־חֶ֥סֶד וֶאֱמֶֽת׃
נֹצֵ֥ר חֶ֙סֶד֙ לָאֲלָפִ֔ים נֹשֵׂ֥א עָוֺ֛ן וָפֶ֖שַׁע וְחַטָּאָ֑ה
וְנַקֵּה֙ לֹ֣א יְנַקֶּ֔ה פֹּקֵ֣ד ׀ עֲוֺ֣ן אָב֗וֹת עַל־בָּנִים֙ וְעַל־בְּנֵ֣י בָנִ֔ים עַל־שִׁלֵּשִׁ֖ים
וְעַל־רִבֵּעִֽים׃

> So Yahweh passed by [Moses] and called out:
> "Yahweh, Yahweh, a God compassionate [**rahum**] and gracious [ha-
> nun], slow to get angry but great in his *hesed* and *'emet*,
> who maintains *hesed* to thousands, and takes away wrongdoing
> ['avon], transgression [pesha'] and sin [hatta'ah],
> who will certainly not fail to punish, who will visit the fathers'
> wrongdoing ['avon] on the sons' sons, up to the grandchildren and
> great-grandchildren."

Hesed appears twice. Both the content and the context suggest that the essence of *hesed* is to surpass what has been earned. They have earned the death of the entire nation under the terms of the covenant. In v. 6, the greatness of God's *hesed* and *'emet* is set alongside his slowness to anger. In v. 7, God's willingness to forgive the assorted iniquities of thousands is described as his maintaining *hesed*, while his punishment is again much more limited. H. J. Stoebe points out that compassionate [*rahum*] and gracious [*hanun*] may be God's general disposition, but the following words indicate clearly his response to sin, so that his general attitude to

---

39. Moberly, "אָמַן," 1:428.

his people survives their failure to keep covenant. That is where *hesed* comes in.[40]

The self-revelation of Yahweh's character thus suggests that *hesed* is something which he guards by forgiving sin to a vastly greater extent than his prosecution of guilt.

> Divine חֶסֶד counteracts God's wrath. At times the biblical text suggests that God's *own* response to human sin runs in opposite directions. . . . The insight that, while both anger and love are appropriate divine responses, the latter outlasts the former, is an important one for biblical theology.[41]

> The *hesed* that is mentioned here cannot ignore human sinfulness, *but depends on, and consists of, the willingness to forgive sins.*[42]

The similarity with the formula in the Decalogue, but with the intensification of *hesed*, invites reflection on intervening events. God's gracious forbearance with the nation goes much further than his covenant obligations, and indeed overlooks their obligations. It is expressed in the ensuing renewal of the covenant in v. 10.[43] Thus, God's *hesed* is not only his electing to make an undeserved covenant, nor is it only his slanting the terms of the covenant to be more generous in rewards than he is severe in punishments. No, *hesed* here goes much further: when the nation breaches the most fundamental terms of that covenant and turns away from God entirely, God does not hand them over to the covenant sanctions, but forgives them.

This does not mean that *hesed* *always* goes beyond the covenant. While Num 14:19 appeals to *hesed* for the ongoing forgiveness of sin which Israel has persistently enjoyed, Deut 7:12 assures them that the covenant rewards will be enjoyed if they obey. Their reward for obedience is grounded in God's *hesed* to Israel's forefathers, in accordance with the

---

40. Stoebe, "חֶסֶד," 1:612–13.

41. Baer and Gordon, "חסד," 2:214.

42. "Das hier zugesagte *ḥǽsæd* kann nicht menschliche Sündhaftigkeit ignorieren, sondern *hat zur Voraussetzung und besteht in der Bereitschaft, Sünden zu vergeben*" (Stoebe, "חֶסֶד," 1:613; italics added).

43. Harris sees the sense of mercy clearly in Exod 34 and argues that it must always have been latent in the Exod 20 and Deut 5 texts, which only seem to speak of just retribution: loving those who love, cursing those who hate (Harris, "חסד," 306). I think this overlooks the imbalance in the detail of how that retribution is promised in those passages: it is not simply latent.

covenant.[44] Yet, behind this sense of faithfulness, there is God's persistent, undeserved disposition to bless the nation. As with the golden calf, so with the exile: Deuteronomy presents a covenant which anticipates national apostasy on a greater scale (Deut 29), and yet promises that even after that there will be gracious restoration for those who call on him (Deut 30). Since some psalms, and groups of psalms, are concerned with these great acts of redemption, we need to be especially careful not to misread the implications of finding *hesed* there.

Glueck's case was that *hesed* could involve grace in covenants, indirectly. The grace could be involved in entering into a covenant, but not in how it is administered. *Hesed* would involve enforcing a divine covenant in a strictly legal way, with no gracious latitude. However, as we have seen in Exod 32–34, that does not fit either the reality of God's covenant at Sinai or the way that *hesed* describes God's dealings, in two significant ways. First, the terms of God's covenants include a magnanimous asymmetry between reward and punishment, described as *hesed*. Second, even then, faced with human apostasy from the covenant, God's *hesed* drives him to go further than even those generous covenant stipulations and to show love and kindness in the face of recalcitrant behavior which is condemned by the covenant. Thus, God's *hesed* here gives rise to a covenant that is inherently *gracious*.[45] Moreover, *hesed* is not constrained by the terms of the covenant. On the contrary, *hesed* far exceeds the faithful application of the obligations of the covenant. As Hannes Olivier puts it:

> The promise of God's pardoning of sin and remittance of guilt is therefore to be seen as the basis of all God's blessings, *fundamentum huius beneficii* (Calvin). To designate God as the merciful redeemer from, and forgiver of, sins is perhaps the greatest achievement of OT times.[46]

From the terms of the covenant at Sinai, and God's response to apostasy from that covenant at the golden calf, we see that *hesed* has no *necessary* connection with obligations or faithfulness to covenant stipulations.[47] Even though obligation to a covenant or other arrangement

---

44. See also Mic 7:20; Ps 25:7; 89:50; 119:41, 76 (Baer and Gordon, "חֶסֶד," 2:216).

45. Von Rad points out that, while חֶסֶד is God's behavior arising from the covenant (as Glueck argued in *Das Wort hesed*, 38), yet Deuteronomy anchors God's decision to cut a covenant in the first place in his freely given oath to the Patriarchs (Von Rad, *Das Gottesvolk*, 69).

46. Olivier, "סָלַח," 3:262.

47. So also Zobel, "חֶסֶד," 5:70–71.

is frequently in the context of *hesed*, that obligation is not part of the meaning of *hesed*, but is indicated by the context.[48] *Hesed* is a loving kindness proper to God, by which he chooses to make a covenant with an undeserving nation. *Hesed* graciously slants the terms of that covenant to reward obedience more lavishly than it punishes disobedience. *Hesed* faithfully metes out the rewards for obedience, and yet is famous for withholding the punishment due for disobedience altogether. *Hesed* foresees the sinful collapse of the covenant and plans to respond once again by withholding the wages of sin and showering blessings on undeserving sinners: "the covenant comes in to reinforce the commitment to חֶסֶד in a situation where its exercise is not naturally to be expected or is likely to be put under strain by future circumstances."[49]

As a result, sinners can seek divine pardon by appealing to God's *hesed*, as in Num 14 above, and even ask God to choose between remembering sins or acting in *hesed*: Ps 25:7; 51:3.[50]

This need not mean, however, that particular sins are always in view when *hesed* is appealed to. R. Laird Harris notes that it is often paired with terms for mercy and concludes: "This attitude is parallel to love, *raḥûm* goodness, *ṭôb*, etc. It is a kind of love, including mercy, *ḥannûn*, when the object is in a pitiful state."[51] As we will see below, a pitiful state is not the same as a particular sin.

In conclusion, in the human sphere (which is the minority of occurrences) *hesed* does not involve strict merit, but goes beyond what is expected or required.[52] Similarly, God's *hesed* never falls short of giving the benefits promised when the stipulations have been met; however, when they are not met, *hesed* means mercy, gives more than is deserved and withholds punishment. *Hesed* responds to a background of sin, and shows a loving disposition towards undeserving sinful creatures. Its overarching historical expression is acts of deliverance that respond mercifully to national and personal sins.

A good gloss for *hesed* might therefore be "steadfast love." "Covenant love" leaves itself open to being understood as bound by the terms of the covenant. "Faithful love" could be taken the same way. "Lovingkindness"

---

48. Kellenberger, *ḥäsäd wä' ämät*, 48.

49. Baer and Gordon, "חֶסֶד," 2:212.

50. Baer and Gordon, "חֶסֶד," 2:216.

51. Harris, "חסד," 307.

52. Rad, *Theology of Israel's Historical Traditions*, 372n6; Stoebe, "חֶסֶד," 1:607–9.

and "goodness" are too general. God's *hesed* is a love that remains *steadfast* in the face of covenant breaking, even while rewarding covenant obedience. However, we will need to establish in each context what is in view: *hesed* as a kind of loyalty between people, or as Yahweh's determined loyalty? In either case, will it be a loyalty that gives what has been *earned*, or a *merciful* loyalty? In some cases, the ambiguity might be deliberate. We will see that in Ps 109 one use (fair treatment between people) is put in a context of a different use (divine mercy) and in turn points to another (merciful, rather than fair, treatment of enemies). We will therefore transliterate *hesed* throughout, to avoid prejudging the issue.

2.B.II. *The Meaning of* אֱמֶת *('emet)*

Its close association with *hesed* requires that *'emet* be treated here too: of only forty appearances in total, thirty-seven are in the Psalter, and sixteen of those are in parallel with *hesed*.[53]

The root אָמַן (*'aman*) denotes faith in the sense of confidence in something dependable, not possibility or vain hope.[54] In its various stems it can carry the sense of support or firm establishment.[55] The connection between subjective trust and objective salvation is seen in Isa 7:9, אִם לֹא תַאֲמִינוּ כִּי לֹא תֵאָמֵנוּ, "if you do not trust (*hip'il 'aman*) you will not be established (*nip'al 'aman*)."[56]

'emet is often a description of God's character and highlights his dependability and especially the trustworthiness of his words. It is extended to those who are in saving relationship to God as those who are trustworthy.[57]

If *hesed* is often linked with mercy, *'emet* is linked to justice:

> [I]t is often linked with "righteousness" (צְדָקָה / צֶדֶק) and sometimes also "justice" (מִשְׁפָּט) and other moral terms (e.g., Ps 15:2; 85:10 [11]; Isa 48:1; 59:14; Jer 4:2). The general significance of this is that Yahweh's faithfulness towards Israel is combined with

---

53. Wildberger sees the Psalms as the place where אֱמֶת comes to prominence (Wildberger, "אמן," 1:204–5).

54. Scott, "אָמַן," 51.

55. Scott, "אָמַן," 51–52.

56. Scott, "אָמַן," 52; Moberly, "אָמַן," 1:432. Moberly adds 2 Chr 20:20 (Scott, "אָמַן," 1:431).

57. Scott, "אָמַן," 52–53.

a strong sense of moral integrity and is in no sense morally lax or indifferent.[58]

As a result, the trustworthiness of God's commandments is an ethical one:

> When, however, the psalmist celebrates Yahweh's torah and commandments as אֱמֶת (Ps 119:43, 142, 151, 160), he does not just mean that they are true as opposed to false, but that they also have the character of being trustworthy and reliable for people to base their lives on. OT usage of אֱמֶת characteristically takes on such wider moral implications.[59]

On the other hand, Moberly argues that in Exod 34 the term indicates "Yahweh's willingness . . . to show his true nature through renewing the covenant with Israel despite their sin with the Golden Calf."[60]

I have argued as much for *hesed*, but *'emet* here might not refer to God's dishing up of undeserved grace, but rather to his faithfulness to the promises that he made to Abraham. That is the basis of Moses's appeal, to which God has responded. In Exod 32:12 Moses warns Yahweh that if he destroys Israel, he will come across as having evil intentions towards Israel; that would contradict his *hesed*. In v. 13 Moses appeals to the promise to the Patriarchs; to forfeit those promises would violate his *'emet*.

Contrary to Glueck's contention that *'emet* is epexegetical of *hesed*, the two terms are distinct.[61] *Hesed* is why Yahweh makes a commitment with Israel in the first place, why he makes a gracious covenant, and why he overlooks the breach of covenant; however, when that commitment is expressed in promises, *'emet* describes God's dependability to keep those promises. As Edgar Kellenberger argues, *'emet* relates to perseverance in one's intention.[62]

---

58. Moberly, "אָמַן," 1:429.
59. Moberly, "אָמַן," 1:428.
60. Moberly, "אָמַן," 1:428.
61. Wildberger, "אמן," 1:201–2. See the extended discussion of the two terms in Kellenberger, *ḥäsäd wä' ämät*.
62. Kellenberger, *ḥäsäd wä' ämät*, 98.

2.B.III. *The Meaning of* חָנַן *(hanan)/* חֵן *(hen)*

Hanan refers to bestowing favor. It is unilateral, freely given, does not entail any kind of commitment, and can be summarily withdrawn.[63] It is always from a superior to an inferior and involves condescension.[64]

It need not always be a response to sin: the righteous are promised that they will find *hen* (Prov 3:3–4).[65] However it certainly is not reserved for the perfect: it is offered to the repentant in Isa 30:19.[66] In Ps 41:5, God is asked to act according to *hen*, *because* the psalmist has sinned. God's willingness to forgive is thus expressed by *hen*.[67]

Hanan, then, is condescending favor, and God's character is such that he even shows it in the face of sin. That is an expression of *hesed* or of *raham*, to which we now turn.

2.B.IV. *The Meaning of* רָחַם *(raham),* רַחַם *(raham).*

In general, *raham* meets a need arising from trouble, weakness or sinfulness.[68] "The basic meaning of the root is . . . a compassion which goes the second mile, which is ready to forgive sin, to replace judgment with grace."[69] The verb especially stands in opposition to deserved wrath from God.[70] It is almost always God who stands behind *raham*: either as the agent, or as the one requiring that humans act in *raham*.[71]

Leonard Coppes summarizes as follows: "This root refers to deep love (usually of a 'superior' for an 'inferior') rooted in some 'natural' bond." It involves "natural mercy for the helpless." He brings out three elements: (1) unconditional election; (2) forgiveness despite guilt and worthiness of judgment, but only following repentance; (3) withholding judgment while people remain unrepentant. He sees unconditional election especially in the divine self-declaration which links this root with

---

63. Freedman et al., "חָנַן," 3:23–27.

64. Stoebe, "חנן," 1:590; Yamauchi, "חָנַן," 302–4.

65. Freedman, "חֵן," 3:32–40.

66. Fretheim, "חָנַן," 2:205.

67. Stoebe, "חנן," 1:595–96.

68. Simian-Yofre and Dahmen, "רחם," 7:475.

69. Butterworth, "רָחַם," 3:1094.

70. Stoebe, "רחם," 2:766.

71. Simian-Yofre and Dahmen, "רחם," 7:474.

hanan (Exod 33:19), "And I will be gracious to whom I will be gracious, and will show mercy on whom I will show mercy."[72]

In the Psalter, *raham* is naturally appropriate to sinners needing not only undeserved favor, but also favor when they have deserved wrath. That is the application to sinners of the "compassion to the helpless" which is the basic idea.

2.B.v. Combined Meaning in Exodus 34:6-7

Yahweh reveals his character in these terms, after failing to destroy Israel following their apostasy with the golden calf. We might explain the contribution of each term as follows. God *favors* (חָנַן, *hanan*) Israel, even in spite of this most grievous sin. Their sin puts them in mortal peril, and he *pities* them (רָחַם, *raham*) in their peril, and rescues them. His favor is therefore shown by being *slow to show the anger* which their sin has earned so spectacularly. They could hardly have breached the covenant more brazenly and totally; yet he keeps them under the blessings of the covenant, which not only vastly exceeds what they deserve but is positively the opposite of what they deserve: his *love* is *steadfast* (חֶסֶד, *hesed*) in the face of their betrayal. All of this, especially the covenant renewal, shows his determination to bless his people because of his own purposes, not being moved by their behavior. Even following their total apostasy, he displays *faithfulness* (אֱמֶת, *'emet*) to his purpose, as promised to Abraham.[73]

In Exod 34:9 Moses confesses the people's sin and yet dares to ask for Yahweh to act as he does to those who love him. Yahweh is, by nature, the one who "takes away wrongdoing, transgression and sin" (v. 7). That is why Moses can beg: "forgive our wrongdoing and our sin and keep us as your inheritance" (v. 9). Yahweh does so and renews the covenant.

For all this, we must note that the fullest display of the four grace terms and the terms for forgiveness, does not imply the absence of all punishment. In 32:27–35, three thousand are killed by the sword, and Yahweh further sends a plague. Similarly, David was restored and forgiven after his sins with Bathsheba and Uriah. The punishment he deserved was vastly commuted, but he was not without punishment (2 Sam 12:13–14).

---

72. Coppes, "רָחַם," 841–42.

73. For alternative accounts of how these terms relate in this verse, see: Stuart, *Exodus*, 715–16, who holds to a view similar to Glueck concerning חֶסֶד.

This pattern continues in other texts that allude to Exod 34:6–7: Num 14:18; Joel 2:13. In Num 14 Moses intercedes for the people as in Exod 34, Yahweh pardons them (Num 14:20) and yet all are punished by not entering the land (v. 22). In Joel 2, a great punishment would be averted on repentance (vv. 12–14, 20), but Joel 1 indicates that a lesser punishment has already begun (vv. 16–18).

2.B.vi. *These Terms for "Mercy" Do Not Always Imply Sin*

Each of the terms we have examined above are appropriate to situations where a person, or the whole nation, has sinned and is in need of forgiveness. However, they all have broader uses. We have seen that *hesed* can apply to giving a covenant partner what they have earned. Blessing such a partner is still an expression of faithfulness (*'emet*). Showing favor and pity on a covenant partner who is in trouble through no fault of their own can be expressed by *hanan* and *rahamah*. The same is true for words of salvation, such as deliverance, redemption, etc. (Hence my use of the broader "rescue" instead of "salvation.")

Christian readers of English translations of the Psalms habitually detect a confession of sin where there is none; we will need to look for actual indicators of wrongdoing and guilt.

2.C. Exodus 34 and the Structure of the Psalter

Even just in the opening verses of Ps 51 we find the terms for both grace (*rahum, hanun, hesed* and *'emet*) and sin (*'avon, pesha', hatta'ah*) that Yahweh used in his self-disclosure:

³חָנֵּנִי אֱלֹהִים כְּחַסְדֶּךָ כְּרֹב רַחֲמֶיךָ מְחֵה פְשָׁעָי:
⁴הֶרֶב כַּבְּסֵנִי מֵעֲוֹנִי וּמֵחַטָּאתִי טַהֲרֵנִי:
⁵כִּי־פְשָׁעַי אֲנִי אֵדָע וְחַטָּאתִי נֶגְדִּי תָמִיד:
⁶לְךָ לְבַדְּךָ ׀ חָטָאתִי וְהָרַע בְּעֵינֶיךָ עָשִׂיתִי לְמַעַן תִּצְדַּק בְּדָבְרֶךָ תִּזְכֶּה
בְשָׁפְטֶךָ
⁷הֵן־בְּעָווֹן חוֹלָלְתִּי וּבְחֵטְא יֶחֱמַתְנִי אִמִּי:
⁸הֵן־אֱמֶת חָפַצְתָּ בַטֻּחוֹת

3 [1] Be gracious [*hanan*] to me, O God, according to your *hesed*
     according to the greatness of your compassion [**rahamah**], rub out
         my transgressions [*pesha'*].
4 [2] Cleanse me thoroughly from my wrongdoing ['*avon*]
     and from my sin [*hatta'ah*] deem me clean.
5 [3] For my transgressions [*pesha'*] are what I know
     and my sins [**hatta'ah**] confront me constantly.
6 [4] It is against you—you alone—that I have sinned [**hatta'**]
     and what is evil in your sight is what I have done;
      so that you are justified when you make pronouncements
      and vindicated when you pass judgments.
7 [5] Look! It was in wrongdoing ['*avon*] that I was procreated,
     and in sin [*hatta'ah*] that my mother conceived me.
8 [6] Look! It is *'emet* that you delight in inwardly.

Claus Westermann correctly identifies Exod 32–34 as "breach and renewal of the covenant" entailing national apostasy. He saw it as the first of certain similar events in the history of Israel, which McCann expands to make the paradigm for all of Israel's history.[74] He sees the golden calf in the background of Ps 51 and concludes: "Israel's story, David's story, and the psalmist's story testify to the same reality—sin pervades the human situation."[75]

David, as king, was Israel's representative head, and broke five of the ten commandments in that episode.[76] According to the superscription, he confesses this incident in Ps 51. His allusions to that national apostasy might acknowledge his awareness that the sin of the king is on a par with national sin.[77] Such corporate solidarity with the nation was not unknown to David: 2 Sam 21:1; 24:10–14.

74. Westermann, *Elements*, 50; McCann, *Psalms as Torah*, 103–4.

75. McCann, *Psalms as Torah*, 103.

76. McCann, *Psalms as Torah*, 102.

77. Eaton sees Ps 51 as the king taking upon himself the burden of the whole people (Eaton, *Kingship*, 178). Wenham suggests that in this Psalm David is interceding for the whole nation's sin, like Moses (Wenham, "Reading the Psalms Canonically," 51).

David, in Ps 51, is not only acknowledging the extent to which his behavior was a high-handed rebellion against Yahweh. He is also making a connection with the nation. Psalm 3 had shown a typological correspondence between David being punished after the incident with Bathsheba, and the fate of Israel after the apostasy that led to exile. Now David connects himself to the first great act of national apostasy.

There are three further references to Exod 34:6–7 in the Psalms: Pss 86:15; 103:8; 145:8.[78] All three are David psalms and suggestively placed: Ps 86 is the only David psalm in Book III, while Pss 103 and 145 are each the last psalm of the last David collection in Books IV and V, respectively. The latter introduces the final doxology, so David figures as the representative of Israel, enjoying God's mercy after national apostasy, not only in every Book, but also framing the Psalter. Psalm 3 follows the Psalter's introduction, and Ps 145 precedes, and leads to, its conclusion. We will see this in more detail when we examine the structure of Book V.

Wilson had claimed, controversially, that David and the Davidic kingdom recede after Book III and the exile. Others see David remaining highly relevant post-exile in the Psalter. Martin Kleer has traced the various groups of David psalms through their place in the Psalter, and argues that a story emerges encompassing the five Books of the Psalter. He sees a future David being promised in Book V who addresses the issues of exile. The David superscriptions particularly gave the exiles a point of identification.[79] David offers them solidarity, as they partake of his fate.[80] Gillingham, similarly, sees the connection between David and the Levites as founders of the cult in the temple. The Psalter's 73 David superscriptions connect the personal piety of David with the Temple cult over which they presided together. In this way, the post-exilic Levites stand in the place of Moses and of David as teachers of the nation in the cult.[81]

To this general sense that David teaches the exilic and post-exilic nation through his psalms, we add the way that Ps 3 introduces him as a type of exilic Israel, and the way that Ps 51 re-introduces David as a representative king, who received mercy after apostatizing, as the nation had after the golden calf.

---

78. Scharbert, "Formgeschichte und Exegese," 133.

79. Kleer, *"Der liebliche Sänger,"* 86.

80. Kleer, *"Der liebliche Sänger,"* 93.

81. Gillingham, "The Levites," 209; see also Blenkinsopp, *David Remembered*, 111.

As Tobias Häner notes, Ps 51 could be expected to disqualify David as model follower and teacher of Torah, since he has fallen so far short with his sin. The opposite turns out to be true: he is an excellent model of Torah, and teacher of Torah, because his contrite response to his sin, his repentance are part of what those who love Yahweh must display when faced with sin. Moreover, he stands for the whole nation as he does so.[82]

For the exiles, the prayers of David provide highly relevant instruction in how to pray. Like David, they have earned their punishment and it has been prophesied. Like Absalom, Babylon was acting wickedly even while being the means of punishment. In both cases, a divine word promised respite. As we have seen, David in Ps 3 teaches the nation to pray from a position of needing mercy and to the end of blessing their enemies.

Hossfeld specifically suggests that *exilic* redactors wanted Ps 3 to be read against the Absalom narrative.[83] McCann argues that Ps 1 (dealing with judgment) and Ps 2 (dealing with national issues) is followed by a book of individual laments (3–41), in order to teach exilic Israel how to deal with exile as the "I" of David's laments.[84] This is further reinforced when we place the Book of Psalms in its canonical context.

---

82. Häner, "David als Vorbeter," 28.

83. Hossfeld-Zenger I:57.

84. McCann 661.

8

Retribution in Book I

Psalm 7

IN THESE NEXT TWO chapters, we examine retribution in two notorious Psalms within Book I of the Psalter: Psalm 7 in this chapter, Psalm 18 in the next. Psalm 7 is generally considered to be imprecatory, while Ps 18 is an extended celebration after victory over enemies.

We are testing the ethical distance between the OT and the NT in these Psalms, and especially examining the assumption that psalms of retribution: require perfect innocence; appeal to merit with no awareness of the speaker's need for mercy; fail to display any mercy to the opponent; and are incapable of conceiving of forgiving the enemy or of the possibility that the enemy could repent.

While I do not claim that every psalm dealing with enemies displays the opposite of these assumptions, I will show that at least some psalms falsify this assumed ethical distance, as we were led to expect by the opening of the Psalter. Whatever differences there are between the Psalter and the NT cannot be attributed simply to the psalmists' epochal blindness, because such blindness would lead to a consistent display of these failures in every psalm.

We saw in Ps 1 that there is judgment to vindicate the righteous and defeat the wicked. Psalm 2 warns about this judgment, throwing open the invitation of repentance and refuge to the wicked. Psalm 3 shows that the righteous does not always desire retributive justice against his enemies, but sometimes desires that they live and be blessed. In the light of Pss 1 and 2, this implies that they repent, seek refuge, and find blessing.

In Book I, we also find three basic stances of desire for the wicked, apart from the urgent desire of relief through judgment. First, there is a general disposition in some psalms to warn and teach those who might act wickedly, so that they escape judgment. Second, when the enemy is defeated, celebration and prayer does not always focus on destruction, but instead on the repentance and blessing of the defeated enemy. Even though this may not be the dominant note of the Book, we have seen that it is frequently assumed in discussions of imprecations and the Psalms, that no-one in the OT could love their enemies or imagine the possibility of their repentance. Third, some psalms ask for much less than proportional retribution. They may not outright ask for blessing on enemies, but they stop short of asking for what is deserved, which is thought to be inconceivable (or even immoral) in the OT.

Book I is the most negative towards the enemy, and where most of the imprecations are found.[1] Palmer Robertson writes of Book I: "It is difficult, if not impossible, to find a single passage in which some form of blessing might be extended towards an enemy."[2] These examples in Book I are surprising and significant. We will see that they are seeds of an attitude which is displayed more fully in Book V.[3] This is not to deny that proportional retribution is found in Book I, but to show that it is not *always* there.

In Psalm 7, we will see that the supplicant is neither perfect nor self-righteous. He does protest innocence of crimes from which he is falsely accused, but that is not the same as delusions of perfection. We will further see an attitude to the enemy that warns them about judgment, desiring them to repent. Moreover, he is content for the repentant enemy to escape justice. There is no hint of vengeance.

---

1. So Jauss, "Fluchpsalmen beten?," 107–15.

2. Robertson, *Flow of the Psalms*, 102–3.

3. Some see a direct instance of prayer for the enemy in 41:11 [10]. Goldingay argues for translating "and I will be friends with them," meaning that David desires victory over enemies so that he can then *make peace* (in line with the use of שׁלם in the previous verse), rather than the more natural translation of שׁלם as *repay* (Goldingay 1:581, 586–87). However, in poetry the positive sense of שׁלם involves fulfilment of a vow, while the only other sense is of repayment of a debt, including retaliation (Eisenbeis, *Die Wurzel שׁלם*, 312). Either sense excludes rewarding good for evil. See also Erbele-Küster, *Lesen*, 124–25.

1. The Setting of Psalm 7

Unusually, the superscription places the prayer in an incident which is named but not identifiable.[4] The imagery of Ps 7 fits a number of possible situations, so that the perspective of one incident can be used to reflect on "a wide sweep of David's experiences."[5] Somebody is trying to kill David (vv. 2–3 [1–2]), accusing him of a crime (vv. 4–6 [3–5]), with malicious intent (vv. 10 [9], 15–17 [14–16]). David appeals for a divine verdict to settle the matter (vv. 4–12 [3–11]). Yahweh's judgment will be just (v. 12 [11]), and therefore vindicate David (v. 11 [10]). The central issue in the psalm is false accusation.

Two broad scenarios can be imagined. First, the enemy might be using the courts to kill David, accusing him of a capital crime, in which case David's appeal to Yahweh is part of the judicial process.[6] Second, the enemy might be waging war against David, justifying the action through accusations of sin: the Absalom usurpation which we examined in Ps 3 would be a good example. In that case, the appeal would be metaphorically judicial: the enemy's military defeat would be the divine judge's vindication of David.

The enemy is plural in v. 2 [1] (מִכָּל־רֹדְפַי, *mikkol-rodfay*, "all who pursue me") but singular in v. 3 [2] ("in case he tears [יִטְרֹף, *yitrof*] my life apart like a lion"). This leads to emendations which lack textual support.[7] However, those who adjust these two verses are being too selective: the psalm switches between singular and plural throughout: for example, v. 6

---

4. Johnson, *David in Distress*, 133–39.

5. Berger, "The David-Benjaminite Conflict," 290–91.

6. Ruppert, *Jesus*, 17n9.

7. There is no uncertainty in the Hebrew MSS: L and Alep all have a plural in v. 2 and singular in v. 3. So also LXX (Rahlfs, *Psalmi*, 87). These verses are lacking in DSS. L agrees with Alep entirely, save in the pointing of the vocal *shevah* in vv. 5, 7, where L has צוֹרְרָי and צוֹרְרָי (*LC* 744 is very clear; reflected in *BHS*; *BHL*) and Alep has צוֹרְרָי, and צוֹרְרָי (*AC*, תפד has faded consonants in places, but the pointing is very clear; reflected in *MGH* I:20). The *Masorah* mark this as a *hapax* in v. 5 in both MSS—a warning to scribes not to "correct" what looks odd. Such compound *shevahs* under non-gutturals are not unusual (GKC §10g; Joüon §9b). Kraus and Leveen emend מִכָּל־רֹדְפִי in v. 2 to מֵרֹדְפִי (Kraus 1:190; Leveen, "Textual Problems," 439), though there is no MSS evidence for this. ESV translates v. 3 with a plural, as do many English translations, perhaps following Craigie's logic: "'They'; literally, 'he,' though the reference is to the 'pursuers,'" (Craigie, *Psalms 1–50*, 97). LXX makes v. 5 plural (Rahlfs, *Psalmi*, 87).

[5] is singular, v. 7 [6] plural.[8] The superscription points to an individual (Cush); however, like Absalom, Cush may be the head of a more numerous enemy. He should certainly be understood to belong to a multitude.[9] The heads of armies represent the whole.[10] The alternating singulars and plurals of MT are widely retained.[11]

The imagery of war and hunting is apt both for a physical confrontation (from which David would appeal to God's metaphorical law court) or for a capital crime accusation in court. In either scenario, life hangs in the balance.[12] It can therefore serve as a model for anyone facing false charges that lead to death, whether in a literal court, armed insurrection, or mob justice.[13]

2. A Conditional Self-Malediction: vv. 2–5 [1–4]

The psalm opens by pleading for deliverance from pursuers lest they tear him apart.

2 [1] save me from all who pursue me [רֹדְפַי, *rodfay*]
3 [2] lest, like a lion, they tear me [נַפְשִׁי, *nafshi* "my neck," a common metaphor for the self, often rendered "soul"] apart

Then David invites God to let them do exactly that:[14]

6 [5] let the enemy pursue [יִרְדֹּף, *yirdof / yeraddef*[15]] me [נַפְשִׁי, *nafshi*] and overtake me

8. ESV *does* translate a singular in v. 5b; Kraus claims there are elsewhere only singulars, but he himself translates with a plural in v. 7b. Targums follow MT (*Tg. Ps.* 7:2–5).

9. Firth, *Surrendering*, 23. For example, Targums identify him as Saul the son of Kish (*Tg. Ps.* 7:1). Other options include Kirkpatrick 1:29; Goldingay 1:144.

10. *Contra* Buttenwieser: "Since, then, 'the enemy' of verses 3, 5–6, and 14–17 is a hostile force, the view that the psalm is the plea of an individual has no basis in fact" (Buttenwieser, *Psalms*, 414).

11. Kirkpatrick 1:30–31; Kimhi, *Psalms*, 41; Ravasi 52; Seybold 45; Goldingay 1:142; Vesco 131n1; Ross 1:279–80; Ḥakham, *Psalms 1–57*, 33; Hossfeld-Zenger I:75; Darby, LEB, NASB, YLT, and *Tg. Ps.* 7:2–3.

12. Goldingay 1:152.

13. Firth, *Surrendering*, 21–22.

14. Craigie, *Psalms 1–50*, 101.

15. "[T]he vocalisation of יִרְדֹּף Ps 7.6 indicates that one can read it either as Qal יִרְדֹּף or Piel יְרַדֵּף" (Joüon §16g; so also Kraus 1:191). This is found in L (*BHS; BHL*) and Alep (*MGH* I:20). The difference in *binyan* does not seem significant (*HALOT*

This perplexing invitation is contingent on his guilt of a particular charge:[16]

4 [3] Yahweh, my God, if I have done this,[17]
    if there is wrongdoing in the palms of my hands,
5 [4] if I have repaid evil to one who was at peace with me,

The final verset is notoriously difficult.[18] Of course, it invites numerous conjectural emendations, none of which are convincing.[19] Here are three possible ways of understanding it:

1191–92; *BDB* 922–23).

16. The two אם protases lay out the charges (Kirkpatrick 1:30; Ravasi 54).

17. Leveen's emendation of זאת to זמת "as there is nothing antecedent to which it can refer" (Leveen, "Textual Problems," 440) is not compelling. True, the relative pronoun usually refers to its antecedent (Joüon §§145c, 158a; GKC §§138, 155). However, Gesenius does not let his own rule stop him in discussing this verse: "e. g. Ps 7:4 ff. 'ג וְ רֹדֵף ... אִם־עָשִׂיתִי זֹאת *if I have done this . . . , let the enemy pursue my soul*, &c." (GKC §159m). It takes a certain lack of imagination to fail to see the poet's device here. The pursuit of David's life is through a courtroom setting, with false charges. The antecedent then is the metaphorical pursuit described in the previous verse, which the psalm will go on to identify as false accusation, with murderous intent. Kraus defends the text *contra* Gunkel's entirely conjectural emendations (Kraus 1:191). MT is followed by Seybold 45; Kirkpatrick 1:30.

18. A comprehensive survey of historical views is given by Tigay, "Psalm 7.5," 178–86.

19. LXX has, sometimes, ἀποπέσοιν ἄρα ἀπό, from ἀποπίπτω, "to fall from" or "miss" or "fail." Other traditions have ἀποπέσοιμι, which cannot be found in any standard lexicon (LSJ; L&N; BDAG; Lust et al., *Lexicon of the Septuagint*; Muraoka, *Lexicon*). Rahlfs directs us to the reference grammars by Curtius and Kühner, presumably for this reason (Rahlfs, *Psalmi*, 87). Kraus reports only this verb: "ἀποπέσοιμι ἀπό = וְאֶלְחֲצָה," in line with Syriac and Targums, but retains MT with "beraubt" (Kraus 1:191–92). However, I cannot find this verb given as a translation for לחץ, nor attested in this verse, in either of Muraoka, *Septuagint*; Tov, *Parallel Aligned Text*. Certainly the simple transposition of לחץ for חלץ is elegant, and the meaning of "oppress" is somewhat fitting. Targums also imply such a reading (Stec, *The Targum of Psalms*, 35n8). Targums and both LXX options are probably best explained as trying to make sense of the final floating adverb. L (*BHS*; *BHL*) and Alep (*MGH* I:20) agree with each other. Both mark the word as a *hapax*—a warning to scribes against corrections. MT is retained by Kraus 1:191; Seybold 45; Ravasi 52; Hossfeld-Zenger I:74n5b; Kirkpatrick 1:31n7; Ross 1:274n7.

5b [4b] [*or have despoiled my enemy empty of cause*[20] OR
rather I have rescued the one who was against me empty of cause[21]
OR *and have set free my enemy in vain*[22]]

All interpretive options of this verset are part of a protestation of innocence and develop the third protasis. None of the options undermine
the basic idea that David is denying a particular charge.

Thus, if David has done what he is accused of, acting without provo-
cation and repaying evil for peace (cf. 35:12; 38:21–22 [20–21]), he agrees
that his pursuers have just cause and should prevail. Requests for retribution in the Psalms must cause the one praying to consider that someone
might be entitled to pray against him.[23]

---

20. רֵיקָם always means empty, usually empty-handed (Gen 31:42; Exod 3:21; 23:15;
34:20; Deut 15:13; 16:16; 1 Sam 6:3; 2 Sam 1:22; Isa 55:11; Jer 14:3; 50:9; Job 22:9; Ruth
1:21; 3:17). It is an adverb, not an adjective (cf. רֵיק), so it cannot mean that the enemy
was empty-handed when plundered. This translation implies that in Ps 7, in context,
the hands are empty of due cause for despoiling the enemy. Lexica seem to create a
needless separate sense of "without cause" (*HALOT* 1229; Clines, "רֵיקָם," 7:485), which
is an attestation of the same sense. Translations in this vein include Seybold 45; Ravasi
52. Another option is that it is the enemy who was empty, that is to say, unsuccessful as
an enemy, going away from an attack empty handed (*BDB* 938). In that case, the idea
would be that the psalmist has gone and despoiled the enemy even though the enemy
had not actually managed to steal anything. Either way, the psalmist would have no
due cause for his actions against the enemy. The major difficulty is that the *pi' el* חלץ
means "rescue" and is not attested as meaning despoil.

21. This option understands חלץ as "rescue," and רֵיקָם as modifying the enemy (as
the option above). See Kirkpatrick 1:31; Ross 1:274. A hybrid of the two options above
is given by Kraus: "und beraubt den, der grundlos mich bedrängt" (Kraus 1:190),
which implies that David is being oppressed by someone who claims that David stole
from him, when he did not. That fits the overall idea of the psalm. So also Hossfeld-
Zenger I:73–75. All the above are represented in English translations, and NET has yet
another option: "or helped his lawless ally."

22. Berger has cogently argued for this understanding, where רֵיקָם modifies not
the enemy but the rescue; he convincingly criticizes the various textual emendations,
argues against the implausible meaning of "plunder" for חלץ, but also insists that רֵיקָם
cannot modify the enemy (Berger, "The David-Benjaminite Conflict," 286–87). Particularly elegant is the context of the superscription: Berger argues that this verset
looks back to the cave at En-Gedi, where David indeed set Saul free, rather than killing
him at the urging of his men. Now, he finds himself persecuted by Saul again; thus,
his earlier act of setting Saul free has been for nothing (Berger, "David-Benjaminite
Conflict," 288). Targums strengthen what is unique to Berger's translation: they render
רֵיקָם as מגן (*Tg. Ps.* 7:5), which has the senses of gratis and of in vain (Jastrow 729), and
can only really qualify the rescue and not the enemy. (But, as noted above, Targums do
not see the main verb as "rescue," but as "oppress.")

23. Zenger, *God of Vengeance?*, 76; Davis, *Getting Involved with God*, 28.

The fact is that he has not "done this." Klaus Seybold even renders these verses as a contra-factual condition.[24] David may not be sinless, but he is innocent of whatever charges they are bringing against him. If he were guilty of the *specific* sins at issue, he would have no grounds for asking God to deliver him.[25] He admits as much, and demonstrates his innocence by expecting deliverance, as we will see in the following verses. First, we will briefly notice his second line of defense: the accusation against him is malicious.

3. Malicious Perjury, Not Mistaken Testimony: v. 15 [14]

David's second line of defense is the malicious intent behind the accusations. The accusers are not innocently mistaken: they are wicked manufacturers of false testimony:[26]

15 [14] Look!
> He is pregnant with evil,
>> and[27] he has conceived harm,
>> and he has begotten perjury [שֶׁקֶר, *sheqer*].

As we saw in ch. 6, §4 (pp. 108–11), the use of שֶׁקֶר (*sheqer*) strongly suggests false accusation, hence "perjury." It indicates a breach of law, especially by lying witnesses. Where an individual is pleading in a psalm, it always concerns perjury in court.[28] There is special legislation where an accuser is bringing a case that would lead to the physical punishment of the accused (Deut 19). Both parties must present themselves to the presence of Yahweh, namely, the priests and judges.[29] The outcome is that either the guilty accused is punished, or the false witness receives the exact same punishment. In the absence of witnesses, an oath as part of

---

24. "wenn ich das getan hätte, wenn . . . wäre . . . Wenn . . . hätte" (Seybold 45).

25. Craigie, *Psalms 1–50*, 100–101.

26. Goldingay 1:144; Schaefer, *Psalms*, 21; Kirkpatrick 1:33; Firth, *Surrendering*, 21.

27. Nothing much hinges on whether the *waw* of וְהָרָה is omitted. It is present in L and Alep, marked as occurring twice by the *Masorah* (*MGH* I:תפד; *LC*, 744). According to *BHS* it (presumably, καί) is lacking in some few LXX MSS (so also Leveen, "Textual Problems," 443), though Rahlfs does not mention this (Rahlfs, *Psalmi*, 88).

28. Klopfenstein, *Die Lüge*, 45, 80.

29. This may imply a visit to the sanctuary; that is what Schmidt envisages in classifying this psalm as a "Gebet des Angeklagten" (cited by Eissfeldt, *The Old Testament*, 119). So also Merrill, *Deuteronomy*, 280; K&D 1:938; *contra* Tigay, *Deuteronomy*, 184.

a judicial ordeal could sometimes suffice in court.[30] However, not so in this type of accusations. Deuteronomy 19 leaves David no choice but to submit to the investigation of the priests and judges.[31] The only way David can avoid death is by Yahweh's issue of a righteous judgment through the court.

His self-imprecation in v. 6 [5] means that he is not wagering on the court's failure to uncover his guilt, but appealing to God for a righteous outcome. David is relying on justice, not trying to save his skin unjustly (unlike his cover-up following his adultery in 2 Sam 11). If God does not act, there will be "no deliverer" (v. 3 [2]; אֵין מַצִּיל, 'en matsil).[32] The justice of God is at stake when the innocent are on trial.[33]

There is some disagreement over חבל (habal) in the first verset, and the significance of the tense of the three verbs. The general point is clear enough. I have represented the different tenses so that the first two versets show a process that has not yet borne fruit (the evil of a death sentence on David, for which the accusers hope) while the final verset shows what has already been brought forth, namely the false witnessing that has David in court already. David is praying for a miscarriage within the metaphor, not a miscarriage of justice. While the evil and harm have not yet happened, the perjury has.

We saw David at prayer in the Absalom incident in Ps 3. He was falsely accused by Absalom, but conscious that this false accusation was divine judgment against him. In Ps 7, matters are different. There is no indication that David has earned the evil that is against him. How will he

---

30. Vaux, *Ancient Israel*, 157; Ravasi 54.

31. Johnston assesses the case for finding certain specific ordeal rituals in the Psalter, and concludes that they are lacking (Johnston, "Ordeals in the Psalms?," 271–92).

32. פָּרֵק in this verset causes some confusion and suggested emendations, as described by Kraus 1:191. However, this need not detain us, because the verb is redundant. As it stands, it repeats the idea of the first line (tearing to pieces); *pace* Kraus' argument that this would require emendation to a *yiqtol* and placement before the *atnah*. If it is read with Kraus, adding a second אֵין, it restates the idea of the final verb (no-one to rescue). If the text is left alone, it is a good example of Alter's idea of intensification (not only tearing in pieces, but also without rescue) and of Berlin's demonstration of poetic changes in verb form (from *yiqtol* in the first verset to participles in the second). The imagery would then be vivid: "picture me being torn and *still* no-one saving me." MT is identical in L (*BHS*; *BHL*) and Alep (*AC*, תפד), and retained by Seybold 45; Kirkpatrick 1:30; Ravasi 52; Hossfeld-Zenger I:75n3. *Contra* Leveen, "Textual Problems," 440.

33. Kraus, *Theologie der Psalmen*, 195.

pray about his enemies when they have no leg to stand on and when he has no reason to doubt the justice of his own case?

4. May God Stop Their Evil Deeds: vv. 7–10 [6–9]

David asks Yahweh to defend him against his enemies:

7 [6] Arise, O Yahweh, in your wrath!
> Lift yourself up against[34] the rage of my enemies!
> Awake, O my God:[35]
>> a judgment you have commanded.[36]

. . .

10 [9] Let the evil of the wicked cease,[37]

34. This is taking ב as adversative in בְּעַבְרוֹת, (cf. Joüon §133c, and so Kraus 1:191; Ravasi 52; Seybold 47; Hossfeld-Zenger I:75; Vesco 132). Targums understand this differently: ברוגזא על מעיקי "lift yourself in fury against my oppressors" (Stec, *The Targum of Psalms*, 36).

35. It does not make a difference to this point whether אֵלַי be understood as "for me" (אֶל + suffix) or "my God" (אֵל, with a plural of majesty, + suffix). Both options are offered by Vesco 132n1. On "for me" see Kraus 1:190; Kirkpatrick 1:1:32; Seybold 45; Tg. Ps. 7:7; Kimhi, *Psalms*, 43. On "my God" see Goldingay 1:143g; Ravasi 52; Hossfeld-Zenger I:73.

36. The implicit relationship between the clauses is taken in different ways and with minor emendations (GKC §156d; Rashi, *Psalms*, 194; Seybold 45; Kirkpatrick 1:32; Ravasi 52; Vesco 132n1). However, some move the first phrase of v. 9 to here and change the perfect to an imperative (so EÜ, and described in Kraus 1:191, rejected by Hossfeld-Zenger I:75). These are needless, and destroy the consistent triads of this poem: three pleas (vv. 2b, 3); three אִם clauses (vv. 4b, 5); three self-imprecations (v. 6); three petitions (v. 7); two triads of judgment (vv. 9, 10).

37. MT has יִגְמָר־נָא (L and Alep, clearly readable in *LC*, 744; *AC*, תפד), a straightforward fientive *yiqtol*, where the loss of stress has reduced the final *holam* to a *qamtes-hatuf*. The verb is not very common, but the use in 12:2 would be similar: the subject will come to an end. In this case, the evil of the wicked is to come to an end, with נָא implying a jussive meaning. Kraus thinks that to make the verb intransitive (which it already is, on the above reading), it should be read as יִגְמַר, (Kraus 1:191). However, this would make it stative, which is unnecessary; it is already intransitive. *HALOT* 197, similarly solves the non-problem by repointing as an imperative, removing the י as dittography from the close of the preceding verse. MT is kept and translated intransitively by common translations, including Seybold 45; Kirkpatrick 1:33; Hossfeld-Zenger I:76. Craigie is convincing: "Though it is possible that the verb גמר 'finish, end' may carry the sense 'avenge' in certain contexts, that sense is unlikely in this context. The simplest way of interpreting the alternation from 3rd pers (יגמר) to 2nd pers (תכונן) 'establish') is to understand רע 'evil' as the subject of the first verb, and יהוה 'Lord' (v 9—implied here) as the subject of the second" (Craigie, *Psalms 1–50*, 98). Harmonizing this apparent problem is Ravasi 52, who translates both verbs as imperatives. All of

but establish the righteous,[38]
tester[39] of hearts and kidneys—
O righteous God![40]

David responds to the threat by appealing to an incorruptible court. His case is simple: the accusations are false. He lays out his defense in two parts: first, he is innocent of the charges; second, the accusers are malicious liars. Both arguments rest on Yahweh's infallible justice.

David asks God to act against the enemies, but not for retribution; after all the pleas for God to rouse himself against them (vv. 7–9 [6–8]), in v. 10 [9] it is the evil deeds, not the people themselves, which David wants to see at an end.[41] David wants his accuser to cease and desist. It is this very thing which is supposed to be impossible for David, "the Old Testament saint." It is denied that he could view the sinful acts apart from the person committing them. It is alleged that David saw the destruction of wicked *evildoers* as the only possible end of their wicked *deeds*; repentance is supposed to have been alien to OT thinking (ch. 2, §5.B, pp. 11–14). Here, David sees that the wicked will only be judged if they fail to repent.

It would be tempting to go further and accept a suggested repointing of רַע (*ra'* evil/trouble) to רֹעַ (*roa'* wickedness).[42] This would not merely

---

the suggested readings agree on one thing: "no more wickedness of the wicked, please."

38. Leveen's assertion: "This verse member seems to be incomplete" is groundless; the text makes sense as it stands (Leveen, "Textual Problems," 441).

39. Leveen's suggestion that ו be understood as misreading י so that the *waw*-particle is a *yiqtol*, in line with the opening verb, is attractive. L is perfectly legible (*LC* 744), while Alep is illegible here in facsimile (*AC* תפד), though transcribed as L in *MGH* I:22. Nonetheless, the *Masorah* offer nothing here and the early corruption is not to be ruled out as a possibility. However, the syntax is explained by Delitzsch 104.

40. Verse 10 ends with אֱלֹהִים צַדִּיק, which Rashi calls God's name (Rashi, *Psalms*, 195), and Kimhi takes as the subject of the second half of the verse (Kimhi, *Psalms*, 45; so also Goldingay 1:148). LXX moves צַדִּיק to the start of the next verse, with different traditions having different forms (δικαία or δικαίως). This is presumably because of the difficult opening of that verse. Leveen offers all manner of cutting, pasting and emendations (Leveen, "Textual Problems," 441). The basic point remains: while MT explicitly ends v. 10 by calling God righteous, LXX tells us that the help which David receives from God in v. 11 is righteous, and names God explicitly as the examiner of hearts and kidneys in v. 10. If the one who thoroughly examines David gives him *righteous* help, then he must be a righteous judge. There are various other small textual issues listed by *BHS* for v. 10, but they are inconsequential to our investigation.

41. Delitzsch 104.

42. Leveen, "Textual Problems," 441. Kraus accepts the change and translates

ask that the evildoer stop these evil acts against David, but that they be ethically transformed as well. This is not inconsistent with the theology of the Psalter elsewhere.[43] However, the textual evidence within the MT is firmly against such a change, with a very explicit warning to scribes not to tamper with this word.[44]

5. David Is Not Guilty and God Will Judge Rightly: vv. 9–12 [8–11]

He appeals to a judge who is unfailingly righteous, who tests the inner man infallibly. David had begun by claiming that he would deserve his persecution if he were guilty, and then appealed for God to bring the evil against him to an end, indirectly asserting his innocence. He also states this outright:

> . . .
>
> 9b [8b] judge me, O Yahweh, according to my righteousness
>> and according to my perfection [וּכְתֻמִּי עָלָי, *uketummi 'alay*].[45]

"Bosheit" (Kraus 1:191), as does Hossfeld (Hossfeld-Zenger I:76). Ravasi seems to hedge, by exegeting as *"malizia"* (malice), despite his translation as *"male"* (evil/trouble; Ravasi 54, 52). Ravasi's equivocation suggests why it would have been easy for the LXX to translate as they did and why commentators—especially in the Christian tradition—favor the emendation: it is in the spirit of Mark 7:20–23. The thought is similar, whichever word is chosen. Seybold does not mention the issue and translates "Frevel" (Seybold 45; likewise, Kirkpatrick 1:33). The repointing would be supported by LXX πονηρία, which in the singular refers to a wicked attitude, and only in the plural to wicked deeds (LSJ, *ad loc*).

43. Wenham, *Psalms as Torah*, 115.

44. Both Alep and L clearly show רַע| (*LC* 744; *AC* תפד). The text as pointed could mean either "evil" or "trouble," and this is clarified for us in *Mp*, which notes that it is unusual to point רַע with a *patah* rather than a *qamets*: "One of nine cases of רַע; and רַע also occurs in all cases where the reference is to speaking evil, an evil imagination or intention, doing evil, or appearing evil in one's eyes, with 7 exceptions" (Kelley et al., *The Masorah*, 76). According to *Mp*, then, ethical evil and not unfortunate trouble is in view, but evil can include either deeds or attitudes, even if not quite the abstraction of "wickedness."

45. The consonants in Alep are very faint (*AC* תפד), but in my judgment clearly עָלָי, as transcribed by *MGH* I:22. L is very clear (*LC* 744). Various explanations of MT as it stands are in Kraus 1:191; Goldingay 1:148; Seybold 45; Hossfeld-Zenger I:76; Ross 1:275n15. Emendations are offered by Ravasi 52; Leveen, "Textual Problems," 441. *All* these options still clearly imply that perfection is the grounds for action, since the phrase twice appeals "according to *my* righteousness" and "according to *my* perfection."

. . .

11 [10] My shield is God—[46]
    rescuer of those with upright heart.
12 [11] *Elohim* is a righteous judge
    and a god[47] who is indignant every day.[48]

     David expects God to inspect the evidence and vindicate him. What is he claiming? First, as we have seen, David is not claiming to be completely sinless all the time, and therefore axiomatically "not guilty" of any crime.[49] This does not accord well with the way that he has been introduced to Book I via Ps 3. It also does not make good sense of David's lengthy explanation that he *would* deserve punishment if he were guilty followed by his entrusting himself to God who will judge the facts. One who were always sinless could say as much more compactly. I have rendered תֹּם (*tom*) above as "perfection" to avoid hiding the issue, but it is often rightly taken to mean something more qualified, such as "integrity" in various contexts.[50] As Giovanni Diodati comments, his defense is "not any way concerning . . . the rigour of the law."[51] Second, while John Goldingay rightly notes that "the world can be divided into the faithful and faithless," I do not think that here "the suppliant claims to belong to the

46. Following Ravasi 53. The textual problem of מָגִנִּי עַל־אֱלֹהִים (my shield is on God) seems overblown. Psalm62:8 has עַל־אֱלֹהִים יִשְׁעִי וּכְבוֹדִי (on God is my salvation and my glory), which is perfectly intelligible. The *Masorah* (L and Alep) point us to that text by marking עַל־אֱלֹהִים as ב. Remembering that "shield" is a common metaphor for protection, frequently used in the Psalms of divine protection, the sense seems clear enough, and translations such as the Targum "My shield is with the Lord" capture it well (Stec, *The Targum of Psalms*, 36). LXX has a variety of efforts (Rahlfs, *Psalmi*, 87–88) and it is omitted in Syr. See further the proposals in Kraus 1:190; Goldingay 1:143; Seybold 45–47; Hossfeld-Zenger I:74n11a; Kirkpatrick 1:33n10.

47. The switch from אֱלֹהִים to אֵל perhaps contrasts Israel's God with the gods of the nations, by virtue of his dependably just judgment.

48. The phrase וְאֵל זֹעֵם בְּכָל־יוֹם causes some difficulties. Early LXX MSS do not offer an equivalent phrase for it, others move it to before a phrase that has no Hebrew equivalent (Rahlfs, *Psalmi*, 88). However, in the main, LXX captures this theological point well, while formally changing the meaning of the Hebrew; אֵל is most often read as אַל (μή), and many versions add, after "righteous judge," καὶ ἰσχυρὸς καὶ μακρόθυμος, "and strong and patient." MT is retained by Ravasi 53; Hossfeld-Zenger I:74n12b; Vesco 132; Kimhi, *Psalms*, 45; Goldingay 1:143l; Horsley, *Psalms*, 203G; Kraus 1:191; Seybold 45–46; Kirkpatrick 1:34n11.

49. So also Goldingay 1:145; Harman, *Psalms 1–72*, 126; Kidner, *Psalms 1–72*, 64; Kirkpatrick 1:33; Kraus 1:197–98; Tigay, "Psalm 7.5," 178.

50. *HALOT* 1744.

51. Diodati, *Annotations*, Ps VII, V. 8.

former group."[52] Rather, finally, David is claiming to be innocent of *this* crime. He has set up his petition so that the outcome hinges only on "if I did *this*," the specific accusations of vv. 2–5 [1–4], then the punishment desired by the enemy should follow (v. 6 [5]). He is not defending himself based on his character in general, but on his innocence, righteousness, and perfection in the matter at issue.[53] In order to be rescued, David must be innocent of the accusations against him, not perfectly sinless.[54]

It is these verses that should shock us, because they are so tame. This psalm is a desperate plea for rescue from evildoers who are proffering false witness against an innocent man, with the express purpose of seeking his judicial murder. The emphasis, throughout, is on respite, not vengeance. David appeals to Yahweh for refuge; begs for his verdict; and asks him to rouse himself martially against the enemy. As we will see, he even celebrates his daily indignation and his death-dealing judgment; commends his ordering of the courts so that evildoers are hoisted on their own petards; and vividly describes his readiness to deal out imminent death to the wicked. This is all from the mouth of one who is hunted by "lions"; who has God, and only God, for a shield; and who is desperate for the evil assailants to be thwarted. God's judgment would be *good news* for the oppressed.[55] Yet, despite all this, the psalmist stops short of asking for retribution. He asks that the evil deeds stop, not that the evildoers be killed.

Chrysostom pointed out that David's joy is not in the death of the enemy, but in divine justice.[56] Even this does not go far enough. David knows that they can avoid their divine punishment by repenting of their false accusation.

6. The Enemy Can Repent: vv. 13–14 [12–13]

13 [12] If he does not turn, he sharpens his sword,
       his bow he has bent and is aiming;

---

52. Goldingay 1:145.

53. *Contra* Goldingay 1:148.

54. Creach rightly uses this psalm as an example of how protestations of innocence are a response to false accusation, and that this is essential for understanding imprecations (Creach, "The Destiny of the Righteous," 58).

55. Goldingay 1:147, 49.

56. PG 55 col 104, cited in Ravasi I:176.

14 [13] he has made ready his vessels of death for him[self];
his arrows he has made into burning things.

These verses are ambiguous, even in context. Andrew Macintosh outlines the bewildering variety of ancient translations and interpretations.[57]
Kraus rightly rejects all emendations, on the grounds that they simply
wrestle with the *sense* and lack all textual evidence.[58] The key interpretive questions are: (1) Is the opening subject God (carried over from the
previous verse) or the wicked man (as in the following verses)? (2) Either
way, who is the subject of the other verbs in these two verses: God, or
the wicked? (3) Is the opening אִם־לֹא (*ʾim-loʾ*) introducing a protasis ("if
not") or an emphatic statement ("surely")?[59]

Paul Raabe suggests that the ambiguity is deliberate. "Upon reflection, the reader realizes all options are true. Unless God repents, the
wicked will die. And unless the wicked repent, they will die by killing
themselves."[60] He argues that this is a device for sustaining attention,
which would be lost if we "prematurely resolved the ambiguity by textual
emendation or otherwise."[61] Such a multifaceted meaning is a known
Hebrew poetic device.[62]

Nonetheless, one line of reading probably commends itself more:
God will judge, unless the evildoer repents.[63] In that case, the subject of
all but the first phrase is God, extending the description of him as a rescuing judge which began in v. 9 [8].[64] It is also in v. 9 [8] that we find the

57. Macintosh, "Psalm 7:12f," 481–87.

58. Kraus 1:191; cf. the extensive bold emendations offered by Leveen, "Textual
Problems," 442–43.

59. There are subsidiary questions too. The main options are well described by
Hossfeld-Zenger I:74n13–14; Vesco 135. See further Kraus 1:190–99; Firth, *Surrendering*, 25–26; Ravasi 53; Ḥakham, *Psalms 1–57*, 36–37; Seybold 47–48; Calvin, *Psalms*,
1:87–88; Ross 1:276; Weber I:68; VanGemeren, *Psalms*, 133; Kimhi, *Psalms*, 46.

60. Raabe, "Deliberate Ambiguity," 225.

61. Raabe, "Deliberate Ambiguity," 225.

62. Alter, *Biblical Poetry*, 72–73.

63. So Kirkpatrick 1:34; Vesco 135; Goldingay 1:149; Schökel I:207; Delitzsch
104–5; Theodoret of Cyrus, *Psalms 1–72*, 80; Hengstenberg, *Psalmen*, 158–59; Alter,
The Book of Psalms, 20n13; Kidner, *Psalms 1–72*, 64–65; Wilcock, *Psalms 1–72*, 37;
Bonar, *Christ and His Church*, 26; Eaton, *Psalms*, 79; Craigie, *Psalms 1–50*, 103; Perowne, *Psalms*, 1:150; Horsley, *Psalms*, 9–10, 203G; Schökel I:198.

64. Whether לוֹ in v. 14 is reflexive or the indirect object does not change the overall
sense: God prepares them for himself, to shoot with them; or he prepares them for the
wicked, to shoot at him.

subject of the opening phrase of v. 13 [12]: the wicked. The alternation between singular and plural need not detain us, since it is a feature of this psalm. God deals with wicked people in general (singular, "any one"), and will deal with the specific wicked who assail David (v. 9 [8], plural). The LXX even renders this as a warning: "unless you (plural) change tack."

Only this fits the courtroom scene. God cannot turn from vindicating the righteous in court: that is David's sole hope throughout the Psalm (vv. 7, 9–12, 18 [6, 8–11, 17]). The wicked can repent of making the accusation and save himself. The self-inflicted harm of the accusers (vv. 15–16 [14–15]) is God's verdict acquitting the innocent, which simultaneously and necessarily causes the sentence to rebound on the wicked accuser.[65] It is self-imposed punishment, because they have chosen to bring the false accusation. He is condemned by his own court-case: he falls into his own pit and his violence lands on his own skull.[66]

This is the picture set up in Ps 2. God is a judge who stands ready and able to deal out death to the wicked: he has already tensed his bow; he is aiming it; it is loaded with an arrow; he has plenty; and has already set them aflame. For the avoidance of doubt, they are specified as weapons of death. Turn quickly before his wrath flares.

The bow *remains* bent, not yet fired. "These are not words of punishment, note, but of threat."[67] There is a condition: *if* the wicked man does not turn. There is time to turn. The confidence throughout the psalm of God's *just* judgment is a warning to the perjurer. Delitzsch even understands זָעַם (za'am "indignant") in v. 12 [11], as God audibly warning the evildoer to turn.[68] The artful repetition of יָשׁוּב (yashub), meaning "return, as in desist" in v. 13 [12] and "return, as in rebound" in v. 17 [16] emphasizes that there are only two options: repentance or self-returning death).[69]

---

65. *Contra* Mark Seifrid, neither vv. 10 nor 12 are confessions of sin on David's part (Seifrid, "Gottes Gerechtigkeit," 33); Seifrid sees this as one of a minority of cases where the root צדק applies to Yahweh condemning rather than saving. In fact, in this psalm the two go together: it is because Yahweh is righteous that he saves the upright by acquitting them in v. 10, even while he condemns their wicked enemies in v. 12 (so also Backhaus, "'JHWH,'" 154).

66. While the subject of v. 15 is not stated, the opening הִנֵּה highlights that something has changed.

67. Theodoret of Cyrus, *Psalms 1–72*, 80; Craigie, *Psalms 1–50*, 102.

68. Delitzsch 104–5.

69. Goldingay 1:151.

Goldingay points out that the possibility of repentance and forgiveness is the starting point of the Psalm.[70] Nor is this a Christianized, nor even Modern, imposition on the Psalms. Here is the Talmud:

> Rabbi Me'ir prayed that God should have mercy on them so that they die. His wife, Beruria, said to him, 'On what verse do you rely [that you pray for the death of these hoodlums]? If it is based on the verse 'May *hatta' im* be ended on earth' [Ps. 104: 35], it does not say *hot' im* [sinners] but *hata' im* [sins]. Furthermore, look at the end of the verse, 'and the wicked will be no more.' [From this we learn that] when sins have ended, the wicked will be no more. Pray, therefore, that God have mercy on them that they do repentance.' He prayed for them to do repentance, and they repented.[71]

David Blumenthal comments: "Actually, Beruria has misread the grammar of the verse. *Hatta'im* means sinners and not sins, it being a professional noun form. The Talmud ignores this grammatical error and takes the lesson for its moral meaning."[72] Whether or not Beruria's exposition of that psalm was accurate, the Talmud unambiguously records the distinction between ending a sinner and ending their sin, and a preference for the latter.

7. Mercy Triumphs over Justice

David is far more generous with his enemy than with himself. In vv. 4–5 [3–4], he was willing to suffer judgment and death if he had in the past been guilty of the offence at issue. In dealing with the enemy, he does not insist that past actual guilt be acted on; he is prepared for the enemy to *repent*, and escape judgment. The threefold אם ('*im*, "if") clauses there set up the surprise of David's attitude: if I ever did anything at all, let them kill me; but *if only* my mortal enemy would repent, he should escape unharmed. The contrast is not in the severity of the punishment for himself, but in its contingency.

This merciful stance is surprising, in light of *Torah*. The law of false accusations for capital crimes does not allow the false witness to escape

---

70. Goldingay 1:145. Similarly, Alter, *The Book of Psalms*, 20n13; Kidner, *Psalms 1–72*, 64–65.

71. *b. Berakot* 10a.

72. Blumenthal, "Liturgies of Anger," 199.

with his life. The sentence they had tried to bring on David rebounds on to them (Deut 19:19) *without exception* (emphasized in vv. 20–21). The *lex talionis* could usually be commuted with monetary payment (Exod 22:21), but that was strictly forbidden for the death sentence (Num 35:31).[73] If the accused is acquitted of a capital crime, the false witness is executed instead. It is not the case that the sentence only falls on the accuser if the innocent has already been wrongfully executed.[74]

The appeal to Yahweh in Ps 7 is an all-out wager, with an unavoidable self-malediction. However, it is also necessarily a wager against the accuser, with unavoidable malediction. David has no choice but to invite what he warns about in vv. 13–17 [12–16]. If he is innocent and the accuser persists in the accusation, then Yahweh (through the priests and judges of Deut 19) will kill the accuser (vv. 13–14 [12–13]). The death sentence which the accuser desires will land on his own skull (vv. 16–17 [15–16]).[75] It is out of David's hands. Either David or the wicked must die, and Yahweh will certainly bring justice, as David has professed about him and as he ends the psalm: "I will praise Yahweh because of his justice" (אוֹדֶה יְהוָה כְּצִדְקוֹ, *'odeh Adonai ketsidqo*).[76]

---

73. K&D 1:839; Vaux, *Ancient Israel*, 158; Rad, *Theology of Israel's Historical Traditions*, 32; Merrill, *Deuteronomy*, 280–81; Budd, *Numbers*, 384.

74. This was a point of contention between Sadducees and Pharisees (Christensen, *Deuteronomy*, 430). However, the plain sense is that the sentence falls instead of a conviction on the accused, as Tigay argues, which is also consistent with Mesopotamian law (Tigay, *Deuteronomy*, 378n50). In fact, the very first law of Hammurabi deals with a charge of homicide which goes unproven, not which is overturned: "§1 If a man accuses another man and charges him with homicide but cannot bring proof against him, his accuser shall be killed" (COS 2.131:337).

75. Goldingay notes that a pit, such as dug by the enemy in v. 16, is used to catch lions, which is also how the enemy is described earlier (Goldingay 1:151).

76. *BHS* reports that a few MSS replace כ with ב, while Syr. has a 1cs suffix. We have fragments of Ps 7 in ḤevPs, which is as MT כצדקו according to Flint's transcription (Charlesworth et al., *Miscellaneous Texts*, 146), though I confess to finding the evidence not beyond all doubt in Col III of 5/6ḤevPsalms (Charlesworth et al., *Miscellaneous Texts*, plate XXV). Alep agrees with L and marks as a *hapax* (MGH I:24). LXX MSS are unambiguous in agreeing with MT (Rahlfs, *Psalmi*, 88). MT is followed almost universally without comment; see e.g., Delitzsch 100; Kimhi, *Psalms*, 47; Rashi, *Psalms*, 195; Kirkpatrick 1:35; Kraus 1:190; Craigie, *Psalms 1–50*, 97; Bratcher and Reyburn, *Book of Psalms*, 76; Hossfeld-Zenger I:76; Seybold 46; Schaefer, *Psalms*, 22; Ḥakham, *Psalms 1–57*, 38; Goldingay 1:144; Vesco 133; Ravasi 53; Schökel I:198; Ross 1:276. The further emendation in few Targum MSS of שֵׁם־יְהוָה to שׁום אלהא עילאה (the name of the most High God) unfortunately removes the keyword chain link with 8:2, 10; 9:3, which Günter Bader noticed (Bader, *Psalterspiel*, 23n86).

Despite the Law, David leaves repentance open to them, and is content for them to escape unharmed if they will stop trying to kill him. He does not ask for the justice prescribed in the Law.[77]

One objection to contemporary use of imprecatory psalms is that God's judgment is postponed, and now is the time for forgiveness (ch. 2, §5.A, p. 11). Others are so convinced that the Old Testament could not envisage the repentance or forgiveness of the enemy, that they refuse to believe that Ps 7 was ever a single poem. It must, they think, be a combination of two independent poems, leading to a contradiction.[78]

This sharp opposition of judgment and forgiveness is not a true reflection of the theology of the Psalter. In Ps 7, reliance on judgment coexists with a desire for the repentance and conversion of enemies.

The evildoer is always *preparing* to do evil (v. 15), while God is always *preparing* to execute judgment (v. 13). David knows that if the evildoer desists, so will God. In a study of the historical setting of this Psalm, Yitzhak Berger argues "that the poem expresses a theme seen to pervade much of the David story, whereby the text underscores his innocence of wrongdoing and proper requital of the deeds of others."[79] In particular, "the Psalm's focus [is] on the requital of good and evil conduct"[80] and fits with the account in Samuel showing David's "superiority to Saul in the realm of revenge and retribution."[81] Berger concludes by noting "the sustained motif of David's innocence and restraint in his dealings with Saul's supporters—a theme that is central to the wider narrative and shared by the poem."[82] David's restraint is not simply that he waits for

77. Firth sees the striking omission, but assumes that a prayer for *lex talionis* is implied, and that the only possible outcome of this prayer by the innocent is the judgment of the wicked (Firth, *Surrendering*, 23, 27).

78. Aurelius sees two contradictory poems. The first portion, guided by his reading of the superscription, speaks of David's love for Absalom, which he thinks contradicts vv. 11–17 (Aurelius, "Davids Unschuld," 410–11). However, as we have seen in our exposition of Ps 3, if Absalom is the enemy, then vv. 11–16 could be read against that backdrop quite naturally, with David lamenting the fate of Absalom and hoping that Absalom would repent and avoid such a fate. Similarly, Mandolfo detects two contradictory theologies in Ps 7, one petitioning for rescue, the other confident of judgment (Mandolfo, "Finding Their Voices," 39). However, he misses the fact that the judgment (vv. 13–17) will only happen *if the enemy does not repent* (v. 13). Petition and confidence are not necessarily opposites but frequently go together in Biblical prayers.

79. Berger, "The David-Benjaminite Conflict," 280.

80. Berger, "The David-Benjaminite Conflict," 290–91.

81. Berger, "The David-Benjaminite Conflict," 290–91.

82. Berger, "The David-Benjaminite Conflict," 295.

retribution and entrusts it to God; he is conscious that the enemy might repent and escape judgment. David does not say how likely he considers that repentance to be, but it is an outcome he considers.[83] This does not require David to envisage a comprehensive ethical renewal of the enemy, but neither is it inconsistent with that possibility.

To make a first-person statement commits the original writer, and subsequent users, to the ethos of the statement in a particularly intense way.[84] It is equivalent to a command, but more intensely felt.[85] In this case, it is either attached to or part of an oath that includes a self-malediction, which makes it as intense a commitment as it is possible to give. David not only commits himself intensely to God's justice, but also to the possibility of the enemy repenting and saving himself.

8. Psalm 7 in the Context of Book I

Psalms 3–7 see David facing opposition within Israel, culminating with his rule over all creation in Ps 8. Psalm 9/10[86] opens the second sequence of laments, focused this time on the nations that are against David and Israel: גוֹיִם (*goyim*, nations; 9:6, 16, 18, 21 [5, 15, 17, 20]), תֵּבֵל (*tebel*, the whole habitable world)[87] and לְאָמִים (*le'ummim*, poetically-used archaic synonym of *goyim*, nations; v. 9 [8]),[88] עַמִּים (*'ammim*, peoples; v. 12 [11]).[89] These nations "forget God" (9:18 [17]) and in 10:4 they are characterized by thinking that there is no God, renouncing God (v. 13), and thinking that God has forgotten (v. 11). This opening pair of psalms introduces the verdict which is finally made by the concluding Ps 14: the fool says, as 10:4, "there is no God." Psalm 14 confounds the expectation of Ps 8: when God looks down, he finds no-one who is righteous, just as Pss 11–13 have lamented. No-one seeks God and there is no-one "who displays wisdom" (מַשְׂכִּיל, *maskil*). The injunction to the nations to "get wisdom" (הַשְׂכִּילוּ, *haskilu*) in Ps 2:10 has gone unheeded.

83. On the likelihood of repentance, see Wenham, *Psalms as Torah*, 115.

84. Wenham, *Psalms as Torah*, 57–76; Erbele-Küster, *Lesen*, 112.

85. Wenham, *Psalms as Torah*, 57, 151.

86. Pss 9 and 10 form an acrostic when read together, which is further invited by Ps 10 lacking a superscription.

87. *HALOT* 1682–83; Wright, "תֵּבֵל," 4:272–73.

88. *HALOT* 513.

89. *Pace* Keener, *A Canonical Exegesis of the Eighth Psalm*, 73, which does not account for the shift in the identity of the enemies either side of Ps 8.

We have seen in Ps 3 and Ps 7 how David responds to wicked enemies within Israel. In our next chapter, we will see how David responds to the wicked enemy nations.

9. Conclusion

With regard to the claims of righteousness in this psalm, we have seen that it is a specific legal plea. David is not claiming to be perfect, nor even appealing to his membership of the "righteous." He merely claims to be "not guilty of the charges." The charges are maliciously motivated perjury. Surprisingly, he does not display ill will towards his murderous persecutors. He desires an end to their persecution, which will mean their punishment if they persist, but his actual desire is for an end to their evil deeds, not their punishment. If they will put an end to their campaign, he is happy for them to avoid their just deserts.

9

Retribution in Book I

Psalm 18

With a wonderful story to tell of his own salvation, the king undertakes to testify of Yahweh's work before all peoples.[1]

PSALM 18 IS NOT a prayer against the enemy, and does not ask for retribution. However, it is a vivid celebration of victory over the enemy. It shows us what happens when the enemy will not heed the warnings of Pss 2 and 7. We will also see how David responds to the defeat of his enemies: by proclaiming the blessings available to other repentant enemies. He does this on the world stage. Especially in its context within Book I of the Psalter, we find that foreign kings are again being enjoined to turn and benefit from the blessings on offer to those who kiss the son.

1. Who Is the Enemy and What Is the Extent of Retribution in Ps 18?

Psalm 18 shows David celebrating a victory which has left him in an unassailable position over his enemies (vv. 3, 17–20, 32–49 [2, 16–19, 31–48]). He had become the agent of God's judgment (vv. 33–41 [32–40]),

---

1. Eaton, *Kingship*, 182–83.

after God rescued David by giving him victory. David has Yahweh's ear (v. 7 [6]), and the enemy does not (v. 42 [41]).

Following the description of David's victory, he tells us that other nations heard of his victory (vv. 45–49 [44–48]). The fate of those other nations is the main focus of this chapter, but we will briefly discuss what happens to David's original enemies.

As in the opening of the Psalter, we have a picture of comprehensively defeated enemies: 1:4–5; 2:9; 3:8 [7] (in light of the superscription). There is complete annihilation: 18:38–43 [37–42]. David does not stop until he has "finished them off" (v. 38 [37]).[2] They fall under him (vv. 39–40 [38–39]), destroyed (v. 40 [39]) and pulverized (v. 43 [42]).

This could be taken as hyperbolic, or metaphorical.[3] The victory is complete, but the destruction of the enemy is not total. Both the ANE and the OT could be quite fluid with this imagery: for example, the execution of a king might represent the defeat of a nation *even when the defeat does not involve the execution of the king*.[4] Their inability to rise and the image of them falling recalls the *Leitmotif* of judgment in Pss 1–3. Among other lexemes, we have קום (*qum*, arise) in 1:5; 3:2, 8 [3:1, 7]. In 1:5 it describes the inability of the judged enemy to rise; in Ps 3 it serves ironically to reverse the fate of the enemy: they had risen against David, but now God has risen against them. This is what we find in Ps 18. Verse 39 [38] has them unable to rise (קום, *qum*), while vv. 40, 49 [39, 48] describe them as having risen against David (קום, *qum*). God has put David above them: both 3:4 [3] and 18:49 [48] use רום (*rum*, raise) of God lifting David in victory against those who had lifted themselves (קום, *qum*) against him. We could therefore imagine an army defeated, but not destroyed.

However, the language lends itself more naturally to the actual destruction of the enemy forces. Psalm 2 had warned the enemy nations to repent before the son's wrath flares up; Psalm 18 shows us what happens when they ignore the offer of amnesty and restoration: they perish. There is none of the reluctance we saw in Ps 3, or the contingency we saw in Ps 7. Sometimes the enemy will not repent, and Yahweh must save the king by defeating them. "In the report of this slaughter, there is no suggestion

---

2. The relevant sense of כלה as "finish off" is brought out by Gray, *Psalm 18*, 157.

3. Gray, *Psalm 18*, 157–64.

4. Keel, *Die Welt*, 8.

of sadness or regret at an appalling necessity."[5] The scenario resembles
2 Sam 8, not 2 Sam 18. Even if not every single enemy has been killed, it
is still a picture of retribution *beyond* merely winning the war. After his
defeat of Moab, he spares a third of the army, but he executes two thirds
of the survivors (2 Sam 8:2). This is not Ps 3, but Ps 2.

After the victory of 18:32–43 [31–42], David describes his headship
over the nations from which he has been rescued as well as his headship
over nations that were not involved, who merely respond to news of David's might (v. 44 [43]).

> You rescued me from the contention of a people,
>> you set me as head over nations
>>> a people who did not know me began to serve me.

Verse 44 [43] is a Janus verse, since vv. 44–49 [43–48] present this
mixed picture of rescue from one set of nations, and the homage paid by
other nations who respond wisely to David's victory. Before this verse, we
have the defeated enemy; after this verse, a new set of nations. It is not entirely clear at which point the switch happens. If a remnant of the warring
nations is included among David's new subjects, then the nations over
which he is head, and the people who did not know him, could include
the original enemy; otherwise, the transition to the nations described
later begins here.[6] Whether there were survivors or not, our interest is in

---

5. Goldingay 1:274.

6. Some argue that the initial enemies here are within Israel, and not international
(e.g., Hossfeld-Zenger I:128; Kraus 1:294; Delitzsch 182). Three major arguments are
advanced. First, they call upon Yahweh in v. 42; however, we find Balak doing the
same in Num 23, and it is a common ANE practice to enlist foreign gods in battle
(Craigie, *Psalms 1–50*, 176; see the examples supplied by Gray, *Psalm 18*, 165). Vesco
argues that the crying out to Yahweh shows them acting as though they were Israelites
(Vesco 203). A further option is that they are crying out concerning Yahweh, rather
than to him (Ross 1:475; Goldingay 1:275, claim that אֶל should surely have been used
to indicate "crying to," but see the discussion concerning the confusion and merging
of עַל and אֶל in Joüon §133b). Secondly, the unique expression רִיבֵי עָם is taken to
refer to disputes within the nation; that it indicates international strife is argued by
Gray, *Psalm 18*, 169. Third, the parallel text explicitly has a 1cs suffix עַמִּי so that this is
David's own nation (Schökel I:336); this could be explained as an example of the plural
ending without the *mem* (GKC §87f), or as an ancient genitive reflected in Samuel
but not in the period of composition of Ps 18 (Cross and Freedman, "Royal Song of
Thanksgiving," 33n99; cf. GKC §90l). A better explanation notes that it is a parallel
text, not an identical text, with its own context. If David is the head over these nations,
then they *are* his people.

those nations that came to serve David without first being defeated. They heard of his victory and calculated wisely in vv. 45–46 [44–45]:

45 [44] No sooner had they given ear, than they gave obedience to me;
        sons of foreigners fawned on me.
46 [45] Sons of foreigners withered;
        they came out trembling from their enclaves.

Either way, we should note what happens as a result of this victory. Nations come to David in fear and trembling, and he blesses them.

2. Blessing and Repentance in Ps 18

In the opening of the Psalter, we saw the promise of Torah blessing (Ps 1); the son giving wisdom to the repentant enemy who takes refuge in Yahweh by obeying the son (Ps 2); and David desiring that the enemy join God's people and receive this blessing (Ps 3:9 [8] and 2 Sam 19:9–13, 40–42 [8–12, 39–41]). I will argue below that this is what David promises in the conclusion of Ps 18, which he fulfils through Ps 19.

However, there is one more feature of the Psalter's introduction which begins to be fulfilled in Ps 18: the decree of 2:8. As in Ps 2, the enemies are invited to serve the son, and they in fact do so, in fulfilment of the decree of 2:8. Whether or not this includes those whom David has defeated, other nations come along quietly without the need for war.

Verse 44 [43] alludes to the choice available in Ps 2: a people whom I had not known (ידע, yada'), served (עבד, 'abad) me. Psalm 2 ends with either service of the king (עבד, 'abad), or perishing (אבד, 'abad). That choice is equivalent to the two ways that conclude Ps 1, which are either perishing (אבד, 'abad) or being known by Yahweh (ידע, yada'). In 18:44 [43], the king has not known (ידע, yada') them, perhaps in the sense of not having heard of them,[7] or not being his own people,[8] but certainly not yet in a treaty with them.[9] Instead of perishing (אבד, 'abad) they are serving (עבד, 'abad). David's victory does not lead to retribution against these further nations, but to collateral blessing.

Verses 45–46 [44–45] sees those nations coming in fear to the king, continuing the pattern of Ps 2. Fear in 2:11 goes hand in hand with

---

7. Goldingay 1:276; Hossfeld-Zenger I:128; Ḥakham, *Psalms 1–57*, 127.
8. Schökel I:336; Delitzsch 182.
9. Gray, *Psalm 18*, 170.

rejoicing and serving, and that is the very note that David concludes with: he proclaims the excellencies of Yahweh among these nations. What he has said of Yahweh in this psalm: that David loves him (v. 2 [1]), that Yahweh rescues David and is his rock (vv. 2, 46 [1, 45]), that he saves the humble but brings down the haughty (vv. 26–28 [25–27]), and that anyone can take refuge in him (v. 31 [30])—all of this is now true for any who come under David's rule. There is ample rejoicing to be had by the nations who come to David. David is not interested in vengeance, but celebrates their repentance and blessing.[10]

3. Psalms 18 and 19 Read Together: Proclaiming Blessing to the Nations

The next psalm teaches the nations how to rejoice and obtain the blessings which David has obtained in Ps 18. Psalm 19 fulfils the promise on which Ps 18 ended, by proclaiming God's praises to the nations.[11]

50 [49] Because of this, I will praise you among the nations, O Yahweh,
      and to your name I will sing with strings [אֲזַמֵּרָה, root *zmr*].
51 [50] The great rescue of his king,
      and showing steadfast love to his Messiah,
         to David [לְדָוִד, *ledavid*] and to his seed for ever!
19:1 [s] For the director of music: a David [לְדָוִד, *ledavid*] song for strings [מִזְמוֹר, root *zmr*].

It is unusual for David to be named in the body of a Psalm: there are only five other instances in the Psalter. The end of Ps 18 is the first occurrence in the Psalter, and is quite unnecessary, as a repetition of "his anointed." "To David" (לְדָוִד, *ledavid*) has been met in the superscription of nearly every psalm so far, helping us to recognize its exact repetition in the following superscription. David offers to do *zmr* in response to his rescue, rather artificially stating that it is *David* who has been rescued,

---

10. Nonetheless, the notion of "mercy" or "graciousness" imported by some English translations at v. 26 (ASV, Darby, ESV, KJV, NASB, NKJV, YLT) is without much merit: it translates חָסִיד and חֶסֶד, which does not have to imply mercy, as our study of חֶסֶד showed. It can simply mean faithfully dealing according to obligation, as captured by the translations of Craigie, *Psalms 1–50*, 167; Gray, *Psalm 18*, 122; Bratcher and Reyburn, *Book of Psalms*, 175; Delitzsch 170; Kraus 1:281; Goldingay 1:249; Vesco 195; Ravasi 95; Schökel I:316.

11. Barbiero, *Das erste Psalmenbuch*, 240–41.

and Ps 19 is presented as David doing *zmr*, as promised. The end of Ps 18 sets us up to recognize Ps 19 as the content of David's praise.

We will first read the psalms as a pair, and in the next section consider their placement within the structure of Book I.

3.A. The Blessed Life Is Available Globally

The universal creation language of the first half of Ps 19 sets the scene for this proclamation to the nations. There follow the blessings of Torah, not to condemn sinners, but to rescue them. "Proclamation" and "illumination" run through Ps 19 and unify the creation and Torah concerns.[12] That enacts David's purpose in 18:50–51 [49–50]. The structure of Ps 19 helps us to see the connection between the whole cosmos and the Torah. Its three sections each list seven attributes of something: the cosmos (vv. 2–5 [1–4]), Torah (vv. 8–9 [7–8]) and Torah again (vv. 9–11 [8–10]).[13]

The first Torah section of Ps 19 begins by telling the kings of the nations where to find the blessings promised by Psalms 1 and 2.

In Ps 1, "Yahweh's *Torah*" was the delight of the one who finds life, rather than perish with the wicked. In Ps 19, the same "Yahweh's *Torah*" in v. 8 [7] gives life. We see that it causes the נֶפֶשׁ (*nefesh*, self, soul) to do שׁוּב (*shub*). This could mean simply refreshment.[14] However, when applied to David in Ps 18, שׁוּב (*shub*) indicates Yahweh's reward (שׁוּב *shub*). This consisted of rescuing him from death because of his uprightness in 18:21, 25 [20, 24].[15]

> God's word 'revives' (cf. v.7). Its restorative quality gives healing to the whole person by assuring forgiveness and cleansing and by giving life to the godly. It unleashes the promises of God by his gracious redemptive acts (80:3, 7, 19).[16]

---

12. Weber I:112.

13. See the table in Labuschagne, "Psalms," 593. Seeing Ps 19 as a single composition is gaining scholarly ascendancy: Ross 1:467–70; McCann 751; Barbiero, *Das erste Psalmenbuch*, 243n250; Brueggemann, *Message of the Psalms*, 38.

14. Craigie, *Psalms 1–50*, 182.

15. All three verbs are *hipʿil*. שׁוּב in 18:21, 25, is understood as reward, recompense or requital by, e.g., Kraus 1:281; Seybold 77; Ravasi 95; Kirkpatrick 1:93; Hossfeld-Zenger I:127; Vesco 195; Goldingay 1:249.

16. VanGemeren, *Psalms*, 217. See also Goldingay 1:292.

As in Ps 1, then, redemption leading to life is on offer through Torah. The sinful pagan nations of Ps 18 have seen Yahweh save David's life, and now David encourages them to go to the source of that life. Psalm 2:10 commands the kings of the nations to let themselves receive wisdom. It is Torah which gives wisdom to those who lack it (v. 8 [7]). They have shown great folly in opposing David, Yahweh's anointed of Ps 2; but David has good news for them. Torah makes fools wise, and they will live and be saved.

No surprise, then, to find rejoicing and fear next in Ps 19:9–10 [8–9]. Fearing Yahweh and rejoicing is commanded in 2:11. The fear of the defeated nations in 18:42–46 [41–45] is redirected to a positive fear, which produces the blessing of finding refuge (2:12).[17]

The concluding note of the Torah section of Ps 19 is a *warning* which is emphatically given to self as well in v. 12 [11] "even your servant" (גַּם־עַבְדְּךָ, *gam 'abdeka*). From here to the end of the psalm, the law functions to protect sinners from themselves, to keep them in Yahweh's blessing of 1:1 and 2:12. However, the nations and David are on an equal footing here. They have been redeemed from their rebellion and sin, and must each serve Yahweh with fear. David has invited them to join his fate, and now includes himself in theirs. The kings of the nations who feature in the canonical context of the psalm (Pss 18; 20–21) will benefit from the righteousness that gave David victory over them.

3.B. "My Righteousness" in Psalm 18 Is Available in Psalm 19

Psalm 18 attributes David's rescue to Yahweh's delight in David's ethical qualities. This is stated in v. 20 [19] and spelled out in vv. 21–25 [20–24],[18] which are bracketed by an *inclusio*.[19] Only the three italicized words are not repeated:

יִגְמְלֵנִי יְהוָה כְּצִדְקִי כְּבֹר יָדַי יָשִׁיב לִי

וַיָּשֶׁב־יְהוָה לִי כְצִדְקִי כְּבֹר יָדַי לְנֶגֶד עֵינָיו

21 [20] Yahweh *repaid* me according to my righteousness,
            according to the purity of my hands he requited [שׁוּב *shub*, discussed above] me.

---

17. Psalm 19 has little to do with lament *contra* Gerstenberger, *Psalms I*, 102.

18. Identifying three sections within vv. 20–37 is also, e.g., Gray, *Psalm 18*, 56.

19. Wilson, *Psalms*, 345.

25 [24] So Yahweh requited me according to my righteousness,
      according to the purity of my hands *before his very eyes.*

In between these verses, we find the following word families linking to the two Torah sections of Ps 19:[20] צדק (*tsadaq,* "justice, justify, just/righteous," v. 10 [9]), בר (*br,* "pure/purity," v. 9 [8]),[21] שׁוּב (*shub,* [see above] v. 8 [7]), שָׁמַר (*shamar,* "keep," v. 12 [11]), שׁפט (*shafat,* "judge, to judge, judgment," v. 10 [9]), עַיִן ('*ayin,* "eye," v. 9 [8]), תם (*tam,* "perfect/perfection," v. 8 [7]). The next section, 18:26–30 [25–29], emphasizes God's character, as one who rewards the upright. The following link both to the previous section and to Ps 19: בר (*br,* v. 9 [8]), עַיִן ('*ayin,* v. 9 [8]), תם (*tam bis,* v. 8 [7]). Further links to Ps 19 in this section are איר ('*ir,* "to do with light," v. 9 [8]), רוּץ (*ruts,* "run," v. 6 [5]), אמר ('*amar,* "to do with speech," v. 15 [14]). The next section (vv. 31–37 [30–36]) binds to the two previous ones with דֶּרֶךְ (*derek,* "way") in vv. 22, 31, 33 [21, 30, 32], which conceptually is found in אֹרַח ('*orah,* "way") in 19:6 [5]. עָמַד ('*amad,* "to do with standing"), with its sense of secure permanence, is in v. 34 [33] and 19:10 [9]. These are not coincidental link words: they are closely related to the ethical qualifications of Ps 18, which are offered by Ps 19, or to the rewards for such ethics, which are offered by both psalms.

In particular, the conclusion of the Torah section of Ps 19 is אָז אֵיתָם ('*az 'etam,* "then I shall be perfect"). The *tam* root appears four times in Ps 18.[22] It plays a crucial role there: it declares David's ethical uprightness (vv. 24, 26 [23, 25]), describes Yahweh (v. 31 [30]) and combines the two by ascribing to Yahweh David's own uprightness (v. 33 [32]).

None of this is to be understood as sinless perfection, which would have no place in a David psalm, nor among the "Prayers of David," introduced as they are by Pss 3 and 51.[23] This is vital to the function of the Psalm in extending the invitation of righteousness to the nations via Ps 19: they must repent, rather than be sinless. Psalm 2 had already shown

---

20. See table 117 in Barbiero, *Das erste Psalmenbuch,* 242. Some of these are observed by Delitzsch 190, who assumes they prompted a compiler to make these separate psalms adjacent.

21. The root בר only occurs in Pss 18, 19 and 24 (Barbiero, *Das erste Psalmenbuch,* 242n242). We will see the significance of Ps 24 below.

22. Vesco 204.

23. *Contra* Goldingay 1:254. Ross is closer to the mark identifying other psalms that link victory with loyalty (Ross 1:438–49), but even that fails to note the coexistence of sin and righteousness in several psalms.

us that blessing is available to the repentant, not the immaculate, and David has modelled that in Ps 3.

Aside from lexical links, there is a correspondence between the requirement of righteousness in Ps 18 and the means of obtaining righteousness in Ps 19. Torah is the instrument, with universal scope, and David applies this scope to the subjugated kings of the nations, before whom he performs Ps 19 in song, as he promised to do in Ps 18:50 [49]. McCann notes the implication of Ps 19 being nestled within royal Pss 18, 20 and 21 stating: "Psalm 19, especially vv. 7–14, describes the orientation to life that faithful kings were supposed to embody."[24] McCann's account omits vv. 1–6: what they add is the global scope of the kings in question. As in the opening of the Psalter, the blessing of Torah (Ps 1; Ps 19) is juxtaposed with psalms where the repentant enemy kings come to the anointed in fear (Ps 2; Ps 18). The use of "hearing" also serves in this direction: 18:45 [44] reports that as soon as faraway people even hear about David, they come to him.[25] Fittingly, Psalm 19 opens with an extended assurance that creation proclaims the rightness of coming to God, with no corner of the globe left out.[26]

David's approach to the enemy reflects his self-understanding as a recipient of mercy, whose righteousness is precarious. In Ps 18, David fears the enemy but overcomes them and has dominion over them, while in Ps 19 he fears that sins might have dominion over him (v. 14 [13]). This would reverse his victory, since his uprightness was the criterion for Yahweh's intervention. This necessary fear of Yahweh and his law is emphasized by the use of עֶבֶד (*'ebed* servant):[27] in 18:44 [43] nations serve David, but the superscription announced David as Yahweh's עֶבֶד(*'ebed*),[28] which is how he sees himself in the third stanza of Ps 19 (vv. 12, 14 [11, 13] both begin גַּ... עַבְדְּךָ, *gam* ... *'abdeka* even your servant). The transition from nations to sin as cause of concern forms an *inclusio* around the pair of psalms through the "Yahweh as rock" metaphor. Psalm 18

---

24. McCann 751.

25. Delitzsch 182–83; Gray, *Psalm 18*, 171–72.

26. Regardless of whether one understands v. 4b as in apposition to v. 4a or as qualifying v. 4a, the imagery drives forward the idea of 18:44–51, that news has spread far and wide.

27. As Miller notes, 18:1 is the first occurrence of עֶבֶד in the Psalter, and as a self-designation, it is largely clustered in the other major Torah psalm, Ps 119 (Miller, "Kingship," 128).

28. Vesco 204.

opens with God as David's rock (also vv. 32, 47 [31, 46]), who delivers militarily from the nations:

יְהֹוָה סַלְעִי וּמְצוּדָתִי וּמְפַלְטִי אֵלִי צוּרִי אֶחֱסֶה־בֹּו מָגִנִּי וְקֶרֶן־יִשְׁעִי מִשְׂגַּבִּי

3 [2] *Yahweh* is my crag, and my fortification, and my savior;
     my God, *my rock* in whom I take refuge;
          my shield, and the horn of my rescue, my unassailable place.

and Ps 19 ends with Yahweh as his rock and his redeemer, from sin:

יְהֹוָה צוּרִי וְגֹאֲלִי

15c [14c] O *Yahweh*, *my rock* and my redeemer.

David's awareness of his precarious moral standing fits with what we have seen of him in Book I so far. He expresses his moral fallibility in 18:33 [32], where he attributes his own ethical qualifications to Yahweh's gift. David in Ps 19 proclaims abroad the availability of this gift. Here, David is showing the nations how they can experience the joy and blessing of serving Yahweh with fear, which was his desire for them in Ps 18. David's example as servant (עֶבֶד, 'ebed) in Ps 18 who commends a right fear of sinning (יִרְאָה, yir'ah) in Ps 19, takes us back to the invitation of Ps 2 to serve him with fear, using the same vocabulary. As Eaton puts it 18:50 demonstrates that the king is:

> God's witness to the world.... With a wonderful story to tell
> of his own salvation, the king undertakes to testify of Yahweh's
> work before all peoples.[29]

He also views Ps 2 as admonishing the whole world to repent and enjoy blessing. Such international and global proclamation of the excellencies of one's God was not unknown in Mesopotamia.[30] Within Ps 19, the creation section addresses God consistently as אֵל, ('el) a generic and international label for "god," while the Torah sections use his covenant name יְהֹוָה, *Yahweh*, precisely seven times.[31] As we will now see, nations that had denied God in Pss 9/10 and 14 are told that Torah introduces him personally.

---

29. Eaton, *Kingship*, 182–83.

30. Eaton, *Kingship*, 181–85.

31. Delitzsch 191.

4. Psalms 18–19 in the Context of Book I

4.A. Who Will Ascend the Holy Hill?

Book I has been put together to reinforce the connection between the Torah, the blessing of the king, and the kings of the world which we have seen in Pss 18 and 19. Psalms 18 and 19 are prominent in Book I. First, Ps 18 stands out by its length. Second, Pss 18 and 19 are a Torah-Royal pair, following the opening Pss 1 and 2. They are the central pillars of Book I, just as Book V has Pss 118 and 119, another Torah-Royal pair, also including a remarkably long psalm.[32] Finally, Ps 19 is highlighted by the structure of Book I, which has four recognizable sections: Pss 3–14; 15–24; 25–34; 35–41.[33] Each section is organized around a central Psalm: 8, 19, 29, 38.[34] Psalms 8, 15, 19, 24 and 29 stand out by not being laments, unlike almost all else in Book I.[35] These mark the center of the first three major sections, and also the beginning and end of the second section.

Section:	3–14	15–24	25–34	35–41
Central psalm:	8	19	29	38
Non-lament psalms:	8 Center	15 Beginning 19 Center 24 End	29 Center	

Psalm 19 stands at the center of the palistrophic sequence Pss 15→24, whose opening and closing psalms enquire about entering the

---

32. Grant, *King*; Mays, *The Lord Reigns*, 133; Robertson, *Flow of the Psalms*, 66–67, 240–41.

33. Bellinger, "Reading from the Beginning," 122; Barbiero, *Das erste Psalmenbuch.*

34. Hossfeld-Zenger I:12.

35. McCann 661.

Zion sanctuary.[36] The sequence places Torah and Kingship (cf. Pss 1 and 2) at its central turning point.[37]

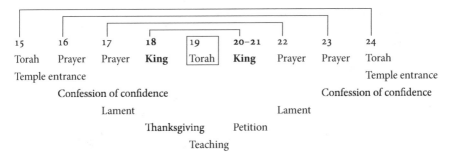

Psalm 14 concluded section I with a rhetorical exclamation:[38]

> [7] O, if only salvation would come out of Zion . . .

This uses an idiom,

מִי יִתֵּן מִצִּיּוֹן יְשׁוּעַת יִשְׂרָאֵל

Who will give salvation from Zion to Israel?[39]

and makes the opening of Ps 15 (the very next verse) seem like a restatement, when it uses the same syntax to ask, also about Zion:

מִי־יָגוּר בְּאָהֳלֶךָ
מִי־יִשְׁכֹּן בְּהַר קָדְשֶׁךָ

> *Who will dwell* in your tent?
> *Who will live* on your holy hill?

The question of who will save *from* Zion is met by the logically prior question: who can *enter* Zion? Section I of Book I had ended with the stark conclusion that neither anyone from Israel nor from the nations can enter. Section II will answer, in the sequence of Psalms 15–24.

---

36. Miller, "Kingship," 127–28; Brown, "'Here Comes the Sun!,'" 260–65; Jacobson, "Imagining," 240.

37. Miller, "Kingship," 128; the diagram is translated from the forthcoming revised edition of Weber, *Theologie und Spiritualität*. Similarly Sumpter, "The Coherence," 186.

38. GKC §151b.

39. Gesenius observes that the literal sense of the idiom is retained sometimes (GKC §151b). This is how LXX renders it: τίς δώσει (no exceptions recorded in Rahlfs, *Psalmi*, 96).

This explains why Pss 18–19 are the turning point of this sequence. The person who enters Zion to bring salvation must meet ethical qualifications which take up the whole of the rest of Ps 15. If Ps 15 looks for a solution to the state of the world in Pss 3–14, it is striking how many connections are made to Ps 15 by Pss 18–19.[40] These "serve to identify the human ruler of Ps 18 with the torah lover of Ps 19."[41] Psalm 24 makes copious word-links to Ps 19 and to Ps 18.[42]

In the center of Book I, Pss 18–19 present David as the one blessed by Torah, who is able to bring justice within Israel (Pss 1; 3–7) and to bring relief to Israel by defeating the enemy nations (Pss 2; 8–14). I argued that the juxtaposition of Pss 18 and 19 could be read as David inviting the foreign kings to *tolle lege* and join in his blessing. This is reinforced by the concluding psalm of the section. Psalm 24:3 restates the question of Ps 15:1, and 24:4 gives a similar answer to 15:2–3. The significant change is how Ps 24 introduces the question.

> 1 Yahweh's is the earth and its fulness,
>   the inhabited world and those who dwell in it.
> 2 For he set it on the waters,
>   and on the rivers established it.

Yahweh has the freehold on the world and all its inhabitants. What Ps 15 offered to Israel, is now offered everywhere. Just as in Ps 19, global creation themes introduce the Torah.

As we have seen, by reading Pss 18 and 19 together, David is enjoying and proclaiming the righteousness that comes from repentance and forgiveness, not perfection. This is what the Torah offers to the nations: blessing, if they imitate David and repent, as Pss 1 and 2 advertised in the introduction to the Psalter. The quest for the savior king of Israel (Ps 15), has become an invitation for all kings to enter the temple (Ps 24), through enjoyment of Torah (Ps 19) and obeisance to the son (Ps 18).

It may be objected that Ps 18 offers nothing better to the nations than subjugation, and that this is hardly benevolent. However, Ps 19 spells out the blessings of Torah in delightful terms: not only giving wisdom but "rejoicing the heart" (v. 9 [8]), better than gold and sweeter than honey (v. 11 [10]), yielding great reward (v. 12 [11]). Despite Israel's chosen status as particularly blessed, that same blessing is offered to the nations, with

40. Barbiero, *Das erste Psalmenbuch*, 311–22.

41. Miller, "Kingship," 128–29.

42. Barbiero, *Das erste Psalmenbuch*, 314, 316; Miller, "Kingship," 129–31.

no mention of any obligation beyond the same Torah obedience which binds Israel. Deuteronomy 4:6–8 envisages nations admiring Israel longingly because of Torah, and here it is on offer to all of them, even after their rebellion. This is just as in Ps 2, which is unequivocal: to surrender and serve the son is *blessing*, the same blessing offered by Ps 1 at the entrance of the Psalter. This note of the nations fearing and rejoicing will grow louder until the Psalter's final "all with breath should hallelujah."

What has David's attitude in victory been? He offers blessing to his enemies. We see this first explicitly in Ps 18, as he proclaims salvation to them. Second, in Pss 18 and 19 holding out Torah as available to bless the enemy kings. Third in the significant placement of Pss 18 and 19 within the sequence of international temple entry (Pss 15→24), answering the problem of enemy nations in Pss 9–14. Fourth in the conspicuous placement of Pss 18 and 19 as a Torah-Royal pair at the center of Book I, making reference to the introductory Torah-Royal pair of Pss 1 and 2, which also holds out the promise of blessing to the nations which kiss the son.[43] David in Ps 18 invites all foreign rulers to join him, and shows them the way.

4.B. David the Exemplary Herald of Good News to the Nations

If Ps 2 warns the kings of the nations to kiss the son before they perish in the way, Ps 18 has shown us the aftermath for those who did not heed the warning. God's anointed has punished them, as judgment from Yahweh. God's anointed has been kept and empowered by his devotion to Yahweh and his Torah, as Ps 1 promised.

As we saw in Ps 7, Yahweh is righteous in all his judgments, and that is why the enemy will perish and the innocent will be protected. So in Ps 18:31 [30]. There it is explicit that he is a shield for *anyone who* makes him his refuge, repeating the promise of Ps 2. That is why David turned his mind to other nations who still have time to repent. David is as evangelical as the anointed in Ps 2: telling of the decree in 2:7 is explicitly done among the nations in 18:50 [49]. We have seen that his message is not one of self-righteousness and one-up-man-ship, but of redemption received by God's mercy following his own repentance. Psalm 19 hints at this, just as much as Ps 3 pointed at it clearly through the superscription.

---

43. Barbiero shows the connections between Ps 1 and 19, and 2 and 18 at length (Barbiero, *Das erste Psalmenbuch*, 249–61).

The message to foreign kings is that they can join David in standing protected by Yahweh, because what is wanted is repentance, not sinlessness.

This is not just about David, but about any reader of the Psalm, and the whole nation. David is an example for them. Here is Leslie Allen, commenting on the connections between Ps 18 and the second part of Ps 19, and on Ps 19 as interrupting the messianic sequence of Pss 18, 20, 21:

> The accumulation of parallels leads to a clear conclusion: the purpose of setting the two psalms side by side was to relate David's experience to the individual pious believer. . . . In his relation with God David was an exemplar for "all who seek refuge in him" (v 30). Ps 19 has been placed next to Ps 18 in order that its second half may develop these hints which explicitly present David as a role model.[44]

We can go further by noticing the first part of Ps 19 and integrating the promise of proclamation to the kings that ended Ps 18. Allen's message for the pious Israelite, and the democratization of David, should lead the pious Israelite to imitate David in proclaiming Yahweh as a refuge to the nations.[45]

5. Conclusion In Book I

We have seen how Psalms 1 and 2 introduce retribution in the Psalter, and how Ps 3 introduces David in the context of retribution. We have examined Ps 7 and have now looked at Ps 18 in its context.

So far, we have found the following. First, is perfect righteousness required to pray against enemies? We have seen that this is contradicted by how David is introduced in the book of Psalms, at the low-point of his ethics. In particular disputes, it is necessary to demonstrate that one is the innocent party, perhaps even a victim, but this is not the same as being generally blameless. We have especially seen this in Pss 3 and 7. Even when David has the upper hand against the wicked nations as God's righteous anointed, as in Ps 18, we have already met him as a restored sinner who has been forgiven. David presents himself in the very next Psalm 19 as far from infallible, but reliant on the Law to correct and restore him, and fearing Yahweh just as the nations were called to do in Ps 2. This also

---

44. Allen, *Psalms*, 125.

45. On the king being a model Israelite, and the corporate solidarity that invites Israel to join the king, see Miller, "Kingship," 131–35.

shows that, second, David is not under any illusions of earned merit, but well aware of his own enjoyment of divine mercy and forgiveness.

Third, do the psalms understand that the enemy is able to repent, or do they imagine that they can only ask for the destruction of the enemy? We have seen that Ps 2 invites repentance and that Ps 7 warns the enemy to repent and wants them to stop their wickedness as an alternative to being judged. Psalm 18 uses military victory against one enemy to celebrate the repentance of other nations, and promises to proclaim this offer of blessing abroad, which is then further expanded in Ps 19.

Finally, do the psalms have any notion of loving the enemy, desiring their blessing, or do they simply demand vengeance? Closely connected with David's awareness that the enemy can repent, we have seen that he offers them the blessings of repentance. This is already clear in Ps 2. More than that, he tempers his desire for them with mercy rather than justice, as we have seen in Pss 3 and 7.

Sometimes the enemy will desist from attacking David and experience the blessing of restoration and repentance. Other times, they will persist, and Yahweh will defend David and judge them. While Ps 18 celebrates the latter outcome, the former is obviously held out as an offer to the enemy, not only in Pss 2 and 7, but also in the declaration to other enemy nations that results from the victory of Ps 18.

This composite picture matches the instinct detected by, for example, Luther and Calvin, when faced with texts concerning judgment:

> So we, too, pray for our angry enemies, not that God protect and strengthen them in their ways, as we pray for Christians, or that He help them, but that they be converted, if they can be; or, if they refuse, that God oppose them, stop them and end the game to their harm and misfortune.[46]

> [T]he righteous would anxiously desire the conversion of their enemies, and evince much patience under injury, with a view to reclaim them to the way of salvation: but when wilful obstinacy has at last brought round the hour of retribution, it is only natural that they should rejoice to see it inflicted, as proving the interest which God feels in their personal safety.[47]

Furthermore, we have seen that David's approach to his enemies is an example to Israelites reading the Psalter. More than that, it is an

---

46. Luther, *What Luther Says: An Anthology*, 1100, cited in Adams, *War Psalms*, 62.

47. Calvin, *Psalms*, 2:378.

example to the nation as a whole, with David teaching them through his model prayers. Further still, there is a typological correspondence between David facing Absalom and Israel facing Babylon in exile. We now turn to examine Book V of the psalms, which responds to the exile.

10

David, Israel's Teacher about Steadfast Love

The Structure of Book V

Give thanks to Yahweh for he is good.
For his steadfast love is forever.
–Psalms, Book V

THE SHAPE OF BOOK V shows us that David is being enlisted as a model for Israel to follow in prayer, and especially as a model of prayer in the light of national apostasy, exile, and restoration. We will see that imprecations against enemies are strategically placed within a clear structure for the book, which highlights David's role as the model supplicant. Central to David's, and Israel's, attitude in prayer is the need for divine mercy, and the fact of having received it.

We begin with an overview of the structure of Book V, and what message may be implied by its editorial shaping. In the next three chapters, we will examine every imprecation in Book V.

1. Steadfast Love and the Structure of Book V

1.A. Pre-existing Collections Are Insufficient

Even though we are interested in the final form, the same evidence is of interest both for diachronic studies and for intentional shaping. Especially in Book V, a later editor or compiler seems to have worked with pre-existing units but woven them into a Book that does not respect their original boundaries. Building on Wilson, Joseph Brennan writes:

> A careful reading indicates that the Psalter has not developed in a haphazard and arbitrary way, but has been carefully woven together in such a manner that previously independent compositions, or smaller collections of such compositions, now comment upon or respond to one another.[1]

Diachronic approaches often recognize the following units:[2]

(105–)107	108–10	111–18	119	120–34	135–36 (137)	(137)	138–45	146–50
Introduction	Penultimate David collection	Egyptian Hallel		Ascents	Great Hallel		Final David collection	Little Hallel

Within such a set of neat divisions, two psalms cause some difficulty. The difficulty of accounting for Ps 119 has been documented by Zenger.[3] Psalm 137 also leads to confusion.[4] I will argue below that, far from being outliers, both of these *imprecatory* psalms fit within a clear arrangement of every imprecatory psalm in Book V, which enlists David psalms to teach the reader how to use them.

Our primary cue as readers will not be the pre-existing collections, but the arrangement strategy that is evident in Book V. Brennan's warning above continued:

1. Brennan, "Some Hidden Harmonies," 126–27. Cf. Wilson, *Editing*, 5.

2. Holladay, *Psalms*, 79; Millard, *Die Komposition des Psalters*, 168; Seybold 2–12; Goulder, *Psalms of the Return*, 16; Zenger, "Composition and Theology," 98; Ballhorn, *Zum Telos des Psalters*, 7–9; Leuenberger, *Konzeptionen*, 278; Hossfeld-Zenger 3:19.

3. Zenger, "Composition and Theology," 87.

4. See the struggle in Millard, *Die Komposition des Psalters*, 168; Ballhorn, *Zum Telos des Psalters*, 362–64.

Hence, for a proper understanding of the Psalter it is not enough to study each of its 150 components in the historical context from which it originally sprang. They must all be studied in their relationship to each other, since all of them together convey more than they do if looked at separately.[5]

This does not mean ignoring the historical context (where known), nor the evidence of grouping psalms (that leads some to speak of pre-existing collections), but it does mean attending to the quite different context suggested by the narrative of the Psalter.[6]

There is a shift in arrangement strategy in Books IV–V. Compared with Books I–III psalms have fewer superscriptions but are additionally organized by refrains in the head or tail of a psalm.[7] This allows the possibility of connecting psalms that are far apart within IV–V, and of using them to form brackets around subgroups.[8] These subgroups divide Book V into three simple sections, which we turn to now.

1.B. Markers of Structure: "Thank Him," "Praise Him," and "His Steadfast Love"

"Give thanks" and "Praise Yah[weh]" are used as refrains. They are spelled differently in Pss 105–50, so I will use *hodu* informally for all variations of הוֹדוּ ("thank") and *hallelujah* for all variations of הַלְלוּיָהּ ("praise Yah"). *Hodu* is an opening refrain, bracketed by *hallelujah* as a closing refrain, identifying three sections for Book V: Pss 107–17; 118–35; 136–50.

This structure is suggested by external evidence, which led Wilson first to propose it. The Dead Sea scroll 11QPsa contains psalms from Books IV–V, in a different order and with a few other poems woven in. It uses two devices for marking the end of sub-collections: psalms that begin with *hodu* and psalms that begin or end with *hallelujah*. Wilson argued from ample evidence of similar devices in ANE temple hymn collections where both *hodu* and *hallelujah* end collections. He noted that the seam between Books IV and V of the Psalter had adapted this, so that

5. Brennan, "Some Hidden Harmonies," 126–27.

6. Walton, "Psalms," 31.

7. Zenger, "Composition and Theology," 99; Ballhorn, *Zum Telos des Psalters*, 61. Note how McFall's scheme for arrangement in Books I–III does not work in Books IV–V (McFall, "The Evidence," 247).

8. Ballhorn, *Zum Telos des Psalters*, 61.

hodu now indicates the start of a sub-collection, while psalms of *hallelu-jah* mark the end.[9] He has been widely followed.[10]

These divisions are within pre-existing collections, and split one psalm from each one: Ps 118 from the Egyptian Hallel, and Ps 135 from the Great Hallel.[11] However, far from isolating connected psalms from each other, those pre-existing units serve to connect the major sections to one another. The Egyptian Hallel straddles sections I and II; the Great Hallel straddles sections II and III.[12]

Hodu and *hallelujah* begin their work as refrains at the end of Book IV. Despite its now-ubiquitous use in liturgy, *hallelujah* is striking there, since it does not appear in the Hebrew Bible until this point.[13]

Psalm 105 begins with *hodu* and ends with *hallelujah*

¹ Give thanks [*hodu*] to Yahweh.

. . .

45c *Hallelujah!*

Psalm 106 begins with *hodu* and ends with *hallelujah*, as well as beginning with *hallelujah*, thus linking it to the end of 105

¹ *Hallelujah!*
Give thanks [*hodu*] to Yahweh for he is good.
For his steadfast love [*hesed*] is for ever.

. . .

48d *Hallelujah!*

This sets us up to notice the structuring refrains that mark the three sections of Book V. Psalm 107 begins with exactly the same *hodu* formula as 106:1, which I will hereafter call "the refrain."

הֹדוּ לַיהוָה כִּי־טוֹב כִּי לְעוֹלָם חַסְדּוֹ׃

¹ Give thanks to Yahweh for he is good.
For his steadfast love is forever.

---

9. Wilson, *Editing*, 124–29.

10. McCann 663–64; Allen, *Psalms 101–150*, 75; Leuenberger, *Konzeptionen*, 265; Ballhorn, *Zum Telos des Psalters*, 362–64; Vesco 1023–24.

11. Zenger, "Composition and Theology," 87–88.

12. For attempts to prioritize the pre-existing collections against this three-fold structure, see: Zenger, "Composition and Theology," 98–99; McCann 1153; Millard, *Die Komposition des Psalters*, 168; Goulder, *Psalms of the Return*, 16, 116, 209.

13. Zenger, "Composition and Theology," 77.

This opens section I. Psalms 111–17 close the section as a *hallelujah* collection: Ps 114 is nestled by two triplets of psalms, each either beginning and/or ending with *hallelujah*.

Psalm 118 opens with the refrain, reuses its second half in vv. 2–4 and ends with it.

> **1** Give thanks to Yahweh for he is good.
> > For his steadfast love is forever.
> **2** Let Israel say:
> > For his steadfast love is forever.
> **3** Let the House of Aaron say:
> > For his steadfast love is forever.
> **4** Let those who fear Yahweh say:
> > For his steadfast love is forever.
>
> . . .
>
> **29** Give thanks to Yahweh for he is good.
> > For his steadfast love is forever.

Section II closes with Ps 135, which begins and ends with *hallelujah*.

Section III begins by expanding the use of the refrain even more than Ps 118. Psalm 136 begins with the refrain, uses the second half in *every* verse, and then ends with the modified refrain.

> **1** Give thanks to Yahweh for he is good.
> > For his steadfast love is forever.
> **2** [. . .]
> > For his steadfast love is forever.
> > [repeat twenty-three times.]
> **29** Give thanks to the God of Heaven.
> > For his steadfast love is forever.

Section III ends with Pss 146–50, which each begin and end with *hallelujah*, and 150 also has two *hallelujah*s per verse.

Reading the psalms in sequence within this structure means not isolating them on the basis of *Gattung*.[14]

This arrangement in three sections will guide us through Book V. Notice how simple the structure of the book becomes, by comparison with the various efforts to divide it by pre-existing compositions. There is no problem with placing troublesome Psalms 119 and 137; they are the first of the body of sections II and III.

---

14. Following Ballhorn, *Zum Telos des Psalters*, 361. Compare the analyses of Whybray, *Reading the Psalms*, 74; Kim, "Strategic Arrangement," 157.

Opening *hodu*	Body of Section	Closing *hallelujah*
107	108–10	111–17
118	119–34	135
136	137–45	146–50

1.C. Pleading and Praising for Steadfast Love: The Seam with Book IV

Hallelujah unites Pss 104–6 at the end of Book IV. In addition each of Pss 105–7 begins with *hodu*, which points forward to the growing refrain that opens each major section of Book V, as we have seen. Thus, Pss 104–6 are marked as a conclusion (and close Book IV), but Pss 105–7 are marked as an introduction, forming a bridge into V.[15]

The content of this bridge is an appropriate segue from Book IV to Book V. The seam of Books IV–V recount the relationship between Israel and Yahweh as covenant partners. Yahweh was faithful and Israel was faithless, ending up exiled.[16] Psalm 107 opens Book V not only answering the lament at the end of Book IV, but the same lament at the end of Book III, where the exile called into question Yahweh's covenant commitment. He is reminded of his covenant with David (89:4 [3]), which he made promising *hesed* (vv. 3, 25, 39, 34 [2, 24, 38, 33]); he is praised for his *hesed* (vv. 2, 15 [1, 14]); and finally asked where his *hesed* has gone (v. 50 [49]). These seven uses of *hesed* are mirrored in Ps 107.[17] As we have seen

15. Ballhorn notes that there are three structuring refrains in the Psalter and Pss 105–7 use all of them: *hodu*, *hallelujah* and doxologies. The *hallelujah*s and *hodu*s trump the doxology, by binding together what the doxology splits up, thus joining Books IV and V (*Zum Telos des Psalters*, 364). The five-book structure is not at odds with the close unity of psalms that straddle the seams (*contra* Kim, "Strategic Arrangement," 151). Wilson's entire proposal hinges on the psalms either side of each seam being closely connected.

16. Firth, "More Than Just Torah," 10.

17. McCann 663. Only five psalms in the whole Psalter have חֶסֶד five or more times. Psalm 119 might be an outlier owing to its length, but the other three are those that hold the refrain of Book V: Pss 107, 118, 136. The only psalm outside Book V is Ps 89, with seven instances. We will see the further significance of all these being historical psalms.

(ch 7, §2.B, pp. 120–31), *hesed* is that disposition of Yahweh not only to be faithful in giving earned covenant rewards, but also his determination to act favorably even when presented with breach of covenant. It is a love for his people that remains steadfast in the face of faithlessness. Reassuringly, the refrain of Book V insists that his *hesed* is forever. It does so as the end of a history lesson that points back to his dependable *hesed*. Psalm 90 answers that lament by pointing to a prior covenant, mediated through Moses, and therefore reminding Israel of a previous deliverance from captivity, at the exodus.[18] This opens Book IV.

Psalms 105–7 tell of the exodus (105), the exile (106), and the return (107). Book IV therefore goes from the exodus to the cusp of a new exodus, the release from exile.[19] This history is summarized in its final two psalms (105–6), which set up the first psalm of Book V as a historical celebration of the return from captivity (107).[20] Book IV ends with a plea for ingathering from among the nations (106:47).[21] Ps 107 answers that plea.[22]

The summons to thanks and praise (*hodu* and *hallelujah*) do not only happen to structure this segue into Book V, but are thoroughly appropriate to the message of the book which they introduce. Psalm 107 "launches Book V as a series of calls for praise to Yahweh for restoring Israel from exile."[23] Psalm 106 ended by pleading for the return from exile with the express purpose of *thanking* (same root as *hodu*) and of *praise* (same root as *hallelujah*). Book V fittingly opens each section with a command to thank (*hodu*) and ends each with a command to praise (*hallelujah*).

What should we thank him for? What led to the end of exile? His steadfast love (*hesed*) which forms the refrain of Book V, as we have seen:

> Give thanks [*hodu*] to Yahweh for he is good.
> For his steadfast love [*hesed*] is forever.

---

18. Wilson argued for the significance of Book IV opening with a psalm "of Moses," and Ballhorn sees Pss 90–106 as a Moses Book pointing back to the exodus (Ballhorn, *Zum Telos des Psalters*, 363–64). Wallace sees Moses as the unifying voice in Book IV (Wallace, *Narrative Effect*, 87–94).

19. Hossfeld-Zenger 3:136.

20. Hossfeld-Zenger 3:19.

21. McCann 662–63.

22. deClaissé-Walford, *Reading from the Beginning*, 93.

23. Allen, *Psalms 101–150*, 79.

Book IV ends by assuring Israel of Yahweh's *hesed* (Ps 105, looking back at the exodus) and showing Israel's desperate need for his *hesed* (Ps 106 looking at the exile).[24]

The seam between Books IV–V emphasizes Israel's sin in history and Yahweh's dependability to respond in *hesed*. It calls to mind the national apostasy at the golden calf, which preceded entrance to the land; the land was entered because of divine *hesed*. This gives hope that the same undeserved *hesed* will bring the nation back into the land after their apostasy that had led to exile. Book V looks back from the return, and is able to declare with certainty that Yahweh's *hesed* is reliable; indeed, "his steadfast love is forever."[25]

Next, we will see that prayers of David are being used in this context of *hesed* to teach Israel how to pray for her enemies. His prayers are full of imprecations, and they are deliberately placed in a structure that highlights David's role as teacher of Israel.

2. David the Model Recipient of Steadfast Love in Book V

2.A. David Displaced in Book V?

Wilson's initial proposal that the monarchy shifts away from David after Book III proved controversial. He refined his thesis in response to criticism several times.[26] Wilson most recently argued that "the role of David is *down-played* in the final form of the Hebrew Psalter" and offers clear evidence for this in the reduction of the proportion of Davidic psalms and especially the striking contrast with the OG and with Psalms among the DSS, where David features in many more superscriptions.[27]

Wilson also shows that there is a distinct emphasis on Yahweh's kingship.[28] He observed that מֶלֶךְ (*melek*, "king" and cognates such as "to rule as king" or "kingdom") is used in IV–V of kingship in general, foreign kings, or Yahweh as king, but never refers to the Kings of Judah. By

---

24. Wallace, *Narrative Effect*, 92.

25. Our concern here is synchronic: what the text seems to indicate in its current form and context; for an overview of vexed diachronic issues, see Beyerlin, *Werden und Wesen*, 1–6.

26. Especially Wilson, "Royal Psalms," 85–94; Wilson, "Shape of the Book of Psalms," 129–42; Wilson, "Understanding," 42–51; Wilson, "Structure," 229–46.

27. Wilson, "King," 401.

28. Wilson, "King," 401–2.

contrast, in Books I–III, *melek* is used of all of these. Where David and his line appear in Books IV–V, they are associated with the roots עֶבֶד (*'ebed*, servant), מָשִׁיחַ (*moshiah*, anointed), רָדָה (*radah*, to rule).[29]

This might support his more moderate proposal. An outright shift from David to Yahweh as king, is not the same as a shift *in emphasis* from David as king to Yahweh as king. The former implies a transfer of kingship, while the latter allows the possibility that both David and Yahweh are kings, even though the Psalter's attention changes focus from the one king to the other.

We will offer our own detailed proposal concerning the place of David in Book V, below.

2.B. David and Israel Have Experienced Steadfast Love

We argued that Exod 34:6–7 is a vital text for understanding various lexemes for mercy and Yahweh's relationship to national apostasy. Various biblical texts refer back to this revelation of Yahweh's character by using the vocabulary of sin and mercy found there.

David does so in Ps 51. He uses the language of Exod 34, and through the superscription, connects his sin with Israel's national apostasy with the golden calf, and Yahweh's forgiveness in both situations. We saw that Ps 3 introduces David to the Psalter by again pointing to the consequences of that same sin. Hossfeld sees a link between 3:9 and 51:20, in that both are beatitudes that put the individual concerns into the cult of the whole assembly, and therefore both of these ask Yahweh to come to the aid of exiled Israel.[30] We discussed in our exegesis of Ps 3 that the verse fits the situation of Absalom and there is little reason to doubt its application to the original situation of David as individual and king, with private and national concerns. Likewise in Ps 51, especially since the sin of the king has repercussions for the nation. There could therefore be an application of David's experience to the nation in exile. As we saw in Ps 3, the Psalter introduces David with a typological correspondence between his flight away from Zion and the exile.

Three more psalms pick up on Exod 34:6–7, and we have seen that these are David psalms, and significantly placed. These five psalms of David, connecting himself to the nation's experience of mercy following the

---

29. Wilson, "King," 402–4.
30. Hossfeld-Zenger I:58.

golden calf, are the first David Psalms of Books I and II, the only one in III, and the final one in IV (103:8) and V (145:8).

Psalm 103 helps us to see the significance of the history lesson of Book IV to the message of Book V. The end of Book IV and the refrain of Book V tell us that his *hesed* is forever. Nonetheless, it is no innovation. When it comes to loving steadfastly, Yahweh has proved himself to Israel and to David. Book IV has set this up. Psalm 103 is about David but also clearly alludes to the golden calf, which Israel survived by *hesed*.[31] The golden calf, and the response of *hesed* is put in the reader's mind as a prelude to the exodus retold in Ps 105. Pss 103 and 106 are bracketed by references to the exodus and the golden calf, through the disclosure of God's character in answer to Moses's prayer.[32] The refrain of Book V (107:1) could well then call Exod 34:6–7 to mind.[33] The return from exile is perhaps shown in Book V as repristinating the liberation from Egypt and entry to the land, all based on Yahweh's *hesed*, for which the book enjoins *hodu* and *hallelujah*. All psalms that have *hodu* or *hallelujah* refrains deal with the exodus and the conquest.[34]

The final such psalm with links to the golden calf, Psalm 145, ends with David summoning all Israel to praise Yahweh: he is Israel's teacher even after the exile. His experience of sin, exile and restoration is normative for theirs. David is again a type of, and a model for, Israel. His prayers about his enemies, following his apostasy and enjoyment of forgiveness, will inform Israel's prayers following the exile.[35]

---

31. Wenham, "Psalm 103," 154.

32. Kirkpatrick 3:602.

33. Hossfeld-Zenger 3:19.

34. Ballhorn, *Zum Telos des Psalters*, 364.

35. Hensley's detailed study of this "grace formula" in the Psalter (Hensley, *Covenant Relationships*, 209–54) omits Ps 51. He concludes that David is a mediatorial leader who intercedes for the people. Hensley states that David leads and teaches the people to proclaim Yahweh's mercy (as we have seen), but "the king's identification with sinners [is] as a petitioner of God's people, not his personal guilt *per se*" (Hensley, *Covenant Relationships*, 254). While there is much to agree with here, the identification of David's own sin and person with the sin and corporate body of Israel, as a *representative* king is clearly seen in Ps 51, and by extension in Ps 3; Hensley's study of the grace formula in Books III–IV could have profited from Book II, at least. Yes, David leads and teaches the people to proclaim Yahweh's grace, but he teaches by modelling his own experience as one who has needed it and experienced it, not as an advocate.

2.C. David Is the Model for the Exiled and Restored Nation

The Psalter presents David as a type of Israel. David, as representative king, likens his experience of sin, punishment, and forgiveness to the national apostasy of the golden calf, in Ps 51. That same apostasy, with its punishment and forgiveness, is linked to the sin that led to exile, and to the restoration. The nation continued to exist after the apostasy at the golden calf purely because of *hesed*. This same *hesed* means that the Davidic king continues even after his apostasy with Bathsheba. It also brings Israel back from exile, just as David was brought back from his exile under Absalom. *Hesed* restores the Davidic monarchy, both in the life of David and the history of the nation.[36] As Kleer has observed, Book V does not shift away from David because of the exile, but presents a future "David" who addresses the issues of exile. The "David" superscriptions particularly gave the exiles a point of identification, with David offering them solidarity, as they partake of his fate.[37]

We will see now that Book V is arranged to highlight David's prayers against enemies, and to teach the nation to use them, in the light of *hesed*.

3. David the Model User of Imprecations

The superscriptions highlight the prominent role of David in Book V, as we should expect if he is exemplary for Israel. We have identified that Book V is divided into three sections, each with a *hodu* opening, a body, and then a *hallelujah* conclusion. David is found only in the body of each section.

---

36. Baer and Gordon, "חֶסֶד," 2:217.
37. Kleer, "*Der liebliche Sänger*," 86, 93.

Introductory *hodu*	Body of Section	Concluding *hallelujah*
107	108–10 All David Psalms (לְדָוִד, *ledavid*)	111–17
118	119, 120–34 3 or 4 *ledavid* in Ascents, and 4 mentions in body of 132	135
136	137, 138–45 All *ledavid*, save 137	146–50

We see at a glance that David is especially prominent in sections I and III, whose body consists almost entirely of the two final David collections. If the opening to Book V encourages a reliance on Yahweh's mercy, David appears as the exemplar of that attitude in these two David collections that frame the book.[38] Wilson, especially, thought that this "Davidic frame" to Book V consisted of model responses by David to the psalms that precede them.[39]

Moreover, David psalms are exemplary for the nation's response. The David psalms in Book V are very similar to the Psalms in Book I, except that they are communal, rather than individual.[40] The connections between carefully placed David collections in Book V and in Book I make sense of the way that Ps 3 and Ps 51 were deliberately placed to introduce David as an example. He received *hesed* following sin and an "exile," so is eminently suitable to be an example in Book V, which teaches Israel to look back on sin and exile after receiving *hesed*.

The overall shape of the Psalter is from lament to praise, so that laments are comparatively rare in Books IV–V.[41] Imprecations stand out in

38. Howard, "Editorial Activity," 63.

39. Wilson, "Shaping the Psalter," 79, 221.

40. Ballhorn and Hossfeld-Zenger argue that links with the first David collection (Book I) have been made deliberately (Ballhorn, *Zum Telos des Psalters*, 368; Hossfeld-Zenger 3:25). Communal doxologies re-cast the psalms of the individual (mostly David) into communal readings. Moreover, *baruk* ("blessed be . . .") formulas are (outside the Psalter) almost exclusively found in the life of David and Solomon so that the whole Psalter is thus seen as connected with David and his offspring (Ballhorn, *Zum Telos des Psalters*, 61).

41. Westermann, *Praise and Lament*, 256; for an outline of the progression see

Book V: they are in Pss 109, 119, 129, 137, 139–44. These are in the *bodies*, not the *hodu* introductions nor *hallelujah* conclusions, and are mostly on David's lips. There is a meaningful progression. The body of section I is all *ledavid* and includes an imprecation. Most psalms in section II have no authorial attribution, and this includes both the imprecations within it (119, 129). What David models in section I is made more general in section II. Finally, section III begins with the final imprecation that is not of David, but is most obviously national: Ps 137. It begins the body of section III, which then consists entirely of David psalms. Psalm 137 is followed by a David psalm that is a model response; there follows a carefully arranged sequence of imprecations by David, and then finally a David response again. Section III, and perhaps the whole of Book V, has been arranged to help us understand how to use Ps 137. Books I and II have also been needed, to set David up as an appropriate type of the nation in Ps 137.

Efforts to discern the arrangement purely based on pre-existing structures struggled to fit two psalms: see the table of presumed pre-existing units in §1.A above (pp. 173–74). One was Ps 137, which we have just discussed. The other is Ps 119. As we will see when we reach section II, there might be more of David in the Psalms of Ascents (120–34), which leaves imprecatory psalm 119 isolated in the body of section II.[42] As with Ps 137, then, the body of section II opens with an imprecation and then uses David to teach us to read it. The final-form structure in three sections, built around the *hesed* refrain and the *hodu* and *hallelujah* brackets, helps us to understand the placement of these two imprecations.

The structure of Book V emphasizes the exemplary role of David at prayer in the situation that Israel found itself in. We have seen the centrality of *hesed* in that structure, and its application to Israel and the nations. We will see both of these more fully in our exposition of each imprecation in Book V, section by section, in the next three chapters.

Hossfeld-Zenger 3:17–18.

42. Wilson remarked that he could not find entirely satisfactory solutions to the central section (Wilson, "Shaping the Psalter," 79).

11

Retribution in Section I of Book V

Psalm 109

Psalm 109 is the most difficult and most
embarrassing psalm for conventional piety.[1]

The most elaborate and the roughest in the OT.[2]

The most vivid imprecatory language of the biblical psalms.[3]

The only pure psalm of imprecation.[4]

The most shocking psalm in the Psalter, the pure vitriol of distilled hatred.[5]

The poorest, most disdained, most ill-treated of all 150 psalms.[6]

And yet:

He would rather love than hate, rather bless than curse.[7]

Ps 109 should be regarded as one of the most Christian prayers.[8]

1. Brueggemann and Bellinger, *Psalms*, 473.
2. Gerstenberger, *Psalms II*, 258.
3. Wright, "Ritual Analogy," 392.
4. Gunkel, cited in McCann 1124.
5. Goulder, *Psalms of the Return*, 132.
6. "[D]er ärmste, verachtetste, geschundenste aller 150 Psalmen." Lohfink, "Drei Arten," 321.
7. Kirkpatrick 3:653.
8. Jung, *Psalm 109*, 130.

1. Exposition of Psalm 109

As THE FIRST SET of quotations above indicate, Ps 109 contains a notorious imprecation. In recent times, about half of commentators have attributed vv. 6–19 to a quotation. This puts the most vicious language on the lips of David's enemies. However, most will then argue that David is quoting the curses against him in order to invoke the *lex talionis*, so that the imprecation is still practically an imprecation by David against the enemy. In this view, David's adversary has issued vv. 6–19 against him as a curse, and David wishes for this curse to rebound. I have argued elsewhere that neither view is correct.[9] There is indeed a quotation, but it is presented as evidence of a conspiracy against David, which has suborned the perjurious accusation against him. He does not only quote what has been asked against him in court, but their machinations beforehand. This evidence is designed to unmask the wider group of enemies, and to save David from an unjust sentence. His prayer against the enemy comes later, and (as is often noticed) is both very different in tenor, and a far cry from retaliation: hence the second set of quotations above.

It is generally agreed that Ps 109 is full of judicial language. David is on trial for his life, whether metaphorically or literally, and appeals to Yahweh as the judge. As part of his defense, he quotes some words from his enemies. We see as follows.

First, in vv. 1b–5, 20–31 the enemies are always plural: David describes his group of enemies. In vv. 6–19 always singular: the enemies are talking about their single enemy, David.

In vv. 2–5, David turns the attention away from the one accuser who has spoken to condemn David in court, and points to the wider cabal who have sent the wicked accuser. The accuser has just spoken vv. 8–19, and David is now setting them in their hidden context. In vv. 6–7, (when the switch from plural to singular begins) David is reporting how this man came to be standing before him in court, making his accusations. The conspirators had said to each other

> 6 Deputize a wicked man against him,
>   let an accuser stand on his right hand-side.

The intention is to secure a guilty verdict (v. 7) against an innocent party. This precludes the possibility that David is quoting vv. 6–19 as an act of

---

9. This section reuses material previously published in Jenkins, "A Quotation in Psalm 109," 115–35, used by the kind permission of the Tyndale Bulletin.

lex talionis. The law does not allow a false accusation to be met with a false accusation. The law would simply require the desired penalty to fall on the accuser instead. As we will further see, David does not ask for this penalty. This is not retaliation.

The following verses present the sentence that was demanded against David. Once they achieve v. 7 and get David falsely convicted, the enemy want vv. 8–15 to happen.

One does not stand up in court and just ask for a sentence, but has to make an accusation, and we find this in vv. 16–19. Despite some unfounded emendations, all the verbs in vv. 16–18 are indicative, making the accusation against David. It is only in v. 19 that we find a petition "let it be" (תְּהִי *tehi*), which wraps up the prosecution by linking back to the seven previous uses of היה (*hayah*) in petitions ("let him/them be") in the desired sentence of vv. 8–15. All volitive uses of *hayah* ("let him/them be" as opposed to indicative uses "I am") are in the quotation.

After quoting their words, he turns to Yahweh and explains what he has just quoted. This has been the plot of conspirators who have sent the accuser (v. 20). Verse 20 is ambiguously terse, so unavoidable translation decisions import a great deal of interpretation into the rest of the psalm:

זֹאת פְּעֻלַּת שֹׂטְנַי מֵאֵת יְהוָה וְהַדֹּבְרִים רָע עַל־נַפְשִׁי:

> This the work/reward of those who accuse me from[?] Yahweh
> and who are speaking evil concerning me.

In the context of the Psalm, I have argued that this means:

> This [what you have just heard in court] has been the doing of those
> who accuse me in Yahweh's presence
> and who are speaking evil against me.

The conspirators had planned to put the accuser at David's right-hand side. He now points out that the accuser has to stand in *Yahweh's* presence to do so, because court proceedings involving violence on the accusation of only one witness happen in his presence (Deut 19:7). That is why David pointedly ends his psalm by stating that Yahweh is at the right-hand side of the oppressed (Ps 109:31).

Verses 20–21 identify the real miscreants (vv. 2–5) behind the work of accusation (vv. 6–19) in verse 20, and turn the matter over to Yahweh for judgment in verse 21. There is no petition in verse 20: what is quoted is *not* turned onto the accuser's head by David.

What follows is a two-fold appeal to the court. First, David is innocent (vv. 22–25). He is accused of ill-treating the afflicted and oppressed (vv. 16–19) but responds that (ironically) he is the afflicted and oppressed who is being ill-treated through this malicious prosecution. Second, because he is innocent, he desires to be acquitted, and his accusers to be shamed (vv. 27–29).

He ends the psalm much as Ps 7 started, with an all-out wager.

> 30 I will thank Yahweh profusely with my mouth,
>   and in the middle of the throng I will praise him.
> 31 For he will stand at the right-hand side of the oppressed one,
>   to save from those who accuse him of capital crimes.

Verse 31 states what is certainly true: whoever is being falsely accused and facing a death sentence will be vindicated. The one who is oppressed has Yahweh at his right-hand side. Whoever is accusing him will be in trouble. According to the enemy, David is the oppressor; according to David, he is the oppressed. Verse 30 shows his confidence that the matter is already decided: Yahweh knows at whose right-hand to stand, and will therefore vindicate David, who in turn will praise him.

This gives us the following structure for Ps 109. A courtroom accusation is presented as evidence for David's defence in God's court.[10]

---

10. While attribution for everything in this section is given in Jenkins, "A Quotation in Psalm 109," 115–35, I restate here that this structure is only a modification of Egwim, "Determining the Place," 112–30.

1a   Superscription

1b   Appeal to divine judge and anticipation of verdict

2–20   David's accusation against his enemies

    2–5   Accusation against plurality of enemies: they have suborned perjury by sending a wicked accuser to court

    6–19   Exhibit A: the private conspiracy of the wicked enemies

       6–7   Their private decision to send a slanderous accuser

       8–19   Their script for the wicked accuser, which has since been heard in court

          8–15   Appeal to the court by false accuser for punishment

          16–19   Evidence brought forward by false accuser, arguing that David has earned the sentence of 8–15

    20   Claim concerning Exhibit A, restating accusation of 2–5. This has been the plot of the wicked enemies, not the good faith accusation of the man who has been heard in court. They are the ones who have dared to send this accusation against David in Yahweh's very presence

21–29   Appeal to divine court for acquittal

    21   Appeal to justice of court

    22–25   Grounds for appeal: protestation of innocence (David is the victim of 16–19)

    26   Second appeal to justice of court

    27–29   Desired sentence from court: acquittal of David, shaming of wicked conspirators

30–31   Protestation of innocence

    30   Implicit protestation of innocence because of 31

    31   All out wager. Yahweh will take the side of the innocent, whoever that may be. David does not refer to himself in the first person here, but employs the terms of the accusation made against *him* as a wicked accuser

       31a   David is innocent. He is not the oppressor of 16, but is himself the oppressed of 22. If he is lying, Yahweh will not take his side

       31b   He must not merely be acquitted from his wicked accuser in court, but generally be rescued from the wicked conspirators who are accusing him

The aim of this section has not been to rescue the Psalter from itself. Nothing in the above argument means that the brutal petition in verses 8–15 is necessarily always wrong; it might well be an appropriate response to someone who is guilty of verses 16–19. Its partial use in

Acts 1:20 might point in that direction. David does not complain that the penalty of Ps 109:8–19 is harsh. If David had, for example, unlawfully decimated the house of Saul, it would be an application of the *lex talionis* for a survivor of Saul's house to pray like this against David. David acknowledges as much in not silencing the curses of Shimei in 2 Sam 16:5–12 along these very lines, a point missed by Brueggemann's claim that Ps 109 is "unrestrained yearning for retaliation"[11] and "surely engages in 'overkill' . . . without recognizing that nobody needs to be or could possibly be violated in that many ways."[12]

What we have argued is that David is innocently accused, as explained in verses 1–7 and then 20, and that his prayer for vindication extends from verses 21–31, with 6–19 forming part of his evidence, not part of his request. What is particularly interesting is the contrast between the evil they wanted for him, and his prayer against them. It is to David's request against the enemy that we now turn.

2. David's Petition in Psalm 109

2.A. Even While Innocent, He Appeals to Mercy . . .

As we have argued in previous chapters, the innocently accused can simply point out that they are not guilty of the crime at issue. This is not self-righteous, nor does it entail perfection nor rewards for merit. In Ps 109, David has shown that he is falsely accused, and that he relies on Yahweh to protect him. However, David does not appeal to Yahweh's justice, nor to his own innocence.[13] He relies on Yahweh to rescue the falsely accused, but does not describe them as such, but rather as "oppressed." The identity of the oppressor and oppressed hinges on who has shown *hesed*. We have seen that *hesed* is significant in Book V, and will go on to see the significance of the "oppressed."

David pleads his innocence implicitly. First, he expects the verdict to acquit him. Second, the enemies bear false witness (v. 2), driven by hatred (v. 3a), and without due cause (v. 3b). His enemies have had to find a wicked accuser, which would not be needed if the charges were not

---

11. Brueggemann, *Message of the Psalms*, 86.

12. Brueggemann, *Praying the Psalms*, 66.

13. Schökel notes that the psalm lacks a typical protestation of innocence: there is no צדק root, no knowledge by the judge (Schökel II:1357).

false.[14] Third, the accusation against him is specific (vv. 16–19). He is not claiming to be perfectly innocent nor relying on his own merit; but he did not do *this*. "This" is about *hesed*.

David refutes the accusation point by point, as follows. The first charge: "he did not do *hesed*" (v. 16a). On the contrary, David loved his enemies (v. 4) and did them good (v. 5); it is they who display the exact opposite of *hesed* by returning evil for good (v. 5), accusing him with hatred in return for his love (vv. 3–4).[15] If David did not show *hesed*, the fitting sentence is that he be shown no *hesed* (v. 12), and that *Yahweh* would always remember his sin and show no mercy to his progeny (vv. 13–15). Yet, David appeals twice to *Yahweh's hesed* (vv. 21, 26). This appeal to *hesed* implicitly corroborates his defense, because only those who display *hesed* can expect divine *hesed*, as David testified in 18:26. "With the ones who show *hesed* you show yourself to be full of *hesed*" (עִם־חָסִיד תִּתְחַסָּד, *'im-hasid tithasad*).

This logic is not inconsequential in Book V. Israel is learning that divine *hesed* had always been their only hope, and the only reason why they have come out of exile. David is enlisted as teacher because he has displayed an ethic that is aware of the need to receive and show mercy, in Books I and II. David teaches that if Israel needs *hesed*, they must display it to others.

Second charge: he pursued one who was "afflicted and oppressed" (אִישׁ־עָנִי וְאֶבְיוֹן, *'ish-'ani we'evyon*), to kill him (v. 16b). In v. 22, David replies that, on the contrary, "*I* am the one who is afflicted and oppressed" (כִּי־עָנִי וְאֶבְיוֹן אָנֹכִי, *ki-'ani we'evyon 'anoki*). That is his ground for deliverance (כִּי, *ki*, "for" connecting with v. 21). We will see the significance of "afflicted and oppressed" in Book V below.

Third, far from curses refreshing him like oil into his bones (v. 18), he has no fat in his body at all (v. 24). Cursing should cling to him constantly from now on (v. 19), but in fact there is no future for him, he is already like a shadow fading in the evening (v. 23). He stands accused of cursing (vv. 17–18), whereas it is his accusers who have cursed him (v. 28).

Finally, as we saw above, David's praise in v. 30 is conditional on his innocence, and is therefore a claim of innocence. Verses 30–31 are not celebrating Yahweh's ability to save his servants regardless of their guilt,

---

14. Seybold 434.

15. Schmidt's removal of the end of v. 5 on the grounds that it is repetitive of v. 4a (Schmidt, *Das Gebet der Angeklagten*, 42n1) is to be rejected.

but implicitly praising him for acquitting the *righteous*.[16] This הלל (*halal* praise) root which closes the psalm, also opened it: "God of my praise" (אֱלֹהֵי תְהִלָּתִי, *'elohey tehillati*). This opening invocation sets up the whole psalm as presuming David's innocence before the divine judge. This *halal* (from which *hallelujah*) and *hesed* are not only structuring devices of Ps 109. They form the structure of Book V. The book teaches Israel to thank and praise, and here we have David at prayer, thanking and praising. The teacher of Israel is showing the way.

2.B. . . . And He Shows Mercy

It has often been assumed that David quotes the curses against him in order to appeal for retribution, in line with the *lex talionis*. Whatever they wanted for me, let it land on them. I have argued above that this cannot be. Nonetheless, he might go on to ask for something like proportional retribution when he asks for Yahweh to intervene (vv. 21, 26). How closely does he turn their clothing metaphor against them in v. 29? What does their shaming mean in v. 28? We might think that it involves their losing the case and facing the punishment that they plotted against him. The sentence sought for David was death and extended family ruin.[17] He was to die (vv. 8–9), his wife and children ruined (vv. 9–12), and his progeny wiped out, finding no mercy from Yahweh (vv. 13–15).

On the contrary, David's requests are minimal. The conspirators are not judicially liable, unlike the false accuser who has appeared in court. David could legitimately pray for God to judge them in a fitting way, but that is not the automatic result of his winning the court case.

The very fact that David re-uses their clothing metaphor helps us to see his mild petition in the light of their breathless baying. They pray for curses (v. 19), and he pointedly does not. He instead asks Yahweh to bless (v. 28). The contrast in v. 28a is elegantly highlighted with redundant pronouns and economy of words: *they* curse, but *you* bless (יְקַלְלוּ־הֵמָּה וְאַתָּה תְבָרֵךְ, *yeqallu-hemmah we'attah tebarek*). Yahweh will bless David, overturning their curse, and the second verset shows the effect on them. If we expect them to receive retribution, not so. In v. 28b, they have risen

---

16. *Contra* Vesco 1050.

17. Seybold 435; Firth, *Surrendering*, 40–41; Vesco 1046–47.

(קָמוּ *qamu*, often used of enemy attack in the Psalms), but the only consequence is that they are shamed.[18]

Putting the enemy and David's requests side by side shows the
contrast:

vv. 17–19

17וַיֶּאֱהַב קְלָלָה וַתְּבוֹאֵהוּ וְלֹא־חָפֵץ בִּבְרָכָה וַתִּרְחַק מִמֶּנּוּ׃
18וַיִּלְבַּשׁ קְלָלָה כְּמַדּוֹ וַתָּבֹא כַמַּיִם בְּקִרְבּוֹ וְכַשֶּׁמֶן בְּעַצְמוֹתָיו׃
19תְּהִי־לוֹ כְּבֶגֶד יַעְטֶה וּלְמֵזַח תָּמִיד יַחְגְּרֶהָ׃

vv. 28–29

28יְקַלְלוּ־הֵמָּה וְאַתָּה תְבָרֵךְ קָמוּ | וַיֵּבֹשׁוּ וְעַבְדְּךָ יִשְׂמָח׃
29יִלְבְּשׁוּ שׂוֹטְנַי כְּלִמָּה וְיַעֲטוּ כַמְעִיל בָּשְׁתָּם׃

They claim he loves cursing (קְלָלָה, *qelalah*), and ask for blessing
(בְּרָכָה, *berakah*) to elude him (v. 17). He instead simply points out that
they are into cursing (יְקַלְלוּ, *yeqalelu*), but Yahweh into blessing (תְבָרֵךְ,
tevarek) (v. 28). They say (v. 18) that he attired (וַיִּלְבַּשׁ, *vayyilbash*) cursing
(*qelalah* again), and that it penetrated into him (like water into his body,
like oil into his bones). As a result, "may it [i.e., cursing] be to him like a
garment wrapped" (v. 19), and like his belt that he wears daily. He, for his
part, subverts their metaphor of wearing garments to ask for much less:
"May my accusers attire dishonor, may they wrap up" in their shame (v.
29).[19] The repetition of attiring, wrapping, brings out the pointed contrast: they wish deadly curses on him, and he *does not* reciprocate.

The lengthy metaphor of v. 18, is absent from v. 29. The explicit petition of v. 19 is matched by one verb (עטה *'atah* wrap) and the simple
metaphor of the garment (כְּבֶגֶד → כַּמְעִיל, *kebeged* "like a garment" →
kame'il "like a mantle"), but the backwards referent to "curse" of v. 19a
is absent, as is the permanently binding belt of v. 19b. Verse 29 is greatly
toned down in metaphors, in length of punishment and in the basic nature of the punishment. Instead of asking for them to be engulfed with
deadly curses, he merely asks for them to be shamed (v. 29).

18. An emendation based on LXX and allegedly supported by parallelism (Kraus
2:919) does not fundamentally change this.

19. כְּלִמָּה, in v. 29, is frequently found in parallel with בוש words, as here (35:26;
69:20; Isa 30:3; Jer 3:25), or in contrast with כָּבוֹד (4:3; 44:16; 69:8; 71:13; Prov 18:3; Job
20:3; Ezek 16:63; 39:23).

2.C. . . . Or Does He Ask for a Death Sentence After All?

Some infer a death sentence in David's prayer for "shaming." First, Pietro Bovati argues that shame was an inseparable element of a guilty verdict and therefore very closely linked with the death sentence. However, it is experienced before that sentence: they are distinguishable. He cites passages where shame is contrasted with honor or joy: Isa 41:11; Pss 31:17; 37:19–20; 71:13; 83:17; 129:5–6.[20] However, in each passage, shaming is the prelude of death. Death is mentioned separately, in every case. David mentions no such thing here. He is asking for shame and *not* for death.

Second, Firth: "the prayer for Yahweh's vindication of the psalmist to be apparent to all (verses 26–29) assumes that the imprecations sought in verses 6–20 are to be applied."[21] Firth assumes that David's vindication and their wrongdoing would only be made public by such an outcome. On the contrary, the mere fact of David *not* suffering the penalty they ask for would already show that he is innocent, whereas their case is wicked. Even if the expected legal outcome were more than shaming, we have already shown that a boomerang of their imprecations would be illegal. Whatever punishment may be appropriate, if the desire is to know who is guilty and innocent (as Firth suggests), then anything short of David's death would do.[22]

As Gerald Downing observes, concerning psalms of innocent suffering:

> [Ps 7] appeals for judgment (v. 8), which means personal protection and the downfall of the poet's enemies and all who are wicked. Only that will establish innocence; compare Pss 31:18, 23; 35:11, 26–27; 64:4, 7; 94:21–23. In every case it is well-being that establishes innocence, and punishment that indicates guilt. . . . But in neither case is a formal verdict sought for its own sake or even as a preliminary.[23]

---

20. Bovati, *Ristabilire la Giustizia*, 341–42.

21. Firth, *Surrendering*, 42.

22. Frank van der Velden's study of shaming lexemes concludes that they are often associated with wider destruction. Nonetheless, he merely concludes about these verses that shaming is *not inconsistent* with the wider destruction of the enemy asked for in vv. 6–19 (Velden, *Psalm 109*, 92–97). Since vv. 16–19 are not David's request, then we *are* left with his petition for shaming and nothing more.

23. Downing, "Justification as Acquittal?," 307. His wider claim, that there is *never* a separate performative declaration, does not seem to account for such passages as Deut 25:1–2; Job 42:7–8. Nonetheless, I believe it to be accurate in the petitions of psalms of innocence.

Generally speaking, Downing is accurately describing how judgment has to work in such cases. That only makes it all the more shocking that David asks for nothing like the judgment that his enemies deserve. He appears quite content to walk away with his own neck, feeling little need for retribution.

2.D. David Repays Malice with Mercy

"Shaming" is so far out of proportion with their imprecation against David, that it is staggeringly merciful. Kirkpatrick concludes: "He would rather love than hate, rather bless than curse."[24] The opening of the psalm had set up the enemy as particularly heinous, returning hatred for love, and evil for good, leading to a sense of utter betrayal.[25] We should therefore consider David to be restrained if he *merely* asked for exact retribution—but he does not even do that. He leaves them alone.

> Ps 109 reminds us of the suffering Christ, who, though maligned, did not return evil for evil . . . but letting his adversaries be (cf. Ps 109,28), completely entrusted himself to God's faithful salvific predilection. . . . Ps 109 should be regarded as one of the most Christian prayers.[26]

To put it negatively, if David were praying vv. 6–19, then Willy Stärk would show us the problem: "If we could erase the major central section of this psalm, verses 6–20, we would have one of the most tender prayers of petition that honest piety ever sent up to God out of the suffering of body and soul."[27] We have the widespread judgment that 6–20 is the worst example in the Bible, so David clearly prays two different things inside and outside that central passage.[28] The most coherent explanation, as I have argued, is that the central passage is David's evidence of a conspiracy.[29] David's actual petition is "one of the most tender prayers." We will see the function of this tenderness in Book V, as David is a model of prayer.

---

24. Kirkpatrick 3:653.

25. Wenham, *Psalms as Torah*, 171.

26. Jung, *Psalm 109*, 130.

27. Cited in Zenger, *God of Vengeance?*, 58.

28. The sharp contrast between the petitions in vv. 6–19 and vv. 21–31 is often noted: Firth, *Surrendering*, 41–42; Creager, "Note on Psalm 109," 122.

29. Jenkins, "A Quotation in Psalm 109," 134–35.

His prayer for the wider conspirators is as striking in its mercy as theirs was in its cruelty. They accused him of not showing *hesed* (v. 16). In answer, he shows them a completely unmerited charity, foregoing the punishment that they have earned—the essence of *hesed* in divine-human relationships. That is what he asks Yahweh for twice (vv. 21, 26). He then imitates the God who blesses in response to cursing (v. 28). He shows *hesed* to his enemy, and he does this as a teacher of Israel.

3. Psalm 109 within the Structure of Book V

As we showed in the previous chapter, Book V is structured in three sections, and each has an opening, with a psalm marked by *hodu* (give thanks), a body and concluding section of *hallelujah* (praise Yahweh) psalms. Psalm 109 is in the body of section I, and that body consists entirely of David psalms.

Introductory *hodu*	Body of Section	Concluding *hallelujah*
107	108–10 All David Psalms (לְדָוִד, *ledavid*)	111–17

This first section sets up David as the teacher of Israel at prayer, and especially at prayer in the light of enemy nations.[30] We will now see how Ps 109 is presented within the context of section I. The concluding *hallelujah* introduces such important new themes that we will treat Pss 107–10 first, and then turn to 111–17.

3.A. David the Model for Israel: *Hesed* and the "Afflicted and Oppressed"

We have seen throughout our exposition that there is an often-recognized connection between David and the nation; each Book of the Psalter presents David, the representative king, as the recipient of mercy. The opening psalms of Book V are connected through word links which further establish the connection between David and the nation in need of Yahweh's *hesed*. Before we explore how David is the model recipient of

---

30. Howard, "Editorial Activity," 63.

hesed, in Pss 107–10, we introduce a further link between David and the nation: David the "afflicted and oppressed."

In our current climate, to identify someone as a victim, to say that they are afflicted or oppressed, is tantamount to calling them righteous.

Two terms frequently occur together in the Psalter to describe the victim: עָנִי (*'ani*, "poor, afflicted," hereafter always "afflicted") and אֶבְיוֹן (*'ebyon*, "needy, oppressed," hereafter always "oppressed"). These terms describe those who are under threat or affliction, whether economic or otherwise.[31] It is the righteous who are frequently described as *'ani*, "afflicted" and *'ebyon* "oppressed."[32] It would be tempting to see David as adopting our modern attitude, where calling himself "afflicted and oppressed" is the new righteousness. However, the picture in the Psalms is more interesting and instructive, both for post-exilic Israel and for our modern culture. As Creach rightly cautions, "their victim status alone does not render them righteous."[33]

When these two terms appear together in Books I and II, they always refer to innocent sufferers (9:19 [18]; 35:10; 37:14; 40:18 [17]; 70:6 [5]), and it is the king's job to defend them (72:4, 12).

In Book III, however, things change. Psalm 74:21 cries out from the perspective of an eyewitness of the final invasion before the exile. The psalm appeals to everything *except for* Israel's righteousness. Nonetheless, they are *'ani* and *'ebyon*, while guilty of national apostasy. The "poor and oppressed" appear again in the only prayer of David in Book III, where he opens his plea by identifying himself as *'ani* and *'ebyon* (86:1). This is the very psalm we have seen before, where David appeals to the mercy revealed in Exod 34:6–7. Nowhere else in Book III do we find *'ani* and *'ebyon* together. Both David and Israel, in Book III, are presented as "afflicted and oppressed" as a result of their own apostasy, on a par with the golden calf: the exile in Israel's case (which is the subject of all of Book III) and the incident with Bathsheba and Uriah referred to in Pss 51 and 3. No longer can Israel simply plead their need, nor the wickedness of their attackers; they are in the situation that David had modelled for them in Ps 3. Wickedly oppressed by human evil, yet deservedly so by Yahweh's righteous judgment. If Yahweh is going to show them compassion because of their affliction, it will have to be by showing *hesed*.

31. Wenham, *Psalms as Torah*, 116n27.
32. Creach, "The Destiny of the Righteous," 50.
33. Creach, *The Destiny of the Righteous in the Psalms*, 5.

In Book IV, there are only two David psalms: 101 and 103. The latter, as we saw above, alludes to the mercy of Exod 34. Psalm 102, nestled between these David psalms, is "a prayer of one afflicted" (תְּפִלָּה לְעָנִי, *tefillah le'ani*). Since David takes over as the lead character in the end of Book IV, he is perhaps here identified as the afflicted one, or as one to model how to pray when afflicted. It is in the David psalms that the theology of the lowly found in Books I–IV reappear in Book V.[34]

As we will see in the rest of this chapter, *afflicted* and *oppressed* will first be applied to Israel in Ps 107, but as the opposite of a plea of innocence: it describes the exile as the outcome of their guilt, and their need for unmerited *hesed*. Psalm 109 uses the terms significantly as part of the accusation against David and his defense; he will model the right behavior of the *afflicted* and *oppressed*. The innocent oppressed might ask for justice, while the guilty must appeal to *hesed*. In Ps 109, innocent David presents himself as the innocent oppressed, yet in need of *hesed*.

David in the Psalter is presented to identify with the needy, the lowly, the oppressed.[35] Yet, he does not wear the titles *'ani* and *'ebyon* as a get-out-of-jail free card. Within the praise that permeates Book V, the harming of enemies is prominent in Pss 108–10.[36] It is as an individual in the face of enemies that David represents Israel, faced by enemy nations.[37] This is especially brought out in Pss 107–10.[38] How does David, modelling national prayer in light of the return from exile, pray for the enemy?

3.B. Psalm 107: Thank Yahweh for His Mercy

Psalm 107 opens with the refrain of Book V, thanking (*hodu*) Yahweh for his *hesed*. In compressed form, this becomes the refrain that structures Ps 107: "let them thank [same root as *hodu*] Yahweh for his *hesed*" (vv. 8, 15, [21,] 31).[39]

---

34. Bremer, "Ps 107," 36.

35. Mays, *The Lord Reigns*, 123; Creach, *The Destiny of the Righteous in the Psalms*, 8.

36. Velden, *Psalm 109*, 126.

37. Velden, *Psalm 109*, 130–31; Goulder, *Psalms of the Return*, 133; Jung, *Psalm 109*, 131.

38. Jung, *Psalm 109*, 116–23.

39. The inverted *nun* suggests we treat v. 21 with caution; I will avoid building a case entirely on the content of verses which are marked by inverted *nunnim* in this psalm, which are vv. 23–28 (Alep) and vv. 21–26, 40 (L).

Psalm 107 puts this *hesed* and the nation's affliction in a particular context: Yahweh's merciful rescue of *sinful* Israel. *Hesed* need not imply sin, but here the context supplies it. In v. 11 they rebel, and when they are rescued from the consequences (v. 14) they are to thank Yahweh for *hesed* (v. 15).[40] Likewise in v. 17, they sin, Yahweh rescues them (v. 20), and they should thank Yahweh for *hesed* (v. 21). These are two of the four scenes, each ending with the refrain, which describe their situation in exile, the result of their national apostasy, and from which Yahweh has nonetheless rescued them (vv. 2–3).[41] Verses 2–3 thus show that Ps 107 answers the prayer of Ps 106.[42] A plethora of tight linguistic connections make the connection between exilic peril (Ps 106) and return (Ps 107).[43] In v. 17, the exile from which they need merciful *hesed* is described as "they were afflicted" (יִתְעַנּוּ, *yit'annu* same root as *'ani* "afflicted"). They are suffering as victims, but not innocent victims.

After the two scenes of sin and rescue, comes Yahweh's post-exilic provision: a restored homeland (vv. 33–38), and his protection from the nations (vv. 39–42).[44] If this could refer to providential care for all nations, in context it shows how to understand the return from exile.[45]

The psalm ends with an explicit message: think carefully about your situation (these things just described, v. 43a), and bear in mind that they flow from Yahweh's *hesed* (v. 43b).[46] Yahweh's *hesed* is the theme of the psalm; it presents recognizable instances of *hesed* which are to be pondered.[47] The wise will know (v. 43) that their current prosperity (vv. 33–38) is the opposite of what their sins deserve (vv. 1–32).

Israel deserved their affliction, but were rescued from the nations because of *hesed*. The nations were defeated (vv. 39–42), not because of Israel's uprightness, but because of God's mercy. This is also how Book

40. Vesco 1025.

41. Kirkpatrick 3:637–38.

42. Vesco 1025; Hossfeld-Zenger 3:142; Seybold 428. Some deem vv. 2–3 redactional, because the following descriptions do not match the exiles (Kraus 2:911; Ravasi III:202; Seybold 428). However, the connection is tight: the four episodes describing the exiles follow from the four cardinal points that describe their ingathering from exile in v. 3 (Hossfeld-Zenger 3:142).

43. Hossfeld-Zenger 3:145; Vesco 1025.

44. Kirkpatrick 3:637–38.

45. Hossfeld-Zenger 3:144; Kraus 2:914–15.

46. Hossfeld-Zenger 3:144.

47. Seybold 428.

IV had ended: Yahweh's *hesed* is both dependable (Ps 105) and necessary because of sin (Ps 106). As in Ps 109, there is no explicit retribution
against the enemy. Wickedness shuts its mouth (v. 42); even if these are
the wicked enemy, all that happens is that they are silenced, not punished.[48] This calls for reflection among the restored exiles: how should
they think of their former enemies? In order to help them, the Psalm
ends by describing the rescue of Israel as "the oppressed out of affliction"
(using the roots of *'ani* and *'ebyon*, v. 41). These are the titles David has
given himself to identify with the nation. We are then given three David
psalms, in the middle of which he will claim this pair of titles.

3.C. Psalm 108: How Shall We Pray about Edom?

David, the "afflicted and oppressed" in need of *hesed*, is introduced here
with a psalm (Ps 108) spliced from two halves of David psalms from
Book II. First, Ps 57, which is an individual psalm; then Ps 60, which was
a national one. David the individual and David the national representative are brought together. The portion quoted from Ps 57 expands the
conclusion of Ps 107 individually, while the portion quoted from Ps 60
expands the same conclusion nationally: to consider Yahweh's *hesed*.

   The second part of Ps 108, from Ps 60, will involve the extensive
defeat of enemy nations. This sounds promising in the light of exile.
However, David does not begin there. He begins with Ps 57 and an even
more extensive, indeed universal, activity than this defeat. He will praise
Yahweh on heaven and on earth—everywhere (vv. 2–6 [1–5]). Specifically, he will thank (same root as *hodu*) Yahweh internationally (v. 4 [3])
because of his *hesed* (v. 5 [4]). Psalm 107 ends by telling the wise to consider this *hesed* shown to Israel; the refrain of Book V, repeated within Ps
107, enjoins thanking Yahweh for his *hesed*. David then vows to do that
among the nations of the world. Psalm 108 picks up on Yahweh's rescue
of Israel because of his *hesed* (108:7–14 [6–13]) as described at the end
of Ps 107 (vv. 33–38). But, as we saw in Pss 18 and 19, this turns into
international proclamation of Yahweh's rescuing disposition.

   The global scale which the Psalter anticipated in Ps 2 and on which
it will end in Ps 150, reappears in Pss 107–8. *Hesed* is a double-edged
sword. Undeserved kindness is Israel's only hope against the enemy nations; but why should the nations not "deserve" *undeserved* kindness? In

---

48. Hossfeld-Zenger 3:157.

Ps 109, David is accused of failing to show *hesed*. He appeals to Yahweh not for his justice (though, being innocent, he could) but for his *hesed*. He displays *hesed* in his lack of prayer for punishment against his enemies. What does this teach Israel to pray against their defeated enemy nations?

If Book V is addressing the returnees from exile, vengeance against Edom would loom large (Obad 15–21; Ps 137). Edom is prominent as the climax of the list of nations in 108:11 [10] and appears twice. In Ps 60, this is reinforced by the superscription of Ps 60, which further mentions Edom.[49] Edom enters Book V noticeably in the first David psalm, and will only reappear in Ps 137, as we will see. (The only other mention in the psalter is Ps 83:7, where Edom is profiting over Israel's exile, as in Ps 137.) The placement of Ps 109 after the mention of Edom is suggestive.[50]

Hesed, is prominent in the context of Ps 109 (Book V and Pss 107–8, as described) and central to the structure of Ps 109 itself. David had to have shown *hesed* in Ps 109, otherwise he would have been condemned. Yet in Book V, *hesed* involves God's forgiveness of Israel, allowing a merciful return from exile, instead of the judgment which has been earned. Now Ps 109 appears, with David and his enemies as models of Israel and the exilic enemies. How would this inform the reader as he ponders Edom?

The relationship between Israel and Babylon is similar to that between David and Absalom in Ps 3, as we have seen. However, in Ps 109, we have a relationship more closely paralleled by Israel and Edom (rather than Babylon). The enemies in the psalm are off stage. They do not take part in the punishment against David; rather, they conspire to bring about the punishment, and they engage the accuser in court. This is how Edom is presented in Ps 137:7, egging Babylon on to destroy Jerusalem. They too were off stage, while Babylon did the work. It is no surprise to find Ps 108 celebrating Yahweh's triumph over nations and homing in on Edom. We will return to Edom in Ps 137.

We should review how David prays for his enemies in Ps 109 as an example for restored Israel.

---

49. Rashi appears to discern this prominence, since without explanation he identifies the wicked of 109:2 as Esau (Rashi, *Psalms*, 640).

50. McCann 1125. I am therefore less convinced that Edom in Ps 108 "is the eschatological archenemy" (*contra* Allen, *Psalms 101–150*, 79).

3.D. Psalm 109: Receive Mercy, Show Mercy

In Ps 109, as we have seen, *hesed* is a key structuring device and is central
to the accusation against David.[51] It also links Ps 109 to its context. In the
preceding psalm, when Yahweh is thanked (same root as *hodu*) in 108:4
[3] it is for *hesed* (v. 5). As Goulder notes, this means that the closing "I
will give thanks" (same root as *hodu*) in Ps 109:30 "recalls the refrain of
Psalm 107, and 108.4."[52] Psalm 109 ends by promising to fulfil the command of Ps 107, by thanking Yahweh.[53] Moreover, Psalm 109 twice asks
Yahweh to show him *hesed* (vv. 21, 26). Thus, Psalm 109:30 has David
personally modelling the response that Book V is demanding of Israel:
he thanked Yahweh for his *hesed*. Psalms 107–9 are a sequence of psalms
that connect David and Israel: David as the representative and exemplary
king, models how to give thanks to Yahweh for *hesed*. His history in Ps
109 has been one of being shown *hesed*, and showing *hesed* to his enemies
in return. Israel's history has been one of receiving *hesed*. How should
they then respond to their enemies?

Psalm 109 should give pause to the reader who is thirsty for Edom's
blood after reading Ps 108. First, it portrays an enemy whose prayer
against David is at least as vicious as Edom's design for Israel. Surprisingly, even though David is confident of righteous victory, he does not
explicitly ask for appropriate retribution.

Second, David does not ask for acquittal according to his innocence
or Yahweh's justice. He begs for rescue according to Yahweh's *hesed*. This
is remarkable since David makes it clear that he *is* innocent. This focus
on *hesed* is what links David and Israel. In isolation, *hesed* in Ps 109 could
simply mean the application of justice, without implying that sin is forgiven. However, we have seen that *hesed* in Book V has a more slanted
history. Israel relies on divine *hesed* for restoration, because of her sin,
in Ps 107. In Ps 108, Yahweh rescues Israel because of *hesed* (108:5 [4],
13–14 12–13]), despite her sin (108:12 [11]). In Ps 109, Yahweh stands
not at the right hand of the righteous, but the afflicted and oppressed (*'ani
we'ebyon* 109:16, 31). In its context, Ps 109 may be read in the light of the

---

51. McCann calls חֶסֶד the keyword of the psalm (McCann, *Psalms as Torah*, 115),
while Brueggemann sees the four uses of חֶסֶד as the key to understanding the Psalm
(Brueggemann, "Psalm 109," 149).

52. Goulder, *Psalms of the Return*, 141.

53. McCann 1125.

victory over the nations of Ps 108.[54] Psalms 107–9 invite the question: why should Yahweh not stand at the right hand of the wicked nations when they become afflicted and oppressed? Why not show them *hesed* when they need it? This becomes quite pointed, as we see next.

Third, Ps 109 centers on the accusation that David failed to show *hesed* to the *'ani we'ebyon* and loved to curse. David pleads with God that he himself is the *'ani we'ebyon*. In Book V, David is the *'ani we'ebyon* who represents Israel when the nation is *'ani we'ebyon*. Israel was so because of sin leading to exile; the restoration from exile was *merciful hesed*. What attitude would that foster towards Edom, mentioned in Ps 108? If Edom becomes *'ani we'ebyon* because of their own sin, and Israel were to demand divine retribution against them, would that not leave Israel open to the exact charge-sheet of 109:16–18? They might notice that Ps 109 ends by assuring us that God is on the right-hand side of the oppressed *'ebyon*. In its context, David's appeal to *hesed*, refutation that he loved to curse, silence on retribution, and reliance on the God who blesses, should be arresting for anyone tempted to curse Edom and to ask for retribution. Whoever prays Ps 108, with Edom in focus, commits himself to appreciating God's *hesed*.

5 [4] For great over the heavens is your *hesed*

The placement of Ps 109 is suggestive, with its focus on *'ani we'ebyon*, the wicked cursing, the godly showing *hesed* and relying on divine *hesed* and blessing. All this is within Book V which has highlighted the response to *hesed* of thanking and praising. Israel is taught by David not only to imitate David's attitude to his enemies but also to imitate Yahweh's *hesed* towards Israel. The extended emphasis on the destruction of children (vv. 9a, 10, 12b–15), and especially the withholding of *hesed* from them (v. 12, in parallelism) is a striking link with Ps 137, where Edom is the target. David's attitude in Ps 109 corresponds to Goulder's description of David earlier in the Psalter, as expected if Book V is using the same David to teach Israel: David relied on Yahweh's mercy, and *therefore* expressed it to his enemies, fasting and praying for them, limiting his imprecations against them.[55]

Psalm 107 set up Israel as the "oppressed" exiles, having been rescued by Yahweh. Psalm 108 is a petition for rescue against worldwide

---

54. Vesco 1046; McCann 1125.
55. Goulder, *Psalms of the Return*, 141.

foes. Psalm 109 is a petition of rescue by the oppressed from the wicked. What is true of David in Pss 108–9 is therefore applied to the nation of Ps 107. David stands for the oppressed collectively in Pss 108–9. This sets up Ps 110, so that the enemy are the nations, and the oppressed are rescued by Yahweh's world-king.[56]

3.E. Psalm 110: Repent or Perish

One way to summarize the plot of Ps 109 is that the wicked had placed a perjurious accuser at David's "right-hand side" (109:6), but Yahweh can be depended on to defend the oppressed (*ʾebyon*) at their "right-hand side" (final verse). In the first verse of Psalm 110, David quotes Yahweh's invitation to his own Master: "Sit at my right-hand side" (v. 1).[57] The one oppressed in Ps 109 is enthroned in Ps 110.[58] David here represents the whole of God's "oppressed" people at any point in history.[59]

Psalm 110 announces victory and judgment over all nations.[60] This puts the nations in need of the *hesed* that Israel has enjoyed. Psalm 108 commits the reader to proclaiming God's *hesed* among the nations (108:2–6 [1–5]). That *hesed* means rescue for undeserving sinful Israel. How will they go about the nations of 108:8–11 [7–10] proclaiming such a message of *hesed* while simultaneously demanding retribution against those same nations?

The David of Book I received *hesed* because he showed it (18:26 [25]), and he is the teacher of Book V. With an eye to the presumed dissonance between the Psalter's ethics and Jesus, we might consider the rationale for the Lord's Prayer in Matt 6:14–15: "For if you forgive people their transgressions, your heavenly father will indeed forgive you; but if you do not forgive people, neither will your father forgive your transgressions." Or Jesus's parable of the unforgiving servant "Were you not also bound to show mercy to your fellow servant, just as I myself showed mercy to you?" (Matt 18:33).

---

56. Leuenberger, *Konzeptionen*, 291.

57. Lohfink, "Drei Arten," 336.

58. Ballhorn, *Zum Telos des Psalters*, 365.

59. Lohfink, "Drei Arten," 336.

60. E.g., Zenger, "Composition and Theology," 90–91; Leuenberger, *Konzeptionen*, 291.

The victory of Ps 110 is an expression of the option given to the nations in Ps 2—victory by glad surrender or crushing defeat. David in Pss 18 and 19 proclaimed Yahweh's life-giving word to the nations. Now he teaches Israel to desire the victory to come through nations receiving mercy in surrender, not retribution in defeat.

3.F. Response to Enemy in 107–110

The body of section I of Book V (Psalms 108–10) has built on the representative nature of king David. He had been introduced to the Psalter in a type of exile, punished righteously for his sins by Yahweh, oppressed wickedly by Yahweh's agent Absalom, and rescued by Yahweh's undeserved *hesed*. Book V introduced Israel as returned from exile and their *affliction and oppression* also as an act of unmerited *hesed* from Yahweh. However wicked the Babylonian invaders and captors may have been (on which more below), they were Yahweh's chosen agents of judgment. He sent them into exile as a righteous punishment.

The sequence of Pss 108–10 has connected David's personal receipt of mercy with his display of it to the afflicted and oppressed (Ps 109). Psalm 109 has been nestled between psalms that draw attention to the enemies, especially Edom (Ps 108), and which promise divine victory over them (Ps 110). This sequence serves the command on which Ps 107 ends: that the righteous should meditate on *hesed*. David's remarkable restraint against his abominably unrighteous and vicious enemies, his reliance on Yahweh's blessing, and his own awareness of needing *hesed* and showing it to the afflicted, is a model for Israel when they consider their now defeated exilic enemies. Israel has been rescued from oppression by *hesed*. Now their enemies are in need of *hesed*.

Appropriately, *hesed* for Israel's foreign enemies is a theme taken up in the following psalms. The concluding *hallelujah* collection of this section of Book V introduces the nations as those who can enjoy Yahweh's blessing and join in Israel's chorus of thanks and praise: "those who fear Yahweh."

4. Concluding *Hallelujah*: Every Nation Invited to Be "Those Who Fear Yahweh"

The concluding part of section I of Book V is marked by *hallelujah*. It falls into two halves, wrapped around a central psalm. The psalms of the first half each begin with *hallelujah*. Those of the second half each end with it. The psalms that end each half begin and end with *hallelujah*. This wrapper highlights Ps 114, which lacks *hallelujah*.[61] It concerns the exodus, and opens "During the exit of Israel from Egypt." This exodus from Egypt surrounded by Hallelujah has given this collection of psalms the ancient title of "Egyptian Hallel."[62]

	111	112	113	114	115	116	117
Begins:	*hallelujah*	*hallelujah*	*hallelujah*	exodus			*hallelujah*
Ends:			*hallelujah*		*hallelujah*	*hallelujah*	*hallelujah*

The function of this concluding Hallel (Pss 111–17) is to emphasize that *all* nations are being summoned to thank and praise Yahweh for his *hesed*.[63] The psalm which closes the first triad is a call to praise Yahweh globally, especially:

> **3** From the sun's rising to its setting,
>   let Yahweh's name be praised.[64]
> **4** Exalted over all nations is Yahweh
>   over the heavens is his glory.

61. The superficial oddity of it lacking *hallelujah* might explain why LXX has transferred it from the end of Ps 113 to the start of Ps 114 (Rahlfs, *Psalmi*, 280). On this structure see, e.g., Ravasi III:303–5; Vesco 1061–99; Robertson, *Flow of the Psalms*, 233–34.

62. In liturgical tradition, the Egyptian Hallel usually includes Ps 118 (Holladay, *Psalms*, 115, 143; Gillingham, *Psalms*, 44, 111), which Wilson seems sometimes to include and sometimes to exclude (Wilson, *Editing*, 220–21). Even if this liturgical tradition represented an earlier literary group, it is now split by the structuring devices of Book V (Hossfeld-Zenger 3:20–21), just as the narrative of Pss 105–7 has been split across the Books. For arguments that the collection should span 113–18, see Hayes, "Unity," 145–56; Kim, "Strategic Arrangement," 149–50, which both fail to do justice to the evidence that Wilson presents.

63. Hossfeld-Zenger 3:246; he argues that this was the original function of the Egyptian Hallel, before 111–12 were added and 118 removed; I will show that it continues to be the case.

64. We infer the volitive mood for the participial phrase מְהֻלָּל שֵׁם יְהוָה (v. 3b) from the explicitly marked jussive in v. 2a, which is parallel with it, since 2b and 3a each describe the extent of the praise (in time and space respectively) leaving 2a and 3b in synonymous parallelism, with vv. 2–3 in an ABB'A' structure. Further, if v. 3b were indicative, and the name were already being praised everywhere, the volitive of 2a would make no logical sense. See also Delitzsch 692.

The psalm celebrates God's condescension to the lowly.[65] Psalms 107–10 had applied Israel's and David's oppressed status to the nations, and here 113:7 reuses "oppressed" in describing those whom Yahweh lifts up (*'ebyon* as well as דָּל, *dal*, "poor"). Up to that the command to praise Yahweh had included all nations (vv. 3–6).[66] The promise to lift up these poor and oppressed "with the princes of his people" would most obviously refer to the nations, and not Israel. The instruction of v. 3 is that:

> (C.) God's praise is not merely to be ceaseless, but universal; (Z.) not restricted by the limits of Judea, but extending to the utmost bounds of the earth.[67]

Turning to the second triad of *hallelujah* psalms, we find that the nations are observing Israel. The second triad indicates that the nations are watching Israel's fate. Psalm 115 opens with concern for Yahweh's glory, because of his *hesed*, but immediately applies that concern to what the nations will infer about him when they see Israel in distress: where is their god (v. 2)? Verse 3 answers the nations: our god is in heaven, and vv. 4–8 deprecate the worship of the nations' gods. The natural conclusion is drawn in vv. 9–11: trust in Yahweh. The outcome will be that he will bless (vv. 12–13). Who, though, is to trust him, and whom will he bless? They are Israel, the house of Aaron, and "you who fear Yahweh." They become "us" in vv. 12–13, again Israel, the house of Aaron, and "those who fear Yahweh" (יִרְאֵי יְהוָה, *yir'ey Adonai*). Who are these?

The question is ancient,[68] and recent scholarship is unsure.[69] A red herring for the last century has been whether they should be identified with the proselytes or "God fearers" mentioned in the New Testament.[70]

65. Delitzsch 691; Kirkpatrick 3:678–79; McCann 1139.

66. Goldingay notes that since Yahweh has this high honor, either "all earthly political powers" already recognize this or should do so (Goldingay 2:317).

67. Neale and Littledale, *Psalm LXXXI to CXVIII*, 468–69, citing Cassiodorus and Euthymius Zigabenus. Brueggemann views this psalm as a cultic enactment of that eschatological vision (Brueggemann, *Message of the Psalms*, 161).

68. See Jerome, *Comm. Ps.* CXV (PL 26:1176).

69. The following are undecided: Kirkpatrick 3:685; Kidner, *Psalms 73–150*, 441; Wilcock, *Psalms 73–150*, 182; Eaton, *Psalms*, 397; Vesco 1087; Alter, *The Book of Psalms*, 409; Harman, *Psalms 73–150*, 820.

70. Bertholet, *Die Stellung*, 181–82; so also Rashi, *Psalms*, 664, on the basis of *Midrash Tehillim* on 22:4. This category is not to be confused with "righteous gentiles," which is how Ibn Ezra identified them in this psalm (Bakon, "'Fearers of the LORD,'" 250).

This is a later rabbinical category, a technical term which should not be imposed on the Psalms.[71] At face value in the psalm, they are distinct from "Israel" and "the house of Aaron" and they fear Yahweh. Seybold, with elegant simplicity, describes them as "worshippers of Yahweh from other nations."[72] That is indeed how they are presented, especially in a psalm that already has the nations in view.

Some, who are undecided, argue that it does not matter, since the Psalmist calls on "everyone" to respond.[73] This fails to see the relevance of the question: who could "everyone" include? What are the limits on the possible addressees? This is where a canonical reading can be helpful. The preceding verses have discussed the nations and conclude by warning them about the end of idol worshippers (v. 8). The inclusion of pagan converts into the cult of Israel in vv. 9–11 is the obvious and desired outcome of that warning.[74] It would be another example of the offer of Ps 2.

This leaves the wider context of the "Yahweh fearers," beyond Ps 115. Kirkpatrick appealed to the "national and even local spirit" of the psalms to settle the issue.[75] However, we have seen that the entrance to the Psalter invites foreign rebels, even their leading kings and judges, to take refuge and receive blessing by serving Yahweh with *fear*. We have seen the injunction to fear Yahweh repeated as an invitation to the nations, in 19:10. We have just seen that the first triad of this Hallel (Pss 111–13) has a global concern, which we had previously seen in Pss 8, 18–19 in Book I. Moreover, the first psalm of that triad ends by identifying "the fear of Yahweh" with wisdom. Against that backdrop for "fear of Yahweh," Psalm 115 not only discusses the nations in vv. 3–8, but also opens by having them watch Israel and speak about their God (v. 2), and will end by talking of the earth in global terms, contrasting with Yahweh's heaven (v. 16). It seems passing strange to assert that the Psalms in general are parochial.[76]

On a canonical reading of the Psalter, we should avoid seeing "fearers of Yahweh" as a technical term. Verses 9–10 do not only address faithful Israelites, but apply the foregoing to encourage all Israel to be faithful,

71. Becker, *Gottesfurcht*, 156–57.

72. "Verehrer JHWHs aus anderen Völkern" (Seybold 451).

73. VanGemeren, *Psalms*, 841; deClaissé-Walford et al., *The Book of Psalms*, 856.

74. Weiser, *Die Psalmen*, 491–93; Hossfeld-Zenger 3:279, 285–86.

75. Kirkpatrick 3:685.

76. See further Wenham, "The Nations," 161–86; Robertson, *Flow of the Psalms*, 84–121.

to resist (or turn from) futile idols, and trust Yahweh. These verses then put Israel on a level playing field with as-yet-unconverted gentiles, restating the invitation of Ps 2 to them. The Book of Psalms has already issued this invitation to Israelites as well, as it portrays wicked enemies *within* the covenant nation, beginning in Ps 3. The "fearers of Yahweh" were genuine outsiders, like the kings of Ps 2, invited to join Israel by serving Yahweh with fear.[77] They are now addressed: "as many of you as *have come to fear Yahweh.*"

That same triad (Israel, Aaron, and fearers of Yahweh) is immediately repeated with the promise of blessing (115:12–13). Psalm 112 had opened by reference to Pss 1 and 2 with "O, the blessings of the man who fears Yahweh," and as in Ps 2 this is opened to all nations in 115:12–13. At the start of Ps 115, the nations might have asked where Israel's God is (vv. 1–2); by the climactic center of the Psalm, some of those among the nations have discovered where he is and want to join Israel in praising him. This concluding Hallel (Pss 111–17) is not only celebrating the new exodus out of Babylon by reference to the first exodus, but is also inviting the nations to abandon their idols and join Israel in praise of Yahweh (*hallelujah*).[78]

הָאָרֶץ (*haʾarets*, land, earth, world) in the concluding doxology (115:16) is probably the world, not the land, since it is contrasted with the heavens.[79] In the previous verse, it is what Yahweh created, which is not limited to Israel.[80] It is given to the sons of *Adam*, not the sons of Israel. The contrast of vv. 17–18, between the dead who do not praise, and "we" who will praise, is not a contrast between Israel and enemy nations, but a contrast between all who have obeyed Ps 2, heeded the warning of Ps 110, and enjoy Yahweh's blessing and *hesed* with restored Israel.[81]

We have seen that the first triad of *hallelujah* psalms (111–13) opened with *hallelujahs* to celebrate the victorious judgment of the world (of Ps 110). This is followed by a celebration of the exodus, applied to Israel's return from exile. Psalm 115 opens the second triad by reminding Israel of the two concluding lessons from Ps 107, which are central to

77. Eaton offers 1 Kgs 8:21 as a pre-exilic example (Eaton, *Psalms*, 397).

78. Hossfeld-Zenger 3:20.

79. Kraus 2:966–67.

80. Delitzsch 697.

81. On Ps 115 as dealing with the exile, see McCann 1144; Harman, *Psalms 73–150*, 820.

Book V. It is not Israel but Yahweh who saves; he does so because of his *hesed*, not because of Israel's deserts.

Psalm 116 opens with quotations and near-quotations from the opening of Ps 18. We saw in ch. 9 that Ps 18 ends with an invitation to far-flung nations to come to David for blessing, and a prediction that they would. The international dimension reappears now. As in the previous psalm (115:16), the "אֶרֶץ [*'erets*, land, earth, world] of the living" (v. 9) is contrasted with the realm of death, not with other nations (v. 8), and it is every *Adam* who is a liar in v. 11.[82]

This Hallel group is international in its outlook, encompassing all nations. The same *hesed* by which Yahweh rescued Israel from the exile is available to the peoples of the world. They are encouraged to take advantage of it, and to join Israel in *hallelujah*: in praising Yahweh for his *hesed*.[83]

This view is by no means universally held. For example, W. Dennis Tucker objects that the psalms frequently call on the nations to praise Yahweh purely in acknowledgement of his great works for Israel, in which they themselves have no share. In this psalm, he particularly points to *hesed* in v. 2a as "covenant loyalty," restricted to Israel.[84] This objection fails to reckon with all the data. We leave aside whether *hesed* can simply be reduced to loyalty with a covenant partner—for the sake of argument let us grant this. However, the unproven assumption is that the covenant in question can only embrace Israel. Book V has been speaking of the inclusion of the nations into the benefits of Yahweh's *hesed*. I am not arguing that the nations are to experience divine *hesed* without being included in the covenant; the very fact that they are offered divine *hesed* is an invitation to enter the covenant. With a wider Psalter lens, Tucker's objection does not account for the call to the kings of the nations, at the entrance to the Psalter, to turn to Yahweh and serve him with *fear*.

Related to the note of fear, Tucker dismisses Zenger's argument for international inclusion throughout the Egyptian Hallel. His critique is based solely on challenging Zenger's identification of the Yahweh-fearers as converts. Tucker argues that converts are never referred to as 'Yahweh-fearers' and that the term in Second Temple literature always refers to an

---

82. Tucker passes this psalm over in his survey of nations (Tucker, *Constructing and Deconstructing*, 86). While it lacks explicit mention of the nations *qua* nations, they are clearly in view.

83. Weiser, *Die Psalmen*, 496–97; Hossfeld-Zenger 3:306.

84. Tucker, *Constructing and Deconstructing*, 87.

Israelite, not a convert.[85] As I argued above, later Second Temple usage cannot be decisive here. On the first point, as I argue above, we must ask why this should be taken to be a technical term? What *should* we call someone who obeys Ps 2:11 "serve Yahweh with fear"? Why can they not be described in the most obvious way, as "those who serve Yahweh" and "those who fear Yahweh"? We should consider the opening of the Psalms, the content of Book I, and the structure and progression of Book V so far, where David is being enlisted to teach Israel. What he teaches is quite at odds with the idea that the nations are called on to celebrate Israel's blessings as mere spectators: they are to become his protected servants (Ps 2), instructed by the covenant law (Pss 18–19), and are no more unworthy of divine mercy than rebellious Israel (Book V). The view I am propounding here is in a minority, but it is no coincidence to find it among authors such as Zenger: it is the application of *canonical* readings that allows some knotty problems to be seen in fresh light. As we will see in section III of Book V, my observations about the proclamation of *hesed* to the nations as *partakers* (*contra* Tucker) is supported by those very authors who pay attention to the shape of the Psalter.

All nations are being called to benefit from Yahweh's *hesed* and to join Israel in praising him for the same. That is the note on which this Hallel (Pss 111–17) closes section I of Book V, with the message tightly compressed in Psalm 117:

$$^1\text{הַלְלוּ אֶת־יְהוָה כָּל־גּוֹיִם שַׁבְּחוּהוּ כָּל־הָאֻמִּים:}$$

$$^2\text{כִּי גָבַר עָלֵינוּ חַסְדּוֹ וֶאֱמֶת־יְהוָה לְעוֹלָם הַלְלוּ־יָהּ:}$$

1 Praise (*hallelu*) Yahweh, all nations (*goyim*),
   sing his praises, all peoples (*'ummim*)!
2 Because mighty for us is his steadfast love (*hesed*),
   and Yahweh's faithfulness is forever!
   Hallelujah!

Book V opened with the refrain that we have noticed above, enjoining thanks to Yahweh "because his *hesed* is forever," and each of these words (*ki le'olam hasdo*) are repeated in v. 2 of Ps 117 in the exact same inflected form. The refrain began Book V, functioned to structure the opening Ps 107 and introduced *hesed* as a significant structuring device in Ps 109. That same refrain now closes section I of Book V.[86] Moreover,

---

85. Tucker, *Constructing and Deconstructing*, 90.

86. As Wilson saw, Psalm 107 constantly calls on the people to praise Yahweh for

it is immediately repeated in opening section II (Ps 118:1). The lack of superscription on Ps 118 makes it hard to miss the repetition of Ps 117:2.

In this way, the first verse of Ps 117 simply states what the concluding Hallel of section I has been building up to: an address to the *goyim* and *'ummim*. These two terms described the rebel nations in Ps 2:1, where they were enjoined to serve Yahweh with fear and be blessed. Now, *all* of these nations have been invited to become fearers of Yahweh and experience his rescuing *hesed*. All of them are to join in Israel's *hallelujah*: the praise of Yahweh because of his endless *hesed*.

It is easy to wish blessings on "all," but the biting challenge is to extend such good will to our enemies—the more brutal the enmity the more difficult the mercy. Exilic enemies, such as Babylon and Edom, surely cannot be included in the invitation to receive blessings, even merciful *hesed*, from Yahweh who rescued Israel from them. Any holding on to such doubts need to review Psalm 109 in its context. The most brutal enemy imaginable is not met with retribution by David. Rather, the need for David to show undeserved, merciful *hesed* as a condition of his receiving undeserved, merciful *hesed* from Yahweh. This condition is put center stage at the very point that Edom was remembered as the vilest of enemies, and which immediately precedes the assurance of worldwide conquest by the Israelite king. In the remaining sections of Book V, we will see that significant imprecations, including Ps 137, are similarly presented in the context of David's prayers, to teach Israel about Yahweh's merciful purpose for the nations.

---

his steadfast love (vv. 8, 15, 21, 31, 39–43), and Ps 117 fulfils this (Wilson, *Editing*, 188–89).

12

Retribution in Section II of Book V

Psalms 119, 129

The people of God live ultimately by the grace of a steadfastly loving God, who is willing to bear opposition from all
sides, including Israel and the church (see Ps 130:7–8).[1]

THE YAHWEH-FEARERS WHOM WE met in the Egyptian Hallel are front
and center, and again some prayers concerning the enemy are pointedly
placed. These are no longer on David's lips, but on the lips of an unspeci-
fied leader who represents the nation. Book V begins to look forward to
future crises and how to pray for enemies when they are defeated. We are
taught to pray for, and expect, the repentance and blessing of the kings
of the nations.

1. Opening *Hodu*: Psalm 118

This psalm bridges sections I (107–17) and II (118–35): the message
to the nations on which section I ended begins section II.[2] The triad of
Aaron, Israel, and Yahweh-fearers of the closing Hallel (Ps 115) appears

1. McCann 1203.

2. See the table in chapter 13, below, showing how the opening and closing seams
of each section of Book V relate to each other.

again in Pss 118 and 135, framing section II.[3] The nations are called to
abandon idols; the same warning about them (they have form but not
function) is repeated from 115:6 in 135:17.[4] Psalm 118 opens with the
refrain of Book V (107:1), celebrating *hesed*, and each of the three groups
from section I has the second half of the refrain put in its mouth:

> [1] Thank Yahweh for he is good,
>   for his *hesed* is forever.
> [2] Let Israel say:
>   "for his *hesed* is forever."
> [3] Let the House of Aaron say:
>   "for his *hesed* is forever."
> [4] Let those who fear Yahweh say:
>   "for his *hesed* is forever."

Section I of Book V transformed *hesed*: what began as Israel's privilege became international. Section II opens on that inclusive note: *hesed*
is to be declared *by* all from among the nations who have turned from
their idols to Yahweh in obedience to Ps 2, as in Ps 115.[5] Foreigners
are not merely hearing about *hesed* but joining in the thanksgiving for
a *hesed* which they have experienced. That *hesed* is the subject of Psalm
118 in its entirety.[6]

The speaker of Ps 118 is mysterious.[7] He begins resembling David,
then morphs into Moses and finally appears as a future representative
leader of Israel. The call to the Israelites, Aaronides, and Yahweh-fearers
of vv. 1–4 is on the lips of an individual like David in vv. 5–9, with echoes
of earlier David psalms, such as Ps 18.[8] He leads the nation in praise
following a rescue. His testimony reinforces the message of Book V that
Israel depends on Yahweh for rescue. The victor of the nations from Ps
110 underlines the point of Ps 115: the nations should forsake their idols
in favor of Yahweh. This will lead to saying "his *hesed* is forever."

---

3. Wilson, *Editing*, 188–89; followed by, e.g., Allen, *Psalms 101–150*, 78; Ballhorn,
Zum Telos des Psalters, 364.

4. Giménez-Rico, "Dos Contrarios Irreconciliables," 13.

5. Hossfeld-Zenger 3:322.

6. Kraus 2:985.

7. See McCann 1153–56.

8. This is a feature of Pss 107–19 (Goulder, *Psalms of the Return*, 208).

From 118:14 onwards, the echoes resemble Moses. Verse 14 is identical to the opening of Moses's Song of the Sea in Exod 15:2.[9] There are other Exodus links, specifically to the Song of the Sea, throughout vv. 14–29.[10] Moses is a fitting representative leader from history, and appeared as such in Book IV.[11] However, in the ensuing verses (especially vv. 18–20, 27) some motifs seem to fit a return from exile better, in keeping with the opening of Book V (which is prominent as the first and also last verse of this psalm).

The surprise comes in v. 25. The allusions to two past events of rescue give way to a petition for future salvation. Book V is looking back on the restoration from exile, but anticipating future needs for national rescue, teaching Israel how to pray when such need arises. The fact that the exodus and the return are viewed in the past, while there also remains a future petition, is in keeping with the post-exilic situation, in which Israel remained far from the kind of restoration hoped for.[12]

> "Exile" does not necessarily mean living outside of the former Kingdom of Judah. People living in the Land of Israel after 538 BCE also felt that they were in exile as long as the Temple was not rebuilt and even afterwards, as long as they were under the rule of a foreign power. Exile is not only a geographic place, it is a religious state of mind.[13]

Not merely independence from foreign powers but a restored monarchy was required.[14] It is therefore fitting for this anonymous future corporate representative to be a king like David. As Israel's teacher in Book V, he intends to thank (*hodu*) Yahweh as instructed in the communal thanksgiving of 106:1; 107:1; 136:1.[15] He teaches not only Israel (118:2) and the Aaronides who regulate their worship (v. 3), but the foreign worshippers of Yahweh (v. 4).[16]

9. Vesco 1107.

10. McCann 1154–55; Hossfeld-Zenger 3:317–19.

11. Ibn Ezra identified Moses as the first king of Israel (Cohen, *Deuteronomy*, 240; Cohen, *Genesis*, 93). I am indebted to Kim Phillips for these references.

12. McCann 1153; Kleer, "*Der liebliche Sänger*," 124; Vesco 1105.

13. Berlin, "Literature of Exile," 65. So also Maró, "Psalm 137," 116–28; Becking, "Does Exile Equal Suffering?," 183–202.

14. McCann 661–62.

15. McCann 1155.

16. Hossfeld-Zenger 3:316–20, 336; Vesco 1107.

2. Imprecations in the Body of Section II (119–34)

We have seen that the opening *hodu* psalm of section II picks up on the call to foreign idol worshippers to turn to Yahweh, enjoy *hesed*, and join Israel in thanking and praising Yahweh for his mercy. We turn now to the body of section II, which consists of the massive Ps 119 and the "Songs of Ascents" (Pss 120–34).[17] We will focus on the two imprecations in the body: Ps 119 and 129. Compared with the bodies of sections I and III, David is harder to find.[18] As we say in the introductory *hodu* of Psalm 118, section II is more gnomic and open to future reuse. This allows all the lessons from David in Book V to be used in as-yet-unknown national situations.

2.A. The Place of Psalm 119

Towering over this section, and indeed over Book V and the whole Psalter, we find Ps 119. As in Ps 109, we find the king embattled by vicious enemies, and he reminds the nation of the criteria that he needs to meet in order to prevail.

Psalm 119 is positioned to make a significant contribution to retribution. As Pss 1 and 2 are a Torah-Royal pair that introduce the Psalter and as Pss 18 and 19 are a similar pair marking the center of Book I, so are Pss 118 and 119 at the center of Book V.[19] In the former examples, we have seen that delight in Torah and the qualified righteousness available there (Pss 1, 19) is essential for the king to fight off enemy nations (Pss 2, 18), just as it proves essential to fighting off his local, private enemies (e.g., in Pss 7, 109). By the time we reach Ps 119, we know that the king is victorious (Ps 110–18). We see him again in strife with enemies, and explaining how to be rescued. The Psalms of Ascents then portray Israel defeated in Ps 129, and remind Israel that they lack innocence (Ps 130). Israel's guilt leaves her in the same position as David in Ps 3: unrighteously persecuted in exile yet as a result of his own unrighteousness.

---

17. The Psalms of Ascents have been recognized as a coherent unit since ancient times: see Jerome, *Helv. NPNF*2 7:337. See modern treatments below.

18. Allen summarizes the situation well: "In the three sections, Pss 107–17, 118–35, 136–50, this framework is set around a collection of Davidic psalms (Pss 108–10) in the first instance; around Ps 119 and the collection of processional songs (Pss 120–34) in the second instance; and around another Davidic collection (Pss 138–45) in the third instance (Allen, *Psalms 101–150*, 276–78).

19. Grant, *King*, 180–88.

Book V so far has featured David as an example of Israel's response, and Ps 118 has introduced an anonymous individual leader with resemblance to David and Moses. Psalm 119 is similarly anonymous.[20] He is presented similarly to Ps 118: an exemplary king modelling prayer for the nation, applicable to any future crisis.[21] Just as Ps 118, the switch between singular and plural helps to show the corporate representation of the individual. The blessed man of Ps 1 ("O! the blessings of the man who . . .") is replaced with a plural (O! the blessings of those whose way is perfect . . ."), but the rest of the psalm concerns the individual exemplar. The second stanza opens by asking how one individual can do what v. 1a enjoins. What does he model and teach in the face of his enemies?

The obvious focus on Yahweh's *Torah* throughout the psalm needs no introduction. It follows the return from exile, which was being presented as a new exodus. After exodus came the giving of the law at Sinai, and after the exile, came the re-publication of the law under Ezra (Neh 8:1–8).[22] In keeping with David's message in Book I, to ask Yahweh for victory over enemies requires that one be in the right, as defined by his law. Thus Ps 119 could be seen as showing how to obtain the rescue that Ps 118 had promised: obedience to Torah.[23] However, as we have already seen in Book I (e.g., in Ps 3), in the connection of David, Israel and the golden calf (Ps 51, Ps 86, Ps 103, and one more to follow), and in the structure of Book V, the pressing question is: what can we expect when we have *not* been righteous? Psalm 109 showed David relying on *hesed* not justice and Book V so far has been bringing that home to Israel. Before examining the place of Torah in Ps 119, we must notice the place of the enemies and the psalmist's self-description.

---

20. Goulder surveys the options in the effort to pin the speaker down (Goulder, *Psalms of the Return*, 199–209).

21. To ask whether the speaker is a true individual or the community personified is a false dichotomy: "one can do justice to the community implications in these psalms without detracting from their 'real individuality' if the speaker is assumed to be the king" (Soll, *Psalm 119*, 139). It seems safe to see Ps 119 as depicting a generic king at prayer in the face of enemies, left open enough for future situations, and as a model for the nation to follow.

22. Vesco 1113.

23. So Leuenberger, *Konzeptionen*, 365.

Psalm 119 is a lament and not a hybrid.[24] It features enemies and even contains imprecations.[25] It includes an extended protestation of innocence in the qualified sense that I have been arguing for. The extensive space given to innocence justifies praying against the enemy:

> 53 Rage seizes me because of the wicked
>   those who forsake your instruction.
> 84 How long are the days of your servant?
>   When will you execute judgment against my persecutors?

See also vv. 21, 22, 78, 85, 86, 87, 113, 115, 119, 126. Psalm 119 therefore begins section II with a representative king modelling prayer against enemies.

Those who try to place Ps 119 in its context usually argue that it teaches the importance of Torah righteousness for the return from exile.[26] However, in light of Book V so far, it should also help Israel relate to enemy nations rightly.

2.B. Attitude to Self in Psalm 119

Psalm 119 is often wrongly seen as claiming perfect innocence. We have seen that psalms involving enemies will either appeal to innocence of a particular charge or to their integrity by comparison with slanderous accusers. So here, many of the verses that protest innocence are lamenting the affliction brought on by enemies and false accusations:

> 69 Insolent ones smear me with false testimony
>   [whereas] I keep your precepts with a whole heart.
> 157 Many are my persecutors and enemies
>   I do not turn aside from your testimonies.

Such verses (vv. 22, 23, 51, 61, 70, 95, 110, 115, 121, 141, 143, 153, 161, 166, 173, 174) are characteristic of the psalm.[27]

24. Soll, *Psalm 119*, 59–86, following Mowinckel, *Psalms*, 2:78. This is not to deny that Ps 119 makes wide-ranging connections to the Psalter and, thus, "is rooted in a range of existing psalm types" (Firth, "More Than Just Torah," 3).

25. McCann 1167; Goulder, *Psalms of the Return*, 206; Botha, "Function," 253–56; Adams, *War Psalms*, 116.

26. E.g., Hossfeld-Zenger 3:23. The majority report on the significance of the placement of Ps 119 is one of agnosticism, as reported at length in Nielsen, "Why Not Plough?," 56–63.

27. Soll, *Psalm 119*, 79; similarly Reynolds, *Torah as Teacher*, 46.

In fact, four times he calls himself "afflicted" using the same root we have met before (עָנָה, *'anah* from which comes *'ani*). In Ps 109, the accusation was that he had failed to show *hesed* to one "afflicted and oppressed"; David protested that he was the one "afflicted and oppressed"; and David relied on Yahweh to stand ready to defend the oppressed. He deflected from his status as deserving justice, and appealed instead to his needy condition, desperate for the same *hesed* that he did not fail to show to others. Israel was invited to consider this in view of their afflicted enemies when they were afflicted as a result of Israel receiving undeserved *hesed*.

The author of Ps 119 confesses that his affliction was all to the good. Before it happened, he had lost his way (v. 67). Affliction was to his benefit, it led to him learning Yahweh's statutes (v. 71). He acknowledges that the affliction was the result of Yahweh's *'emet*, the disposition to do good to his covenant partner because of his promise (v. 75b), because Yahweh's judgments are righteous (v. 75a). In other words, his sinfulness had earned his affliction,[28] which was used by Yahweh to restore him to the paths of his instruction, not to punish him. This was all retrospective. In his present affliction (v. 107), he asks for life, but he does not focus on deliverance from the enemy but on Yahweh's "word" which is one of the eight synonyms for Yahweh's *Torah* which are used in every stanza of the psalm. He does not ask for more instruction but for the gifts of better understanding and living in its light more fully.[29] He has fallen short and needs to be restored; that is his pressing concern even while beset by enemies. This is especially clear in the *yod* stanza. After his confession that the affliction was righteous (v. 75), he confesses that what he needs is *hesed* (v. 76). He offers to be a teacher of those who fear Yahweh (v. 74, v. 79)—the nature of his teaching is as expected, that of one forgiven, one who has enjoyed undeserved, merciful *hesed*, and is eager to point others to it. In the context of Book V, where *hesed* is a response to Israel's culpability in the exile, his sin advances his national representation. He is constantly in need of *hesed*; Israel is in constant need of *hesed* because of their rebellion.[30]

The whole psalm ends by describing the psalmist in language reserved for the wicked.[31] The reliance on Torah cannot then be a marker

28. So also McCann 1171.

29. Hossfeld-Zenger 3:350.

30. McCann 1171; further connections via Ps 107 are offered by Hossfeld-Zenger 3:358.

31. McCann 1175.

of earned righteousness. Torah in Ps 119 as life-giving and liberating and not an oppressive burden or alienating duty. The sense of growing into Torah and of a mystical union with Yahweh, the teacher of Torah, is worthy of Jer 31:33–34.[32]

> Psalm 119 does not lay out at length a series of precepts to be observed. It never speaks of man being justified before God through obedience of the commandments. It prefers to celebrate the richness and the value of the instruction which God supplies to the one who desires to hand his heart over to him.[33]

The Psalm is a dual confession: of God's grace and the psalmist's need of that grace.[34] This is precisely what Book V is teaching Israel about *hesed*.

The extended protestation of innocence should, again, qualify any thirst for revenge among Israelites who are aware that the exile fell upon them because of their thoroughgoing lack of righteousness and repeated rejection of Torah. The timeless (arguably even eschatological) character of Ps 119 would serve Israel in future times of distress,[35] and reinforce a particular way of seeing the enemies. We turn now to see how.

2.C. Attitude to the Enemy in Psalm 119

In v. 46 the psalmist tells foreign kings about Yahweh's law.[36] The stanza opens with the first of seven occurrences of *hesed* (v. 41).[37] This accords with the message of Book V so far: *hesed* is to be proclaimed to the nations. This stanza has remarkable similarities to Ps 18.[38] I argued above that Ps 18 involves the king proclaiming the *Torah* among the nations following his victory, so that they will be blessed as he has been. Zenger sees this as in line with other psalms (2:10–12; 72:10; 102:20–23; 138:4–6) and Isa 2:1–5; 42:1–4.[39] He goes on to note that the stanza ends with Torah in the place of Yahweh: lifting up the hands is an act of divine

32. Hossfeld-Zenger 3:390–91.

33. Vesco 1160; he also shows that the psalmist resembles the tax collector, and not the Pharisee, in the parable (Vesco 1152).

34. Wenham, *Psalms as Torah*, 92.

35. McCann 1167.

36. Soll, *Psalm 119*, 140.

37. McCann 1170.

38. Hossfeld-Zenger 3:368.

39. Hossfeld-Zenger 3:368–69.

worship (v. 48).[40] If nations are being invited to turn from their idolatry, as in Book V so far, Ps 119 applies to them too: Torah is indispensable to worshipping Yahweh.[41]

The *hesed* to be proclaimed among the nations in Book V *fills* the ambiguous הָאָרֶץ (*ha'arets*, "earth" or" land," v. 64). In the immediately preceding verse, the psalmist is a companion of "all who fear you" (v. 63).[42] The psalmist would be a companion of anyone who does what Ps 2 says, and there is no reason to *assume* that it does not include his enemies, as Ps 2 would. In the mid-way point of the psalm (vv. 78–79), these wicked enemies are given the same choice as Ps 2 had given: "those who fear you" are invited to know Yahweh's testimonies (v. 79), just as in Ps 2 the enemy kings who fear Yahweh are instructed to enjoy the blessings of Ps 1. This is bracketed by the psalmist's own precarious standing before the law (vv. 77, 80, see previous section), so that he invites the enemy to learn with him. As in other psalms of forgiveness, the psalmist expects to teach or encourage others, in vv. 74, 79.[43]

There are three psalms closely associated with *Torah*: 1, 19, 119. As we have seen, Ps 1 is followed by Ps 2, inviting the enemy kings to enjoy the blessings of *Torah*, by which the Messiah has defeated them. Psalm 19 has the same function, after Ps 18, and more explicitly. In Ps 119, we find the two ideas combined in a single psalm. The king who needs *Torah* in order to enjoy divine mercy and blessing points his enemy kings to the same. What about the enemy who will not repent? While there is disdain for the wicked, and a desire to be free from them, McCann is right to note: "neither is there any trace of the psalmist's commitment to a rigid retributional scheme."[44]

2.D. Psalm 129 in the Songs of Ascents

The Songs of Ascents are clearly marked as a collection by their super-scriptions, and have been analyzed extensively in modern times as a

40. Hossfeld-Zenger 3:369; so also Ravasi III:470.

41. The proclamation in v. 46 is promised as the result of the very חֶסֶד and תְּשׁוּעָה that is asked for at the start of the stanza (v. 41). *Contra* Soll, who seems to isolate v. 46 from the rest of the stanza (Soll, *Psalm 119*, 140).

42. חָבֵר is rare but consistently has that sense of companionship; so here Hakham, *Psalms 101–150*, 235; Kraus 2:989.

43. McCann 1171.

44. McCann 1175.

coherent group.[45] Our interest in their progression and structure is limited to Ps 129, which contains an imprecation.

The start line is distress (120:1), from which "I called to Yahweh, and he answered me." The final line (134:4) is a prayer that Yahweh would bless you, and Yahweh is described as "maker of heaven and earth." Just as the first and last psalms are connected, other psalms are connected pairwise as you move in towards the center. The collection uses lexical and thematic links to produce a palistrophic arrangement (or chiasm) in the collection. For example: hills and forevermore (Pss 121, 133), house (Pss 122, 132), lifting the eyes, looking to the Lord (Pss 123, 131), hope in Yahweh—while enemies *rise* vs. out of the *depths* (Pss 124, 130). Psalms 125 and 129 are more obviously connected by the way they open. Both open with a statement, then break it off with "let Israel say" (יֹאמַר־נָא יִשְׂרָאֵל, yo'mar-na' yisra'el), then the original statement of each psalm restarts and continues.[46]

Before we examine what Israel is taught to say in Ps 129, let's examine what they are taught to say in Ps 124. Verses 1–2 show that Israel has been rescued from enemy nations only because "Yahweh was for us." The psalm ends with a confession which is repeated verbatim within the collection:

124:8 Our help is in Yahweh's name,
  maker of the heavens and the earth.

It is a restatement of a confession near the beginning of the collection.

121:2 My help is from Yahweh,
  maker of heaven and earth.

The same description is the final note of the whole collection:

---

45. See: Hengstenberg, *Psalmen*, 4:337–47; Liebreich, "Songs of Ascents," 33–36; Keet, *Psalms of Ascents*; Seybold, *Die Wallfahrtspsalmen*; Viviers, "Coherence," 275–89; Crow, *Songs of Ascents*; Goulder, *Psalms of the Return*, 20–113; Satterthwaite, "Songs of Ascents," 105–28; Hunter, "The Psalms of Ascents," 173–87; Ayres, "'Devices and Desires,'" 131–51.

46. Apart from this palistrophe, other proposals for structure still end up linking Pss 124 and 129: Viviers, "Coherence," 278–83, 287; Vesco 129; Hossfeld-Zenger 3:590.

134:4 May Yahweh bless you from Zion,
   maker of heaven and earth.

To recap, this threefold repetition of *"maker of heaven and earth"* functions as the second half of three verses. First, near the start of the collection, which began in distress, an individual confesses that his help is from Yahweh. Second, a celebration of rescue from the nations, where the same confession becomes corporate ("our help"). Third, the Songs of Ascents collection ends with a prayer for blessing. The second of these three uses of *"maker of heaven and earth"* is in Ps 124, which is variously connected to Ps 129, and which especially reuses a curious formula to teach Israel to say something. In Ps 124, they are taught that only Yahweh's support has rescued them from the enemy nations. What are they taught to say in Ps 129? An individual confesses that enemies have troubled him since his youth, but they did not succeed. Israel is taught that this is *their* corporate history, when they were afflicted by various nations.[47] This is the kind of thing we have come to expect in Book V: a representative individual standing for the people as a whole and modelling how to respond to their past torment at the hand of enemy nations. The Songs of Ascents as a whole are generally understood either as referring to the pilgrimages to Zion in the land after the exodus (Pss 111–18) and Sinai (119), or to the return to Zion from exile (111–18) and the republication of the law (119).[48] Since Book V presents the return from exile as a new exodus, we do not need to choose. On either reading, Israel remembers that they only made it into the land because *Yahweh mercifully rescued* them from enemy nations. Book V is continuing to teach Israel how to look back on their exilic enemies, and preparing the people to respond to any similar future events.

How does Ps 129 teach Israel to respond? With a curiously negative imprecation. Instead of asking for trouble, they ask for the absence of blessing. The Song of Ascents collection ends by praying for Yahweh's *blessing* on someone, and follows this with "maker of heaven and earth," linking to earlier distress (Ps 121) and rescue from distress (124, 129). However, Ps 129 would exclude some from that blessing. Speaking of all who hate Zion (v. 5), the psalm ends:

---

47. Schaefer, *Psalms*, 309; K&D 5:774.

48. On restoration settings for Ps 120, see Wilson, *Editing*, 224; Hengstenberg, *Psalmen*, 4:348; Goulder, *Psalms of the Return*, 38–39; Kirkpatrick 3:757.

⁸ and let⁴⁹ the passers-by not say:
"Yahweh's blessing to you,
   we bless you in Yahweh's name."⁵⁰

The imprecation is not only a prayer for downfall: it ends by desiring that no-one who sees the final state of the enemy should offer them the blessing on which the Songs of Ascents have ended, nor the merciful *hesed* that Book V celebrates. Psalm 129:8 contradicts the blessing of the opening *hodu* of section II, 118:26:

Blessed whoever comes in Yahweh's name,
   we bless you from Yahweh's house.

That blessing was to include the Yahweh-fearers from among the nations, while Ps 129 instructs Israel to desire the curse of their international enemies.

The placement of Ps 129 in its context helps us to read this desire. The psalms either side put it in a particular light. In Ps 128 the blessing is:

¹ O, the blessings of *all who fear Yahweh*,
   who walk in his ways.

This brings us right back to the introduction of the Psalter, which opened "O, the blessings of . . ." (אַשְׁרֵי, *ashrey*, 1:1) for those who "walk in the way" (1:1, 6; 2:12), including foreign enemies who turn and *fear Yahweh*

---

49. There are no explicitly marked jussives in this Psalm, but נָא identifies the first *yiqtol* (v. 1b) as volitive. Accordingly, Kraus translates all the *yiqtols* in vv. 5–8 as indicative (Kraus 2:1043). Kirkpatrick favors this option, while noting that the majority is against it (Kirkpatrick 3:757n5). Some leave it open (McCann 1203; Weber II:305; Goldingay 3:514). In light of vv. 1–2, we should see vv. 5–8 most naturally as celebrating the cursed state of the enemy (whether current or hoped-for). Accordingly, we find volitive translations in: Ravasi III:615; Seybold 490; Ḥakham, *Psalms 101–150*, 333; Vesco 1215–16; Hossfeld-Zenger 3:551; Schökel II:1515.

50. Kraus sees v. 8b, after the *'atnaḥ*, as outside the quotation, giving a final blessing to Israel, after the imprecations against the enemy (Kraus 2:1046). Targums insert between b and c an explicit indication that someone is replying, but they do not state who the parties are (*Tg. Ps.* 129:8). Some take v. 8c as a redactional addition (e.g., Weiser, *Die Psalmen*, 533). Vesco has it as a single quotation, and reports the suggestion that the psalm was to be performed by a complex cast, with Levites handing over to a choir at v. 8a, and a priest picking up v. 8c (Vesco 1216). Zenger, based on Ruth 2:4, thinks that harvesting had taken up this quasi-liturgical formula so that v. 8c is part of a single original quotation. Verse 8b then cites a divine blessing, and the same speakers apply that blessing to the harvesters in v. 8c (Hossfeld-Zenger 3:562–63). For all this, one thing remains clear, v. 8a desires that the blessing of at least v. 8b, perhaps also v. 8c, should be withheld.

(2:11). In this psalm, the repentant from among rebel nations receive blessing from Zion (v. 5), as in Book V. Those who are excluded from blessing are, as in Pss 1 and 2, the "wicked" (רְשָׁעִים, *resha'im* 129:4). As in Pss 1 and 2, to be marked as "wicked" it is not enough to sin (like David and Israel), but one must hate God's purposes:

> **129:5** Let them be shamed and be turned back—
> all those who hate Zion!

Thus Ps 129 is put in a context that reinforces the opening of the Psalter: some will reject the offer of amnesty and be destroyed. They will reject the invitation to be blessed, and so they should not be blessed.

The psalm that follows (Ps 130) restates one of the features we have seen in David's prayers for enemies. Just as in Ps 128 it is not the sinless but the Yahweh-fearers who are blessed, so in Ps 130 this blessing is for those who confess sin. With good reason has Ps 130 been a penitential psalm. Verses 3–4:

> **3** Were you to be on the look-out for iniquities, O Yah,[51]
> Master: who would be left standing?
> **4** For with you there is forgiveness,
> in order that you may be feared.

Any tally of iniquities will condemn; the only hope is forgiveness. The fear (v. 4) and hope (vv. 5–6) are, as in Ps 2, the property of repentant rebels. Israel's own iniquity is the issue in v. 8, as well as v. 3. Here, as in the wider context of Book V, *hesed* and other terms for divine favor are a response to sin, not to ill fortune. If the imprecation in Ps 129 arose because of Israel's need of rescue from enemies, Ps 130 turns attention to the prior cause of their trouble with enemies. Yahweh is judging them because of their rebellion. They had been *greatly* (רַב, *rab*, 129:2, *bis*) troubled by enemies, but actually need to be *greatly* (130:7, הַרְבֵּה, *harbeh*) redeemed.

> The juxtaposition of Psalms 129 and 130 is fortunate. Lest the people of God be tempted to self-righteousness by their suffering for God's sake, Psalm 130 is an eloquent reminder that the opposition to God is internal as well as external. The history of Israel may be one single passion narrative, but it is also one singularly marked by Israel's persistent faithlessness and disobedience (see . . . Psalms 51; 78; 106). The people of God live ultimately by the grace of a steadfastly loving God, who is willing to

---

51. The first half of the divine name, often used, as in hallelu-*jah*.

bear opposition from all sides, including Israel and the church (see Ps 130:7–8).[52]

This correction away from self-righteousness is used to help understand one of the coldest imprecations in the psalter. Not a prayer for harm but for the withdrawal of blessing, even undeserved blessing. Psalm 109 showed that this is not something to be desired. Psalm 129, as Ps 2 and Ps 18, shows that there is a time when the wicked do rightly face judgment. They have forsaken the offer of mercy, and the offer expires. That is not an invitation to self-righteousness, as Pss 1–3 and Pss 18–19 had made clear.

The imprecation in the Psalms of Ascents advances the message of Book V. An individual like David is teaching Israel to pray amidst enemy nations.[53] The distinction between "us and them" is no longer "Israel vs. nations" but a matter of relationship with Yahweh. Israel was exiled by being on the wrong side of that relationship, and has no grounds for presumption. Anyone from "all nations" is able to turn to Yahweh and join redeemed Israel in praising Yahweh. There is no room for grudges against repentant sinners, either looking back on the exile from the restoration, or in future conflicts.

3. Concluding *Hallelujah*: Psalm 135

The Hallel that closes section II builds on the international picture that has been emerging in Book V. We saw that the concluding Hallel of section I used the triad of Israel, Aaron's House, and Yahweh-fearers to indicate that thanks for Yahweh's *hesed* is open to non-Israelites who repent. The call to thank him for his *hesed* opens section II (118:1) as the refrain of Book V. Immediately afterwards, we find the same triad of Israel, Aaron's House, and Yahweh-fearers (118:2–4).

We now find that triad in the closing Psalm of section II (135:19–20). If the Hallel of section I ended by calling all nations to participate, this is picked up here by the Hallel in Ps 135.[54] Israel, Aaronides, and Yahweh-

---

52. McCann 1203.

53. Vesco observes that this psalm of an individual, who is confident that Yahweh *is* love, pardon and rescue, and therefore waits on Yahweh, now serves to educate exilic Israel to wait on Yahweh in the same way (Vesco 1226).

54. Wilson noted many connections between Pss 135 and 118, including the fact that both enjoin trust in Yahweh alone, and that Ps 118 has an international scope appropriate to the sequel of Ps 117, and so does Ps 135 (Wilson, *Editing*, 223).

fearers take up a "hallelujah" on their lips as they stand in the temple (vv. 1–3). While he has chosen Israel (v. 4) his might is global (vv. 5–7) and he defeated all enemy nations to establish Israel in the land (vv. 8–12). By contrast with his enduring dependability and mercy (vv. 13–14), the idols and gods of other nations are powerless snares (vv. 15–18). This repeats the Hallel of section I, especially Ps 115: God doing as he pleases; heaven and earth; supremacy over all gods. As in the "Egyptian Hallel" of section I, the nations he defeated are those of the exodus.

Were Ps 135 to end at v. 18, or even v. 20a, this could be an exclusive enjoyment of the God who has uniquely chosen Israel to enjoy his benefits. Instead, the closing call to *bless* Yahweh includes the Yahweh-fearers: "House of Israel, House of Aaron, House of Levi, and fearers of Yahweh" (vv. 19–20). Temple worship now includes Yahweh-fearers from the nations. The message of Ps 2 continues to be one of sober invitation to joy: death by idols, or life by Yahweh.

Section II of Book V ends by confirming that, just as *undeserved hesed* was Israel's only hope, so too it is now equally the hope of every *undeserving* nation.

4. Book V So Far—Lessons from the Past for Israel's Future

As we have noted previously, "historical psalms" do not retell history, but teach something from it.[55] Interestingly, the three psalms that open sections of Book V are all historical psalms: Pss 107, 118, and 136. The familiar historical events that they retell are being applied to new situations.

In section I of Book V we saw that (1) Israel looks back on the restoration of the exile and is instructed that Yahweh brought them out mercifully because of his *hesed*, and (2) the nations are to experience and proclaim this too, in view of impending global judgment. David was enlisted to teach Israel that enjoying mercy and then failing to show it to the enemy nations is incongruous. Among those nations Edom is prominent, which would be particularly poignant when remembering the Babylonian Exile, as Ps 137 will remind us. David is enlisted as Israel's teacher, applying his experience in prayer to Israel, as they remember exilic enemies with bitterness, and in anticipation of ongoing and future troubles with enemies.

---

55. Alter, *Biblical Poetry*, 27.

In section II, David has receded, replaced by anonymous psalms and allusions to national leaders (including David and Moses). We saw that Ps 119 by not being a David psalm, contributes to this gnomic picture so that the lessons from section I become applicable to future situations.[56] Psalm 119 is imprecatory and reinforces the Davidic lessons we have seen in Book I and in the introductory psalms of the Psalter. In Pss 128–30, we find an individual teaching the nation how to respond, based on his historical experience.

If Ps 119 reinforces the need for innocence in order to pray against enemies, Pss 128–30 show the flip side. Blessing is supposed to go to anyone who fears Yahweh (Ps 128). Israel may wish to withhold that blessing from those abundantly troubling the nation in connection with the exile (Ps 129). However, the exile was brought about through Israel's abundant sins (Ps 130), so Israel should by rights be disqualified from praying against the enemy. Any such rescue, as in Ps 3, will be an act of undeserved mercy. Psalms 119 and 130 knock self-righteousness out of those who pray about enemies. While there are adumbrations of blessing for enemies in Ps 119, it is the Hallel structure that gives pause to cursing. The enemy nations are invited to fear Yahweh and join Israel in praising him for his mercy.

---

56. Kleer had understood Ps 107 to anticipate a future rescue by a future David (Kleer, "*Der liebliche Sänger*," 121–23).

13

Retribution in Section III of Book V

Psalms 137, 139–44

Psalm 145 invites us to live by this truth, and to join all creation in making known to all people the good news that God's
power is manifest in gracious, compassionate love.[1]

My people, in its widest sense, including Israel and
the Gentiles who were to be added to the kingdom
of David under the reign of the Messiah.[2]

In the end, the burden of proof is upon those who suggest
the illocutionary stance of the New Testament is incom-
mensurate with the illocutionary stance of the Psalter.[3]

PSALM 137 IS THE central problem being addressed by the structure of
section III. Book V would not be complete without it. The Book opens
by commanding thanksgiving for the return from exile, and will end
by climaxing its invitation to all nations to receive and celebrate divine

---

1. McCann 1261.
2. Alexander, *Psalms*, 551.
3. Barker, "Divine Illocutions," 14.

mercy. Psalm 137 makes explicit an obvious emotional and ethical sticking point: why should our wicked enemies receive blessing, why should we celebrate it if they do, and even more, why should we be agents of delivering blessing to them? David's psalms are used to deliver the answer that we have seen from the Psalter's own introduction onwards: for Israel to want to share divine blessing with the enemies requires Israel to understand that Israel's own blessing is *undeserved mercy*.

1. Opening *Hodu*: Psalm 136 and the Structure of Sections I–III

The opening note of section III is hard to miss: thanking Yahweh for his *hesed*. This opening builds on the opening and closing of sections I and II.

Psalm 136 would be a fitting end to Book V. Using the Book's refrain, it celebrates God's *hesed* in every verse. The first three lines reassert Yahweh's international supremacy over all other gods (v. 2) and other masters (v. 3) and his standing alone as the one who does great saving wonders (v. 4). His status as creator of all, which we have seen in Book V (vv. 5–9), introduces his saving work in the exodus (vv. 10–15) and conquest (vv. 16–22).[4] Verses 23–25 could allude to the return from exile,[5] which is the perspective that began Book V. We might expect to find here the fulfilment of 135:14, but instead the whole perspective of section III is anticipation of *future* rescue.

In Ps 137, we have returned to the end of Book IV: Babylonian captivity. The David laments which follow in the final Davidic collection seem fitting for teaching a nation that remains in exile, troubled by enemy nations. It may therefore be that David teaches post-exilic Israel how to pray after Edom and Babylon are brought low, which is predicted in Ps 108 and wished for in 137:7–9. The international focus of Book V, and the proclamation to the nations of *hesed*, wherein nations are enjoined to repent and enjoy blessing, would require Israel to deal with their thirst for vengeance if that proclamation is to include Edom and Babylon.

Whatever the past and future of Israel, Yahweh's *hesed* is broader, in keeping with the theme of Book V. He gives food "to all flesh" (136:25). Because God is the creator and provider of all, Israel's past experience of

---

4. Ravasi III:740–41.

5. Leuenberger, *Konzeptionen*, 365.

common and special grace must now be extended throughout all geography.[6] We will see this fulfilled at the end of section III, where Yahweh feeds "all that lives" because of his universal kingship (145:15–16), so that "all flesh" can now praise him.[7]

The *hodu* of section III introduces two series of imprecations and the concluding Hallel, as we see in the following table:

---

6. Ravasi III:742; cf. Tucker, who notes the future applications of this psalm, but to Israel alone (Tucker, "The Role of the Foe," 187–88).

7. Leuenberger, *Konzeptionen*, 366.

	Opening *hodu*	Closing *hallelujah*
Section I	Ps 107	Pss 111–17
	First verse is the refrain of the Book, with focus on *hesed*.	Final verse calls on all nations to praise Yahweh, with focus on *hesed*.
		Ps 115 has introduced the triad of Aaron, Israel, and Yahweh-fearers with focus on *hesed* (v. 1).
Section II	Ps 118	Ps 135
	Opens and closes with the refrain, focusing on *hesed*.	Opening verse picks up on the servants standing in the house of God from the final Psalm of Ascents. The triad concludes the Psalm. Yahweh-fearers are now standing in God's house, thanking him for his *hesed*. The triad are blessing Yahweh from Zion, in Jerusalem (v. 21).
	Opening combines the refrain with the triad of Ps 115: each member is called to say the second half of the refrain. Yahweh-fearers become recipients of Yahweh's *hesed* to Israel (vv. 2–4).	
Section III	Ps 136	Pss 146–50
	Opens with the refrain.	These take up David's commitment in 145:21 to assemble all that has breath to *hallelujah*.
	Every verse uses the second half of the refrain as its second half, leading to pervasive focus on *hesed*.	Retribution on the kings and nations of Ps 2 is finally meted out, but universal praise is the dominant and final note of the Psalm.
	Final verse repeats refrain, as Ps 118, but changes "to Yahweh" to "to the God of heaven," consistent with global dominion.	
	The story told by the psalm goes from creation to the conquest of Canaan, so that we are left to expect his victory over the deporting enemies. Psalm 137 is thus partly expected: it deals with the deporting enemies, but from a standpoint of captivity, desiring their defeat, and not looking back on it yet.	

Yahweh's acts against the nations were a merciful rescue of undeserving Israel. It has been the note developed in Book V, as *hesed* becomes an insistent reminder of Israel's sin and Yahweh's mercy. Of all the things that could last forever, such as Yahweh's righteousness, or his instruction, it is his *hesed* which endures in every verse of Ps 136. For Israel to understand why Yahweh would show mercy to their enemy nations, they must first understand the extent to which Yahweh has shown mercy to Israel, through Exod 34, the connection with David in Ps 51, and the refrain of *hesed* as mercy in Book V.

2. Body of Section III (Pss 137–144): Imprecations Are Followed by Universal Praise for *hesed*

As we noted earlier, scholars have struggled to account for the presence of Pss 119 and 137 within the structure of Book V. We argued that section II makes lessons from David about imprecations more generally applicable to future situations. Now section III enlists David to teach Israel how to pray Ps 137 in appropriate future circumstances.

2.A. The Puzzling Placement of Ps 137

Some have offered helpful observations concerning the relationship of Ps 137 to its surroundings, but none of these adequately explain why it was included at all. They rightly note that surrounding psalms have to respond to the note of exilic trouble sounded by Ps 137.[8] But why is that note of distress included at all?

Allen rightly sees the focus on Edom and Babylon as significant:

> The editorial use of Ps 137 was to provide a hermeneutical interpretation for these enemies, identifying them as a veritable Babylon and Edom, eschatological enemies that loom larger than life, and taking דוד, "David," in the headings of the following psalms as representative of the community, as indeed he functions in Ps 144.[9]

I would add that David is not merely a community representative: if he were, a sequence of communal psalms would serve here instead. David is also a teacher of the community by his example. The hermeneutical interpretation runs in the opposite direction to Allen's suggestion. Babylon and Edom do not explain the enemies of Pss 138–44. Rather, Book

---

8. See, e.g., Wilson, *Editing*, 221–22; Zenger, "Composition and Theology," 96; Leuenberger, *Konzeptionen*, 365; Seybold 12; Ballhorn, *Zum Telos des Psalters*, 368; Lohfink, "Psalmengebet," 13–14.

9. Allen, *Psalms 101–150*, 78.

V enlists certain psalms of David, where he deals with his enemies (Pss 138–44); Book V uses these to teach Israel how to pray about Babylon and Edom (Ps 137).[10] The open-ended presentation of the nation's leader in section II means that those David psalms here point back to the historical David and the nation's historical enemies, and do so as examples for any future conflict. Put boldly, Ps 137 is not an interruption to the structure of Book V. The structure of Book V *teaches Israel how to pray Psalm 137.*

2.B. Structure of Section III: David Responds to Psalm 137 with Psalms 138–145

Psalms 138–45 are marked as a unit by their David superscriptions. Notice the placement of imprecations:

Series	Imprecation	Celebration of rescue involving promise for all nations
1	137 **Israel**	138 **David**
2	139-44 **David**	145 **David** (145:21 → 146–50)

Each series of imprecations is followed by a single psalm. In the first series, David responds to the imprecation with Ps 138; in the second series, David prays the imprecations, and also responds with Ps 145, remarkably similar to Ps 138.[11] Psalm 137 is not an interruption in Book V, as though it broke up the *hodu* (Ps 136) from the final David collection (Pss 138–45). On the contrary, the final David collection is set in place to respond to Ps 137.[12] Only after this response, can David usher in the final Hallel (145:21), which answers the *hodu* of Ps 135.[13]

---

10. The future reappearance of David or the monarchy is therefore not the topic, and not the reason for including these David Psalms near the end of Book V; *contra* Wallace, "Gerald Wilson," 203–4.

11. Zakovitch lists ten linguistic similarities, as well as more obvious thematic ones (Zakovitch, "Ordering of Psalms," 216–17).

12. Zakovitch believes that Ps 136 was originally followed by Ps 138, and offers six points of contact; he thinks that Ps 137 has been inserted to separate them (Zakovitch, "Ordering of Psalms," 215). Our study is not diachronic, but we should note that two very similar psalms, or tightly connected psalms, need not ever have been adjacent.

13. Lohfink argues similarly, that Ps 138 presents David as *answering* the lament of Ps 137. It does not cancel Ps 137, but both need to be uttered in sequence (Lohfink, "Psalmengebet," 14).

The editorial shape of Book V invites us to read Pss 138–45 with Ps 137 as the body of section II, where David offers a model response to the exilic concern of Ps 137.[14] Not only the significant pair of "afflicted and oppressed" (see ch. 11, §3.A, pp. 196–98) in 140:13, but a pervasive sense of powerlessness, serves to identify David with Israel as an exemplary victim.[15] This final David collection opens with David in one of his usual exiles from Zion.[16] In 138:2, "I bow towards your holy temple" matches Ps 5:8, where the context is absence from the temple. It also alludes to Dan 6:11, so that David responds to the cries of exile (Ps 137) in the same vein as Daniel, "both as *witness* to the nations and as *paradigm* to the exiles."[17]

Psalm 137 looks back on the exile and reports the sentiments of the past.[18] The celebration of return in Ps 107 is not a matter of forgetting the exile, but of learning how to respond to it afterwards, led by a leader who (like Solomon) stands in the shoes of Moses and David. Even though Book V as a whole is set after the return, Pss 137–38 are remembering the exile.

2.C. Psalm 138: Response to Imprecations (I)

David's opening praise (vv. 1–3) is preparatory for the hymn of praise that is expected from all the kings of the earth (v. 4), which is cited in short form in vv. 5b–6, anticipating the conversion of all the kings of the world, to be brought about when they observe Yahweh's mighty rescue of the "lowly," namely, Israel scattered among the nations.[19]

David models the response that Book V has called from both Israel and Yahweh-fearers. In Ps 137, the exiles remembered Zion but refused to sing on foreign soil. David responds, in Ps 138:1, by turning towards

---

14. As Vesco puts it: "C'est le personage de David qui unifie [Pss 138–45]. La figure du roi symbolise Israël opprimé parmi les nations et demandant à Dieu d'être délivré de ses ennemis" (Vesco 1284). That identification may be strengthened by the use of the familiar pair of אֶבְיוֹן and the root ענה in 140:13. These identified David with Israel as an exemplary victim.

15. Tucker, "Powerlessness," 228–43.

16. Recall the observation by Hossfeld-Zenger and by Goulder that the David psalms in Book V reach back into earlier psalms for their material.

17. Wilson, *Editing*, 222; similarly Lohfink, "Psalmengebet," 14.

18. Krüger, "Psalm 137," 79.

19. Lohfink, "Psalmengebet," 14.

the temple and bursting forth in the presence not only of the captors, but of their gods.[20] He calls on the kings of the nations to worship Yahweh.[21]

David thanks (same verb as *hodu*) Yahweh, and the rest of the Psalm is bracketed by an inclusio of *hesed*. The refrain of Book V called all to *hodu* for *hesed*, because it is forever. The final use of *hesed* reminds us that it is "forever." The body of the psalm is chiastic with the outer part recalling God's rescue of David (vv. 3, 7), and the center predicting, or desiring, that "all the kings of the earth" will know Yahweh, having heard the words of Yahweh's mouth, and will praise him for his rescue (vv. 4–6).[22] Given this content, v. 1 would suggest that the gods before whom David is singing Yahweh's praise are the gods of the nations.[23] This is how their kings will come to hear of it. Yahweh's *hesed* is celebrated, and this is a fitting contrast to other gods.[24] We have seen hints of this in Pss 18–19, and it has been a building theme in Book V, but here it is quite explicit in the center of the Psalm. Yahweh's protection is on all who fear him, regardless of nationality. The final note brings us crashing back to the ongoing need for rescue: "do not let go of your handiwork" (v. 8b).

Future rescue remains in view, despite the post-exilic setting of section I (Pss 107–17); this fits with the gnomic setting of section II (Pss 118–35), and prepares us to understand the exilic situation of Ps 137 as a type of any future perils which Israel will need to pray through.[25] We see how the same themes are developed in Ps 145, which terminates the second series, as Ps 138 had terminated the first one.

2.D. Psalm 145: Response to Imprecations (II)

Despite the heading of the whole Psalter as תהלים (*tehillim*, "praises"), Ps 145 is the only תְּהִלָּה (*tehillah*, "praise"), and it sets the tone for the final

20. Lohfink, "Psalmengebet," 13.

21. Vesco 1285.

22. Allen, *Psalms 101–150*, 314.

23. Lohfink argues this point from the placement of the Psalm, and sees it as self-evident: "Die 'Götter' sind im Problemkontext, der durch Ps 137 geschaffen wurde, natürlich die Gottheiten, die die anderen Völker 'fern, auf fremder Erde' (137,4) verehren. Viele Übersetzungen machen aus ihnen leider die hier völlig deplazierten 'Engel'" (Lohfink, "Psalmengebet," 14). Versions that struggled with אֱלֹהִים, giving rise to various modern translations, are discussed by Allen, *Psalms 101–150*, 311.

24. Schaefer, *Psalms*, 324.

25. Krüger, "Psalm 137," 84.

six psalms.[26] The enemy is viewed with optimism. We have noted that each Book of the Psalter establishes a connection between Israel and David through references to Exod 34:6–7. Here, at the end of the final David collection, we find a reference again, but with significant modifications.

Psalm 145, the final David psalm in the whole Psalter, is also the final reference back to the terms of God's grace as experienced when he revealed his name after the golden calf:

> **8** Gracious and compassionate is Yahweh
> slow to wrath but great in *hesed*.

His grace for Israel has progressively expanded throughout Book V to include Yahweh-fearers and all nations. Verse 9 extends the universalizing motif of the Book, especially in light of Yahweh as *universal* creator, which Book V has stressed:[27]

> **9** Yahweh is good to all,
> and his compassion is on all that he has made.

"All that [Yahweh] has made" reappears in the next verse, and they fulfil the refrain of Book V.[28]

> **10a** Let all that you have made give you thanks, Yahweh,
> and let your *hasidim* bless you.

The whole world should give thanks as they experience the same mercy that Israel has received.[29] Among expositors of the Psalms, those with an eye for the shape of the Psalter tend to see this point, as we will continue to show below: Lohfink, McCann, Zenger, Leuenberger, Vesco, Hossfeld, Wenham.

The same verse has a more restrictive category: his חֲסִידִים (*hasidim*), who imitate David in making Yahweh known (vv. 11–12). Who are these? Wenham observes, "though it would be going too far to claim that the golden calf experience was in the psalmist's mind whenever he spoke of

---

26. Alter, *The Book of Psalms*, 500n1.

27. Verse 10a could refer to global inanimate creation, by contrast with more local saints in 10b (Kirkpatrick 3:816). I do not think it makes the best sense in Book V (e.g., 138:8c) nor in this psalm, where *hesed* is for people, not things (v. 8).

28. The *yiqtol* is commonly understood to be jussive: Kraus 2:1126; Weber II:364; Vesco 1338; Hossfeld-Zenger 3:790; Schökel II:1634.

29. This means both that the world gives thanks for the mercy that Israel has received, and also that they are invited to partake of that same mercy and then celebrate it (Vesco 1288–89; Wenham, "The Nations," 185–86).

God's *ḥesed*, it does at least appear that the Exodus version of that event was very influential in their thinking."[30] It *might* be going too far, but we have seen that there are other links to the golden calf, through the association with David's apostasy in Books I–IV, and through the structural prominence of *hesed* in Book V as the grounds for the return from exile. While חָסִיד (*hasid*) in v. 10 and elsewhere, is normally taken to indicate those who *display hesed*, by being faithful or holy, it is tempting to understand them in Book V as those who have *received* divine *hesed*.[31] They will make known Yahweh's deeds not to Israel but to everyone: the sons of Adam/man (v. 12b).

Verse 14 shifts focus to those in peril, in terms that relate both to exiled Israel and all nations, using the universal language that Book V has been developing.[32] In vv. 14–20, the invitation is almost monotonously universal with כֹּל (*kol*, "all") appearing twice in each verse. It is easier to notice how similar the doxology of Book V and the proclamation of the apostles are, if the way that "all" saturates the second half of Ps 145 is compared with Matt 28:18–20; Phil 2:9–11. In this universal context, the double use of "all who call on him" of Ps 145:18 turns into the now familiar יְרֵאָיו (*yereʾay*, "those who fear him"). While David desires *all* flesh to bless Yahweh (v. 21),[33] the choice of Ps 2 reappears in vv. 19–20: fear him and be saved, but "all the wicked" will be destroyed.

Psalm 3 introduced David to the reader, and he there included all Israel, even the rebel enemy northern tribes, in Yahweh's blessing. Now he includes the whole world, even Israel's enemies.

---

30. Wenham, "Golden Calf," 181.

31. Allen translates חֶסֶד as "recipients of [Yahweh's] loyal love" throughout Pss 145, 148, 149, despite his more mainstream translations in Pss 116, 132 (Allen, *Psalms 101–150*). Kirkpatrick in 145:10 gives two options: "Thy beloved, or, thy godly ones" (Kirkpatrick 3:816).

32. This acrostic is missing a line with נ, which would coincide with this shift, going between vv. 13 and 14. The line is absent in all but one Hebrew MS, but is reflected in DSS, LXX and Syr (Flint, "Dead Sea Psalms Scrolls," 25–26). In the missing verse Yahweh is נֶאֱמָן, which would fill in the missing grace lexeme from Exod 34 by adding the idea of אֱמֶת. Nothing in this exposition changes significantly whether the verse is present on absent.

33. Leuenberger notes that vv. 15–16 fulfil the final note of Ps 136, since Yahweh now feeds כָּל־חַי, as a result of his universal kingship, and כָּל־בָּשָׂר can finally praise Yahweh (Leuenberger, *Konzeptionen*, 366).

Psalms 2 and 149 do not let us imagine that everyone without exception will turn and be saved.[34] Nonetheless, the idea that Babylon and Edom should be excluded from the offer because of their wickedness towards Israel in the past could not be countenanced either. That has been made plain by the juxtaposition of Pss 108 and 109, and by the unbounded invitation to all nations through Book V. David is hopeful and thankful for every nation's inclusion in his final psalm.

That is why the *hallelujah*s throughout Book V are imperatives.[35] That is why the final note of this psalm (Ps 145) commits David to praising Yahweh, and then summons praise universally, which leads into the five concluding psalms of *hallelujah*:[36]

> **21** Yahweh's praise is what my mouth will speak
> and let all flesh bless his holy name forever and ever.

Joining in the praise is not the automatic response of all creation. David insists that *all flesh* should join in the praise of Yahweh. As this Psalm (145) and Book V teaches, those from the nations who have taken refuge in Yahweh and fear him are to join David in making this universal appeal.[37] Israel, looking back on the exile in Ps 137, finds that the conclusion of these two series of imprecations is simple: if you have received mercy, proclaim mercy and earnestly desire all to take hold of it.

We have seen that the outer frame of the final David collection (Pss 138–45) reinforces the message of Book V emphatically.[38]

---

34. Wenham, "The Nations," 171.

35. Ballhorn argues that *hallelujah* in the closing five Psalms are not liturgical, but literary, binding together the closing doxology for the reader (Ballhorn, *Zum Telos des Psalters*, 369).

36. As Kimelman puts it: "The correspondence between the psalmist's 'I' blessing God's name forever at the outset and the expectation of all in the end doing so animates the whole psalm that it sets the initial tone and shapes the final cadence" (Kimelman, "Psalm 145," 40–41).

37. McCann 1261.

38. That outer frame is seen also by Buysch, who sees the entire set concentrically arranged (Buysch, *Der letzte Davidpsalter*, 326).

Imprecations	Frame—*hesed* for Nations
	138 David
139–44 David	
	145 David

This structure allows Book V to slot Ps 137 in so neatly. Because every-thing inside the frame are imprecations, placing a further imprecation in front of the series suggests an equivalence between imprecatory Ps 137, and the series of imprecatory David psalms.

Imprecations	→	Response—*hesed* for Nations
137 Israel	→	138 David
139–44 David	→	145 David

The psalms that respond to the imprecations are linked by the promi-nence of *hesed*.[39] *Hesed* is central to their message, which is how we might expect Book V to respond to imprecations.

How does this teach one to read Ps 137? Is it mere contradiction? David answers the question implicitly by providing a series of impreca-tions in the second set, Pss 139–44. We have seen that David serves as a representative example and teacher for post-exilic Israel in Book V. However, we will now see that David was presented in the opening of the Psalter in a way that especially fits Israel in Ps 137.

3. How and When to Pray Psalm 137: Lessons from David

3.A. As David in Psalm 3, so Israel in Psalm 137

We saw in Ps 3 that David reaps the results of his own sin. Nathan had prophesied a punishment that Absalom fulfils, but Absalom does so un-righteously by making false accusations. While David is suffering deserv-edly because of his guilt, he is also suffering *unjustly* at the hands of God's

39. McCann 664.

appointed agent. David's "exile" from Zion is analogous to the Assyrian and Babylonian exiles in that respect.

Yahweh called Assyria to judge the North, but then judged Assyria for the boastful way that they judged Israel (Isa 10:5, 15–16). He similarly sent Babylon to punish Israel, quite justly, and equally justly punished Babylon for their actions, and even Edom for their complicity.

Just so, he sent Absalom to punish David (2 Sam 12:11), and then punished Absalom for his wicked and unjust treatment of David. When 2 Sam 17:14 tells us: "Absalom and all the men of Israel said, 'Hushai the Archite's counsel is better than Ahithophel's counsel.' Yahweh had determined to nullify Ahithophel's *good* counsel, with the express purpose that Yahweh should bring harm against Absalom."

> There can be little doubt that Yahweh's decree in 17:14 has the violent death of Absalom in view as punishment. . . . Absalom is a divine instrument whom Yahweh intends to destroy.[40]

In the case of the enemy of Ps 137, Babylon and Edom, the prophetic announcements are even more explicit and detailed. While Obad 10–14 warns Edom not to gloat, Ezekiel goes further and promises retribution: Ezek 35:5–15 (esp. 6, 11, 15). In Isa 47, a chapter of prophetic judgment against Babylon, we find:

> ⁵ Sit quietly, and go off into darkness, <u>O daughter of the Chaldeans</u>!
>   because you will not be called 'mistress of kingdoms' again.
> ⁶ I got angry against my people, I ruined my inheritance and so gave
>   them over into your hand;
>   you did not ordain mercy for them; even on the elderly you made
>   your yoke most heavy
> ⁷ You said: "I will be mistress forever."
>   You had not yet got these thoughts out of your heart.
>   You did not remember what comes next.
> ⁸ But now, listen to this, O luxurious one who lived confidently
>   saying to yourself, "I, I and no other,
>   I will not live as a widow
>   <u>nor will I know the loss of my children</u>!"—
> ⁹ "These two things will come upon you in a trice, on a single day:
>   <u>bereft of your children</u>; widowed."

Note the similarity in the underlined portions with Ps 137, especially "daughter of the Chaldeans" || "daughter of Babylon." Even more closely

---

40. Smith, *The Fate of Justice*, 187–88.

connected with Ps 137, Isa 13 prophesied the Persian overthrow of Babylon:

> **16** <u>Their infants will be shattered</u> before their very eyes.
> Their houses will be plundered,
>   and their wives violated.[41]

"Their infants" (עֹלְלֵיהֶם, *'olelehem*,) matches "your infants" (עֹלָלַיִךְ, *'ola-layik*) in Ps 137. Psalm 137 has long been identified as a direct fulfilment of this prophecy.[42]

So, in light of the parallels with Ps 3, Ps 137 need not imply Israel's innocence, any more than Ps 3 implied David's. Israel confesses this explicitly in Lam 1:18, 21–22, even while asking for retribution against their divinely-sanctioned enemies. Israel is confident that justice involves repayment to those who watched on (Lam 3:64). Unlike situations such as Ps 7, where one party is innocent and the other guilty, David was a guilty victim facing a guilty adversary (Absalom). Yahweh could justly have chosen either one of them to be victorious. Israel, attacked by Assyria and Babylon, were guilty of the breach of covenant that caused Yahweh to punish them; Assyria and Babylon were also guilty of the way they went about it. Israel's rescue at Yahweh's hands from Babylon is like David's from Absalom: undeserved mercy for sinners, which is Yahweh's *hesed* at work.

3.B. The Imprecations in Psalm 137

> **7** Remember, Yahweh, against the sons of Edom,
>   the day of Jerusalem:
> they who said,
>   "Raze it, raze it
>   right down to its base!"
> **8** Daughter of Babylon, devastated-in-waiting:
>   O the blessings of whoever pays you back
>   your due payment
>   for what you paid out to us!
> **9** O the blessings of whoever grabs
>   and smashes your little ones against the rock!

41. On the MT softening from K to Q, without change in meaning, see Watts, *Isaiah 1–33*, 194.

42. Calvin, *Psalms*, 5:197–98.

In this section we will first establish that this text means what it says on the surface: any efforts to soften this text by appeals to metaphor are a blind alley. Second, we will see where it fits historically, and so how it serves to address the readers of Book V.

The imprecations are directed first against Edom, then Babylon.[43] Against Edom, in v. 7, we have poetic justice. Edom did not attack Israel but egged on Babylon against her. Likewise, now, Israel does not attack Edom but eggs on Yahweh against her. Verse 7 is not a prayer for retribution; it is retribution.

Against Babylon, v. 8 looks forward to retributive judgment, to exact retribution.[44] Verse 9, the most troubling, longs for the targeted slaughter of children.[45] That last horrific detail cries out to be softened, and many have tried, in various ways, the most plausible of which appeal to metaphor.

Did we not see that the martial language in Pss 2 and 3 is metaphorical but nonetheless signifies literal force? "Crushing" may refer to subduing rather than literal grinding, even if it does involve military strength. "Breaking the teeth" may mean disarmament and not orthodontics, though, again, it did not happen without casualties in Absalom's army. Therefore, might the infanticide on the surface of 137:9 perhaps signify some less gruesome form of retribution? Granted, it will not be entirely free of gore, but can we spare the children? Such proposals are made frequently. However, infants are in view, for two reasons.

First, without thereby being excused, it did fit contemporary customs of warfare.[46] As a way of wiping out a people or a city, the next

---

43. "Daughter of Babylon" is not a metaphor for Edom, but a synecdoche, as found in Isa 47:1 and similar to "sons of Edom." VanGemeren, *Psalms*, 952; Gerstenberger, *Psalms II*, 393. A discussion of the alternative view is found in Allen, *Psalms 101–150*, 308.

44. Scoralick, "Gerechtigkeit und Gewalt," 129–30.

45. Verse 9 could be, and often has been, understood as spelling out what the *lex talionis* of v. 8 will amount to. However, we are not told explicitly that the Babylonians killed children in the fall of Jerusalem. This is often assumed with good reason (e.g., Dimock, *Books of Psalms*, 315; Eaton, *Psalms*, 455; Calvin, *Psalms*, 5:197; Theodoret of Cyrus, *Psalms 73–150*, 324–25; Steenkamp, "Violence and Hatred," 306). However, that is only an assumption: v. 9 might be going beyond strict repayment (Scoralick, "Gerechtigkeit und Gewalt," 129–30). It would be arguing in a circle to insist otherwise.

46. This is frequently observed, e.g., Steenkamp, "Violence and Hatred," 307; Simango, "Psalm 137," 227.

generation was killed too. We find biblical references to Assyria and Syria doing just this in 2 Kgs 8:12; Hos 10:14; Nah 3:10. On the latter passage:

> [T]he attackers cruelly destroyed even the infants of Thebes. The picture of dashing in pieces conveys the most barbaric treatment imaginable. The invaders crushed the infants against the stones and buildings of the city. Such cruelty abounded in ancient times. . . . 'At the head of every street' refers to the fact that these atrocities occurred in public places in full view of everyone. All over the city and without shame or remorse the invaders cruelly destroyed the innocent children of Thebes.[47]

Could that very fact not soften the passage? If this is so common during invasions, could it be a metaphorical reference to invasion, a synecdoche? The death of some children (heirs to the throne) would end the Babylonian empire, but without wholesale infanticide.[48] However, it would be special pleading to argue that the concrete example chosen to signify that invasion (the death of children) is the very thing excluded from the invasion.

More tellingly, second, the prophecies anticipating Ps 137 are specific. Isaiah 13 prophesied the actual killing of children, in accordance with the expectations of war. This psalm does not merely expect the death of children because that was the done thing, but because it had been prophesied.

If, as has seemed apparent since Ps 107, Book V positions itself after the exile, looking back on the exilic enemies after the return, is this prayer not anachronistic? Had Babylon not already been recompensed with Persian violence? On the contrary, the timing explains the impatience of the final prayer. The fall of the Babylonian empire is not the same as the destruction of the city of Babylon itself, since the city surrendered peacefully to Cyrus but was later laid waste by Darius.[49] After the return from Babylon, but before the sacking of the city, the psalmists would still be waiting for "repayment" against Babylon. Eventually, the Babylonians themselves killed their own children.[50] Only later, in 300 BC, was the city

---

47. Barker, *Micah*, 233.

48. Keel, *Die Welt*, 8B; see further his evidence that the suckling babies of rulers were depicted as killed in symbolism of the defeat of nations (Keel, *Die Welt*, 209A–B).

49. Plumer, *Studies*, 1156.

50. Plumer, *Studies*, 1156.

destroyed completely.[51] The Psalm is therefore naturally placed after the return from exile, when the Babylonian empire has fallen but while the city still stands within the Persian empire.[52] The psalm knows that the city is under sentence of destruction (hence my "devastated-in-waiting"). This explains why the psalm focusses on the city, not the empire.[53]

The question to ask now is how the Psalter indicates that this psalm should be *used*. The culture of the day is not enough: "an interpretative approach needs to take cognisance of the role of ancient social values in the cultural and religious world of post-exilic Israel."[54] We have seen that the desire against Babylon is not based on surrounding culture, but on the *lex talionis*. Even so, the Psalter into which Ps 137 has been artfully woven might not allow the matter to rest there.

3.C. The Final David Collection (Pss 138–45) Teaches the Use of Psalm 137

As we have seen, Psalm 137 delights in a judgment that had been prophesied in detail. It is not strictly a prayer, even though it is addressed to God.[55] In terms of speech-act theory, this is *behabitive* language, where a plain statement "blessed be" does more than convey information. It implies the same commitment to the outcome as a prayer would do.[56] Psalm 137:8–9 belongs among the imprecations.

Considering how the Psalter introduced David in Ps 3, the prophecies of Isa 13 and 47 are analogous to the messengers coming to David at night (2 Sam 17:21 / Ps 3:6b [5b]). Their message shows that God has chosen David (and Israel) over Absalom (and Babylon), so that David (and Israel) can *confidently* pray against their enemies. But how *did* David pray at the equivalent point in the episode that introduced him to the Psalter? How *should* Israel therefore pray?

51. Vos, *Theopoetry of the Psalms*, 272.

52. Vesco 1279; *contra* Giménez-Rico, who understands Ps 137 as "the dramatic *Sitz im Leben* of 120–35, retroactively" (Giménez-Rico, "Dos Contrarios Irreconciliables," 4).

53. Widely recognized, e.g., by Hartberger, *An den Wassern*, 224; Seybold 509.

54. Steenkamp, "Violence and Hatred," 308.

55. Daly-Denton, *Psalm-Shaped Prayerfulness*, 182.

56. See the discussion of behabitive language in the Psalms in Wenham, *Psalms as Torah*, 69–70; on this passage as functionally equivalent to prayer, see Weber II:334; Gerstenberger, *Psalms II*, 392–93.

The Psalter began by offering the nations restoration if they repented (2:10–12). To Israel, who had suffered unjustly at the hand of the Babylonians in exile, it presented David, suffering unjustly at the hand of Absalom in exile from Zion. It showed David's unjust suffering as the result of his own sin, as duly prophesied, and reminds Israel that if they had suffered unjustly under Babylon, they too were being punished for their sin. David prayed without presuming on divine favor. He prayed for his enemies to be defeated by minimal force: being disarmed. He prayed, once victorious, for his enemies to be blessed as God's people.

As well as the typological connection between David and Israel when facing the "exiles" of Absalom and Babylon, we have also seen a further connection. Israel's national apostasy at the golden calf is presented as equivalent to the sin of the national representative king in Ps 51. That event is then presented as (quite naturally) also typological of Israel's exile. In all three cases (golden calf, David's sin, exile) it is Yahweh's nature, and especially his *hesed* that is solely responsible for rescuing Israel and David.

Book V has been applying that *hesed*: the same mercy that brought Israel out of exile is to be offered to the nations. David has shown that anyone who has received such mercy cannot begrudge the same mercy being enjoyed by his enemies. A David Psalm (Ps 138) is placed in immediate response to Ps 137, celebrating his own enjoyment of *hesed* and the enjoyment of the same by all the kings of the earth (as we showed in §2.C, pp. 235–36). The following series of David imprecations leads to Ps 145, with the same universal celebration of *hesed* again. How is all this to be reconciled with the sentiment of Ps 137? We will examine the ensuing series of imprecations, and notice that David is reminding Israel of the criterion of specific innocence for praying imprecations. That is an apposite reminder to the reader of Book V, because Psalm 137 does not show a hint of awareness of guilt, which is very unusual among psalms that deal with the exile.[57]

In Book V, David teaches exiled Israel by being a model of one "afflicted and oppressed," as they are. However, in Book V, Israel's affliction is the direct result of sin, just as David's in Ps 3. One of the functions of this final collection of David imprecations is to set up the final Hallel (Pss 146–50), at which point there is a shift of subject. No longer David, but

---

57. Weber II:336.

the afflicted of Israel are the agents and singers.[58] The model teacher hands over the baton to the pupil: afflicted David gives way to afflicted Israel.

Psalm 145, which announces that final Hallel, introduces the חֲסִידִים (*hasidim*) who imitate David. David promises "O God, a new song I will sing to you" in 144:9, and in 149:1 it is the *hasidim* who command the hearers of the psalm to "sing to Yahweh a new song." The final David collection (Pss 138–45) is preparation for understanding how to sing the final Hallel. That preparation is needed because of the situation faced in Ps 137 (the exile and its memory).[59] If it was hard enough to sing Yahweh's song when on foreign soil, how are they supposed now to sing a song that celebrates the well-being and inclusion of their erstwhile captors? That is why the David collection, making up the body of section III, is full of imprecations.[60]

3.D. David's Innocence Criterion Applied to Psalm 137 in Psalms 139–44

The universal proclamation of *hesed* is the final note and goal of the David collection, as we saw above.[61] What do we read on the way to that endpoint? In Pss 139–44, the strength of imprecation is commensurate with the degree of innocence in each psalm. As McCann observes, the placement of these psalms applies "the individual expressions of petition and profession" to "the post-exilic community."[62] In other words, these David psalms provide instruction to the nation for future conflicts, as we have observed above. We will examine each psalm in turn.

---

58. Hossfeld-Zenger 3:26.

59. The enemies are prominent throughout 137–44, with Edom and Babylon center stage (Allen, *Psalms 101–150*, 77–78).

60. Harm van Grol comes closest to this view, by seeing Pss 138–45 as responding to the problem of Ps 137, and as clearing the way to sing the praises of Pss 145–50. He sees the setting as the crisis with the Hellenists, with references to "exile" as a symbolic key ("*chiffre*") for that conflict (Grol, "David and His Chasidim," 334–36). In view of the paradigmatic experience of exile, with future application for the nation, there is no reason to exclude that particular conflict, but neither does it need to be tied down to it.

61. Zenger, "Composition and Theology," 96; Leuenberger, *Konzeptionen*, 366.

62. McCann 1240.

3.D.1. Psalm 139

Psalm 139 is often seen as disjointed: first a celebration of God's attributes, especially his omnipresence, to delight any lecturer of dogmatics (vv. 1–18). A horrid cranking of gears moves us from sweet adoration to brutal imprecation against the wicked (vv. 19–24).

> The last parts of Psalm 139 . . . seem to be disgustingly inferior to the noble, humble, and open kind of thinking presented in vv. 1–18. Some modern Bible translations do away with the vengeful sections (vv. 19–22) in order to stay with a "morally clean" text.[63]

Is this not what we have come to expect? An imprecation against enemies requires a demonstration of relevant innocence. What better way to confess innocence in any given matter than to point out to God himself that there is nowhere for David to hide his guilt.[64] Yahweh has thoroughly examined David and knows him inside out (vv. 1–6). Were David to hide his behavior from Yahweh, where would he do so? He cannot flee from his presence (v. 7): not to heaven, Sheol, sea, darkness, or night (vv. 8–12). David's inner being is Yahweh's specialist subject because it is Yahweh who made David (vv. 13–16). All this amounts to saying, "whether I want to or not, I have to make full disclosure." Of what crime is David innocent? In vv. 17–18 he loves God and his thoughts. Not so the wicked, who hate God and slander him (vv. 19–22). He ends with an invitation to be examined thoroughly in his thoughts to prove that he does love God (v. 23). Far from any delusions of perfection, he wants Yahweh's examination to reveal faults and then correct them (v. 24). This is in the spirit of Ps 19.[65] His prayer against the wicked is supported by his declaration of his own innocence.[66]

All this is exemplary for post-exilic Israel.[67] It will not do to look at Edom and Babylon and say that they are wicked and hate Yahweh (as in

---

63. Gerstenberger, *Psalms II*, 404.

64. On our canonical reading, we note that the editors of the psalter are attaching the psalm to David (if it was not already so attached), and that its individual content is consistent with David as an *individual* being an example for the nation as a whole, without any royal cultic festival in view, for the reasons we have argued in the structure of Book V and the developing persona of David in the Psalter. *Contra* Kraus 2:1094; Kirkpatrick 3:786.

65. On the integrity of the poem as a unified whole, see Seybold 515.

66. Vesco 1294.

67. Vesco 1294.

vv. 19–22), without first being in a position to declare one's innocence (vv. 17–18) and prove it (vv. 1–16). Post-exilic Israel knows that they were in no position to demand that Yahweh take their side against their enemies: they were paying for their guilt in Babylon. Yahweh did take Israel's side and punish their enemies; this was purely because of his mercy, not their merit. Were it not for the prophecies of Isa 13 and the like, they would be like David at the start of Ps 3: with no right to pray against the enemy. This they must remember when faced with enemies in future.

3.D.11. Psalm 140

Verse 13 [12] may seem promising to Israel, in that Yahweh is for the well-known pair of "afflicted and oppressed."

> I know that Yahweh will handle the case [דִּין, *din*] of the afflicted
> and the judgment [מִשְׁפָּט, *mishpat*] of the oppressed.

Din and *mishpat* are legal terms. The promise is not of unconditional care, but of justice. Even the afflicted and oppressed will be handled justly, not preferentially; they need to be innocent for God to side with them.[68] The next verse closes the psalm by making the point. David's only hope of rescue from the wicked is that it is the *righteous* who will be able to thank Yahweh, and the *upright* who will enjoy his presence (v. 14 [13]).[69] It was not enough for David to show that he was in need of rescue from enemies; it is because his enemies are acting unrighteously against him (v. 10b [9b]), and he is not the one in the wrong, that Yahweh will rescue him from his affliction at their wicked hands.

Against that strong backdrop of innocence, we find an equally strong and lengthy imprecation in vv. 9–12 [8–11]. As with Ps 139, prayer against the enemy requires a demonstration of one's own standing. For Israel, being afflicted and oppressed at the hands of Babylon and Edom turns out not to be enough for praying against them. Psalm 137 was the fruit of Yahweh's extraordinary choice of Israel, not their entitlement. But for that, they would not have been able to sing the imprecation in Ps 137.[70]

68. *Contra* Beyerlin, *Die Rettung der Bedrängten*, 33.

69. I am taking the parallelism as distributive, as in Prov 10:1 (cf. Schökel, "Poética hebrea," 195). The righteous *and* the upright will thank *and* be with Yahweh.

70. This is still true even though, as McCann observes, "the issue in vv. 8–11 is not personal revenge, but justice for the victimized" (McCann 1241). Israel could not appeal to justice in Ps 137, any more than David could in Ps 3.

Psalm 140 shows as much: David could only pray against his enemies when he was not at fault.

3.D.III. Psalm 141

Psalm 141 develops this criterion of innocence by juxtaposing the previous protestations of innocence with an awareness of precarious standing.[71] Verses 3–5 are in the style of Pss 19 and 119, asking for prevenient grace from sin. In v. 8, David's confidence is not in innocence, but in his relationship with Yahweh, taking refuge like the repentant of Ps 2. David is so aware of his sinful nature that he welcomes corrective chastisement (v. 5). The imprecation here is correspondingly weak. In v. 5b, David's prayer is בְּרָעוֹתֵיהֶם (beraʿotehem, "their wicked acts"), preceded by the preposition bet). Even if we take bet as adversative, which is the majority report but by no means certain, it would still be a prayer against their wickedness or their wicked deeds, not against them personally (as in Ps 7, see ch. 8, §4, pp. 143–45).[72] However, bet could also indicate praying "for" them,[73] praying "even in" (perhaps "despite") their wickedness,[74] and praying "about" their wickedness.[75] A further imprecation resembles Ps 7: David asks for safety from their traps, and that they themselves should fall into them; this is at most the lex talionis, and with very tame imagery.[76]

The shift to plural in protesting the current state of affairs ("our bones have been scattered before *Sheol*," v. 7b)[77] is evocative if the Baby-

---

71. The tight literary connections between Pss 140 and 141 are described by Hossfeld-Zenger 3:751; Goldingay 3:653–54.

72. So Perowne, *Psalms*, 2:452; Jebb, *Psalms*, 296; Ravasi III:846; Seybold 521; Allen, *Psalms 101–150*, 338; Vesco 1312; Alter, *The Book of Psalms*, 488; Goldingay 3:657; ESV; GNB; HCSB; LEB; MSG; NASB; NIV; NRSV; RSV. On the adversative בְּ, cf. Joüon 133c.

73. Darby.

74. Kraus 2:1107; Hossfeld-Zenger 3:743; Schökel II:1607; ASV.

75. YLT. Delitzsch elegantly leaves the ambiguity with "Denn noch begegn' ich ihren Tücken nur mit Beten" (Delitzsch 795), and the UBS Handbook suggests three options (Bratcher and Reyburn, *Book of Psalms*, 1143). Only NCV has David praying "against those who do evil." NLT paraphrases "against the wicked and their deeds," which seems an unwarranted overspecification.

76. Judicial wickedness is mentioned in v. 6. This may not be a literal courtroom but a description of wicked movers and shakers (Hossfeld-Zenger 3:749).

77. Goldingay rightly translates the *qatal* as past and rejects the smoothing emendations in 11QPsa and versions, which retain a singular psalmist and plural enemies

lonian exile is in the background, especially since the only other instance of סֶלַע (*sela'*, "rock, cliff") in Book V is 137:9. Wright further detects in v. 8 that the psalmist "sees personal and private prayer as the functional equivalent of being in the Temple—a necessity, of course, for the great majority of Jews even before the destruction of the Temple in AD 70."[78] We saw in Ps 1 that engagement with Torah is a functional equivalent of temple presence, in that it leads to blessing, and that Ps 3 presents David as experiencing something analogous to the exile, and praying to Zion from a distance. This final David collection is therefore not only useful for Israel in looking back on the exile, but also in anticipating future exiles or, as McCann suggests, if the exile continued even after Ezra and Nehemiah's restorations.

The kind of innocence in view has shifted between Ps 140 and 141. The former is more focused on the enemy as a danger, and the latter is more focused on internal sin as a danger:

> Psalm 141 participates in the response of Book V to the ongoing crisis of exile and its aftermath [which] involved not only protection against powerful enemies . . . but also the persistent temptation to conclude, in effect, 'If you can't beat them, join them.'"[79]

There is less claim of innocence, and the confession of precarious moral standing (as we saw in Ps 19) is more in the foreground. When faced with a situation such as Ps 137, if we cannot make the claims of righteousness found in Pss 139 and 140, can we at least attain to the lesser claims of righteousness found in Ps 141? In the case of Israel looking back on Babylon and Edom, hardly. As the exile fell on Israel, they did not show the desire of v. 4 to be kept from evil and kept from evil company, much less the willingness to be chastised (v. 5) for the sake of moral correction. They broke the law, joined in idol worship with others, and persecuted the prophets. Once again, Ps 137 was the result of *hesed*, not righteousness.

---

consistently (Goldingay 3:653). On the variety of emendations in vv. 5–7, see McCann, who argues that the hard MT should be retained over the various conjectures (McCann 1244).

78. Wright, *Finding God*, 99.

79. McCann 1243.

3.D.IV. Psalm 142

In Ps 142 we have the only historical notice outside the "prayers of David" (Pss 3–72). The "cave" mentioned offers two possibilities: 1 Sam 22 or 24. The latter, when David spared Saul at Engedi, is a better fit:

> Support for an En-gedi reference was adduced by E. Slomov-ic... who plausibly suggested that the historicization resulted from the linguistic affinities between v 8 of the psalm and Saul's words outside the cave there. He saw wordplays of a midrashic kind in מסגר, "prison" (cf. סגרני, "he delivered me," 1 Sam 24:19 [18]); צדיקים, "righteous" (cf. צדיק in 1 Sam 24:18 [17]); and תגמל, "treat well" (cf. this root twice in the sense "repay" in 1 Sam 24:18 [17]).[80]

What purpose does this serve?

> Here by means of intertextuality David is presented as a role model for the *individual* sufferer.[81]

What lessons might there be for corporate Israel? The intertextual links point to the end of the episode, 1 Sam 24:18–22 [17–21]:

> **18 [17]** [Saul] said to David: "you are more righteous than I, because <u>you have requited me with good, whereas I have requited you with evil.</u> **19 [18]** Thus you have shown today how you have dealt well with me, <u>when Yahweh had handed me over into your hand and yet you did not kill me.</u> **20 [19]** For when someone finds an enemy, does he send him on his way well? May Yahweh repay goodness to you because of this that you have done to me today. **21 [20]** Now then, look, <u>I know that you will definitely become king,</u> and that the kingdom of Israel will arise when it is in your hand. **22 [21]** <u>So now, swear to me by Yahweh that you will not cut off my seed after me, nor will you wipe out my name from my father's house.</u>"

The underlined portions are instructive if David is a model for Israel in considering Babylon and the sentiments of Ps 137.[82] David wants to be delivered from his enemies and makes no mention of revenge, but rather

---

80. Allen, *Psalms 101–150*, 348; so also Buysch, *Der letzte Davidpsalter*, 225.

81. Allen, *Psalms 101–150*, 348; italics added; so also Hossfeld-Zenger 3:756, who further notes that the David of Books I and II are being appealed to, precisely by the inclusion of *any* historical notice, since these appear in those books.

82. McCann, once again, sees this psalm as part of the communal response "to the exile and its aftermath," and that the original setting is fitting (McCann 1246).

the familiar intention: "so that I might thank [same verb as *hodu*] your name" (v. 7). This was the purpose of being brought out of exile, the final prayer of Book IV, 106:47, which Book V is supposed to be answering (ch. 10, §1.C, pp. 177–79). Considering the episode in Samuel, David was as righteous as he could be, yet he repented of even cutting off some of Saul's garment. If the psalm is read in this light, then even when David was righteous, that did not automatically entitle him to seek revenge against the enemy. David did not think that it entitled him even to cut off the corner of his garment as a warning, let alone avenge himself on him.

Saul was appointed by Yahweh as king. Despite Yahweh's promise to David, and despite Saul's sinful kingship, and Yahweh's promise of judgment against Saul, David was not entitled to forget that Saul was Yahweh's anointed. He had to wait patiently for Yahweh to fulfill his promise to David in his own time. While Israel waited for Yahweh to fulfil his promises of restoration to Israel (as far back as Deut 30) and of judgment against Babylon (Isa 13), their prayer in Ps 137 had to be one of faithful waiting.

3.D.v. Psalm 143

Psalm 143 is one of the seven penitential psalms and opens with an appeal for mercy followed by a general confession:

> **2** But do not enter into judgment with your servant,
>   for no-one alive can be vindicated in your presence.

In the Psalms of Ascents, an imprecation was followed by a confession of inability to withstand divine judgment (Pss 129→130). Here, a series of imprecations (Pss 139→144) includes the same acknowledgement. It is immediately after David's confession that the enemy is presented as punishing him; compare David's self-malediction in 7:6:

> 7:6 [5] *let the enemy pursue me* [יִרַדֹּף אוֹיֵב נַפְשִׁי, *yiradof 'oyeb nafshi*] and
>   overtake me
>   and *let him trample my life to the ground* [לָאָרֶץ חַיָּי, *la'arets hayyay*].
> 143:3 for *the enemy has pursued me* [רָדַף אוֹיֵב נַפְשִׁי, *radaf 'oyeb nafshi*]
>   and *crushed my life into the ground* [לָאָרֶץ חַיָּתִי, *la'arets hayyatiy*].

If David is to survive the night, it will be through undeserved *hesed* (v. 8). This goes further than preceding psalms and resembles Pss 19 and 119. David pleads with Yahweh to instruct him in righteousness (vv. 8b–10), in light of his confession of moral inability. This suggests that "in your righteousness" (vv. 1b, 11b) is not appealing to divine justice as grounds for being rightfully acquitted but appealing to Yahweh's righteousness in keeping his promises to David. That is why it is paired with *'emunah* "faithfulness to covenant commitment."[83] (See the discussion of the root *'emet* in ch. 7, §2.B.II., pp. 127–29) As we saw, Yahweh's *'emunah* is not an attribute of mercy in itself, but it causes him to act mercifully for the sake of being faithful to his covenant promises. In Exod 34 it is his covenant to Abraham, here to David. David discovers that in Yahweh he does not face either righteousness or mercy, but always both, as related aspects of his dealings with him.[84] However, Yahweh's righteousness in keeping his covenant commitments is not the same as dishing out the punishments that unrighteous behavior would deserve, as seen in David's confession in the next verse. His righteous commitment to faithfully discharge his covenant promise will sometimes mean acting in undeserved mercy to the covenant breaker: that is his steadfast love, his *hesed*.

Verse 11b is the second of four appeals in the final verses: to Yahweh's name, to his *hesed*, and because of David's status as "your servant";[85] none of the other three appeals imply righteousness on David's part. They are parallel in an ABB'A' structure so that the appeal to "your righteousness" (v. 11b) matches the appeal to *hesed* (v. 12b).[86]

It will be by undeserved mercy by heeding Ps 2 and turning to Yahweh for refuge, returning to his instruction as a contrite sinner (vv. 9, 11), that David will be rescued (v. 10).[87] For Israel looking back on the exile, David serves as a model, relying no longer on a righteous vindicating judgment but on Yahweh's *hesed*.[88] Luis Alonso Schökel puts it simply:

---

83. Allen's rendering as "by your consistency" in both places captures this (Allen, *Psalms 101–150*, 351, see discussion in 355).

84. Buysch, *Der letzte Davidpsalter*, 261.

85. So also Hossfeld, who argues that this self-abasement ("Niedrichkeitsaussage") is the result of David's *lack* of membership of the righteous (Hossfeld-Zenger 3:772).

86. Buysch, *Der letzte Davidpsalter*, 261.

87. This psalm is entirely unsuitable for one facing false accusation, since innocence is the one thing that he claims not to have (Beyerlin, *Die Rettung der Bedrängten*, 36; *contra* Goldingay 3:672).

88. McCann directly applies the confession of v. 2a to exilic Israel (McCann 1252). The lack of explicit royal language need not limit its application to an individual (*contra* Eissfeldt, *The Old Testament*, 115–16); neither need the exemplary royal character here *limit* its application to a future eschatological Davidic King (*pace* Singer, "The Literary Context," 373).

"the supplicant . . . appeals to God to ask for grace, not justice."[89] If Israel's enemies will be destroyed, it is only because Israel is Yahweh's "servant" (v. 12). "Servant of Yahweh"—this puts Israel on a par with the repentant sinning ruler of any of the nations who answer Ps 2 by "serving Yahweh with fear." David has brought Israel through some imprecations that they are in no position to pray and finally shows them their actual standing: relying on God's mercy alone.[90] That is why Book V keeps calling on Israel to thank God for his eternal *hesed*. That is the sole ground for the prophecy that stood behind their expectation in Ps 137.

3.D.vi. Psalm 144

This reliance on undeserved *hesed* has a consequence for the enemy nations. It reappears in 144:2. Psalm 144 is the most reduced imprecation in this final David collection.[91] It opens by alluding to the rock that bracketed Pss 18 and 19, then quotes a phrase from 18:35, distributed across two parallel phrases:

18:35 [34] The one *who trains my hands for war*
>   and then my arms bend a bronze bow.
>   144:1 David's.
>   Blessed be Yahweh my rock,
>>   *who trains my hands* for battle
>>   my fingers *for war.*

Psalm 144 makes such extensive use of Ps 18 that Gunkel and others consider Ps 144 to be simply an imitation of Ps 18.[92] McCann is more plausible:

---

89. "El orante . . . acude a Dios para pedir gracia, no justicia" (Schökel II:1622).

90. Seybold notes the constant judicial pleading in these psalms (Seybold, "Zur Geschichte," 379–89).

91. It is so reduced, compared to the previous ones, that some take Ps 143 as the end of the series of prayers (Buysch, *Der letzte Davidpsalter*, 274; Hossfeld-Zenger 3:772). The structure of this David collection and the content of Ps 144 makes it more likely that we are to see it as the final, very reduced, imprecation. It is no coincidence that it is both the final and the least of the imprecations: David has been leading Israel through a decreasing series of protestations of innocence, and increasing confessions of sinfulness or actual guilt, and therefore reducing the imprecations accordingly. David continues to represent the nation in Ps 144 (Allen, *Psalms 101–150*, 78).

92. See Kraus 2:1122; Delitzsch 808; Vesco 1331; Allen, *Psalms 101–150*, 363–64; Saur, "Die Theologische Funktion," 694.

What is puzzling and problematic from a form-critical perspective, however, makes more sense when one considers the placement of Psalm 144 within the Psalter.... Psalm 144 offers ... a rereading of Psalm 18. It is significant that this reflects the realities of the exile and its aftermath.[93]

With such a widely-seen similarity between the two psalms, prayers against the enemy are conspicuously limited in Ps 144, compared with the extensive celebration of victory in Ps 18. The theophanic language of bowing the heavens and coming down to rescue David is there (vv. 5–7, cf. 18:10), but the language of David finishing off the enemy is absent. Instead, they are merely scattered by Yahweh (v. 6). The enemy is not destroyed; instead, the blessing of having Yahweh as God is made universally available at the close of the Psalm. As in Ps 18, so here David announces a proclamation which describes the following psalm well. The "new song" that David announces in v. 9 concerns Yahweh who gives victory to kings, plural, not just David in v. 10. As we have seen, this final note in David's imprecations fits not only the theme of Book V, but the two David psalms that follow the sets of imprecations in section II (Pss 138, 145). Psalm 145 comes next, bringing us back to this repeated note of Book V.[94]

Before we turn there, we should consider the significance of v. 2b. Does David's God subdue "my people under me"? J. J. Stuart Perowne explains the problem: "It is certainly not easy to understand how any but a despotic ruler, or one whose people had taken up arms against him, could thus celebrate God as subduing his own nation under him."[95] The context and the parallel in Ps 18 / 2 Sam 22 would also suggest that many peoples are subdued under David. The textual evidence is neatly summarized by Peter Flint: MT and LXX are singular, while DSS, some Hebrew MSS, Syriac and Targums are plural.[96] To this we add that the Masoretes (*Mp* in both L and Alep) warn us explicitly against turning this singular

---

93. McCann 1254.

94. An ancient MS tradition links 144:15 to Ps 145, as does modern Jewish liturgy (Ḥakham, *Psalms 1–57*, viii). The universal kingship note is reinforced by borrowing from Ps 8. Verse 3 quotes the opening refrain of Ps 8. Further, the final phrase of v. 1, while semantically parallel with the phrase borrowed from Ps 18, uses vocabulary from Ps 8: אֲאַלְפֵּ is only found in these two psalms. Links to, even quotations from, Ps 8 are seen by, e.g., Allen, *Psalms 101–150*, 363; Saur, "Die Theologische Funktion," 694.

95. Perowne, *Psalms*, 2:465; Kraus similarly thinks that the verb is inherently violent and therefore cannot be directed at his own people (Kraus 2:1121).

96. Flint, "Dead Sea Psalms Scrolls," 28–29.

into a plural,[97] and that Ps 18:44 (shortly before the re-used verse in Ps
144) and 2 Sam 22:44 also differ here, with the same Masoretic warning.
Ps 18:44

תְּפַלְּטֵנִי מֵרִיבֵי עָם

You delivered me *from the strife of* a people.

2 Sam 22:44

וַתְּפַלְּטֵנִי מֵרִיבֵי עַמִּי

And you delivered me *from the strife of* my people.

Before we let context change the text, we should give the flexible
reuse of Ps 18 (or 2 Sam 22) a chance to prove its worth, spurred on by the
Masoretes' insistence. The introduction to the Psalter can guide us again.
In Ps 3, we have two peoples at war (Israel and Judah). Yahweh subdues
Israel under David, and David ends by praying for the combined nation
as a single people. This meets Perowne's objection that a ruler would
hardly "celebrate God as subduing his own nation under him" (above).[98]
In Ps 2, we have many nations promised to the son as his inheritance and
possession, both nouns being singular. Psalm 18 / 2 Sam 22 is a partial
fulfilment of that promise, so it is hardly surprising to find the former
enemy nations, now part of David's inheritance, referred to both in the
plural and in the singular.[99] As Joseph Alexander puts it: "My people, in

---

97. ג סביר עמים וקר עמי in *BHS* and *MGH* II:230. On סביר see Kelley et al., *The Masorah*, 156–57; the other two passages are 2 Sam 22:44 and Lam 3:14.

98. Goldingay (rightly, in my view) observes: "MT and LXX have a much more interesting declaration about Yhwh subduing 'my people'" (Goldingay 3:685). Far too many emendations remove what is interesting in the text, especially in poetic texts.

99. While I am of course arguing that this interpretation of Ps 144:2 is at least as old as the shape of the Psalter, it is found explicitly as early as Hilary of Poitiers, also citing Ps 2: "*Who subdueth my people that is under me.* Taking the words as those of Christ, the earlier ones, S. Hilary tells us, need no explanation, (H.) so clearly are they set forth in the Gospels by Christ's revelation of His Father and ascription of all things to Him; but this last clause points especially to the conversion of the Gentiles, and is the Lord's thanksgiving for the fulfilment of that promise, 'Desire of Me, and I shall give Thee the heathen for Thine inheritance: and the uttermost parts of the earth for Thy possession. Thou shalt bruise them with a rod of iron: and break them in pieces like a potter's vessel'" (Neale and Littledale, *Psalm CXIX to CL*, 371).

its widest sense, including Israel and the Gentiles who were to be added to the kingdom of David under the reign of the Messiah."[100]

Psalm 144 fittingly concludes the series of imprecations, Pss 139→144, by returning to the idea that many nations will join Israel in receiving and celebrating Yahweh's mercy. This is the note on which the David collection began (Ps 138), and is the note of the next psalm, Ps 145. This in turn ushers in the concluding Hallel, which resounds with that note in fulfilment of the theme of Book V and of the Psalter as begun in the introductory psalms. Its openness allows it to serve those looking back on the exile as well as any future generations:

> Although Psalm 144 would have had special relevance to the post-exilic community, it portrays the position which the people of God perpetually occupy.[101]

Psalm 137 longs for Edom and Babylon to be excluded from that mercy. That longing is not contradicted by the David collection. David does remind the nation of the criteria for praying Ps 137—an innocence that they lack in their conflict with these nations. It is only because Yahweh freely chose to forgive Israel and not Babylon, and prophesied as much, that Israel knows Babylon and Edom will face the fate of Ps 137. They were in no position to invent and ask for such an outcome on their own initiative. The innocent sufferer is entitled to approach Yahweh for rescue and even for fair judgment against enemies, but that was not Israel's situation.

David presents a graduated series of imprecations that ask for less retribution each time, with correspondingly weaker requirements to prove innocence. In the end, the guilt leading to exile is such that none of these imprecations would have been fair game for Israel against their exilic enemies. The nation is left with the message that the *hesed* they have enjoyed is one that they should celebrate, even when it is experienced by their enemies. They could be confident that what they await in Ps 137:8–9 will happen, but only because of the prophecies of Isa 13. There may be future conflicts when any or all of Pss 137 and 139–44 can be prayed by the nation, given the requisite innocence; if they cannot, it will not be a problem with the imprecation but with the one who is disqualified from wielding it. Even when they are entitled to pray like this, the example of David in Book I, re-enlisted in Book V, still demonstrates

---

100. Alexander, *Psalms*, 551.

101. McCann 1256.

that the completely innocently accused one should prefer the repentance and blessing of their enemy; *hesed* should be displayed *to* the enemy by praying for *hesed* to be received *by* the enemy. This is in keeping with Yahweh's purpose to rescue and bless all nations.

4. Closing *Hallelujah*: Psalms 146–50

This Hallel does triple duty: it is the concluding *hallelujah* of section III, the doxology of Book V, and the conclusion to the Psalter.

The universal note, which embraces all foreign kings and the whole cosmos, grows from the individual of 145:21→146:1, through to Zion in 146:10, and finally blossoms in 148:11 when the politicians of Ps 2 reappear: the "kings of the earth" of 2:2, the "peoples" of 2:1, and the "judges of the earth" of 2:10. Even the "princes" who were the enemy in 119:23, 161 reappear. As in Ps 145, it is "all" of them who are in view. Here, in Ps 148, the cosmic extent of the praise is most fully expressed, including the heavens and the earth.[102] They are being enjoined to praise: 148:7, 13. The contrast of 145:11 reappears, where his *hasidim* are the ones given power, who are enjoying the result of Yahweh's *hesed*. Time will run out for these international statesmen. In the next psalm, the *hasidim* will, finally, not only execute that command to praise (149:6a) but also take up swords (149:6b) and execute judgment (149:7). Here we find the "nations" and "peoples" of 2:1. The kings and nobles who in 2:2 wanted to unbind the peoples from Yahweh's rule are themselves bound (149:8). The justice promised in Ps 1 is executed on them (149:9a), as they had been warned in Ps 2. "The *nations, peoples* and *kings* who seek to throw off Yahweh's authority in 2:1–2 become the object of his retribution in 149:7–9."[103] They received their final summons in the previous psalm (148:11).[104]

That will be honor of his *hasidim* (149:9b). Their joy in vv. 5, 9 corresponds to their blessing in 2:12, so that the Psalter ends by confirming the proclamation of Ps 2: the Messianic King is victorious over the nations, so that those who take refuge in Yahweh are triumphant in 149:4–5.[105]

102. Vesco 1363–65.

103. Brennan, "Psalms 1–8," 26.

104. Vesco shows that Pss 148–49 are closely knit together, giving praise for this judgment, but with "praise" being the dominant note (148:1, 2, 3, 4, 7, 13, 14; 149:1, 3, 9) and with its universal scope again identified by כל (148:2, 3, 7, 9, 10, 11; 149:9; Vesco 1365–66).

105. Vesco 1371.

It will be the honor of *all* his *hasidim*: those from any nation, who have answered the call of Ps 2 and the insistent call of Book V.[106] They now say *hallelujah* (v. 9c), and they finally call on absolutely everything that has survived the judgment to *hallelujah* (Ps 150). Just as section I (Pss 107–17) had ended with them exiting Egypt (and being at the tabernacle) and section II (118–35) had ended with them arriving at the new temple in Zion, so section III (136–50) ends with them using all the instruments of the temple cult,[107] at the crescendo of *hallelujah*,[108] which finally concludes:

> 150:6 *All with breath* should praise Yah [*hallelujah*].
> Praise Yah! [*hallelujah*]

In fact, it does *not* conclude. It has assembled the worshippers and arranged the orchestra, but the performance is what the whole world is to do after the end of the Psalter.[109] Psalm 150 is the end of the conflict:[110] between the wicked and the righteous, the Messianic King and his vassals, the nations and Israel, Yahweh and his rebellious creation; it is therefore the end of *retribution*.

---

106. The link with Ps 2 is also seen by Vesco, who argues that the "judgment written" in 149:9 refers, as discerned through a canonical reading of the Psalter, to the judgment announced in 1:5 and its matching precept in 2:7 so that Pss 148–50 are a conclusion to the Psalter, corresponding to Pss 1–2 as its introduction (Vesco 1370–71). As reported above, it has been noted that Book V, and the seam with Book IV, is answering the crisis of Ps 89. However, Ps 89 (along with Ps 72) is a framing psalm leaning on the promises as expressed in Ps 2 (Ḥakham, *Psalms 1–57*, 11). It is therefore no surprise to find that Book V ends both by answering the question of Ps 89 and by fulfilling the promise of Ps 2, both in terms of Yahweh's חֶסֶד: the complaint of Ps 89 was precisely that the promise of Ps 2 was not being fulfilled and therefore Yahweh was not acting in חֶסֶד towards David. As Heim puts it, Ps 89 demands that Yahweh "fulfil his covenant obligations," which can only happen through the end of the exile and restoration of the Davidic monarchy (Heim, "The (God-)Forsaken King," 306). Universality is one of two themes that Janowski sees as linking the "Proömium Pss 1–2" with Ps 150 (Janowski, "Ein Tempel aus Worten," 302).

107. Hossfeld-Zenger 3:876.

108. McCann 1278.

109. Weber, *Theologie*, 208.

110. Vesco 1376.

5. Summary: Retribution in Section III (Psalms 137, 139–44)

We will now summarize what this final section of Book V teaches concerning retribution. In the next section, we will conclude our exposition of Book V as a whole with a summary of our conclusions. In the final chapter we will present our conclusions concerning retribution in the whole Psalter.

We have seen that the final collection of David psalms is within the body of section III. It consists of a series of imprecations (139–44). These are framed by two David psalms that celebrate rescue through unmerited grace, that desire the same for the kings of the nations, and finally (Ps 145:21) usher in the resounding series of five *hallelujah* psalms that close the whole psalter with all that lives praising Yahweh for his mercy after the final rescuing judgment.

The only other element in the body of section III is notorious Ps 137, where Israel is wrathful against her exilic enemies. We have seen that this is immediately followed by the first of the David psalms (138), pointing to *hesed* for the nations, even the enemy nations. It is then followed by the series of David imprecations, which lead to the final David psalm (145), which likewise points to *hesed* for the nations.

Psalm 145 not only concludes the instruction on how to take up Ps 137 but also fulfils the call of Ps 107 and of the whole of Book V:

> Ps 145 therefore fulfills the programmatic intent of the fifth book, as it has been enunciated in its opening verse (Ps 107:1 . . .): to give thanks unto Yhwh, for he is good, for his love endures for ever. . . .
>
> Once it was Moses from Sinai, but now it is David from Zion, who proclaims the genuine character of the God of Israel. All the peoples of the earth are called to share this revelation and to seal a covenant with Yhwh.[111]

All of this was introduced by the opening *hodu* psalm (136), whose message is impossible to miss: *all* of Yahweh's acts for Israel are the result of his *hesed*, each of them being explained (almost monotonously) as "for his *hesed* is forever." The psalm opens and closes by calling forth thanks (*hodu*) for his mercy. Just as Israel owes their return from exile to

---

111. Coniglio, "Gracious and Merciful," 42.

Yahweh's undeserved kindness, so should the nations, even enemy nations, even barbarous exilic foes, be invited to enjoy the same.

5.A. Are These Imprecations Self-Righteous?

The series of imprecations (139–44) responds to Ps 137 by containing a gradation of imprecations, which fit the protestations of innocence, declarations of sinfulness, or confessions of guilt. This is offered to postexilic Israel as a model to follow.

Psalm 137 distinguishes itself by its lack of confession of sin. There is no hint that there is anything wrong with this psalm. However, the final David collection (138–45) forces this question on Israel: would you have been *qualified* to ask for this against Edom and Babylon, or is your rescue from them akin to David's rescue from Absalom—an undeserved act of divine mercy to you? Had Yahweh not taken the initiative and predicted the brutal overthrow of the enemy, Israel would (like David in Ps 3) have had to wait in their guilt. Like David praying to the temple from exile, they had no right to call on Yahweh to arise and give them military victory: the ark of the covenant was rightly removed from them.

Nothing could be further from self-righteousness than Psalms 139–44, and that lesson is central to the right appropriation of Ps 137.

5.B. Is Perfect Righteousness Required to Pray Imprecations?

This does not mean, however, that only one who is completely sinless could pray imprecations. The David collection responding to Ps 137 does not stop imprecations as soon as guilt appears: it moderates them in accordance with sinfulness. Book V has been pressing on Israel that it is only by *hesed*, unmerited mercy, that Israel was brought back from exile. The fact that Babylon and Edom were defeated had nothing to do with Israel's righteousness.

Even in a position of lacking righteousness, like David in Ps 3, the assurance of Yahweh's *hesed* towards Israel entitled David to pray against Absalom and his army and entitled Israel to desire the punishment prophesied against Edom and Babylon and, thus, to pray Ps 137.

However, having such an assurance of rescue, what place is there for further retribution? What has David, from Ps 3 on, modelled?

5.C. Cannot the Enemy Repent and Be Blessed?

What Israel waits for in Ps 137 is inevitable: it has been prophesied. Israel can no more wish for Babylon to go unscathed than David could wish for Absalom to keep the throne. The final collection of David psalms looks forward to future situations and teaches how to pray for enemies such as Edom and Babylon. It moderates what Israel can legitimately pray for, as we have just seen in the previous two sections.

It goes further, though. These David psalms present a different hope altogether in the framing of Psalms 138 and 145, which fits the overall message of Book V: the inclusion, on a global scale, of repentant sinners from among the nations, including their kings, as envisaged in Ps 2. They are to be shown the same *hesed* that Israel has enjoyed from Yahweh, and Israel is to rejoice in the salvation of the nations. This does not mean that there will be no judgment for the unrepentant enemies: it is a necessary penultimate note before universal praise, in Ps 149.

This is over-played by Derek Wittman, who points out that the first and last references to foreign kings are in Pss 2 and 149:[112]

> [T]he psalmists display an overwhelming tendency to portray foreign nations in a negative light when they refer to them explicitly" and that Pss 2 and 149, by their strategic position, "create in the mind of the reader a lasting negative impression of foreign nations and kings as enemies.[113]

There is a lot to his case, but Ps 2 does not leave the kings as unredeemable enemies: they are invited to repent and be blessed. It will not do to consider only Pss 2 and 149: there is a progression within the Psalter of how the nations are viewed. Book V both implicitly and explicitly calls on the nations to join in Israel's blessing. Psalm 149 is a vital piece of that picture, but, crucially, it is not the final word about the nations. The judgment promised in Ps 149 is the final word for the *unrepentant* nations. The final message is Ps 150, which calls on all that has breath, including all foreign repentant nations and kings, to *hallelujah* with Israel. Judgment of the wicked is penultimate; blessing of the repentant is ultimate.[114]

---

112. Wittman, "Let Us Cast Off," 53–70.

113. Wittman, "Let Us Cast Off," 66–67.

114. It therefore will not do to say that these final Hallel psalms have a multi-voiced approach to the nations: sometimes judgment, sometimes blessing. They speak with one voice: recalcitrant nations will face judgment; the others have taken up the offer of repentance and blessing. *Contra* Neumann, "Israel und die Völker," 334–35.

5.D. Does David Teach Israel to Hate the Enemy?

As section I and the position of Ps 109 highlighted, so section III continues with the clear implication: Israel has received *hesed* from Yahweh despite behaving as an undeserving enemy; Israel must display *hesed* to equally undeserving enemies.

Consider the counter-claim:

> The Christian faith teaches a new way, the pursuit of forgiveness and a call to love. Both its intrinsic non-nationalism and its ability to fall back on an eschatological final reckoning, the last judgment, facilitate such a course.[115]

The global, trans-national concern of the Psalter is part of the context of Ps 137. The same context teaches Israel to show forgiveness as Israel has received forgiveness. Psalm 137 is surrounded in Book V by Yahweh's purposes which are better than non-national: they are international, global, universal. Not only individuals, but nations are invited in as nations, complete with their kings. Psalm 137 is in a context that looks beyond the judgment of Israel's exilic enemies, to the very "eschatological final reckoning" that Allen describes. Israel is commanded to rejoice in having all nations joining in celebrating Yahweh's *hesed*. Israel must celebrate the inclusion of enemy nations, which requires their forgiveness. *Hesed* is, in the context of Book V, a love to the undeserving, wicked enemy. Allen's "pursuit of forgiveness and a call to love" is not a new way in the NT: it is the way of the Book of Psalms.

As Kit Barker concludes, reflecting on Ps 137:

> In the end, the burden of proof is upon those who suggest the illocutionary stance of the New Testament is incommensurate with the illocutionary stance of the Psalter.[116]

6. Conclusion: David, Israel's Model of Imprecation in Book V

Over the last four chapters we have examined Book V overall, and we have expounded each of its many imprecations in the light of how Book V presents them.

115. Allen, on Ps 137 (Allen, *Psalms 101–150*, 309).
116. Barker, "Divine Illocutions," 14.

Book V looks back on the exile and on Israel's brutal enemies. David is enlisted as the exemplary and representative king: he had been set up at the start of the Psalter as facing an analogous "exile" from which Yahweh rescued him despite his guilt. His situation and Israel's exile were typologically similar to the apostasy at the golden calf, where Yahweh revealed his gracious nature and rescued the nation from their own sin. Book IV leads into Book V with a retelling of the history of Israel's constant rebellion and Yahweh's merciful rescue through the exodus and the restoration from exile, all attributed to his merciful *hesed*. Through this lens, David models prayers against enemies.

The enemy nations are undeserving, as David and Israel had been. Yahweh's purpose, throughout Book V, is to show the same gratuitous mercy to the nations as he had shown David and Israel. Not just some nations, but all flesh is called to worship Yahweh and enjoy his forgiveness.

> In the MT Psalter tradition, David is at the end remembered for directing Israel in the worship of Yahweh through unconditional praise, a praise resounding from every corner of the cosmos, Yahweh's macro-temple.[117]

The bitter pill for Israel is that this must include their most barbaric and hateful enemies, both looking back on the exile and looking forward to all future conflicts.

In Ps 109, David's behavior is consistent with his prayers in Book I: he is aware of his sinfulness, does not appeal to earned merit, and has no interest in vengeance but, instead, repays malice with mercy. Further, David is an example of receiving and then displaying *hesed*, and this example is placed suggestively after a psalm that has an exilic enemy, Edom, in view (anticipating Ps 137). Israel did not earn Yahweh's rescuing mercy; they must be happy for him to show the same favor to others who do not deserve it, even Israel's enemies. After an affirmation of certain victory by Yahweh's anointed against all enemy nations, the sequence of *hallelujah* psalms remembers the exodus and invites all nations to join Israel in fearing Yahweh (as invited in Ps 2, at the start of the Psalter). The command that opened Book V is extended to them and is delightful: taste Yahweh's goodness and his everlasting mercy and thank him for it.

Turning to the second section of Book V, we find anonymous imprecations of an individual king (Ps 119) and of the nation (Ps 129), making it easier to see that the lessons of the Psalter are not restricted

---

117. Ramantswana, "David of the Psalters," 458.

to past, known situations but are a light for future conflicts. Psalm 119, even in the midst of a famously breath-taking commendation of Torah, shows awareness of the psalmist's own sin and need of mercy; he points enemy kings to develop the same awareness. Psalm 129 is set in the context of one of the most far-reaching confessions of sin in the Bible. Israel's sin and experience of undeserved forgiveness will not allow grudges against enemy nations; not nationality, but relationship with Yahweh, is what brings blessing. The closing *hallelujah* psalm brings this home to the nations: their gods do not rescue them, but they are invited to fear and worship Yahweh and join Israel in testifying that he is good and enjoying his *hesed* forever.

This brings us to the current chapter, where the everlasting mercy enjoyed by Israel is shown to be the ground of all Israel's history (verse by verse through Ps 136). As we have seen, David becomes the teacher of how to appropriate Ps 137, through his own telling examples of prayer. We have seen that his rescue in Ps 3 is relevant here. He was guilty and had not grounds for expecting Yahweh to rescue him, but Yahweh prophesied that he would rescue David and condemn the enemy. Israel faced the same privilege against Babylon. Psalm 137 was not something they could have dreamt up as a matter of justice or entitlement; the desires within it were simply for fulfilment of prophecy. What had been prophesied had not been earned but was Yahweh's gracious favor to Israel. In David's ensuing psalms (138–45), the Psalter reinforces the lessons learned so far. Yahweh cannot be called on to help in a conflict when we are the guilty party in that conflict; that does not mean that perfect righteousness, nor anything like it, is needed or even possible. The enemy nations can and should repent, and Israel should be like David, in rejoicing in the salvation of the enemy. Any hatred for the enemy has to give way to the Psalter's growing insistence, which climaxes in David ushering in the praise of Pss 146–50: all nations, everything with breath, should repent, experience Yahweh's salvation, and praise Yahweh for his mercy.

Yahweh's display of *hesed* to the nations should be no surprise. His *hesed* to Israel, as we have seen, meant saving and protecting them even when they broke the terms of his covenant, and this was grounded in Yahweh's *'emunah*: his faithful determination to bring about the purpose of his covenant. The purpose of the covenant at Sinai and the covenant with David are repeatedly grounded in his covenant with Abraham. Moses averted Yahweh's wrath after the golden calf and secured his self-disclosure as full of *hesed* by appealing to the promise to the Patriarchs

(Exod 32:13). That promise, from the very beginning, was designed to bless all nations, Gen 12:3:

> I will bless those who bless you, but whoever belittles you I will curse. *All the families of the earth will be blessed in you.*

Yahweh continued to be merciful to Israel after the exile for the sake of blessing the enemy nations.

14

Conclusion

Give thanks to Yahweh for he is good.
For his steadfast love is forever.

WE SET OUT IN our quest through the Book of Psalms to answer five
questions:

1. Do prayers against enemies require perfect righteousness?

2. Alternatively, do such prayers stem from a deluded self-righteousness, which is unaware of the supplicant's own need for mercy and
   forgiveness?

3. Is suffering a sufficient qualification for praying against enemies?

4. Do the psalms understand that the enemy is able to repent, or do
   they imagine that they can only ask for the destruction of the enemy?

5. Do the psalms have any notion of loving the enemy, desiring their
   blessing, or do they simply demand vengeance?

These questions were based on assumptions about the theology of
the psalmists, both what they believed and what they could not possibly
understand. The Psalms have overturned each assumption.

1. Imprecations Do Not Require Perfect Righteousness (Real or Imagined)

In a conflict where judgment is required, the one praying for justice must be innocent of the charges at issue. They need not be sinless in general, and certainly not perfectly righteous. It is simply not the case that only a perfectly sinless supplicant could ever pray imprecations: that is a flawed assumption imported to the psalms.

We have shown this in a number of psalms, and we have also shown that it is built into the guide for the reader of the whole book, especially how David is introduced and how imprecations are framed in Book V. The lesson for individuals can be summarized easily enough in Ps 51, for example:

> 5 [3] For my transgressions are what I know
> and my sins confront me constantly.

For the nation it is no different, Ps 130, for example:

> 3 Were you to be on the look-out for iniquities, O Yah,
> Master: who would be left standing?

The imprecations are cut from this very same cloth. There is no perfection in those who rightly prayed them. The news that I am a sinner is not a NT innovation.

2. Imprecations Are Not a Symptom of Self-Righteousness

Neither is it the case that the supplicant is delusional, believing himself to have earned God's favor through his own upright behavior or character. That too is a flawed assumption imported into the Psalms.

A supplicant may be aware that his rescue from injustice will not only be a matter of righteousness, but also of divine mercy. Even though he is in the right in the dispute at issue, his own pervasively sinful character means that other sins disqualify him from divine favor. Even plain justice, that is, rescue from flagrant injustice, is not his right. Psalm 3 makes this abundantly plain at the opening of the Psalter, both for individuals and for the people as a whole, through the person of David. For another example, after his victory against wicked enemies in Ps 18, David identifies the real threat. It is not the wicked out there, but the wickedness within him, in Ps 19:

14 [13] Also from presumptuous sins restrain your servant,
     do not let them govern me!

Self-righteousness is not what animates imprecations in the Psalter. This awareness of fallibility and of actual guilt brings out one of the most glorious lessons in the Psalms. Yahweh's character is revealed most wonderfully by rescuing the oppressed *even when they do not deserve it.* When they have no right to ask for his intervention, he intervenes anyway. Seeing this in the Psalter should transform how the reader thinks of the pagan nations, even the enemies.

3. Victimhood Is Not Righteousness

That rider, "even when they do not deserve it" is important today. We have noticed that the mere fact of victimization is not enough to appeal to Yahweh's defense. Contrary to some contemporary sentiments, the Psalms do not offer evidence that the oppressed are automatically entitled to divine favor. Israel, when oppressed in exile, had no claim on Yahweh to rescue them. They were oppressed because of Yahweh's just judgment against their sin.

David did not presume on Yahweh when he was guilty, in Ps 3. When innocent, in Ps 7, he models to individuals that it is only because he has not done what his enemies accuse him of, that he can appeal to Yahweh:

4 [3] Yahweh, my God, if I have done this,
     if there is wrongdoing in the palms of my hands,
     . . .
6 [5] let the enemy pursue me and overtake me.

In Book V, David models this for the nation as a whole, by responding to the bitter prayer against their enemies (Babylon and Edom), namely Ps 137. He demonstrates that divine justice must be just; Yahweh cannot be called on to attack our enemies when we are the ones at fault (Pss 139–44).

As we have briefly noted, this is in keeping with the message of the NT. First Peter 2:20 will not let beatings or ill-treatment be a cloak for Christians who have earned their punishment. Jesus did not pronounce blessed any who were persecuted for any reason, but only those persecuted *for the sake of righteousness* (Matt 5:10). In the next verse, we should also not excise some key qualifiers: being reviled, persecuted, and having evil spoken against one is not a mark of blessing. They are blessed when persecuted *for Christ's sake*, and when the evil alleged against them *is not true*. The Christian canon speaks with one voice against the easy presumption that ill-fortune, even malicious attack, puts me in the right. Being asked to comment on murderous and unrighteous persecution of his contemporaries at the hands of Pilate, Jesus's shocking answer was: "unless you repent, you will all perish" (Luke 13:5; much like Pss 1:6; 2:12).

This is why the Psalms taught, and continue to teach, that asking Yahweh for help against enemies is only an upright thing to do when the enemies are not prosecuting a just cause against you. This is neither self-righteous nor the exclusive domain of a perfectly sinless person.

It is no surprise that Peter's second warning only to suffer punishment for doing *good* (1 Pet 3:13–14) follows his injunction not to return evil for evil, but instead to bless (v. 9), and then proves the point by quoting, of all things, the Book of *Psalms* (vv. 10–12). We turn now to that question of blessing enemies in the psalms.

4. The Enemies Are Redeemable: Even Enemy Kings and Nations Are Invited to Repent and Be Blessed

Allegedly, the minds behind the Psalms could not imagine that the enemy was capable of repentance. At least as early as Ps 2 (if not Ps 1), this assumption proves to be so much chaff, awaiting the wind.

> 10 Now then, O kings, get wisdom;
>> submit to retraining, O judges of the earth.
> 11 Serve Yahweh fearfully,
>> rejoice and tremble.
> 12 Kiss the *Sohn*
>> lest he anger so that you perish while on the way
>> because suddenly kindled is his ire.
> O, the blessings of all who take refuge in him!

In Ps 7, David wants the enemies to stop being wicked against him; it would have been news to him that they could only stop being wicked by dying. He expected that they might repent.

This desire for the enemy to be restored might not be present in every psalm. However, we certainly cannot go on claiming that the psalmists could not have known about the repentance and forgiveness of their enemies, since they want this very thing in at least some psalms.

Moreover, taking the Book of Psalms as a whole, this repentance of the wicked is no sideshow. In the theology of the Psalms, it is the preferred option for the enemy. The repentance of all the wicked is the desire on which the whole Psalter ends, as we will see next.

5. The Psalms Would Rather Bless the Enemy Than Be Avenged

Even imprecatory psalms show concern for the welfare of the enemy, including not only leniency in punishment but also forgiveness and a desire for their repentance and blessing.

After the invitation of Ps 2, which we have just quoted, comes Ps 3, where David models this merciful attitude to his defeated enemies:

> 9 [8] It is to Yahweh that rescue belongs!
> May there be a blessing upon *your* nation!

Once again, I do not claim that every psalm shows such a desire to bless the enemy. Nonetheless, some do. It will not do to say that the psalmists lived at a time when they simply knew no better than to hate their enemies.

At the national level, the whole of Book V has been built around the growing call for all nations to join Israel in celebrating a salvation that is undeserved. The reader cannot remain happy to enjoy Israel's rescue from national sins without desiring the whole world to accept the invitation to be blessed. Just as Israel received undeserved mercy, so undeserving nations (including enemy nations) are to do likewise. Each section of Book V opens by calling Israel to give thanks for Yahweh's *hesed*, and then each section ends by inviting the nations to join in.

> 117:1 Praise Yahweh, all nations,
> sing his praises, all peoples!
> 2 Because mighty for us is his steadfast love,
> and Yahweh's faithfulness is for ever!
> *Hallelujah!*

> 135:19 O Israel's House: bless Yahweh!
> O Aaron's House: bless Yahweh!
> 18 O Levi's House: bless Yahweh!
> *O fearers of Yahweh*: bless Yahweh!

150:6 *All with breath* should praise Yah[weh].
Praise Yah[weh]!

6. A Missing Theology of the Cross?

The questions we set out to answer were in large measure determined by unsympathetic concerns, which assume a large ethical gap between us and the Psalms. At the far more sympathetic end, we find Derek Kidner, for example:

> It would be better, in fact, to speak of [the psalmists] attuning our ears to the gospel than of our adjusting to their situation, for we cannot truly hear its answers until we have felt the force of their questions.[1]

Even with such an open attitude to the Psalter, many will agree with him that the Psalms are noticeably pre-Christian. Kidner posits that the cross brings an assurance of final judgment unknown to the psalmists, as well as awareness of sin. For that reason, the Christian cannot pray these prayers:[2]

> To get fully in tune with the psalmists on this issue we should have to suspend our consciousness of having a gospel to impart (which affects our attitude to fellow sinners) and our assurance of a final righting of wrongs (which affects our attitude to present anomalies). Without these certainties, only a cynic could feel no impatience to see justice triumphant and evil men broken; and these authors were no cynics.[3]

Has our exposition left room for such a gap between the Psalms and the gospel?

We need an "assurance of a final righting of all wrongs." Such psalms as 149 already supplied it. The gospel which we have to impart tells of God saving undeserving sinners by grace. We need look no further than Psalms 2 and 3 and the many other passages we have examined. Does our view of the enemy need to be tempered by self-awareness of sin? We have seen a pervasive awareness of the psalmist's own sinfulness, which has served as a model for Christians down the

1. Kidner, *Psalms 1–72*, 26.
2. Kidner, *Psalms 1–72*, 32.
3. Kidner, *Psalms 1–72*, 26.

ages: it is to the seven penitential *psalms* that the liturgies of the church have turned for contrition.

Are we really taught to be more patient for justice than the psalms? David in the backstory of Ps 3 waits patiently to see whether God will save him. The "How long?" cries of the Psalter are echoed often enough in the NT's "How long?" (Rev 6:10) and such passages as Luke 18:7–8. Whatever "impatience" the Psalms show is not un-Christian, just un-British.[4]

7. Contemporary Use of Imprecations

How should the modern reader, and modern congregations, make use of some difficult psalms? Recovering the time-tested practice of regularly traversing all the psalms in order will be of considerable help—something which many churches find sensible with every other book of the Bible. Such sequential reading, without leaving any psalms out, will reinforce the sense that there is a time when we may pray for divine justice against our enemies and a time when we may not. The psalms will throttle any lingering sense of our moral superiority and self-sufficiency. Even when we may pray against enemies, we are to prefer an end to the evil through repentance and forgiveness, over the end of the evildoer through justice and judgment. There is a time to pray for relief against enemies for our oppressed kin in troubled parts of the world. Yet even then, the psalms make us aware that even the persecuted are in need of divine mercy, and should show it to their persecutors.

These psalms prove that God cares for the victims of sin even now, and can intervene before final judgment. They also show why his final judgment has not landed to end all suffering: God is still waiting for wicked nations to repent.

Ultimately, none of us can stand on our own merits before the judge of all the earth. The tune of the Psalter is that the judge is the willing savior. He is immovably determined to bring all nations into his choir. That is why his anointed leads us in singing:

145:21 Yahweh's praise is what my mouth will speak
      and let all flesh bless his holy name forever and ever.

---

4. Villanueva, "Preaching Lament," 64–84.

Bibliography

Adamo, David. "Reading Psalm 109 in African Christianity." *OTE* 21 (2008) 575–92.

Adams, James E. *War Psalms of the Prince of Peace: Lessons from the Imprecatory Psalms.* Phillipsburg, NJ: P&R, 1991.

Alexander, Joseph. *The Psalms: Translated and Explained.* Edinburgh: Elliot & Thin, 1864.

Allen, Leslie C. *Psalms 101–150.* Rev. ed. WBC 21. Dallas: Word, 2002.

———. *Psalms.* Word Biblical Themes. Waco: Word, 1987.

Alter, Robert. *The Art of Biblical Narrative.* 1981. Reprint, New York: Basic, 1983.

———. *The Art of Biblical Poetry.* 1985. Reprint, New York: Basic, 1987.

———. *The Book of Psalms: A Translation with Commentary.* New York: Norton, 2007.

———. *The Prophets.* Vol. 2 of *The Hebrew Bible: A Translation with Commentary.* New York: Norton, 2019.

Althann, Robert. "Atonement and Reconciliation in Psalms 3, 6, and 83." *JNSL* 25 (1999) 75–82.

———. "The Psalms of Vengeance against Their Ancient Near Eastern Background." *JNSL* 18 (1992) 1–11.

Ambrose. *De paenitentia.* In *St. Ambrose Select Works and Letters,* edited by Philip Schaff and Henry Wace, vol. 10 of *NPNF2,* 327–59. 1890–1900. Reprint, Grand Rapids: Eerdmans, 1983–88.

Ames, William. *Conscience with the Power and Cases Thereof.* Amsterdam, 1639.

Anderson, A. A. *2 Samuel.* WBC 11. Dallas: Word, 1989.

Aquinas, Thomas. *Commentaire sur les Psaumes.* Translated by Jean-Éric S. de Saint-Éloy. Paris: Cerf, 1996.

Athanasius. *Epistula ad Marcellinum de interpretatione Psalmorum.* In *On the Incarnation,* translated by a Religious of C.S.M.V. Popular Patristics Series. Crestwood, NY: St. Vladimir's Seminary, 1996.

Augustine. *Saint Augustine: Expositions on the Book of Psalms.* Vol. 8 of *NPNF1,* edited by Philip Schaff. 1886–1889. Reprint, Grand Rapids: Eerdmans, 1969–88.

Aurelius, Erik. "Davids Unschuld: Die Hofgeschichte und Psalm 7." In *Gott und Mensch im Dialog: Festschrift für Otto Kaiser zum 80. Geburtstag*, edited by Markus Witte, 391–412. BZAW 345/I. Berlin: de Gruyter, 2004.

Auwers, Jean-Marie. *La composition littéraire du Psautier: un état de la question*. CahRB 46. Paris: Gabalda, 2000.

Ayres, Robert A. "'The Devices and Desires of Our Own Hearts': Reflections on Blessing and Curse in the Songs of Ascent." In *Poets on the Psalms*, edited by Lynn Domina, 131–51. San Antonio, TX: Trinity University Press, 2008.

Backhaus, Franz Josef. "'JHWH, mein Gott, rette mich!': Menschliche Gewalt und göttliche Gerechtigkeit in Psalm 7." *BK* 66 (2011) 150–58.

Bader, Günter. *Psalterspiel: Skizze einer Theologie des Psalters*. HUT. Tübingen: Mohr Siebeck, 2009.

Baer, David A., and Robert P. Gordon. "חָסַד." In *NIDOTTE* 2:211–18.

Bakon, Shimon. "Who Were the 'Fearers of the LORD' (Yirei Hashem) in Psalms?" *JBQ* 42 (2014) 250–54.

Ballhorn, Egbert. *Zum Telos des Psalters: der Textzusammenhang des Vierten und Fünften Psalmenbuches (Ps 90–150)*. BBB 138. Berlin: Philo, 2004.

Barbiero, Gianni. *Das erste Psalmenbuch als Einheit: eine synchrone Analyse von Psalm 1–41*. ÖBS 16. Frankfurt am Main: Lang, 1999.

———. *L'asino del nemico: rinuncia alla vendetta e amore del nemico nella legislazione dell'Antico Testamento (Es 23,4–5; Dt 22,1–4; Lv 19,17–18)*. AnBib 128. Roma: Pontificio Istituto Biblico, 1991.

Barker, Kenneth L. *Micah, Nahum, Habakkuk, Zephaniah*. NAC 20. Nashville: Broadman & Holman, 1999.

Barker, Kit. "Divine Illocutions in Psalm 137: A Critique of Nicholas Wolterstorff's 'Second Hermeneutic.'" *TynBul* 60 (2009) 1–14.

Basil, Saint. *Exegetic Homilies*. Translated by Agnes Clare Way. FC 46. Washington, DC: Catholic University of America Press, 1963.

Basson, Alec. "'Rescue Me from the Young Lions': An Animal Metaphor in Psalm 35:17." *OTE* 21 (2008) 9–17.

Bauckham, Richard. *The Bible in Politics: How to Read the Bible Politically*. 2nd ed. Louisville, KY: Westminster John Knox, 2011.

Bauer, Walter, F. W. Danker, W. F. Arndt, and F. W. Gingrich, eds. *A Greek-English Lexicon of the New Testament and Other Early Christian Literature*. 3rd ed. Chicago: University of Chicago Press, 2000.

Bavinck, Johan Herman. *An Introduction to the Science of Missions*. Translated by David Hugh Freeman. Philadelphia: Presbyterian and Reformed, 1960.

Becker, Joachim. *Gottesfurcht im Alten Testament*. AnBib 25. Rome: Pontificio Istituto Biblico, 1965.

Becking, Bob. "Does Exile Equal Suffering? A Fresh Look at Psalm 137." In *Exile and Suffering: A Selection of Papers Read at the 50th Anniversary Meeting of the Old Testament Society of South Africa OTWSA / OTSSA, Pretoria, August 2007*, edited by Bob Becking and Dirk J. Human, 183–202. Leiden: Brill, 2009.

Beckwith, Roger. *The Old Testament Canon of the New Testament Church and Its Background in Early Judaism*. Grand Rapids: Eerdmans, 1985.

Bellinger, William H., Jr. *Psalms: Reading and Studying the Book of Praises*. Peabody, MA: Hendrickson, 1990.

――――. "Reading from the Beginning (Again): The Shape of Book I of the Psalter." In *Diachronic and Synchronic: Reading the Psalms in Real Time: Proceedings of the Baylor Symposium on the Book of Psalms*, edited by Joel S. Burnett et al., 114–26. LHB/OTS 488. New York: T. & T. Clark, 2007.

Bergen, Robert D. *1, 2 Samuel*. NAC 7. Nashville: Broadman & Holman, 1996.

Berger, Yitzhak. "The David-Benjaminite Conflict and the Intertextual Field of Psalm 7." *JSOT* 38 (2014) 279–96.

Berlin, Adele. *The Dynamics of Biblical Parallelism*. 2nd ed. Biblical Resource Series. Grand Rapids: Eerdmans, 2008.

――――. "Psalms and the Literature of Exile: Psalms 137, 44, 69, and 78." In *The Book of Psalms: Composition and Reception*, edited by Peter W. Flint et al., 65–86. VTSup 99. Leiden: Brill, 2005.

Bertholet, Alfred. *Die Stellung der Israeliten und der Juden zu den Fremden*. Freiburg: Mohr, 1896.

Beyerlin, Walter. *Die Rettung der Bedrängten in den Feindpsalmen der Einzelnen auf institutionelle Zusammenhänge untersucht*. FRLANT 99. Göttingen: Vandenhoeck u. Ruprecht, 1970.

――――. *Werden und Wesen des 107. Psalms*. BZAW 153. Berlin: de Gruyter, 1979.

Blenkinsopp, Joseph. *David Remembered: Kingship and National Identity in Ancient Israel*. Grand Rapids: Eerdmans, 2013.

Block, Daniel I. *Judges, Ruth*. NAC 6. Nashville: Broadman, 1999.

Blumenthal, David R. "Liturgies of Anger: The Lost Art of Imprecation." *Cross Currents* 52 (2002) 178–99.

Boda, Mark J. *A Severe Mercy: Sin and Its Remedy in the Old Testament*. Siphrut, Literature and Theology of the Hebrew Scriptures 1. Winona Lake, IN: Eisenbrauns, 2009.

Bonar, Andrew. *Christ and His Church in the Book of Psalms*. 1859. Reprint, Stoke-on-Trent: Tentmaker, 2001.

Bonhoeffer, Dietrich. *Life Together and Prayerbook of the Bible*. Edited by Geffrey B. Kelly. Translated by Daniel W. Bloesch. Dietrich Bonhoeffer Works 5. Minneapolis: Augsburg Fortress, 1996.

――――. "Sermon on a Psalm of Vengeance—Psalm 58." In *Meditating on the Word*, translated and edited by David McI. Gracie, 84–96. Cambridge, MA: Cowley, 1986.

Botha, Phil J. "The Function of the Polarity between the Pious and the Enemies in Psalm 119." *OTE* 5 (1992) 252–63.

――――. "The Ideological Interface between Psalm 1 and Psalm 2." *OTE* 18 (2005) 189–203.

Botha, Phil J., and Beat Weber. "'Killing Them Softly with This Song . . .': The Literary Structure of Psalm 3 and Its Psalmic and Davidic Contexts. Part II: A Contextual and Intertextual Interpretation of Psalm 3." *OTE* 21 (2008) 273–97.

Bovati, Pietro. *Ristabilire la Giustizia: Procedure, Vocabolario, Orientamenti*. AnBib 110. Rome: Pontificio Istituto Biblico, 1986.

Bratcher, Robert G., and William David Reyburn. *A Handbook on the Book of Psalms*. UBS Handbook Series: Helps for Translators. New York: United Bible Societies, 1991.

Bremer, Johannes. "Ps 107 als programmatischer 'Armenpsalm' des 5. Psalmenbuches Ps 107–45." *Jahrbuch der Philosophisch-Theologischen Hochschule SVD St. Augustin* 4 (2016) 27–38.

Brennan, Joseph P. "Psalms 1–8: Some Hidden Harmonies." *BTB* 10 (1980) 25–29.

———. "Some Hidden Harmonies of the Fifth Book of Psalms." In *Essays in Honor of Joseph P. Brennan*, edited by Robert F. McNamara, 126–58. Rochester, NY: St. Bernard's Seminary, 1976.

Brodersen, Alma. *The End of the Psalter: Psalms 146–150 in the Masoretic Text, the Dead Sea Scrolls, and the Septuagint.* Berlin: de Gruyter, 2017.

Brown, Francis, S. R. Driver, and Charles Briggs. *Hebrew and English Lexicon: With an Appendix Containing the Biblical Aramaic.* Oxford: Clarendon. 1906.

Brown, William P. "'Here Comes the Sun!': The Metaphorical Theology of Psalms 15–24." In *The Composition of the Book of Psalms*, edited by Erich Zenger, 259–77. BETL 238. Leuven: Peeters, 2010.

———. "The Psalms and 'I': The Dialogical Self and the Disappearing Psalmist." In *Diachronic and Synchronic: Reading the Psalms in Real Time: Proceedings of the Baylor Symposium on the Book of Psalms*, edited by Joel S. Burnett et al., 26–44. LHB/OTS 488. New York: T. & T. Clark, 2007.

———. *Psalms.* Interpreting Biblical Texts. Nashville: Abingdon, 2010.

———. *Seeing the Psalms: A Theology of Metaphor.* Louisville, KY: Westminster John Knox, 2002.

Brueggemann, Walter. *The Message of the Psalms: A Theological Commentary.* Augsburg Old Testament Studies. Minneapolis: Augsburg, 1984.

———. *Praying the Psalms: Engaging Scripture and the Life of the Spirit.* 2nd ed. Eugene, OR: Wipf & Stock, 2007.

———. "Psalm 109: Three Times 'Steadfast Love.'" *WW* 5 (1985) 144–54.

Brueggemann, Walter, and William H. Bellinger Jr. *Psalms.* NCBC. New York: Cambridge University Press, 2014.

Budd, Phillip J. *Numbers.* 2nd ed. WBC 5. Dallas: Word, 1998.

Bullock, C. Hassell. *Psalms 1–72.* Teach the Text Commentary. Grand Rapids: Baker, 2015.

Buttenwieser, Moses. *The Psalms: Chronologically Treated with a New Translation.* Chicago: University of Chicago Press, 1938.

Butterworth, Mike. "רָחַם." In *NIDOTTE* 3:1093–95.

Buysch, Christoph. *Der letzte Davidpsalter: Interpretation, Komposition und Funktion der Psalmengruppe Ps 138–145.* SBB 63. Stuttgart: Katholisches Bibelwerk, 2009.

Calvin, John. *Commentary on the Book of Psalms.* Translated by James Anderson. 5 vols. Edinburgh: Calvin Translation Society, 1846–49.

Certain Learned Divines. *Annotations upon All the Books of the Old and New Testament Wherein the Text is Explained, Doubts Resolved, Scriptures Parallelled and Various Readings Observed / by the Joynt-Labour of Certain Learned Divines, Thereunto Appointed, and Therein Employed, as Is Expressed in the Preface.* London, 1645.

Charlesworth, James, et al. *Miscellaneous Texts from the Judaean Desert.* DJD 38. Oxford: Clarendon, 2000.

Cheyne, Thomas K. *The Book of Psalms: Translated from a Revised Text, with Notes and Introduction.* 2 vols. London: Paul, Trench, Trübner, 1904.

Childs, Brevard S. *The Book of Exodus: A Critical, Theological Commentary.* OTL. Louisville, KY: Westminster John Knox, 2004.

———. *Introduction to the Old Testament as Scripture.* Philadelphia: Fortress, 1979.

———. "Psalm Titles and Midrashic Exegesis." *JSS* 16 (1971) 137–50.

Christensen, Duane L. *Deuteronomy 1:1—21:9.* WBC 6A. Dallas: Word, 2001.

Clines, David J. A. "Psalm 2 and the MLF (Moabite Liberation Front)." In *Interested Parties: The Ideology of Writers and Readers of the Hebrew Bible*, edited by J. Cheryl Exum, 244–75. JSOTSup 205. Sheffield: Sheffield Academic, 1995.

———, ed. "רִיקָם". In *DCH* 7:485.

Cohen, Menachem, ed. *Deuteronomy*. Mikraʾot Gedolot 'Haketer': A Revised and Augmented Scientific Edition of 'Mikraʾot Gedolot'. Based on the Aleppo Codex and Early Medieval MSS. Ramat Gan, Israel: Bar Ilan University Press, 2011.

———, ed. *Genesis, Part II*. Mikraʾot Gedolot 'Haketer': A Revised and Augmented Scientific Edition of 'Mikraʾot Gedolot'. Based on the Aleppo Codex and Early Medieval MSS. Ramat Gan, Israel: Bar Ilan University Press, 1999.

———, ed. *Psalms: Part I*. Mikraʾot Gedolot 'Haketer': A Revised and Augmented Scientific Edition of 'Mikraʾot Gedolot'. Based on the Aleppo Codex and Early Medieval MSS. Ramat Gan, Israel: Bar Ilan University Press, 2003.

———, ed. *Psalms: Part II*. Mikraʾot Gedolot 'Haketer': A Revised and Augmented Scientific Edition of 'Mikraʾot Gedolot'. Based on the Aleppo Codex and Early Medieval MSS. Ramat Gan, Israel: Bar Ilan University Press, 2004.

Cole, Robert L. *Psalms 1–2: Gateway to the Psalter*. HBM 37. Sheffield: Sheffield Phoenix, 2012.

Coniglio, Alessandro. "'Gracious and Merciful is Yhwh . . . ' (Psalm 145:8): The Quotation of Exodus 34:6 in Psalm 145 and Its Role in the Holistic Design of the Psalter." *Liber Annuus* 67 (2017) 29–50.

Coppes, Leonard J. "רָחַם". In *TWOT* 2:841–43.

Cradock, Walter. *Divine Drops Distilled from the Fountain of Holy Scriptures: Delivered in Several Exercises before Sermons, upon Twenty and Three Texts of Scripture*. London: R. W., 1650.

Craigie, Peter C. *Psalms 1–50*. WBC 19. Dallas: Word, 1983.

Creach, Jerome F. D. "The Destiny of the Righteous and the Theology of the Psalms." In *Soundings in the Theology of Psalms*, edited by Rolf A. Jacobson, 49–62. Minneapolis: Fortress, 2011.

———. *The Destiny of the Righteous in the Psalms*. St. Louis: Chalice, 2008.

———. "Like a Tree Planted by the Temple Stream: The Portrait of the Righteous in Psalm 1:3." *CBQ* 61 (1999) 34–46.

———. *Violence in Scripture*. Interpretation. Louisville, KY: Westminster John Knox, 2013.

———. *Yahweh as Refuge and the Editing of the Hebrew Psalter*. JSOTSup 217. Sheffield: Sheffield Academic, 1996.

Creager, Harold L. "Note on Psalm 109." *JNES* 6 (1947) 121–23.

Cross, Frank Moore, Jr., and David Noel Freedman. "A Royal Song of Thanksgiving: II Samuel 22 = Psalm 18." *JBL* 72 (1953) 15–34.

Crow, Loren D. *The Songs of Ascents (Psalms 120–34): Their Place in Israelite History and Religion*. SBLDS 148. Atlanta: Scholars, 1996.

Crutchfield, John C. "The Redactional Agenda of the Book of Psalms." *HUCA* 74 (2003) 21–47.

Curtis, Adrian. *Psalms*. Epworth Commentaries. Werrington: Epworth, 2004.

Dahood, Mitchell. *Psalms I: 1–50: A New Translation, with Introduction and Commentary*. AB 16. Garden City, NY: Doubleday, 1966.

Daly-Denton, Margaret M. *Psalm-Shaped Prayerfulness: A Guide to the Christian Reception of the Psalms*. Blackrock: Columba, 2010.

Davis, Ellen F. *Getting Involved with God: Rediscovering the Old Testament*. Cambridge, MA: Cowley, 2001.

Day, John. *Crying for Justice: What the Psalms Teach Us about Mercy and Vengeance in an Age of Terrorism*. Leicester: InterVarsity, 2005.

———. *Psalms*. OTG. Sheffield: JSOT, 1990.

deClaissé-Walford, Nancy L. *Reading from the Beginning: The Shaping of the Hebrew Psalter*. Macon, GA: Mercer University Press, 1997.

———. "The Theology of the Imprecatory Psalms." In *Soundings in the Theology of Psalms*, edited by Rolf A. Jacobson, 77–92. Minneapolis: Fortress, 2011.

deClaissé-Walford, Nancy L., et al. *The Book of Psalms*. NICOT. Grand Rapids: Eerdmans, 2014.

Delitzsch, Franz. *Die Psalmen*. 5th ed. 1894. Reprint, Giessen: Brunnen, 1984.

Dickson, David. *A Commentary on the Psalms*. 2 vols. 1655. Reprint, Glasgow: Dow, 1834.

Dimock, H. *Notes Critical and Explanatory on the Books of Psalms and Proverbs*. Glocester: Raikes, 1791.

Diodati, Giovanni. *Pious Annotations upon the Holy Bible: Expounding the Difficult Places Thereof Learnedly and Plainly*. London, 1664.

Dotan, Aron, ed. *[Torah Nevi'im u-Khetuvim] = Biblia Hebraica Leningradensia: Prepared according to the Vocalization, Accents, and Masora of Aaron Ben Moses Ben Asher in the Leningrad Codex*. Peabody, MA: Hendrickson, 2001.

Douglas, Mary. *Leviticus as Literature*. Oxford: Oxford University Press, 1999.

Downing, F. Gerald. "Justification as Acquittal? A Critical Examination of Judicial Verdicts in Paul's Literary and Actual Contexts." *CBQ* 74 (2012) 298–318.

Durham, John I. *Exodus*. WBC 3. Dallas: Word, 2002.

Durlesser, James A. "Poetic Style in Psalm 1 and Jeremiah 17:5–8: A Rhetorical Critical Study." *Semitics* 9 (1984) 30–48.

Eaton, John. *Kingship and the Psalms*. SBT, 2nd series 32. London: SCM, 1976.

———. *The Psalms: A Historical and Spiritual Commentary with an Introduction and New Translation*. London: T. & T. Clark, 2003.

———. *Psalms of the Way and the Kingdom: A Conference with the Commentators*. JSOT 199. Sheffield: Sheffield Academic, 1995.

Egwim, Stephen. "Determining the Place of vv. 6–19 in Ps 109: A Case Presentation Analysis." *ETL* 80 (2004) 112–30.

Eisenbeis, Walter. *Die Wurzel שלם im Alten Testament*. Berlin: de Gruyter, 1969.

Eissfeldt, Otto. *The Old Testament: An Introduction: The History of the Formation of the Old Testament*. Translated by Peter R. Ackroyd. Oxford: Blackwell, 1965.

Elliger, K., and W. Rudolph, eds. *Biblia Hebraica Stuttgartensia*. 5th ed. Stuttgart: Deutsche Bibelgesellschaft, 1997.

Erbele-Küster, Dorothea. *Lesen als Akt des Betens: eine Rezeptionsästhetik der Psalmen*. WMANT 87. Neukirchen-Vluyn: Neukirchener, 2001.

Ewald, G. Heinrich A. von. *Commentary on the Psalms*. Translated by E. Johnson. 2 vols. London: Williams & Norgate, 1880–81.

Firth, David G. "More Than Just Torah: God's Instruction in the Psalms." Paper presented at the Tyndale Fellowship Old Testament Study Group, Cambridge, July 2014.

———. "Shining the Lamp: The Rhetoric of 2 Samuel 5–24." *TynBul* 52 (2001) 203–24.

———. *Surrendering Retribution in the Psalms: Responses to Violence in Individual Complaints*. Paternoster Biblical Monographs. Milton Keynes: Paternoster, 2005.

———. *1 & 2 Samuel*. Apollos Old Testament Commentary 8. Nottingham: Apollos, 2009.

Flesher, Paul V. M., and Bruce Chilton. *The Targums: A Critical Introduction*. Studies in the Aramaic Interpretation of Scripture 12. Leiden: Brill, 2011.

Flint, Peter W. *The Dead Sea Psalms Scrolls and the Book of Psalms*. STDJ 17. Leiden: Brill, 1997.

———. "The Dead Sea Psalms Scrolls: Psalms Manuscripts, Editions, and the Oxford Hebrew Bible." In *Jewish and Christian Approaches to the Psalms: Conflict and Convergence*, edited by Susan Gillingham, 11–34. Oxford: Oxford University Press, 2013.

France, R. T. *The Gospel According to Matthew*. NICNT. Grand Rapids: Eerdmans, 2007.

Freedman, D. N., et al. "חָנַן." In *ThWAT* 3:23–41.

———, ed. *The Leningrad Codex: A Facsimile Edition*. Grand Rapids: Eerdmans, 1998.

Frensdorff, Salomon, ed. *Die Massorah Magna nach den ältesten Drucken mit Zuziehung alter Handschriften*. Hannover: Cohen & Risch, 1876.

Fretheim, Terence E. "חָנַן." In *NIDOTTE* 2:203–6.

Futato, Mark D. *Interpreting the Psalms: An Exegetical Handbook*. Handbooks for Old Testament Exegesis. Grand Rapids: Kregel, 2007.

Gerstenberger, Erhard S. *Psalms, Part I, with an Introduction to Cultic Poetry*. FOTL 14. Grand Rapids: Eerdmans, 1988.

———. *Psalms, Part II, and Lamentations*. FOTL 15. Grand Rapids: Eerdmans, 2001.

Gesenius, Wilhelm. *Hebräisches und aramäisches Handwörterbuch über das Alte Testament*. Edited by Udo Rüterswörden et al. 18th ed. Berlin: Springer, 1987.

Gilchrist, Paul R. "יצר." In *TWOT* 1:394–95.

Gillingham, Susan. "The Levites and the Editorial Composition of the Psalms." In *Oxford Handbook of the Psalms*, edited by William P. Brown, 201–13. Oxford: Oxford University Press, 2014.

———. *Psalms through the Centuries, Vol. 1*. Blackwell Bible Commentaries. Oxford: Blackwell, 2008.

———. "The Zion Tradition and the Editing of the Hebrew Psalter." In *Temple and Worship in Biblical Israel: Proceedings of the Oxford Old Testament Seminar*, edited by John Day, 308–41. LHB/OTS 422. London: T. & T. Clark, 2005.

Giménez-Rico, Enrique Sanz. "Dos Contrarios Irreconciliables: Dios y los ídolos en Sal 134–37." *Gregorianum* 92 (2011) 1–22.

Glueck, Nelson. *Das Wort hesed im alttestamentlichen Sprachgebrauche als menschliche und göttliche gemeinschaftgemässe Verhaltungsweise*. 1927. Reprint, BZAW 47. Berlin: Töpelmann, 1961.

Goldingay, John. *Psalms*. 3 vols. Baker Commentary on the Old Testament Wisdom and Psalms. Grand Rapids: Baker Academic, 2006–8.

Goshen-Gottstein, Moshe, ed. *The Aleppo Codex: Part One: Plates*. Jerusalem: Magnes, 1976.

Goulder, Michael D. *The Prayers of David (Psalms 51–72): Studies in the Psalter, II*. JSOTSup 102. Sheffield: JSOT, 1990.

———. *The Psalms of the Return (Book V, Psalms 107–150): Studies in the Psalter, IV*. JSOTSup 258. Sheffield: Sheffield Academic, 1998.

———. *The Psalms of the Sons of Korah*. JSOTSup 20. Sheffield: JSOT, 1982.

Grant, Jamie A. "Determining the Indeterminate: Issues in Interpreting the Psalms." *Southeastern Theological Review* 1 (2010) 3–14.

———. *The King as Exemplar: The Function of Deuteronomy's Kingship Law in the Shaping of the Book of Psalms*. Society of Biblical Literature Academia Biblica 17. Atlanta: SBL, 2004.

Gray, Alison R. *Psalm 18 in Words and Pictures: A Reading through Metaphor*. Biblical Interpretation Series 127. Leiden: Brill, 2013.

Gregory of Nazianzus. *Oratio in laudem Basilii*. In *S. Cyril of Jerusalem. S. Gregory Nazianzen*, edited by Philip Schaff and Henry Wace, vol. 7 of *NPNF2*, 422–34. 1890–1900. Reprint, Grand Rapids: Eerdmans, 1983–88.

Gregory of Nyssa. *Against Eunomius*. In *Gregory of Nyssa: Dogmatic Treatises, Etc.*, edited by Philip Schaff and Henry Wace, vol. 5 of *NPNF2*, 35–100. 1890–1900. Reprint, Grand Rapids: Eerdmans, 1983–88.

———. *Gregory of Nyssa's Treatise on the Inscriptions of the Psalms*. Translated and edited by Ronald E. Heine. Oxford Early Christian Studies. Oxford: Clarendon, 1995.

Grol, Harm van. "David and His Chasidim: Place and Function of Psalms 138–45." In *The Composition of the Book of Psalms*, edited by Erich Zenger, 309–37. BETL 238. Leuven: Peeters, 2010.

Gunkel, Hermann. *Die Psalmen: übersetzt und erklärt*. Göttinger Handkommentar zum Alten Testament. Göttingen: Vandenhoeck und Ruprecht, 1926.

Gunkel, Hermann, and Joachim Begrich. *Einleitung in die Psalmen: die Gattungen der religiösen Lyrik Israels*. Göttinger Handkommentar zum Alten Testament. Göttingen: Vandenhoeck & Ruprecht, 1933.

Gurnall, William. *The Christian in Complete Armour: A Treatise of the Saints' War against the Devil*. 1662–64. Reprint, Edinburgh: Banner of Truth, 1964.

Hackett, Jo Ann, and John Huehnergard. "On Breaking Teeth." *HTR* 77 (1984) 259–75.

Hallo, William W., and K. Lawson, eds. *The Context of Scripture*. Leiden: Brill, 1997–.

Ḥakham, Amos. *Psalms 1–57*. Vol. 1 of *The Bible: Psalms with the Jerusalem Commentary*. Jerusalem: Mosad Harav Kook, 2003.

———. *Psalms 101–150*. Vol. 3 of *The Bible: Psalms with the Jerusalem Commentary*. Jerusalem: Mosad Harav Kook, 2003.

Hamilton, James M., Jr. *God's Glory in Salvation through Judgment: A Biblical Theology*. Wheaton, IL: Crossway, 2010.

Häner, Tobias. "David als Vorbeter: Psalm 51 im Kontext des Psalters." In *Miserere mei, Deus: Psalm 51 in Bibel und Liturgie, in Musik und Literatur*, edited by Dominik Helms et al., 11–32. Würzburg: Echter, 2015.

Harman, Allan. *Psalms 1–72*. Vol. 1 of *Psalms*. Rev. ed. A Mentor Commentary. Fearn: Mentor, 2011.

———. *Psalms 73–150*. Vol. 2 of *Psalms*. Rev. ed. A Mentor Commentary. Fearn: Mentor, 2011.

Harris, R. Laird. "חסד." In *TWOT* 1:305–7.

Harrison, R. K. *Introduction to the Old Testament*. London: Tyndale, 1970.

Hartberger, Birgit. *"An den Wassern von Babylon . . .": Psalm 137 auf dem Hintergrund von Jeremia 51, der biblischen Edom-Traditionen und babylonischer Originalquellen*. BBB 63. Frankfurt: Hanstein, 1986.

Hayes, Elizabeth. "The Unity of the Egyptian Hallel: Psalms 113–18." *BBR* 9 (1999) 145–56.

Heim, Knut. "The (God-)Forsaken King of Psalm 89: A Historical and Intertextual Enquiry." In *King and Messiah in Israel and the Ancient Near East*, edited by John Day, 296–322. Sheffield: Sheffield Academic, 1998.

———. "Verbal Violence in Psalm 137." Unpublished Paper.

Hengstenberg, Ernst. *Commentar über die Psalmen*. 2nd ed. 4 vols. Berlin: Dehmigte, 1849–52.

Hensley, Adam D. *Covenant Relationships and the Editing of the Hebrew Psalter*. LHB/OTS 666. New York: T. & T. Clark, 2018.

Holladay, William. *The Psalms through Three Thousand Years*. Minneapolis: Augsburg Fortress, 1993.

Holmstedt, Robert D. *Ruth: A Handbook on the Hebrew Text*. Baylor Handbook on the Hebrew Bible. Waco, TX: Baylor University Press, 2010.

Horsley, Samuel. *The Book of Psalms Translated from the Hebrew*. 4th ed. London: Longman, Brown, Green, and Longman, 1845.

Hossfeld, Frank-Lothar, and Erich Zenger. *Die Psalmen I: Psalm 1–50*. NEchtB 29. Würzburg: Echter, 1993.

———. *Psalmen 101–150*. HThKAT. Freiburg: Herder, 2008.

———. *Psalmen 51–100*. HThKAT. Freiburg: Herder, 2000.

Howard, David M., Jr. "Editorial Activity in the Psalter, a State-of-the-Field Survey." In *The Shape and Shaping of the Psalter*, edited by J. Clinton McCann Jr., 52–70. JSOTSup 159. Sheffield: JSOT, 1993.

Hubbard, Robert L., Jr. "Dynamistic and Legal Processes in Psalm 7." *ZAW* 94 (1982) 267–79.

Hunter, Alastair G. "The Psalms of Ascents: A Late Festival Recovered?" In *Proceedings of the Twelfth World Congress of Jewish Studies*, edited by Ron Margolin, 173–87. Jerusalem: World Union of Jewish Studies, 1999.

Ibn Ğanâḥ, Abulwalîd Merwân. *Sepher Haschoraschim: Worzelwörterbuch der hebräischen Sprache*. Edited by Wilhelm Bacher. Translated by Jehuda Ibn Tibbon. Berlin: Itzkowski, 1896.

Jacobson, Rolf A. "Imagining the Future of Psalms Studies." In *The Shape and Shaping of the Book of Psalms: The Current State of Scholarship*, edited by Nancy L. deClaissé-Walford, 231–46. SBLAIL 20. Atlanta: SBL, 2014.

Jacobson, Rolf A., and Karl N. Jacobson. *Invitation to the Psalms: A Reader's Guide for Discovery and Engagement*. Grand Rapids: Baker Academic, 2013.

Janowski, Bernd. "Ein Tempel aus Worten: zur theologischen Architektur des Psalters." In *The Composition of the Book of Psalms*, edited by Erich Zenger, 279–306. BETL 238. Leuven: Peeters, 2010.

Jastrow, Marcus. *Dictionary of the Targumim, the Talmud Babli and Yerushalmi, and the Midrashic Literature*. Authorised ed. New York: Choreb, 1926.

Jauss, Hannelore. "Fluchpsalmen beten? Zum Problem der Feind- und Fluchpsalmen." *BK* 51 (1996) 107–15.

Jebb, John. *A Literal Translation of the Book of Psalms*. London: Longman, 1846.

Jenkins, Steffen G. "The Antiquity of Psalter Shape Efforts." *TynBul* 71 (2020) 161–80.

———. "A Quotation in Psalm 109 as Defence Exhibit A." *TynBul* 71 (2020) 115–35.

Jerome. *Adversus Helvidium de Mariae virginitate perpetua*. In *St. Jerome: Letters and Select Works*, edited by Philip Schaff and Henry Wace, vol. 6 of *NPNF2*, 334–46. 1890–1900. Reprint, Grand Rapids: Eerdmans, 1983–88.

———. *Epistulae*. In *St. Jerome: Letters and Select Works*, edited by Philip Schaff and Henry Wace, vol. 6 of *NPNF2*, 260–72. 1890–1900. Reprint, Grand Rapids: Eerdmans, 1983–88.

———. *Commentarioli in Psalmos*. PL 26. Paris, 1845.

Johnson, Vivian L. *David in Distress: His Portrait through the Historical Psalms*. LHB/OTS 505. New York: T. & T. Clark, 2009.

Johnston, Philip S. "Ordeals in the Psalms?" In *Temple and Worship in Biblical Israel: Proceedings of the Oxford Old Testament Seminar*, edited by John Day, 271–92. LHB/OTS 422. London: T. & T. Clark, 2005.

Joüon, Paul. *A Grammar of Biblical Hebrew*. Translated and revised by T. Muraoka. 2 vols. *SubBi* 14/1–2. Rome: Pontifical Biblical Institute, 1991.

Jung, Jangpyo. *A Study of Psalm 109: Its Meaning and Significance in the Context of the Psalter*. SBF Thesis ad Doctoratum 424. Jerusalem: Studium Biblicum Franciscanum, 2009.

Kaiser, Walter C. "יׁשׁב." In *TWOT* 1:411–13.

Käsemann, Ernst. "Paul and Israel." In *New Testament Questions of Today*, translated by W. J. Montague, 183–87. The New Testament Library. London: SCM, 1969.

Kaufman, Stephen A., ed. *Targum Psalms: The Jewish Literary Aramaic Version of Psalms from the Files of the Comprehensive Aramaic Lexicon Project (CAL)*. Edinburgh: T. & T. Clark, 2005.

Kautzsch, E., ed. *Gesenius' Hebrew Grammar*. Translated by A. E. Cowley. 2nd ed. Oxford: Clarendon, 1910.

Keel, Othmar. *Die Welt der altorientalischen Bildsymbolik und das Alte Testament: Am Beispiel der Psalmen*. Neukirchen: Neukirchener, 1972.

———. "Tiere als Gefährten und Feinde." In *"Im Schatten deiner Flügel": Tiere in der Bibel und im Alten Orient*, edited by Othmar Keel and Thomas Staubli, 25–26. Freiburg: Universitätsverlag, 2001.

Keel, Othmar, and Christoph Uehlinger. *Göttinnen, Götter und Gottessymbole: neue Erkenntnisse zur Religionsgeschichte Kanaans und Israels aufgrund bislang unerschlossener ikonographischer Quellen*. Quaestiones Disputatae 134. Freiburg: Herder, 1992.

Keener, Hubert James. *A Canonical Exegesis of the Eighth Psalm: YHWH's Maintenance of the Created Order through Divine Intervention*. Journal of Theological Interpretation Supplements 9. Winona Lake, IN: Eisenbrauns, 2013.

Keet, Cuthbert C. *A Study of the Psalms of Ascents: A Critical and Exegetical Commentary upon Psalms CXX to CXXXIV*. London: Mitre, 1969.

Keil, Carl Friedrich, and Franz Delitzsch. *Commentary on the Old Testament*. Translated by J. Martin et al. 25 vols. 1857–78. Reprint, 10 vols. Peabody, MA: Hendrickson, 1996.

Kellenberger, Edgar. *ḥäsäd wä'ämät als Ausdruck einer Glaubenserfahrung: Gottes Offen-Werden und Bleiben als Voraussetzung des Lebens*. ATANT 69. Zürich: Theologischer, 1982.

Kelley, Page H., et al. *The Masorah of Biblia Hebraica Stuttgartensia: Introduction and Annotated Glossary*. Grand Rapids: Eerdmans, 1998.

Kidner, Derek. *Psalms 1–72: An Introduction and Commentary on Books I and II of the Psalms*. Leicester: InterVarsity, 1973.

———. *Psalms 73–150: A Commentary on Books III-V of the Psalms*. Leicester: InterVarsity, 1975.

Kim, Jinkyu. "The Strategic Arrangement of Royal Psalms in Books IV-V." *WTJ* 70 (2008) 143–57.

Kimelman, Reuven. "Psalm 145: Theme, Structure, and Impact." *JBL* 113 (1994) 37–58.

Kimhi, David. *The Longer Commentary of R. David Ḳimḥi on the First Book of Psalms (I-X, XV-XVII, XIX, XXII, XXIV)*. Translated by R. G. Finch. Translations of Early Documents. Series III: Rabbinic Texts. London: SPCK, 1919.

Kirkpatrick, A. F., ed. *The Book of Psalms: With Introduction and Notes*. 3 vols. The Cambridge Bible for Schools and Colleges. Cambridge: Cambridge University Press, 1894–1901.

Kitz, Anne Marie. *Cursed Are You! The Phenomenology of Cursing in Cuneiform and Hebrew Texts*. Winona Lake, IN: Eisenbrauns, 2014.

Kleer, Martin. *"Der liebliche Sänger der Psalmen Israels": Untersuchungen zu David als Dichter und Beter der Psalmen*. BBB 108. Bodenheim: Philo, 1996.

Kline, Meredith G. *Kingdom Prologue: Genesis Foundations for a Covenantal Worldview*. Eugene, OR: Wipf & Stock, 2006.

———. *The Structure of Biblical Authority*. Grand Rapids: Eerdmans, 1972.

Klopfenstein, Martin A. *Die Lüge nach dem Alten Testament*. Zürich: Gotthelf, 1964.

Koehler, Ludwig, Walter Baumgartner, and J. J. Stamm. *The Hebrew and Aramaic Lexicon of the Old Testament*. Translated and edited by M. E. J. Richardson. 4 vols. Leiden: Brill, 1994–99.

Koopmans, William T. "אָחַז." In *NIDOTTE* 1:358–59.

Kraus, Hans-Joachim. *Psalmen 1–59*. Vol. 1 of *Psalmen*. 5th ed. BKAT 15. Neukirchen-Vluyn: Neukirchener, 1978.

———. *Psalmen 60–150*. Vol. 2 of *Psalmen*. 5th ed. BKAT 15. Neukirchen-Vluyn: Neukirchener, 1978.

———. *Theologie der Psalmen*. Vol. 3 of *Psalmen*. 5th ed. BKAT 15. Neukirchen-Vluyn: Neukirchener, 1979.

Krüger, Thomas. "'An den Strömen von Babylon...': Erwägungen zu Zeitbezug und Sachverhalt in Psalm 137." In *Sachverhalt und Zeitbezug: Semitistische und alttestamentliche Studien, Adolf Denz zum 65. Geburtstag*, edited by Rüdiger Bartelmus and Norbert Nebes, 79–84. JBVO 4. Wiesbaden: Harrassowitz, 2001.

Kwakkel, Gert. *According to My Righteousness: Upright Behaviour as Grounds for Deliverance in Psalms 7, 17, 18, 26, and 44*. OtSt 46. Leiden: Brill, 2002.

Labuschagne, Casper. "Significant Compositional Techniques in the Psalms: Evidence for the Use of Number as an Organizing Principle." *VT* 59 (2009) 583–605.

Lam, Joseph. "Psalm 2 and the Disinheritance of Earthly Rulers: New Light from the Ugaritic Legal Text RS 94.2168." *VT* 64 (2014) 34–46.

Laney, J. Carl. "A Fresh Look at the Imprecatory Psalms." *BSac* 138 (1981) 35–45.

Lee, Seong Hye. "The Psalter as an Anthology Designed to Be Memorised." PhD diss., University of Bristol and Trinity College, 2011.

Leithart, Peter J. *A Son to Me: An Exposition of 1 & 2 Samuel*. Moscow, ID: Canon, 2003.

LeMon, Joel M. "Psalms." In *DSE* 644–46.

———. "Saying Amen to Violent Psalms: Patterns of Prayer, Belief, and Action in the Psalter." In *Soundings in the Theology of Psalms*, edited by Rolf A. Jacobson, 93–109. Minneapolis: Fortress, 2011.

Leuenberger, Martin. *Konzeptionen des Königtums Gottes im Psalter: Untersuchungen zu Komposition und Redaktion der theokratischen Bücher IV-V im Psalter*. AThANT 83. Zürich: TVZ, 2004.

Leveen, Jacob. "Textual Problems of Psalm 7." *VT* 16 (1966) 439–45.

Lewis, C. S. Introduction to *On the Incarnation*, by Athanasius, 3–10. Crestwood, NY: St. Vladimir's Seminary, 1996.

———. *Reflections on the Psalms*. London: Bles, 1958.

Lichtheim, Miriam. "Instruction of Amenemope." In *Canonical Compositions from the Biblical World*, edited by William W. Hallo and K. Lawson Younger, 115–23. The Context of Scripture 1. Leiden: Brill, 1997.

Liddell, Henry George, and Robert Scott. *A Greek-English Lexicon*. Rev. ed. Oxford: Clarendon, 1996.

Liebreich, Leon J. "The Songs of Ascents and the Priestly Blessing." *JBL* 74 (1955) 33–36.

Liess, Kathrin. *Der Weg des Lebens: Psalm 16 und das Lebens- und Todesverständnis der Individualpsalmen*. FAT, 2nd series 5. Tübingen: Mohr Siebeck, 2004.

Loewinger, David S. *Masorah Gedolah Shel Keter Aram-Tsovah [Massorah Magna of the Aleppo Codex]*. Jerusalem: Sivan, 1977.

Lohfink, Norbert. "Drei Arten, von Armut zu sprechen: illustriert an Psalm 109." *TP* 72 (1997) 321–36.

———. "Psalmengebet und Psalterredaktion." *Archiv für Liturgiewissenschaft* 34 (1992) 1–22.

Longman, Tremper, III. *How to Read the Psalms*. Leicester: InterVarsity, 1988.

———. "Messiah." In *DOTWPW* 466–72.

Longman, Tremper, III, and Raymond B. Dillard. *An Introduction to the Old Testament*. 2nd ed. Grand Rapids: Zondervan, 2006.

Louw, Johannes P., and Eugene A. Nida, eds. *Greek-English Lexicon of the New Testament Based on Semantic Domains*. 2nd ed. New York: United Bible Societies, 1989.

Lucas, Ernest. *The Psalms and Wisdom Literature*. Exploring the Old Testament 3. London: SPCK, 2003.

Lust, Johan, et al. *A Greek-English Lexicon of the Septuagint*. Rev. ed. Stuttgart: Deutsche Bibelgesellschaft, 2003.

Luther, Martin. *First Lectures on the Psalms I: Psalms 1–75*. Edited by Hilton C. Oswald. Vol. 10 of *Luther's Works*, edited by Jaroslav Pelikan. St. Louis: Concordia, 1974.

———. *Selected Psalms III*. Edited by Jaroslav Pelikan. Vol. 14 of *Luther's Works*, edited by Jaroslav Pelikan. St. Louis: Concordia, 1958.

———. *The Sermon on the Mount (Sermons) and the Magnificat*. Edited by Jaroslav Pelikan. Vol. 21 of *Luther's Works*, edited by Jaroslav Pelikan. St. Louis: Concordia, 1956.

———. *Word and Sacrament I*. Edited by E. Theodore Bachmann. Vol. 35 of *Luther's Works*, edited by Helmut T. Lehmann. St. Louis: Concordia, 1960.

Macintosh, Andrew. "A Consideration of Psalm 7:12f." *JTS* 33 (1982) 481–90.

Mandolfo, Carleen. "Finding Their Voices: Sanctioned Subversion in Psalms of Lament." *HBT* 24 (2002) 27–52.

Mann, Steven T. "Run, David, Run! An Application of Speech Act Theory in a Literary Analysis of David's Departure (2 Samuel 15:14—17:24)." PhD diss., Fuller Theological Seminary, 2011.

———. *Run, David, Run! An Investigation of the Theological Speech Acts of David's Departure and Return (2 Samuel 14–20)*. Siphrut, Literature and Theology of the Hebrew Scriptures 10. Winona Lake, IN: Eisenbrauns, 2013.

Maró, Leonard P. "Psalm 137: Exile—Not the Time for Singing the Lord's Song." *OTE* 23 (2010) 116–28.

Martens, Elmer A. "יצר." In *NIDOTTE* 2:500.

Martin, Chalmers. "The Imprecations in the Psalms." *Princeton Theological Review* 1 (1903) 537–53.

Mays, James Luther. "The David of the Psalms." *Int* 40 (1986) 143–55.

———. "Delight in the Law: Psalm 1." In *Preaching and Teaching the Psalms*, edited by Patrick D. Miller and Gene M. Tucker, 161–63. Louisville, KY: Westminster John Knox, 2006.

———. *The Lord Reigns: A Theological Handbook to the Psalms*. Louisville, KY: Westminster John Knox, 1994.

———. *Psalms*. Interpretation. Louisville, KY: Westminster John Knox, 1994.

McCann, J. Clinton, Jr., ed. *The Shape and Shaping of the Psalter*. JSOTSup 159. Sheffield: JSOT, 1993.

———. "The Psalms as Instruction." *Int* 46 (1992) 117–28.

———. "Psalms." In vol. 4 of *New Interpreter's Bible*, edited by Leander E. Keck, 639–1280. Nashville: Abingdon, 1996.

———. "Psalms." In *DTIB* 645–52.

———. "The Shape of Book I of the Psalter and the Shape of Human Happiness." In *The Book of Psalms: Composition and Reception*, edited by Peter W. Flint et al., 340–48. VTSup 99. Leiden: Brill, 2005.

———. "The Single Most Important Text in the Entire Bible: Toward a Theology of the Psalms." In *Soundings in the Theology of Psalms*, edited by Rolf A. Jacobson, 63–75. Minneapolis: Fortress, 2011.

———. *A Theological Introduction to the Book of Psalms: The Psalms as Torah*. Nashville: Abingdon, 1993.

McCarthy, Carmel. *The Tiqqune Sopherim and Other Theological Corrections in the Masoretic Text of the Old Testament*. OBO 36. Göttingen: Vandenhoeck & Ruprecht, 1981.

McFall, Leslie. "The Evidence for a Logical Arrangement of the Psalter." *WTJ* 62 (2000) 223–56.

Merrill, Eugene C. *Deuteronomy*. NAC 4. Nashville: Broadman & Holman, 1994.

Merwe, Christo H. J. van der, et al. *A Biblical Hebrew Reference Grammar*. Sheffield: Sheffield Academic, 1999.

Millard, Matthias. *Die Komposition des Psalters: ein formgeschichtlicher Ansatz*. FAT 9. Tübingen: Mohr Siebeck, 1994.

Miller, Patrick D. "The Beginning of the Psalter." In *The Shape and Shaping of the Psalter*, edited by J. Clinton McCann Jr., 83–92. JSOTSup 159. Sheffield: JSOT, 1993.

———. "Deuteronomy and Psalms: Evoking a Biblical Conversation." *JBL* 118 (1999) 3–18.

———. "The Hermeneutics of Imprecation." In *The Way of the Lord: Essays in Old Testament Theology*, 193–202. FAT 39. Tübingen: Mohr Siebeck, 2004.

———. "Kingship, Torah Obedience, and Prayer: The Theology of Psalms 15–24." In *Neue Wege der Psalmenforschung: für Walter Beyerlin*, edited by Klaus Seybold and Erich Zenger, 127–42. Herders biblische Studien/Herder's Biblical Studies 1. Freiburg: Herder, 1994.

———. "The Psalms as a Meditation on the First Commandment." In *The Way of the Lord: Essays in Old Testament Theology*, 91–122. FAT 39. Tübingen: Mohr Siebeck, 2004.

———. "Who Are the Bad Guys in the Psalms?" In *Let Us Go up to Zion: Essays in Honour of H. G. M. Williamson on the Occasion of His Sixty-Fifth Birthday*, edited by Iain Provan and Mark J. Boda, 423–31. VTSup 153. Leiden: Brill, 2012.

Moberly, R. Walter L. "אָמַן." In *NIDOTTE* 1:427–33.

Motyer, J. Alec. "The Psalms." In *NBC*, edited by Don A. Carson et al., 485–583. 4th ed. Leicester: InterVarsity, 1994.

Mowinckel, Sigmund. *The Psalms in Israel's Worship*. Translated by D. R. Ap-Thomas. 1962. Reprint, The Biblical Resource Series. Grand Rapids: Eerdmans, 2004.

———. *Segen und Fluch in Israels Kult und Psalmdichtung*. Vol. 5 of *Psalmenstudien*. 1923. Reprint, Amsterdam: Schippers, 1966.

Muraoka, T. *A Greek-English Lexicon of the Septuagint*. 3rd ed. Louvain: Peeters, 2009.

———. *A Greek-Hebrew/Aramaic Two-Way Index to the Septuagint*. Louvain: Peeters, 2010.

Nasuti, Harry P. "The Interpretive Significance of Sequence and Selection in the Book of Psalms." In *The Book of Psalms: Composition and Reception*, edited by Peter W. Flint et al., 311–39. VTSup 99. Leiden: Brill, 2005.

Neale, J. M., and R. F. Littledale, eds. *A Commentary on the Psalms: From Primitive and Mediæval Writers and from the Various Office-Books and Hymns of the Roman, Mozarabic, Ambrosian, Gallican, Greek, Coptic, Armenian, and Syriac Rites*. 4 vols. London: Joseph Masters, 1868–74.

Neumann, Friederike. "Israel und die Völker. Ein Diskurs über Feindschaft und Überwindung der Feindschaft am Ende des Psalters." In *Gegner im Gebet, Studien zu Feindschaft und Entfeindung im Buch der Psalmen*, edited by Kathrin Liess and Johannes Schnocks, 301–38. HBS 91. Freiburg: Herder, 2018.

Nielsen, Kirsten. "Why Not Plough with an Ox and an Ass Together? Or: Why Not Read Ps 119 Together with Pss 120–34?" *SJOT* 14 (2000) 56–66.

Okorocha, Cyril. "Psalms." In *Africa Bible Commentary: A One-Volume Commentary Written by 70 African Scholars*, edited by Tokunboh Adeyemo, 605–746. Nairobi: WordAlive, 2006.

Olivier, Hannes. "סָלַח." In *NIDOTTE* 3:259–64.

Origen. *Contra Celsum*. In *Volume IV: Tertullian, Part Fourth; Minucius Felix; Commodian; Origen, Parts First and Second*, edited by Alexander Roberts and James Donaldson, vol. 4 of *ANF*, edited by A. Cleveland Coxe, 395–669. 1867–85. Reprint, Grand Rapids: Eerdmans, 1979–87.

Owens, Daniel C. *Portraits of the Righteous in the Psalms: An Exploration of the Ethics of Book I*. Eugene, OR: Wipf & Stock, 2013.

Peels, Hendrik G. L. "'I Hate Them with Perfect Hatred' (Psalm 139:21–22)." *TynBul* 59 (2008) 35–51.

———. *Shadow Sides: The Revelation of God in the Old Testament*. Translated by Hetty Lalleman. Carlisle: Paternoster, 2003.

———. *The Vengeance of God: The Meaning of the Root NQM and the Function of the NQM-Texts in the Context of Divine Revelation in the Old Testament*. OtSt 31. Leiden: Brill, 1995.

———. "נָקַם." In *NIDOTTE* 3:154–57.

Perowne, J. J. Stewart. *The Book of Psalms: A New Translation*. 2 vols. 5th ed. London: Bell, 1882–83.

Plumer, William S. *Studies in the Book of Psalms: Being a Critical and Expository Commentary, with Doctrinal and Practical Remarks on the Entire Psalter.* Edinburgh: A & C Black, 1872.

Poole, Matthew. *Annotations upon the Holy Bible: Wherein the Sacred Text Is Inserted, and Various Readings Annex'd, Together with the Parallel Scriptures, the More Difficult Terms in Each Verse Are Explained, Seeming Contradictions Reconciled, Questions and Doubts Resolved, and the Whole Text Opened.* London, 1683.

Poythress, Vern S. *The Shadow of Christ in the Law of Moses.* Phillipsburg, NJ: P&R, 1991.

Raabe, Paul R. "Deliberate Ambiguity in the Psalter." *JBL* 110 (1991) 213–27.

Rabin, Chaim. "An Arabic Phrase in Isaiah." In *Studi Sull'Oriente e la Bibbia, Offerti al P. Giovanni Rinaldi Nel 60 Compleanno Da Allievi, Colleghi, Amici,* 303–9. Genoa: Studio e Vita, 1967.

Rad, Gerhard von. "'Gerechtigkeit' und 'Leben' in der Kultsprache der Psalmen." In *Gesammelte Studien zum Alten Testament.* TB. Altes Testament 8. Munich: Kaiser, 1958.

———. *Das Gottesvolk im Deuteronomium.* BWANT 47. Stuttgart: Kohlhammer, 1929.

———. *The Theology of Israel's Historical Traditions.* Vol. 1 of *Old Testament Theology,* translated by D. M. G. Stalker. London: SCM, 1975.

———. *The Theology of Israel's Prophetic Traditions.* Vol. 2 of *Old Testament Theology,* translated by D. M. G. Stalker. London: SCM, 1965.

Rahlfs, Alfred, ed. *Psalmi Cum Odis.* Vol. 10 of *Septuaginta Societatis Scientiarum Gottingensis.* Göttingen: Vandenhoeck & Ruprecht, 1931.

Ramantswana, Hulisani. "David of the Psalters: MT Psalter, LXX Psalter, and 11QPsa Psalter." *OTE* 24 (2011) 431–63.

Rashi. *Rashi's Commentary on Psalms.* Translated and edited by Mayer Gruber. The Brill Reference Library of Judaism 18. Leiden: Brill, 2004.

Ravasi, Gianfranco. *I Salmi: Introduzione, testo e commento.* Milano: San Paolo, 2007.

———. *Il libro dei Salmi: commento e attualizzazione.* 3 vols. Lettura pastorale della Bibbia 12. Bologna: Dehoniane, 1981–85.

Rendsburg, Gary A. "Addressee-Switching." In *EHLL* 1:34–35.

———. "The Strata of Biblical Hebrew." *JNSL* 7 (1991) 81–99.

———. "Style-Switching." In *EHLL* 3:633–36.

Rendtorff, Rolf. "The Psalms of David: David in the Psalms." In *The Book of Psalms: Composition and Reception,* edited by Peter W. Flint et al., 53–64. VTSup 99. Leiden: Brill, 2005.

Reynolds, Kent Aaron. *Torah as Teacher: The Exemplary Torah Student in Psalm 119.* VTSup 137. Leiden: Brill, 2010.

Riede, Peter. *Im Netz des Jägers: Studien zur Feindmetaphorik der Individualpsalmen.* WMANT 85. Neukirchen-Vluyn: Neukirchener, 2000.

Robertson, O. Palmer. *The Flow of the Psalms: Structural and Theological Considerations.* Phillipsburg, NJ: P&R, 2015.

Rodriguez, Angel M. "Inspiration and the Imprecatory Psalms." *Journal of the Adventist Theological Society* 5 (1994) 40–67.

Rose, Wolter H. "How Will God Deal with Children of Parents Who Have Committed Idolatry?" In *Living Waters from Ancient Springs: Essays in Honor of Cornelis van Dam,* edited by Jason van Vliet, 11–24. Eugene, OR: Pickwick, 2011.

Ross, Allen P. *A Commentary on the Psalms: Volume 1 (1–41)*. Kregel Exegetical Library. Grand Rapids: Kregel, 2011.

———. *A Commentary on the Psalms: Volume 2 (42–89)*. Kregel Exegetical Library. Grand Rapids: Kregel, 2013.

Ruppert, Lothar. *Jesus als der leidende Gerechte? Der Weg Jesu im Lichte eines alt- und zwischentestamentlichen Motivs*. SBS 59. Stuttgart: KBW, 1972.

Sanders, James A. *The Dead Sea Psalms Scroll*. Ithaca, NY: Cornell University Press, 1967.

———. *The Psalms Scroll of Qumrân Cave 11 (11QPsa)*. DJD 4. Oxford: Clarendon, 1965.

Sarna, Nahum. "Legal Terminology in Psalm 3:8." In *Sha'arei Talmon: Studies in the Bible, Qumran, and the Ancient Near East Presented to Shemaryahu Talmon*, edited by Michael Fishbane et al., 175–81. Winona Lake, IN: Eisenbrauns, 1992.

Satterthwaite, Philip E. "Zion in the Songs of Ascents." In *Zion, City of Our God*, edited by Richard Hess and Gordon J. Wenham, 105–28. Grand Rapids: Eerdmans, 1999.

Saur, Markus. "Die Theologische Funktion der Königspsalmen innerhalb der Komposition des Psalters." In *The Composition of the Book of Psalms*, edited by Erich Zenger, 689–99. BETL 238. Leuven: Peeters, 2010.

Scanlin, Harold. *The Dead Sea Scrolls & Modern Translations of the Old Testament*. Wheaton, IL: Tyndale, 1993.

Schaefer, Konrad. *Psalms*. Berit Olam: Studies in Hebrew Narrative & Poetry. Collegeville, MN: Liturgical, 2001.

Scharbert, Josef. "Formgeschichte und Exegese von Ex 34:6f und seiner Parallelen." *Bib* 38 (1957) 130–50.

Schlimm, Matthew R. *From Fratricide to Forgiveness: The Language and Ethics of Anger in Genesis*. Siphrut, Literature and Theology of the Hebrew Scriptures 7. Winona Lake, IN: Eisenbrauns, 2011.

Schmidt, Hans. *Das Gebet der Angeklagten im Alten Testament*. BZAW 49. Giessen: Töpelmann, 1928.

Schökel, Luis Alonso. *Hermenéutica de la palabra*. Vol. 1 of *Hermenéutica biblica*. Academia Christiana 37. Madrid: Cristiandad, 1986.

———. "Poética hebrea. Historia y procedimientos." In *Interpretación literaria de textos bíblicos*, 17–228. Vol. 2 of *Hermenéutica de la palabra*. Academia Christiana 38. Madrid: Cristiandad, 1987.

Schökel, Luis Alonso, and Cecilia Carniti. *Salmos I: (Salmos 1–72) Traducción, introducciones y comentario*. 3rd ed. Nueva Biblia Española. Madrid: Cristiandad, 2008.

———. *Salmos II: (Salmos 73–150) Traducción, introducciones y comentario*. 4th ed. Nueva Biblia Española. Madrid: Cristiandad, 2009.

Schroer, Silvia, and Othmar Keel. *Vom ausgehenden Mesolithikum bis zur Frühbronzezeit*. Vol. 1 of *Die Ikonographie Palästinas/Israels und der Alte Orient: eine Religionsgeschichte in Bildern*. Fribourg: Academic Press Fribourg, 2005.

Schultz, Richard L. "Integrating Old Testament Theology and Exegesis: Literary, Thematic, and Canonical Issues." In *NIDOTTE* 1:185–205.

Scoralick, Ruth. "Gerechtigkeit und Gewalt. Psalm 137 in kanonischer Lektüre." In *Gewalt im Spiegel alttestamentlicher Texte*, edited by Norbert Baumgart and Martin Nitsche, 123–37. ETS 43. Würzburg: Echter, 2012.

Scott, Jack B. "אָמַן." In *TWOT* 1:51–53.

Seerveld, Calvin. "Why We Need to Learn to Cry in Church: Reclaiming the Psalms of Lament." In *Forgotten Songs: Reclaiming the Psalms for Christian Worship*, edited by C. Richard Wells and Ray Van Neste, 139–58. Nashville: B&H Academic, 2012.

Seifrid, Mark A. "Gottes Gerechtigkeit im Alten Testament und bei Paulus: Eine Skizze." *Jahrbuch für Evangelikale Theologie* 12 (1998) 25–36.

Seybold, Klaus. *Die Psalmen.* HAT, 1st series 15. Tübingen: Mohr Siebeck, 1996.

———. *Die Wallfahrtspsalmen: Studien zur Entstehungsgeschichte von Psalm 120–34.* Biblisch-theologische Studien. Neukirchen-Vluyn: Neukirchener, 1978.

———. "Zur Geschichte des vierten Davidpsalters (Pss 138–45)." In *The Book of Psalms: Composition and Reception*, edited by Peter W. Flint et al., 368–90. VTSup 99. Leiden: Brill, 2005.

Sheppard, Gerald T. *The Future of the Bible: Beyond Liberalism and Literalism.* Toronto: United Church, 1990.

———. *Wisdom as a Hermeneutical Construct: A Study in the Sapientializing of the Old Testament.* BZAW 151. Berlin: de Gruyter, 1980.

Silva, Larry. "The Cursing Psalms as a Source of Blessing." In *Psalms and Practice: Worship, Virtue, and Authority*, edited by Stephen Breck Reid, 220–30. Collegeville, MN: Liturgical, 2001.

Simango, Daniel. "A Comprehensive Reading of Psalm 137." OTE 31 (2018): 217–42.

Simian-Yofre, H., and U. Dahmen. "רחם." In *ThWAT* 7:460–77.

Simon, Uriel. *Four Approaches to the Book of Psalms: From Saadiah Gaon to Abraham Ibn Ezra.* Translated by Lenn J. Schramm. SUNY Series in Judaica. Albany: SUNY Press, 1991.

Singer, Dwight C. "The Literary Context of the Fourth Davidic Grouping in the Psalter (Psalms 138–45)." *WTJ* 75 (2013) 373.

Smith, Richard G. *The Fate of Justice and Righteousness during David's Reign: Narrative Ethics and Rereading the Court History according to 2 Samuel 8:15—20:26.* LHB/OTS 508. London: T. & T. Clark, 2010.

Soanes, Catherine, and Angus Stevenson, eds. *Concise Oxford English Dictionary.* 11th ed. Oxford: Oxford University Press, 2004.

Soll, Will. *Psalm 119: Matrix, Form, and Setting.* CBQMS 23. Washington, DC: Catholic Biblical Association of America, 1991.

Stec, David M. *The Targum of Psalms: Translated, with a Critical Introduction, Apparatus, and Notes.* The Aramaic Bible 16. Collegeville, MN: Liturgical, 2004.

Steenkamp, Yolande. "Violence and Hatred in Psalm 137: The Psalm in Its Ancient Social Context." *Verbum et Ecclesia* 25 (2004) 294–310.

Stoebe, H. J. "חנן." In *THAT* 1:587–97.

———. "חֶסֶד." In *THAT* 1:600–621.

———. "רחם." In *THAT* 2:761–68.

Stuart, Douglas. *Exodus.* NAC 2. Nashville: Broadman & Holman, 2007.

Sumpter, Philip. "The Canonical Shape of Psalms 1–14." OTE 32 (2019) 514–43.

———. "The Coherence of Psalms 15–24." *Bib* 94 (2013) 186–209.

Swanson, Dwight D. "Qumran and the Psalms." In *Interpreting the Psalms: Issues and Approaches*, edited by David Firth and Philip S. Johnston, 247–62. Leicester: Apollos, 2005.

Tate, Marvin. *Psalms 51–100.* WBC 20. Dallas: Word, 1991.

Tennent, Timothy C. *Theology in the Context of World Christianity: How the Global Church Is Influencing the Way We Think about and Discuss Theology.* Grand Rapids: Zondervan, 2007.

Theodoret of Cyrus. *Commentary on the Psalms, 1–72.* Translated by Robert C. Hill. FC 102. Washington, DC: Catholic University of America Press, 2000.

———. *Commentary on the Psalms, 73–150.* Translated by Robert C. Hill. FC 102. Washington, DC: Catholic University of America Press, 2001.

Tigay, Jeffrey H. *Deuteronomy: The Traditional Hebrew Text with the New JPS Translation.* JPSTC. Philadelphia: Jewish Publication Society, 1996.

———. "Psalm 7.5 and Ancient Near Eastern Treaties." *JBL* 89 (1970) 178–86.

Tov, Emanuel. *The Parallel Aligned Text of the Greek and Hebrew Bible.* Bellingham, WA: Lexham, 2003.

———. *Textual Criticism of the Hebrew Bible.* 3rd ed. Minneapolis: Fortress, 2012.

Tregelles, Samuel Prideaux, ed. *Gesenius' Hebrew and Chaldee Lexicon to the Old Testament Scriptures.* Plymouth, 1857.

Tucker, W. Dennis, Jr. *Constructing and Deconstructing Power in Psalms 107–150.* Ancient Israel and Its Literature 19. Atlanta: SBL, 2014.

———. "Powerlessness and the Significance of Metaphor in Psalms 140–43." In *"Wer lässt uns Gutes sehen?" (Ps 4,7): Internationale Studien zu Klagen in den Psalmen Zum Gedenken an Frank-Lothar Hossfeld*, edited by Johannes Schnocks, 228–43. HBS 85. Freiburg: Herder, 2016.

———. "The Role of the Foe in Book 5: Reflections on the Final Composition of the Psalter." In *The Shape and Shaping of the Book of Psalms: The Current State of Scholarship*, edited by Nancy L. deClaissé-Walford, 179–91. SBLAIL 20. Atlanta: SBL, 2014.

Ulrich, Eugene, ed. *The Biblical Qumran Scrolls: Transcriptions and Textual Variants.* VTSup 134. Leiden: Brill, 2010.

Van Pelt, Miles V., and Walter C. Kaiser, Jr. "הָגָה." In *NIDOTTE* 1:1006–8.

VanGemeren, Willem A. *Psalms.* Rev. ed. The Expositor's Bible Commentary 5. Grand Rapids: Zondervan, 2008.

Vanhoozer, Kevin J. "'One Rule to Rule Them All?': Theological Method in an Era of World Christianity." In *Globalizing Theology: Belief and Practice in an Era of World Christianity*, edited by Craig Ott and Harold Netland, 85–126. Grand Rapids: Baker Academic, 2006.

Vaux, Roland de. *Ancient Israel: Its Life and Institutions.* Translated by John McHugh. 2nd ed. London: Darton, Longman & Todd, 1965.

Velden, Frank van der. *Psalm 109 und die Aussagen zur Feindschädigung in den Psalmen.* SBB 37. Stuttgart: Katholisches Bibelwerk, 1997.

Vesco, Jean-Luc. *Le psautier de David: traduit et commenté.* Lectio Divina 211. Paris: Cerf, 2006.

Villanueva, Federico G. "Preaching Lament." In *Reclaiming the Old Testament for Christian Preaching*, edited by Grenville J. R. Kent et al., 64–84. Downers Grove, IL: IVP Academic, 2010.

Viviers, Hendrik. "The Coherence of the *Maʿalôt* Psalms (Pss 120–34)." *ZAW* 106 (1994) 275–89.

Vos, Cas J. A. *Theopoetry of the Psalms.* London: T. & T. Clark, 2005.

Wagner, Max. "Beiträge zur Aramaismenfrage im alttestamentlichen Hebräisch." In *Hebräische Wortforschung: Festschrift zum 80 Geburtstag von Walter Baumgartner*, edited by Benedikt Hartmann et al., 355–71. VTSup 16. Leiden: Brill, 1967.

Wallace, Robert E. "Gerald Wilson and the Characterization of David in Book 5 of the Psalter." In *The Shape and Shaping of the Book of Psalms: The Current State of Scholarship*, edited by Nancy L. deClaissé-Walford, 193–208. SBLAIL 20. Atlanta: SBL, 2014.

———. *The Narrative Effect of Book IV of the Hebrew Psalter*. Studies in Biblical Literature 112. New York: Lang, 2007.

Waltke, Bruce K., and Cathi J. Fredricks. *Genesis: A Commentary*. Grand Rapids: Zondervan, 2001.

Waltke, Bruce K., et al. *The Psalms as Christian Worship: A Historical Commentary*. Grand Rapids: Eerdmans, 2010.

Walton, John H. "Psalms: A Cantata about the Davidic Covenant." *JETS* 34 (1991) 21–31.

Ward, Martin J. "Psalm 109: David's Poem of Vengeance." *AUSS* 18 (1980) 163–68.

Watts, John D. W. *Isaiah 1–33*. WBC 24. Dallas: Word, 1985.

Weber, Beat. *Die Psalmen 1 bis 72*. Vol. 1 of *Werkbuch Psalmen*. Stuttgart: Kohlhammer, 2001.

———. *Die Psalmen 73 bis 150*. Vol. 2 of *Werkbuch Psalmen*. Stuttgart: Kohlhammer, 2003.

———. "Psalm 1 als Tor zur Tora JHWHs: wie Ps 1 (und Ps 2) den Psalter an den Pentateuch anschliesst." *SJOT* 21 (2007) 179–200.

———. *Theologie und Spiritualität des Psalters und seiner Psalmen*. Vol. 3 of *Werkbuch Psalmen*. Stuttgart: Kohlhammer, 2010.

———. "Von der Psaltergenese zur Psaltertheologie: der nächste Schritt der Psalterexegese?! einige grundsätzliche Überlegungen zum Psalter als Buch und Kanonteil." In *The Composition of the Book of Psalms*, edited by Erich Zenger, 733–44. BETL 238. Leuven: Peeters, 2010.

Weijden, Athanasius H. van der. *Die 'Gerechtigkeit' in den Psalmen*. Nijmegen: Nimwegen, 1952.

Weil, Gérard E., ed. *Catalogi*. Vol. 1 of *Massorah Gedolah: iuxta codicem Leningradensem B19a*. Rome: Pontificum Institutum Biblicum, 1971.

Weiser, Artur. *Die Psalmen, Zweiter Teil: Psalm 61–150*. ATD 15. Göttingen: Vandenhoeck & Ruprecht, 1987.

Wenham, Gordon J. "The Ethics of the Psalms." In *The Psalter Reclaimed: Praying and Praising with the Psalms*, 103–27. Wheaton, IL: Crossway, 2013.

———. "The Golden Calf in the Psalms." In *A God of Faithfulness: Essays in Honour of J. Gordon McConville on His 60th Birthday*, edited by Jamie A. Grant et al., 169–81. LHB/OTS 538. New York: T. & T. Clark, 2011.

———. "The Nations in the Psalms." In *The Psalter Reclaimed: Praying and Praising with the Psalms*, 161–86. Wheaton, IL: Crossway, 2013.

———. "Psalm 103: The Song of Steadfast Love." In *The Psalter Reclaimed: Praying and Praising with the Psalms*, 147–59. Wheaton, IL: Crossway, 2013.

———. *Psalms as Torah: Reading Biblical Song Ethically*. Studies in Theological Interpretation. Grand Rapids: Baker Academic, 2012.

———. "Reading the Psalms Canonically." In *The Psalter Reclaimed: Praying and Praising with the Psalms*, 57–79. Wheaton, IL: Crossway, 2013.

———. "Sanctuary Symbolism in the Garden of Eden Story." In *Proceedings of the Ninth World Congress of Jewish Studies, Jerusalem, August 4–12, 1985: Division A. The Period of the Bible*, edited by David Assaf, 19–25. Jerusalem: World Union of Jewish Studies, 1986.

———. *Story as Torah: Reading Old Testament Narratives Ethically*. 2000. Reprint, Grand Rapids: Baker, 2004.

Westermann, Claus. *Elements of Old Testament Theology*. Translated by Douglas W. Stott. Atlanta: John Knox, 1982.

———. *Praise and Lament in the Psalms*. Translated by Keith R. Crim and Richard N. Soulen. Edinburgh: T. & T. Clark, 1981.

Whybray, R. Norman. *Reading the Psalms as a Book*. JSOTSup 222. Sheffield: Sheffield Academic, 1996.

Wilcock, Michael. *The Message of Psalms 1–72: Songs for the People of God*. BST. Downers Grove, IL: InterVarsity, 2001.

———. *The Message of Psalms 73–150*. BST. Downers Grove, IL: InterVarsity, 2001.

Wildberger, H. "אמן." In *THAT* 1:177–209.

Willgren, David. *The Formation of the 'Book' of Psalms: Reconsidering the Transmission and Canonization of Psalmody in Light of Material Culture and the Poetics of Anthologies*. FAT, 2nd series 88. Tübingen: Mohr Siebeck, 2016.

Wilhelmi, Gerhard. "Der Hirt mit dem eisernen Szepter: Überlegungen zu Psalm 2:9." *VT* 27 (1977) 196–204.

Wilson, Gerald H. *The Editing of the Hebrew Psalter*. SBLDS 76. Chico, CA: Scholars, 1985.

———. "King, Messiah, and the Reign of God: Revisiting the Royal Psalms and the Shape of the Psalter." In *The Book of Psalms: Composition and Reception*, edited by Peter W. Flint et al., 391–406. VTSup 99. Leiden: Brill, 2005.

———. *Psalms—Volume 1*. NIVAC. Grand Rapids: Zondervan, 2002.

———. "The Shape of the Book of Psalms." *Int* 46 (1992) 129–42.

———. "Shaping the Psalter, a Consideration of Editorial Linkage in the Book of Psalms." In *The Shape and Shaping of the Psalter*, edited by J. Clinton McCann Jr., 72–82. JSOTSup 159. Sheffield: JSOT, 1993.

———. "The Structure of the Psalter." In *Interpreting the Psalms: Issues and Approaches*, edited by David Firth and Philip S. Johnston, 229–46. Leicester: Apollos, 2005.

———. "Understanding the Purposeful Arrangement of Psalms in the Psalter: Pitfalls and Promise." In *The Shape and Shaping of the Psalter*, edited by J. Clinton McCann Jr., 42–51. JSOTSup 159. Sheffield: JSOT, 1993.

———. "The Use of Royal Psalms at the 'Seams' of the Hebrew Psalter." *JSOT* 35 (1986) 85–94.

———. "ישׁב." In *NIDOTTE* 2:550–51.

Wittman, Derek E. "Let Us Cast off Their Ropes from Us: The Editorial Significance of the Portrayal of Foreign Nations in Psalms 2 and 149." In *The Shape and Shaping of the Book of Psalms: The Current State of Scholarship*, edited by Nancy L. deClaissé-Walford, 53–70. SBLAIL 20. Atlanta: SBL, 2014.

Wodehouse, P. G. *Stiff Upper Lip, Jeeves*. Harmondsworth: Penguin, 1975.

Wolf, Herbert. "אזח." In *TWOT* 1:32–33.

Wolterstorff, Nicholas. *Justice in Love*. Emory University Studies in Law and Religion. Grand Rapids: Eerdmans, 2011.

Wonneberger, Reinhard. *Understanding BHS: A Manual for the Users of Biblia Hebraica Stuttgartensia*. Translated by Dwight R. Daniels. 2nd ed. *SubBi* 8. Roma: Pontificio Istituto Biblico, 1990.

Wright, Christopher J. H. *Old Testament Ethics for the People of God*. Leicester: Inter-Varsity, 2004.

——. "תֵּבֵל." In *NIDOTTE* 4:272–73.

Wright, David P. "Ritual Analogy in Psalm 109." *JBL* 113 (1994) 385–404.

Wright, N. T. *Finding God in the Psalms: Sing, Pray, Live*. SPCK: London, 2014.

Yamauchi, Edwin. "חָנַן." In *TWOT* 1:302–4.

Zakovitch, Yair. "On the Ordering of Psalms as Demonstrated by Psalms 136–50." In *Oxford Handbook of the Psalms*, edited by William P. Brown, 214–28. Oxford: Oxford University Press, 2014.

Zenger, Erich. "The Composition and Theology of the Fifth Book of Psalms, Psalms 107–45." *JSOT* (1998) 77–102.

——. *A God of Vengeance? Understanding the Psalms of Divine Wrath*. Translated by Linda M. Maloney. Louisville, KY: Westminster John Knox, 1996.

——. "Psalmenexegese *und* Psalterexegese: eine Forschungsskizze." In *The Composition of the Book of Psalms*, edited by Erich Zenger, 17–66. BETL 238. Leuven: Peeters, 2010.

——. "Was wird anders bei kanonischer Psalmenauslegung?" In *Ein Gott, eine Offenbarung: Beiträge zur biblischen Exegese, Theologie und Spiritualität: Festschrift für Notker Füglister zum 60. Geburtstag*, edited by Friedrich V. Reiterer, 397–413. Würzburg: Echter, 1991.

——. "Zion als Mutter der Völker in Psalm 87." In *Der Gott Israels und die Völker: Untersuchungen zum Jesajabuch und zu den Psalmen*, edited by Norbert Lohfink and Erich Zenger, 117–50. SBS 154. Stuttgart: Katholisches Bibelwerk, 1994.

Zobel, H.-J. "חֶסֶד." In *ThWAT* 5:48–71.

Author Index

Page numbers in bold indicate a discussion of the author's work.

Scripture Index

Page numbers in bold indicate an exposition of the passage.

24	252	15:5	87
24:7 [6]	96	15:7–12	78
24:18–22 [17–21]	252	15:12	79
24:18 [17]	252	15:13–18	90
24:19 [18]	252	15:13	77, 79
24:20 [19]	252	15:20	80
24:21 [20]	252	15:21	80
24:22 [21]	252	15:24–29	99
29:5	98	15:25–28	83
		15:25–26	79, 99
2 Samuel	78, 92, 96, 101,	15:25	79
	102, 119	15:28	81
		15:29–30	83
1	96	15:29	117
1:22	140	15:31	80, 81, 82, 83, 90,
2	115		91
2:9	115	15:34	80, 90
6–10	87	16:5–12	190
6	117	16:8	81
7:14	91	16:10	99
8	157	16:11	80
8:2	157	16:14	81, 83
8:12	115	16:15	81
11–19	**86–91**	16:16–19	81
11	78, 142	16:20–22	79, 81
11:17–25	92	16:20	90
11:27	92	16:23	81, 90, 91
12	51	17:1–3	81
12:10–14	78	17:2	98
12:10	78, 79	17:3	81
12:11–14	51	17:6–13	82
12:11–12	78	17:7	90
12:11	79, 90, 241	17:11	98
12:13–14	130	17:14	82, 84, 90, 91, 241
12:13	51, 93	17:20	82
13–20	80	17:21–22	83
13	78	17:21	245
13:21–23	84	17:22	83
13:33	84	17:23	82, 90
13:34	84	18	157
13:39	84	18:1–4	84
14	78	18:1	98
15–19	77	18:5	84, 99
15–17	91, 117	18:31–32	90
15	77	18:33	84, 99
15:1–4	78	19	84
15:2	87, 90	19:7 [6]	85, 99
15:4	87, 90	19:9–13 [8–12]	158